THE WHOLE JOURNEY

THE WHOLE JOURNEY

SHAKESPEARE'S POWER OF DEVELOPMENT

C. L. BARBER

AND

RICHARD P. WHEELER

University of California Press

Berkeley
Los Angeles
London

University of California Press
Berkeley and Los Angeles, California

University of California Press, Ltd.
London, England

Library of Congress Cataloging-in-Publication Data
Barber, C. L. (Cesar Lombardi)
   The whole journey.

   Includes index.
   1. Shakespeare, William, 1564–1616—Criticism and
interpretation—Addresses, essays, lectures.
I. Wheeler, Richard P. (Richard Paul), 1943-
II. Title.
PR2976.B324   1986   822.3'3   85-20712
ISBN   0-520-06622-7   (alk. paper)

Printed in the United States of America

1 2 3 4 5 6 7 8 9

For Cleo H. Barber

One of the greatest capacities of genius is the
power of development. . . . As with Shakespeare,
his later work must be understood through
the earlier, and the first through the last;
it is the whole journey, not any one stage of it,
that assures him his place among the great.

T. S. Eliot on James Joyce

Contents

Foreword   xi

Note on Texts   xxix

1

The Family and the Sacred in Shakespeare's
Development   1

2

Shakespeare in the Rising Middle Class   39

3

Domestic Comedy   67

4

Savage Play and the Web of Curses in
Richard III   86

5

Titus Andronicus: Abortive Domestic
Tragedy   125

6

Shakespeare in His Sonnets   158

7

From Mixed History to Heroic Drama:
The *Henriad*   198

8

Sight Lines on *Hamlet* and Shakespearean
Tragedy   237

9

Inextricable Ruthlessness and Ruth:
King Lear 282

10

"The masked Neptune and / The gentlest
winds of heaven": *Pericles* and the Transition
from Tragedy to Romance 298

Index 343

Foreword

C. L. Barber did not live to finish this book, in which he had hoped to see the culmination of his life's work on Shakespeare. In a series of telephone conversations in the week preceding his death on March 26, 1980 (when there was reason to believe he had a year or two to live), he asked me to come in on the book project as co-author, so that his years of work on it might be "brought to fruition." I told him that nothing would honor me more than to help him complete the book, but that, because his work was so much—and so strongly—a record of his own long personal engagement with Shakespeare, it would be inappropriate to think of me as co-author. We debated the issue, each sticking to his position, until Barber closed the matter genially by deferring it until we could begin our work when I joined him for the spring break.

I do not know what book would have been produced by the sort of collaboration then envisioned but never begun. After his death I brought back from California a large packing box of manuscripts and notebooks that Joe's wife, Cleo, his colleague John Jordan, and I gathered up from his Santa Cruz office and study. This box contained chapters I had seen before, but it also contained a great deal of draft and fragmentary material that bore closely on the chief concerns of the book. The status of this material in relation to the book project would be determined by how I, in bringing the book to completion, addressed the authorship problem left open at Barber's death.

To an unusual degree, what this book *is*, is bound up with the unusual ways in which it has since come to be. None of the chapters that came to me was in a form that Barber regarded as final. Even his last work on the book was devoted largely to opening it up further to new subjects and to bringing new perspectives or organizational strategies to bear on subjects already explored. There was, however, some finished work, including two essays that are already well known to students of Shakespeare: "'Thou that beget'st him that did thee beget': Transformation in *Pericles* and *The Winter's Tale*"[1] and "The Family in Shakespeare's Development: Tragedy and Sacredness."[2] But the question of how these essays could best be made to serve the interests of the larger project was complicated by an abundance of related material among the unfinished manuscripts.

Along with, and overlapping, the short published essay on *Pericles* and *The Winter's Tale*, there was a larger, unfinished paper on *Pericles*—which, while covering much of the same ground, provided a more extensive reading of the single play—as well as other, more fragmentary material on the romances and their relation to the tragedies. Although the published version of "The Family in Shakespeare's Development" addressed what are perhaps the principal animating concerns of the whole project—the distinctive place tragedy occupies in Shakespeare's development and the crucial place within tragedy of efforts to recover a sacred dimension of feeling in secular experience—this essay represented only a part of Barber's thinking on these matters. The unfinished papers, however, included extensive pertinent materials: in drafts or notes for lectures; in draft chapters started, abandoned, and taken up again, some of them only two- or three-page fragments; in various notes and comments dispersed throughout notebooks and "reading journals."

These two instances are variants of the circumstances that came to shape my relationship to this project at every level of organization. Often, material addressing concerns at the very heart of Barber's enterprise existed only in fragmentary form, whereas the most nearly completed parts of the book did not reflect the fullness of Barber's thinking about its central issues. Again and again I have had to choose between cutting the book back to what was most nearly finished by Barber and moving the book toward the larger design that he had envisaged for it. Whenever possible I have chosen the latter option, which created the paradoxical situation that would repeatedly define my work: the more I tried to make the book responsive to the core, the range, and the personal quality of Barber's study of Shakespeare's development, the more fully I had to take responsibility for the structure and composition of the book

1. *Shakespeare Survey* 22 (1969): 59–67.
2. *Representing Shakespeare: New Psychoanalytic Essays*, ed. Murray M. Schwartz and Coppélia Kahn (Baltimore: Johns Hopkins University Press, 1980), pp. 188–202.

myself. I found it necessary, in short, to share in the authorship of the book much more pervasively than I had originally thought would be the case.

In finishing the book Barber began, I have regarded my revisions, additions, and constructions as an adaptation, fitted to what turned out to be the circumstances of my work, of the collaborative effort Barber had suggested before his death. In clarifying, extending, and organizing what Barber had written, I have tried to produce a book as close as possible in form and scope to the book he had planned to write. Often, in the manuscripts that came to me, central concerns turned up, at times only slightly altered and at times in substantially different form, in draft chapters in varying states of completion, each belonging to a different conception of the design for the whole book. In such instances I have checked each draft against the several others that bear on the same or similar concerns. Throughout I have stayed as near as I could to the language, tone, and conceptual framework of the materials that came to me. Barber regularly, though not always, wrote in the first person, and I have tried to do nothing that would compromise or sharply qualify the distinctive critical presence the first person pronoun represents in his writing. The "I" that establishes itself in the following chapters is, I believe, fully expressive of Barber's deeply personal engagement with the materials of this book, even in sections that I have extensively revised or augmented.

Chapters 3, 4, 5, and 6 already existed as structural units in the manuscripts. I have revised these chapters for clarity, coherence, economy, and organization, and have completed their notes. Each posed different problems. The first section of chapter 3 Barber had adapted from a 1964 essay on *The Comedy of Errors*.[3] But the second section of this chapter and all of chapter 4, on *Richard III*, were written in the fall of 1979. This draft material, the last sustained work that Barber did on *The Whole Journey*, called for extensive rewriting and restructuring. Chapter 5, on *Titus Andronicus*, required expansion and revision to clarify a number of telling points, some of which Barber had marked in the margins as needing further work. Chapter 6 included much from a 1960 essay on the Sonnets,[4]

3. "Shakespearian Comedy in *The Comedy of Errors*," *College English* 25 (1964): 493–97.

4. Introduction to *The Laurel Shakespeare: The Sonnets* (New York: Dell Publishing, 1960); reprinted as "An Essay on the Sonnets," *Elizabethan Poetry: Modern Essays in Criticism*, ed. Paul J. Alpers (New York: Oxford University Press, 1967), pp. 299–320.

though its new format reflected the increasingly pivotal position the Sonnets had come to occupy in Barber's thinking about the whole span of Shakespeare's development. Here my revisions went chiefly into coordinating this chapter with other moments in the book where the Sonnets are called upon to illuminate Shakespeare's art and temperament.

No one working text can account for the structure of chapters 1, 2, 7, 8, 9, and 10. In putting these chapters together, I have relied heavily on my own understanding of Barber's project, acquired first as his student at SUNY/Buffalo in the late sixties and extended as his friend and frequent correspondent in subsequent years. Although I have done substantial writing and reconstruction in each of them, I have added nothing that does not have some basis, however fragmentary in some instances, in Barber's papers. My concern has been not to introduce new perspectives but to develop and integrate lines of thought indicated in the manuscripts I worked with. Barber's own characteristic style of revision, which was to start over with a new format, fitting into the new structure pertinent materials from the old, provided a model for my work.

Chapter 1, particularly the first section, is chiefly developed from the published paper "The Family in Shakespeare's Development." But for considerable portions of this chapter, including most of the second section, I have drawn on many other materials, among them an address given at Sarah Lawrence College in the fall of 1965[5] and several unfinished drafts of 1969–70 (a year Barber spent at the Center for Advanced Study in the Behavioral Sciences at Stanford). Chapter 2 restructures a draft chapter of the same title, "Shakespeare in the Rising Middle Class," and expands it on the basis of materials that include a paper, "From Falstaff to Hamlet: Shakespeare's Route Toward Tragedy," presented at the 1977 meeting of the Shakespeare Association of America. Chapter 7, on *Henry IV* and *Henry V*, is based on the unfinished draft of a chapter that Barber started in the fall of 1977; in augmenting it, I have relied on a variety of materials, including the SAA paper on Falstaff and Hamlet. Chapter 9 is based on the published version of "The Family in Shakespeare's Development"; a paper on *Lear* that Barber wrote before leaving Amherst in 1961; a lecture on *Lear* delivered at the University of Minnesota in 1974; and a brief section on *Lear* from a superseded draft chapter. The last chapter is based on the

---

5. "'Perfection of the Work': The Use of the Drama for Shakespeare," *Sarah Lawrence Alumnae Magazine* 31 (Fall 1965): 13–16.

unpublished paper on *Pericles* mentioned earlier; the published essay on *Pericles* and *The Winter's Tale*; notes for a lecture at the University of Minnesota; and a tape recording of Barber's reflections after a lecture on *The Tempest* he had given at the University of Southern California in the spring of 1978.

With chapter 8, on *Hamlet*'s place in Shakespeare's development of tragic form, I have proceeded with the least authority from Barber's texts and hence added more of my own. The first section is developed from a discussion of "Hamlet and the Burial of the Dead" from a superseded chapter; the last section includes most of a paper on *Othello* as a development from *Hamlet* presented at the 1974 SAA meeting; otherwise I am responsible for the chapter's design. Materials from this chapter included notes for a set of lectures given at Smith College in 1966; drafts from the year at Stanford; and several drafts started during the years Barber spent at SUNY/Buffalo (1967–69) and at the University of California, Santa Cruz (1970–80). From these materials I have evolved a chapter that I hope reflects accurately the enormous importance of *Hamlet* to the dominant concerns of this book.

I am aware that, in providing even so simplified an account of the making of this book, I run the risk of deflecting the attention of its readers away from its substance and onto the uncommon nature of its production. There is nothing particularly unusual, I think, about working into the final form of a book diverse materials that have been written at various times, but it is, of course, unusual for a second person to perform this task with materials originally produced by a first. What has made this task possible, apart from my intellectual sympathy with this project and its points of connection with my own work on Shakespeare's development, is the fundamental integrity and coherence of the critical sensibility Joe Barber brought to his work on Shakespeare and sustained through many interruptions as the ideas of this book took shape.

Barber's earlier exploration of comic form in relation to social custom situated Shakespeare's dramatic art at "a moment when the educated part of society was modifying a ceremonial and ritualistic conception of human life to create a historical, psychological conception." [6] That exploration is continued and amplified in *The Whole Journey* to include other dimensions both of Shakespeare's art and

---

6. *Shakespeare's Festive Comedy: A Study of Dramatic Form and Its Relation to Social Custom* (Princeton: Princeton University Press, 1959), p. 15.

of the historical moment. The lines of continuity linking the present book to Barber's earlier one are many and strong. Many admirers of *Shakespeare's Festive Comedy*, however, are perhaps more likely to be struck by the new book's points of departure, by shifts in conceptualization that have followed from the more intensive concern to comprehend Shakespeare's development through the principal modes in which he worked over an entire career.

Although particularly concerned to clarify the importance of tragedy, Barber found that Shakespeare's use of tragedy could only be understood through a consideration of the place it occupies in the shape of Shakespeare's whole development. Much of what is distinctive about this book derives from a closely interrelated group of issues or problems that the effort to conceptualize the whole journey brought into prominence: the development of Shakespeare's art in response to what can be inferred as stresses on the author's temperament; the relation of dramatic form to the ever present human tendency toward magical thinking; the historical emergence of tragedy in the new secular theater to comprehend needs that in a religious context would look toward sacred resolution; and the uses (and hazards) of psychoanalytic perspectives for addressing these and other concerns raised by Barber's readings of the plays.

In immersing myself in Barber's drafts of many years, watching them coalesce into the project of this book, I have been struck by the increasing power that attends the growth of a simple yet, in relation to the current status of Shakespeare studies, controversial conviction: that Shakespeare's artistic achievement has a human shape. Barber believed that the art met needs in the man who created it and knew himself through it, that it developed in directions that responded to shifts in his relationship to experience and to the needs and structure of his temperament. "Shakespeare's genius makes his temperament, including the special vulnerabilities and powers that went with his creativity, part of the whole process of his work. His art embodies him—an achievement which seems to have made other forms of public self-expression or assertion superfluous."[7] Barber was, of course, fully aware of the difficulties

7. From a manuscript entitled "Everything/Nothing and 'the holy cords . . . too intrinse t'unloose,'" a draft chapter superseded by Barber's published paper "The Family in Shakespeare's Development" (see n. 2 above). Ensuing quotations are from mostly unpublished and often unfinished materials among Barber's papers. Other parts of some of these materials (and of many others) have been adapted for use elsewhere in this book.

attending the effort to see Shakespeare's art as an activity, an endeavor undertaken by a human subject responding to the "vulnerabilities and power" of his own temperament. He instanced the
very different circumstances of *The Divine Comedy*: for Dante,
"what the poem does for him, his need for it and gain from it,
is expressed directly and indirectly" throughout. By contrast,
"Shakespeare's dramatic medium and the autonomous function of
each separate play obviate any such direct expression of the man
working in the work and what the work does for him. . . . But the
fact that, except for the Sonnets and his two early long poems, we
can know him only through his dramatic works, does not mean
that they did not serve his human needs—how could they not have
done so? How could they have been created if they did not?"[8]

One strand of speculation in this book seeks to identify links between Shakespeare's art and what is known about his life from the
biographical record. But more often the emphasis is on seeing the
art as the endeavor of a human sensibility that can be known only
from what the art accomplishes, the directions in which it moves,
the recurrent crises it encounters, and the patterns that emerge
from the different kinds of artistic resolution by which those crises
are mastered. "Shakespeare, one comes to feel, could do almost
anything with language and the theater, and understood almost
everything. . . . 'Others abide our question, thou art free.' Who are
we to set limits to his achievement?" But an essential part of the
critical effort is to attend to what Shakespeare does not do in his
art, the constraints that shape and limit his art and beyond which it
does not or cannot go: "If we do not attend to its limits, we cannot
see its shape. Though he had artistic powers to do almost anything, he elected to do what he did." Barber did not underestimate
the difficulties and traps built into "this formidable undertaking."
"I have become involved in it almost against my will, not from a
desire to write a biographical study, but from fascination with . . .
the meaning each production has as a part of a larger pattern testi-
fying to the artist's power of development. The power of development is exercised against odds, by mobilizing resources of the art
form, of the culture, and of the individual talent."[9]

Barber noted that "the enormous range of varied life which we
encounter in the plays must have come from a man extraordinarily
open to life, fluidly responsive to other identities." Such respon-

8. Ibid.
9. Ibid.

siveness is abundantly present in the poet of the Sonnets. "We can see something of Shakespeare's way of responding to another human being, and so something of the individual temperament which created the plays, because we have his Sonnets." In these poems, "Shakespeare exhibits an unparalleled capacity to live by identification, to lose himself in the realization of the beauty and vitality of another person."[10] In Shakespeare's giving himself over to the realization of the friend's identity we can glimpse a process akin to the dramatist's power to enter into the lives of his characters.

But the experience recounted in the Sonnets also resists needs the poet brings to it. Along with the affirmation of self through another that characterizes the moments of highest fulfillment in these poems,

> we also encounter extremes of selflessness which are troubling, sometimes embarrassing: to make everything of the young nobleman in whom he sees the highest perfections of life, Shakespeare will sometimes make nothing of himself, humiliate himself, in a way which today we can only call masochistic. When one reads the contorted, self-abasing sonnets, one is led to ask how it was possible for Shakespeare to endure his openness to life, his selfless sense of other identities.[11]

He could do so in part, Barber felt, because he had the drama. When we turn from the Sonnets to the plays, we "can see in them how fortunate for Shakespeare's temperament it was that he had the theater for living in and through other identities."[12] For the theater provided Shakespeare with "a way of realizing other identities, . . . while at the same time mastering them. Dramatic form, the perspective on creative life shared in the theater with an audience, enabled him to control the otherness that might have overwhelmed him, providing in the rhythm of tragic and comic creation and destruction a balance between surrender and aggression."[13]

The "nothing" that the sonneteer will sometimes make of himself and that emerges as a dominant theme in the dramatic work, particularly in the tragedies, is very different from that of Borges's well-known parable, "Everything and Nothing," which Barber thought to be a simplification of "Keats's insight about Negative Capability."[14] "There was no one in him," Borges wrote; "behind his face (which even through the bad paintings of those times re-

10. "Perfection of the Work," p. 13.   11. Ibid.
12. "Everything/Nothing."   13. "Perfection of the Work," p. 14.
14. "Everything/Nothing."

sembles no other) and his words, which were copious, fantastic and stormy, there was only a bit of coldness, a dream dreamt by no one."[15] "The parable is engaging," Barber wrote, "because it states a half truth that leaves out, by lumping them together, problematic tensions: 'Everything' in the art is simply poised against the 'Nothing' in the artist, and then justified by a very modern, existential God-the-artist." He read Borges's parable as an eloquent extension of the tendency characteristic of "impersonal theories of poetry," which bracket out from consideration the artist's human stake in the achievement of his art. For Barber, by contrast, the encounter with the self as "nothing" in the Sonnets witnessed to a "potentially destructive stress about selflessness." "The problem of 'nothing,' the terrifying possibility of it, is a central subject of his art—the dread of nothing is, after all, a universal human problem, not just a problem that goes with being an artist. His art permits him to be open to it, and to express the form the threat characteristically takes at different stages for his particular sensibility— 'nothing' is not just an awkward blank at the center. . . . In *King Lear*, the whole action of the play is generated from the great rage of Lear in response to Cordelia's 'nothing.'"[16]

At the other pole from the dread of nothing is the fantasy that one can be everything, the assumption that is grounded in the infantile condition of omnipotence of mind and that persists as magical thinking throughout life. Barber found the tendency toward magical thinking essential to literature and art. "The arts are our civilized versions of magic. They meet the human need for imaginative experience made physical." Fully successful art, however, is a profoundly "social process" grounded in "the common symbolic resources of society"; it not only expresses magical thinking but also provides a means of controlling it, of understanding it ironically. "There is magic in the web of Shakespeare's art." But "the whole situation created by the new theater of the Renaissance made it possible for Shakespeare's drama to provide detachment about magic—a place where the audience could experience magical thinking and at the same time judge it realistically, from where they sat outside the play space. . . . Artists in our time do not have the same kind of communal symbolic resources that he had."[17]

15. Jorge Luis Borges, *Labyrinths: Selected Stories and Other Writings*, ed. Donald A. Yates and James E. Irby (New York: New Directions, 1964), p. 248.

16. "Everything/Nothing."

17. "Magic in the Web of Art," script for a BBC telecast, an Open University program in the Arts Foundation Course, filmed December 1977.

In *Shakespeare's Festive Comedy*, which explores the way "the dramatist must control magic by reunderstanding it as imagination," Barber dealt with magical expectations chiefly in relation to folk superstition, as in *A Midsummer Night's Dream*, or to the misplaced faith in "the magic of the crown," as in *Richard II* (pp. 220, 211). Barber's later interest in magic was primarily focused by tragic situations, understood in relation to the cultural and religious situation of Renaissance England:

> Magical expectation is at the heart of the plays because it is built into the heart of man. But in the Renaissance, such expectation is loose in the world as never before, not under, or intertwined with, a monolithic religion, but conceived as a possible "second world," to use the term of my colleague Harry Berger. And the expectation has a new urgency, because it seemed to many an alternative to religious power. At the core of it—in the text of the Hermetic *Asclepius*, at the core of Giordano Bruno's manic personality—was the old old promise, "Ye shall be as Gods." [18]

"A sound magician is a mighty god," says Marlowe's Doctor Faustus at the beginning of his tragic plunge into heroic blasphemy.

As magic seemed to some an alternative to the established church, so "the theater in the Renaissance becomes a place apart, alternative to the traditional place apart for dealing with magical expectations, the church. In the sacred precincts of the church, magical expectations are vanities of the heart. . . . The two great resources for being realistic about magic have been religion and art. Magical thinking frequently takes over in both disciplines, yet the true practitioners of each discipline, of worship and of art, bring it under control." [19] Barber connected the time's intense interest in magic and in theater with the Reformation renunciation of the efficacy of ritual and iconic resources central to Catholic worship, which gave "so much more physical embodiment to mystery than the Protestants allowed. . . . The theater flourished in the generation after Protestantism took over, and achieved enormous popularity in satisfying needs no longer met in the church." [20] In meeting those needs in its own way, the theater often tended toward situations that evoke the forms of Christian ritual, but with tragic not redemptive outcomes. "When we find suggestive analogies to

---

18. "There's Magic in the Web," paper presented at the annual meeting of the Philological Association of the Pacific Coast, November 1975, San Jose, California.
19. Ibid.
20. "Magic in the Web of Art."

Christian rituals in Shakespeare's plays, I think that the whole context usually leads us to understand them ironically, as magical thinking which proves vain or destructive—as with the potential analogy in *Julius Caesar* to the last supper and holy communion, to drinking the blood of Christ." Brutus and his fellow conspirators "hope to carve up Caesar as a dish fit for the gods and share in his spirit. After the assassination, Shakespeare makes their dipping their arms up to the elbows in his blood into an effort to do this, with what results the sequel shows after his wounds speak to the mob." [21]

Shakespeare puts in dramatic perspective the magical thinking of tragic protagonists, identifying "just those strains of magical or superstitious lore" that answer to their special needs. In *Macbeth*, the "witch cult . . . of the age is understood . . . as it caters to the dependency needs of the hero." In *Othello*, the protagonist's "insecurity about sexuality, his need to sanctify it and keep it virginal, with the cruel potential underneath, is all in his description of the sibyl's making of the handkerchief. . . . To highlight the importance of magic—the understanding which its modes of thought make possible even as their human basis is understood—one has only to recall the remarks for which Thomas Rymer is famous: he called *Othello* 'the tragedy of the handkerchief' and observed that the moral of the play is that 'ladies should look to their linen.' Rymer's comment is such fun because he is so totally blind to the power of the magic in the web—and so relieves us, for a moment, of the burden of tragedy." [22]

Barber was exceptionally open and vulnerable to the burden of tragedy, to the depth of response he found its power and beauty demanded of him. In notes to himself made after a 1961 seminar, he speculated that "perhaps in all tragedy, certainly in some, we experience the almost unnameable qualm and dread that comes from opening the gates to regression—gates which, once opened in our individual minds, make us tremble, regardless of the fate of the fictive protagonists, because *we ourselves* might go through, might go down into the whirlpool. . . . And once one has seen into it, one then asks, what is the relevance of this heart of light or darkness to the rest of the work and to the rest of our experience? This leads one to see—to need to see—how the fullest life is grounded

---

21. "There's Magic in the Web."
22. Ibid.

in this terror." Criticism, for Barber, was grounded in such experience, in the full encounter of our essential equipment for living
with the "imaginative design" (a term he borrowed from his friend
Reuben Brower) we find in the literary work—which can in turn
reshape the sense of life that we bring to it. "One cannot recognize
an imaginative design without constant reference to one's knowledge of life. . . . One cannot honestly read except with one's whole
awareness of life." [23]

Since we, as readers, are situated "in history, imaginative design
is open, always made anew by every reader and every time, and
made with reference always not only to the text but also whatever
else we know" that bears on the text.[24] An essential, shaping contribution to Barber's "awareness," to his own vantage point as a
reader in his own historical situation, was provided by Freud. He
was, certainly, wary of the imperialistic tendency of psychoanalysis
and of other nonliterary methodologies to usurp the distinctive
function of literary criticism. "We tend to be pushed into the residual systematic vocabularies"—religious, Marxist, Freudian—
"three theologies or anthropologies which it is one's constant effort
to avoid being trapped in, because being trapped in them leads you
to be unable to get at the work of art; the work of art becomes an
illustration of the theology, ceases to matter as a separate fact." [25]
But he found "Freudian analysis, though difficult to control, a resource of enormous power," [26] and believed that "Freudian awareness, once it has sunk in, must be coped with, must be used, wher-
ever it is relevant. . . . It seems to me that a fuller understanding of
literature is made possible by developing the Freudian understanding of the mind and body—a fuller understanding not only of the
experience presented *in* the work, but of the function of the work
in relation to experience. In other words, a fuller understanding of
what artistic form does for us adds a dimension of meaning to
works of art." [27]

That Barber should refer to Freudian "awareness" and "understanding," not to Freudian theory, is characteristic. The "disci-

23. From manuscript pages (dated May 14 to June 1, 1961) grouped under the
heading, "Notes after May 12 Ford Humanities Project Seminar."
24. Ibid.
25. Transcript of a lecture, "Piety and Outrage in Kyd's *Spanish Tragedy* and in
Hamlet," given as part of a Humanities Colloquium series at SUNY/Buffalo, Spring
1969.
26. Copy of a letter to Richard Schlatter, May 26, 1962.
27. "Notes" (see n. 23 above).

pline" of psychoanalysis was for him a way of being aware, a way of knowing that "sank in," that must be "coped with," that could be "used"; it presented itself to him as a "way we have been taught to pay attention" more than as a theoretical system responsible to its own inner, abstracted coherence. Freud, he found, sustained, even as he added a new dimension to, the cultural "conversation [that] is the ground for written currency." He was uneasy with post-Freudian developments that tended to isolate psychoanalysis from this conversation. "Freud and his generation" he found more available because "in moving into their special world, each took some of the larger world with him. The epigoni, by contrast, live in a world almost sealed off by professionalism from general discourse."[28]

By "temperament and taste" Barber was uncomfortable writing criticism that was not oriented primarily toward his own direct experience of works of literature. He found psychoanalysis useful because it conditioned his awareness of what he found most vital in his experience of the world and hence of his reading of literature. But, as he wrote to his friend Richard Schlatter (May 1962), after a frustrated effort to integrate a theoretical discussion of psychological criticism into the work he was then doing on Marlowe, "when I write critical evaluations, in general terms, of various modes of interpretations, . . . I find that I am in a false position. Not so when I have my sights on Marlowe and the general issues at the side of my eye."

The reading of Freud that has shaped the work in this book is illuminated by an unfinished commentary entitled "Freudian Resources for Interpretation." Barber began with the following statement: "Freud began as a student of desire; his studies led him to become a student of conscience and worship." The focus here was on those developments that led Freud "more and more to see a given form of sexual fantasy or behavior as *expressing* more fundamental attitudes which are determined as much by identification and dependence as by specific sexual drives." Freud's "increasing preoccupation with identification—the identification of the child with a parent which contributes to the formation of the superego, the identification of the group with the leader which can have such drastic consequences for conscience"—pointed for Barber to the dynamics of worship and piety before the larger powers of life first encountered in the parents, and consolidated, in a stable religious

28. Ibid.

society, both by the individual act of worship and by group solidarity within the communal, institutional structure of the church.
"My goal will be to show how Freud's ideas can be related to the
need for worship and to the aberrations resulting when that need
does not find an adequate object. This of course is not Freud's point
of view: he maintains stoutly his nineteenth-century scientist's
scorn of religion . . . in the midst of studies which, as I read them,
profoundly illuminate man's nature as a worshipping being inescapably involved with conscience."[29]

In what ways, or how fully, the recurrent delays and blocks that
interrupted Barber's own writing on this book were related to
the ways he experienced such need within himself, in relation to
the artistic and religious resources of his own time, are matters well
beyond my knowing. But the tragedies are tragic, in his readings,
in large part because they dramatize worlds in which such need becomes the source of destructive and self-destructive action when
invested in secular, human "objects" who are not, and cannot be,
"adequate" to it. Even the great resonance Barber felt between tragedy and the writings of Freud was in part due to what he saw as
analogous in the historical contexts from which each emerged. In
an unfinished supplement to his study of Shakespeare's "post-
Christian" art in "The Family in Shakespeare's Development,"
Barber meditated on the "post-religious" predicament of psychoanalysis. He began by quoting the 1930 preface to the Hebrew
translation of *Totem and Taboo*. There Freud declared himself "completely estranged from the religion of his fathers—as well as from
any other religion," but observed that he was himself "in his essential nature a Jew." Freud also noted, however, that the book itself
"adopts no Jewish standpoint and makes no exceptions in favour of
Jewry." Barber's brief commentary, marked "abandoned" at the top
of the first page, but which was still on his mind when I last visited
him in his home three months before his death, reads as follows:

> Though Freud does not quite say so here, it seems to me that psycho-
> analysis is a post-religious development of thought and culture, not
> an irreligious development, and that his moving Preface to the He-
> brew Version of his study of "the origin of religion and morality" re-
> flects this fact. . . . I do not know enough about Jewish religion to
> judge whether Freud was right about his having kept any of its dis-

29. Unfinished draft (April 1963) of an appendix to Barber's then projected study
of Marlowe's use of tragedy.

tinctive assumptions out of his study. But I have always been struck by what seems an incongruous assumption in Freud's account of the aftermath in his "tumultuous mob of brothers" after killing "the violent primal father"—"their burning sense of guilt" and their "longing for the father." Within the frame of his hypothetical narrative, their Hobbesian fear of one another is easy to credit, with its consequences in clan prohibition of murder and totemic exogamy. But why a longing for the utterly brutal father as Freud describes him domineering over the patriarchal horde? When Freud goes on to argue that "at bottom God is nothing other than an exalted father," he has shifted over to basing his argument on "the psychoanalysis of individual human beings" in his own culture, a post-Christian culture where the idea of God surely shaped the idea of the human father in the sort of families with which he and other analysts dealt.

When we look at the later nineteenth century's anthropology, on which Freud drew so heavily in *Totem and Taboo*, we can see now that its authors were looking in "primitive" societies for equivalents of Christianity's "dying god," in a period when that god was fading away in their own culture. We are now, we hope, less ethnocentric, and in most cases [we are] further still from religious resources of our own tradition. The educated avant-garde in the "nineteenth century and after" looked in the nursery as well as in exotic cultures for what it was in the process of losing in the church, so [the English reviewer's] calling *Totem and Taboo* Freud's "Just-So Story" neatly placed it culturally. One can also see it, in form—and dignity—as something like a Euripidean tragedy, with expositions, often assignable to a sort of learned chorus, on "The Horror of Incest," on Taboo, Animism, Omnipotence of Thoughts, rocking and expanding the frame of reference before the sudden, final Agon, followed by an Epiphany. I suspect that, for many of us and for "future generations," access to religious understanding and feeling may be as much through reading Freud's literary masterpiece and others of the post-religious period as through the reading, in a retrospective arrangement, of sacred and/or anthropological texts themselves. And I wonder whether the whole psychoanalytic movement may not come to be seen as a post-religious moment, during which, for example, the reliability of the patient's transference to the analyst depended on residues of religious feeling within the family structure which may not be there in future [patients]—which have not been there, as I understand it, for the increasing number of patients who are classified as "borderline."

Far from being antithetical to religion, however "completely estranged" Freud was on a doctrinal level, psychoanalysis, in practice, for those who have lost some dimensions of belief, may be an art which does mend religion, change it rather—and I can perhaps go on with "But / The art itself is nature." Certainly one can say that many people who in another time would have maintained themselves by religious discipline now are or have been in analysis or therapy. And in literary studies. One can notice, too, that a very vital development in psychoanalysis since Freud has been a secular equivalent of the cult of the Madonna, itself a later development in Christianity, after the initial worship of the father through the son. The recent tender study of mother-child interaction, growing out of or in resonance with Melanie Klein's explorations of pre-oedipal experience, has followed on the tough, heroic oedipal agons of Freud and his generation.[30]

In the new Elizabethan theater Shakespeare perfected an art fully responsive to the needs of his temperament and to the "form and pressure" of a historical moment marked by deep religious crisis. He could cherish in this art the identities it enabled him to create and control, never more tenderly than when surrendering them to the tough, heroic agons of the tragedies. Psychoanalysis was one of the resources of Barber's own culture that contributed to his understanding of Shakespeare's power to use and transform the theatrical resources of his.

I have not tried to assemble the names of persons whose assistance Joe Barber would have acknowledged. I should, however, like to express my gratitude to his colleagues at the University of California, Santa Cruz, whose encouragement in this project has been heartening.

Generous and indispensable support from the University of Illinois, Urbana, has taken many forms: a semester appointment at the Center for Advanced Studies, a sabbatical semester, a semester of reduced teaching arranged by the Department of English. The Research Board funded a graduate assistant, Willard Rusch, who provided several kinds of help with skill and diligence. Sherri George accurately typed the long and often tangled manuscript, and Mary Soliday diligently sought out and corrected dozens of errors I had managed to introduce into its many quotations. My colleagues Cary Nelson, Arnold Stein, and Jack Stillinger responded with helpful comments to a draft of the Foreword. Jan Hinely gave me painstaking and perceptive assessments of the roughest drafts of the most difficult chapters.

I could not have completed this work without the frank and supportive criticism and encouragement of several persons at a number of other universities: Janet Adelman, Peter Erickson,

30. Two typed pages (November 3, 1977) entitled "Freud's Relation to Religion, and Shakespeare's."

Stephen Greenblatt, Joel Fineman, Norman Holland, Coppélia Kahn, Norman Rabkin, Murray Schwartz, Edward Snow. I take great pleasure in acknowledging the help of these friends of Barber's, and friends of mine, who have translated their eagerness to see this book completed into assistance of various kinds, including critical, suggestive readings of its chapters. David Bevington, Frederick Crews, and Marianne Novy have provided illuminating formal readings of the entire book, which have shaped my further revisions repeatedly. Carol Neely has read and exactingly criticized every chapter, staying with each through successions of revised drafts that must have seemed endless; she has seen deeply and sensitively into the problems and the promise of this work, and my debt to her is enormous.

It has been a pleasure to work again with the University of California Press; I wish especially to thank Doris Kretschmer for her able and strategic support of the whole project, Marilyn Schwartz and Gladys Castor for their masterful editorial work, and Barbara Roos for her skillful preparation of the index. I have received other kinds of no less essential support from Joanne Wheeler, from Clifford and Irene Wheeler, and from Natalie, Gregory, and Ellen. George Putnam Barber, Lucie Barber Stroock, and Robert Ennis Barber have amply encouraged my work with the manuscripts of their father. The generosity, trust, and cooperation of Cleo Barber have sustained my work on this project from the beginning; to Joe's wish that this book be dedicated to her I am grateful to add my own.

Note on Texts

Quotations from the Sonnets are from *Shakespeare's Sonnets*, edited with analytic commentary by Stephen Booth (New Haven: Yale University Press, 1977). All other Shakespeare quotations are from *The Riverside Shakespeare*, ed. G. Blakemore Evans (Boston: Houghton Mifflin, 1974); contemporary references to Shakespeare are quoted from Appendix B of that volume. Shakespeare's sources are quoted from Geoffrey Bullough, ed., *Narrative and Dramatic Sources of Shakespeare*, 8 vols. (London: Routledge and Kegan Paul; and New York: Columbia University Press, 1957–75), and cited as *Sources* in the notes. References to Freud are to *The Standard Edition of the Complete Psychological Works of Sigmund Freud*, trans. and ed. James Strachey et al., 24 vols. (London: Hogarth, 1953–74), and cited in the notes as *Standard Edition*.

1

The Family and the Sacred in Shakespeare's Development

The loss that we feel in some of Shakespeare's greatest tragedies is not just the loss of human beings, though that is part of it; nor yet the loss of heroic human beings, though that is a great deal of it. I think our deepest sense of loss in the greatest tragedies is of what one may call the sacred-in-the-human. The qualm of awe we feel comes from the fact that the sacredness the tragedy generates is shown by the logic of the tragic action to be something that human life and society cannot sustain, something indeed whose pursuit can be destructive, leading to tragic consequences. This experience of sacredness does not, in my judgment, involve a religious, supernatural eschatology. On the contrary, it seems to me that Shakespeare's extraordinary relevance to the modern age that begins in his period comes partly from his having so consistently done without any religious supernatural. He takes up into his tragedy human needs that might look to religious fulfillment; but the tragic situation he presents is the natural world. He thus presents what can be called the post-Christian situation. One way to put it is that in these tragedies he dramatizes the search for equivalents of the Holy Family of Christianity in the human family.

My goal in this chapter is to see how this kind of drama comes out of the situation in which Shakespeare wrote, how it expresses the new cultural moment of the Renaissance and Reformation. But we must also look to the distinctive shape of Shakespeare's development as an artist, the place tragedy occupies in the whole journey from the early plays and poems to the late romances. In speaking of an artist's "power of development," we obviously refer to a many-sided process. In setting up Shakespeare as the standard of comparison for other Elizabethan dramatists, T. S. Eliot made his fullest statement of the conception of integral development instanced, in another version, in the epigraph to this book:

This standard set by Shakespeare is that of a continuous development from first to last, a development in which the choice both of theme and of dramatic and verse technique in each play seems to be determined increasingly by Shakespeare's state of feeling, by the particular stage of his emotional maturity at the time. What is "the whole man" is not simply his greatest or maturest achievement, but the whole pattern formed by the sequence of plays; so that we may say confidently that the full meaning of any one of his plays is not in itself alone, but in that play in the order in which it was written, in its relation to all of Shakespeare's other plays, earlier and later: we must know all of Shakespeare's work in order to know any of it.[1]

If, in the necessarily imperfect effort to keep this ideal of comprehension in view, one asks what Shakespeare uses his power of development for, the most general answer is that he uses it to deal with the predicaments of a new historical situation. His works, in one aspect, are a titanic work of knowing his age. In a complementary aspect, what we see in Shakespeare's development is his work of knowing himself as his works. Shakespeare uses the resources of poetry and theater to cope with and fulfill a temperament and a situation in life shaped by the family in Shakespeare.

"The family in Shakespeare" refers at once to the handling of the family in his works and to the internalizing of the family situation in his own sensibility, which actively informs his works. Shakespeare's art is distinguished by the intensity of its investment in the human family and especially in the continuity of the family across generations. This investment is extended out into society and up into the royal family. The man Shakespeare, of course, is beyond direct knowledge and would be so even if we knew vastly more than we do about his parents and his childhood. The next chapter offers some speculations about how Shakespeare's works can be placed in relation to what is known about his life. But what we chiefly have are his works. I think we can see in them something of the contribution of the individual sensibility that makes them distinctive, hazardous as this attempt has often proved. Shakespeare's power of development in this individual sense is his capacity in his works to engage creatively the inner constellations that shape temperament. Such development, in great art, always will involve "action or struggle . . . in the soul of the poet"—again the phrasing is Eliot's.[2]

1. T. S. Eliot, *Selected Essays*, rev. ed. (New York: Harcourt, Brace and World, 1950), p. 170.
2. Ibid., p. 173.

FAMILY AND GENDER IN SHAKESPEARE'S
DEVELOPMENT

A salient fact in Shakespeare's development is that tragedy does not become his central form of expression until more than half of his plays, chiefly comedies and histories, have been written. The whole tragic period can be seen as a reckoning with the problem of inheritance from one generation to the next. The problem dramatized at the core of heritage is that of achieving and maintaining masculine authority, shaped by male-to-male Oedipal confrontation and the crucial stresses brought into such conflict by relationship to the feminine. The early works, by contrast, dramatize ways of maintaining heritage that do not involve confronting and internalizing the self-asserting male egoism of a father. But we can see in them that, from the beginning, relationship to the feminine—most deeply, naturally, to the maternal—is especially problematic for Shakespeare. The major tragedies come late because, as I see it, his sensibility is shaped by a constellation of family relationships in which, initially, female or maternal power is more important than paternal. The classic Oedipal confrontation, with its possibility of atonement by identification with the father, is postponed because for him there are alternative ways of achieving identity. After the effort to shift the prime allegiance to heroic manhood in the great tragedies, the romances again show the female as predominant; with the exception of the artist-dominated *Tempest*, male identity is lost when relationship to women is lost, and regained as their gift when relationship is recovered.

The early comedies and histories, along with *Titus Andronicus* and the narrative and lyric poems, reveal a double pattern. At one pole, there is a very strong identification with the cherishing role of an infant's parents that is deeply grounded in early modes of relating to the mother. Such identification tends to submerge or transcend conflict, a tendency brought out most clearly, perhaps, in the role the poet adopts in cherishing the young man addressed in the Sonnets. Yet behind this identification with cherishing, maternal attitudes, motivating it at deep levels, is the danger of being abandoned or overpowered. At the opposite pole from maternal identification, there is a preoccupation with overpowering women— both being overpowered by them and overpowering them. There are domineering women like Margaret, the virago queen of weak, saintly Henry VI, and Shakespeare's special version of Venus, her passion frustrated by an unresponsive Adonis. And there are instances of the overpowering of women, as in *The Rape of Lucrece* or in Richard III's ruthless wooing of Anne. But Richard is himself the physical embodiment of maternal rejection, shouldering his crookbacked way through a gauntlet of curses by bereft women, including his mother, who bestows a final maternal curse. In *King John*, near the end of the first body of work, we have on the one hand the marvelous expression of Constance's grief for her son, Arthur, along with the struggle she and Queen Elinor conduct to secure the kingship for their sons, and on the other hand the Bastard's humiliation and rejection of his local-gentry mother as he leaves family and lands to take his chances as a noble, as the illegitimate son of Richard Cordelion.[3]

The strange transformation of Titus, the official martial hero who becomes the embodiment of maternally cherishing fatherhood, calls attention to Shakespeare's preoccupation with cherishing fathers in these early plays—including, in *Titus Andronicus*, the villainous Moor, Aaron, who takes over the nurture of his black infant son, born to Tamora, when her older sons are ready to destroy it. But more characteristically, figures of adult male authority are weak or vulnerable, and they command loyalty or sympathy.[4] There are generous but weak figures like Henry VI and like Titus helpless before the monstrous Gothic queen. After Titus dies by his own hand, his revenge finally consummated, Lucius with "obsequious tears" performs the "last true duties of thy noble son" (V.iii.152, 155). There are also heroic fathers, like Talbot and York, who command unlimited, sentimental loyalty from sons, including

---

3. This classic "family romance," elaborated from a chronicle episode historically unconnected with John's reign, yields Shakespeare a freewheeling, liberated figure of wit and strength to prop up John, England, and his play. Shakespeare's chronicle sources commonly provide the subject matter for such treatment of men, women, and families in the early histories, as notably with Margaret of Navarre and Henry VI. And the whole structure of his society, with the institution of inherited monarchy at its core, predicates dealing with society and heritage as extensions of the family, with dynastic continuity as the central issue. But Shakespeare's selection, emphasis, and invented additions in the history plays consistently reflect the preoccupations I am tracing, as they do in the early comedies, where sources are less determinative.
4. Coppélia Kahn's splendid book, *Man's Estate: Masculine Identity in Shakespeare* (Berkeley and Los Angeles: University of California Press, 1981), deals extensively with the vulnerability of men in Shakespeare from the vantage point of infantile individuation/separation and the anxieties this early maturational process bequeaths to later life.

York's son Richard Crookback. Male-to-male violence is typically between men of the same generation, not between father and son; violence between brothers, as in Richard's destruction of Clarence, is its fullest realization.[5]

In the comic mode, Shakespeare's strong family orientation appears early in *The Comedy of Errors*. He transforms Plautus's libertine comedy into a thoroughly domestic affair that begins with a helpless father condemned to death and ends with a moving family reunion presided over by a holy abbess—who proves to be the lost mother. But the concern with domineering women also emerges here: we have the taming of a shrew, made possible by the Abbess's intervention. Soon Petruchio turns Katherina into good household Kate in a spirited counterstatement to the rule of female predominance in the early works. In *Love's Labor's Lost* a group of men bind themselves together, first to repudiate women, then to conquer them, only to have their amorous quest miscarry when the women take control. Love's labor is lost because the Princess and her ladies are not bamboozled by Navarre and his company, not even by Berowne, who in his game of running with the hare and hunting with the hounds anticipates later predominating heroines.

As the festive form of comedy comes into its own, what is dramatized is release from family ties on a tide of communal, seasonal holiday feeling. The younger generation leaves the family to go out into what Northrop Frye has called "the green world," to go through something like a saturnalian revel, and in the process to experience a release from family sexual taboos.[6] Release brings clarification about the claims of nature within the natural and generational cycles. *Romeo and Juliet*, which starts out, under the aegis of Mercutio, almost as a festive comedy, is in many ways more closely related to these plays than to either *Titus* or the tragedies that follow. Its brilliant power and beauty find expression in the liminal situation, neither Capulet nor Montague, that Romeo and

5. Titus's slaying of his son Mutius (I.i), who has opposed his father's insistence that Lavinia marry Saturninus, is an exception that helps prove the rule, since the play is unable to make any use of the implications of this act in its subsequent dramatization of familial feeling. See the extended discussion of *Titus Andronicus* in chapter 5, pp. 125–57.

6. "The Argument of Comedy," in *English Institute Essays 1948*, ed. D. A. Robertson, Jr. (New York: Columbia University Press, 1949), pp. 58–73. For the relation of saturnalian revels to Shakespeare's comic form, see C. L. Barber, *Shakespeare's Festive Comedy* (Princeton: Princeton University Press, 1959), especially chap. 1.

Juliet dare to enter and enjoy before the hero is compelled, by Mercutio's death, to rejoin the family feud. Because the family ties that destroy young love are not contained within, but poised in opposition to, the passion of the lovers, the tragedy does not have the depth of those that come later, though it has its own kind of simpler beauty and its own internal logic.

The festive comedies provide virtually no male-to-male confrontation. Orlando's wrestling proves his physical virility in *As You Like It*, but the struggle with his elder brother is mysteriously resolved without direct confrontation, as is the animosity between the usurping and rightful dukes. In contrast to standard New Comedy, the action of festive comedy typically does not turn on the capacity of young men to overcome the obstructions of an older generation or a paternalistic society. When, in *The Merchant of Venice*, paternal wrath is vilified in Shylock, it is Portia who meets the challenge. After Hero's humiliation and mock death in *Much Ado about Nothing*, her outraged father and uncle dramatize their own helplessness when they attempt to force a confrontation with Claudio. In *Twelfth Night* there is no older generation, except Sir Toby Belch, whose young niece subsidizes *his* rule-breaking revelry.

Violence central to the action is not needed, because the comedies typically dramatize a movement into a moment or a world where nature and community join in sanctioning a "cleanly wantonness."[7] Presiding over this movement are generous, masterful young women whose femininity is frequently hidden by a page's disguise and who often must themselves elude the obstacles, among them authoritarian fathers, that block romantic union. The man is fulfilled in yielding to the female's predominance, which in the festive comedies proves to have been in the service of the women's reassuring surrender. When serious male-to-male violence seems on the verge of erupting in *Twelfth Night*, the man whom Orsino jealously threatens turns out to be a woman after all, so that, with the wonderful Shakespearean ambiguity about just what the Duke plans to do to Cesario-Viola, we can read her acquiesence as the expectation of yielding *sexually* after revealing her sex:

ORSINO: I'll sacrifice the lamb that I do love,
To spite a raven's heart within a dove.

7. Robert Herrick, "The Argument of His Book": "I write of youth, of love, and have access / By these to sing of cleanly wantonness."

VIOLA: And I most jocund, apt, and willingly,
To do you rest, a thousand deaths would die.
(V.i.130–33)

Much Ado about Nothing, a play which is not fully "festive" in the way *As You Like It* and *Twelfth Night* are, recalls in some respects the earlier comedies—Petruchio's assault on Kate's shrewishness in *Taming of the Shrew*, the precarious solidarity of men in confrontation with women in *Love's Labor's Lost*. *Much Ado* explicitly makes the precariousness of mutuality between the sexes its subject. The merry war of Benedick and Beatrice charmingly dramatizes the two sexes' fascination with and resistance to each other as objects, while the slandering of Hero exhibits in a critical perspective male degradation of a woman as object, such as we get in the sonnets to the mistress. The play sets up, and apart, male and female solidarity: the prince and the martial hero and his boon companion Benedick fresh back from the wars, the women richly in communication with each other in the world of the household. The "practice" in which the men persuade Benedick that Beatrice loves him desperately, as the women do conversely for Beatrice, provides both with the needed trust to move across the sexual line. In the play's finest dramatic moment, when Beatrice challenges Benedick to "kill Claudio," Benedick discovers that he has given up a primary male relationship for allegiance to the much richer female world. *Much Ado* is so satisfying as a comedy because it shows up the callowness and the callousness of male solidarity and suspicion while moving through confusions to a consummation that does not promise too much. The great delight of it, of course, is the way Benedick and Beatrice, in their mocks and in their final commitment, are *conscious* of the precariousness and are resolved to live with it. What makes such consciousness and commitment possible is that whole gracious, sociable world evoked in easy conversation and incarnated most fully in Beatrice's poised wit.

These comedies, taken as a group, suggest an exceptional capacity in Shakespeare for identification with women. His use of comic form tends to make women the center of an awareness shared with the audience, their dominant role combining the cherishing of men with the sort of control that depends not on overtly asserted power but on subtle manipulation guided by superior understanding. The women's enabling dominance partly incorporates cherishing, maternal attitudes in leading the men toward sexual bonds. The entire absence of actual mothers in the festive comedies is consistent with the protection of these emerging bonds both from the threat of overpowering women prominent in the earlier works and from incestuous undercurrents that become prominent in the tragedies and the late romances.

In the Sonnets we can see most clearly the recourse of incorporating the cherishing parental role to cope with a problematic relationship to the maternal. Much of the strangeness in the attitudes we find expressed in the sonnets to the young man becomes comprehensible when we recognize relationships to parental attitudes and, more deeply still, to childlike feelings of total dependence, as they are now shaping relationships within a single generation or half-generation. In urging the young man to have a child, the first seventeen poems encourage him to make of himself a renewing mirror image such as the poet soon makes for *himself* of the young man:

> Look in thy glass and tell the face thou viewest,
> Now is the time that face should form another.
> (Sonnet 3)

The lines describe exactly what Shakespeare himself does in later poems with the young man as mirror:

> My glass shall not persuade me I am old,
> So long as youth and thou are of one date.
> (Sonnet 22)

The poet's renewal by identification is compared to that of a parent with a child. In Sonnet 37 it is a father:

> As a decrepit father takes delight
> To see his active child do deeds of youth,
> So I, made lame by fortune's dearest spite,
> Take all my comfort of thy worth and truth.

In Sonnet 3 it is the youth's own mother:

> Thou art thy mother's glass, and she in thee
> Calls back the lovely April of her prime;
> So thou through windows of thine age shalt see,
> Despite of wrinkles, this thy golden time.

Relationship by identification is less familiar from our conscious social experience than relationship to people as objects, because it is less observable. We observe our objects, but people whom we take into ourselves by identification are matter less for our observation than for our conservation. In fact, as Freud's later writings and more recent studies deriving from them insist repeatedly, identification is particularly important not only in relationship to parents but generally as a means of dealing with the loss of objects by estrangement or death. And a person lost, who has been internalized and so preserved, as well as grieved for, can often be found again in a new object. One of the most extraordinary of the Sonnets, 31, makes explicit the beloved's function as heir to earlier attachments:

> Thy bosom is endearéd with all hearts,
> Which I by lacking have supposéd dead;
> And there reigns love and all love's loving parts,
> And all those friends which I thought buriéd.

The third quatrain specifies that those lost become "parts of" the poet, now projected in the friend:

> Thou art the grave where buried love doth live,
> Hung with the trophies of my lovers gone,
> Who all their parts of me to thee did give;
> That due of many now is thine alone.
> Their images I loved I view in thee,
> And thou, all they, hast all the all of me.

There is no reference here to parental figures; the earlier figures are "lovers" in the broad Elizabethan sense, but the kind of feeling for them, "dear religious love" calling forth "many a holy and obsequious tear" (lines 6 and 5), is consistent with original familial love.

The poet's identification with the young man and passive dedication to dependence on his love are far more visible than the poet's identification with the cherishing parent, because for the most part the parenting is expressed or embodied in the process of creating the sonnet. What is crucial for the whole view of Shakespeare's development in its early stages is that the adoption of a cherishing role permits a reception of heritage and the maintenance of a self grounded in it, without confronting centrally the problem of manliness. The poet in effect becomes the nurturing parent(s), in his (her, their) earliest desirable function, the function that creates and validates life.

Relationship by cherishing links the Sonnets both to the festive comedies, with their enabling heroines, and to the greatest of the history plays. In the same period when the comedies center on witty, loving heroines, Shakespeare develops in Falstaff a marvelous burlesque of cherishing by an older man who seeks to appropriate the very highest aristocratic substance. Falstaff's role brings forth ironic potentials suppressed or averted in the relationship to the friend of the Sonnets, including the self-reflexive egotism animating the poet's devotion. But Prince Hal is also everything to Falstaff for "spiritual" reasons, as the romantic critics liked to insist: by reflection, in Harry's company, Falstaff can feel that to banish plump Jack is to banish all the world. Like the poet of the Sonnets, Falstaff in Hal's abundance is sufficed, and by a part of all his glory lives. In chapter 7 we will look at how the Chorus in *Henry V* extends such vicarious participation in another's manhood—leaving behind the ironies of Falstaff's bond to Hal and seeking fulfillment through a very different object from that of the Sonnets poet.

The second group of histories, together with the festive comedies, the works from about 1595 to 1599, exhibit a significant moratorium on certain kinds of man-woman stress. The separation of genres in this period, between male-dominated history and festive comedy with its delightful, enthralling heroines, keeps apart areas of conflict that come together in the major tragedies and the problem comedies.[8] Even in the histories of this very productive period, however, where the role of women is minimal, the dominant protagonist is, finally, the nation, thought of as female: "This nurse, this teeming womb of royal kings" (*R2* II.i.51). As the men's struggle for dominance transforms the "fresh green lap of fair King Richard's land" (*R2* III.iii.47) into a battleground, Henry IV dreams of a foreign war to end the "intestine shock":

> No more the thirsty entrance of this soil
> Shall daub her lips with her own children's blood,
> No more shall trenching war channel her fields.
> (*1H4* I.i.5–7)

His son will end this civil strife, win France for England, and gain a wife for himself by ravishing, and threatening to ravish, French "cities turn'd into a maid . . . girdled with maiden walls that war

---

8. On the separation of genres in the period preceding the major tragedies, see Richard P. Wheeler, *Shakespeare's Development and the Problem Comedies: Turn and Counter-Turn* (Berkeley and Los Angeles: University of California Press, 1981), pp. 154–79.

hath never ent'red" (*H5* V.ii.321–23). But actual relationship to women will not contribute significantly either to the troubled reign of Henry IV or to Prince Hal's emergence as Henry V.[9]

We often first encounter an insuperable problem in thinking we have solved it. Shakespeare's power of development seems to me involved in such a moment of apparent resolution in the two parts of *Henry IV* and their triumphant finale in *Henry V*. Here, where Shakespeare for the first time dramatizes tensions between a son and a strong father, he uses every resource, social and dramatic, to represent the son's inheritance from the father as successful. Hal internalizes his father to become, officially, all king and a guiltless man, "th' offending Adam" whipped out of him by "Consideration" (*H5* I.i.28–29). After *Henry V*, the series of major tragedies begins with Brutus's prophetic qualm of self-recognition:

> Into what dangers would you lead me, Cassius,
> That you would have me seek into myself
> For that which is not in me.
>
> (*JC* I.ii.63–65)

Soon Hamlet will cry out across terrifying uncertainties to the apparition of the heroic manhood that is not in him. Beginning with *Julius Caesar*, the tragedies dramatize a series of failures to preserve or vindicate heritage by taking on the authority of the father or the figure of authority. The hostility of the young to the old, the impulse to destroy them and so take over, becomes progressively more overt and savage in the sequence of tragedies that climaxes with *Lear* and *Macbeth*. With it goes the tragic recognition, in various forms, that in fact one can take over from the older generation only by becoming them, which their destruction prevents.

Shakespeare postpones until *Julius Caesar* the dramatization of the tragic potential in the problem of achieving full adult authority, full manhood. Then, with *Hamlet* he situates his protagonist in relation to the ghost of a heroic father murdered by a usurping father, whom the Prince must in turn seek to destroy to vindicate his own manhood and the heritage of the dead king. Like Falstaff, a figure

---

9. In "Fathers, Sons, and Brothers in *Henry V*," chap. 2 of his *Patriarchal Structures in Shakespeare's Drama* (Berkeley and Los Angeles: University of California Press, 1985), Peter Erickson observes: "Both Henry V and Hamlet are poised between the two incompatible options of male and heterosexual ties. In both cases, forms of male bonding take precedence at the expense of relations with women. *Hamlet* more directly confronts alienation from women, but the ending of *Henry V*, in raising yet not fulfilling festive marital expectations, reveals the problem" (pp. 64–65).

endowed with such wit, imaginative energy, and dramatic resource that he dominates an action in which the design gives him a subordinate role, Hamlet is endowed with the dramatist's powers to the point where he tends to come out of the control of the play. Like the self-effacing Chorus celebrating the heroic manhood of Henry V, Hamlet stands rapt before the royal presence of his father's ghost. But whereas Falstaff and the Chorus are versions of the cherishing and dependent role of the Sonnets poet, finding vicarious enjoyment in the friend's manhood and high birth, Hamlet is potentially the thing itself, a prince who "was likely, had he been put on, / To have prov'd most royal" (V.ii.397–98). The last histories begin the shift to heroic investment in the thing itself by banishing Falstaff in favor of unqualified identification with the young hero king. But the heroic mode of *Henry V* diminishes the range of ironic understanding achieved in balancing comic Falstaff against noble historical action in *1 & 2 Henry IV*. The struggle to achieve full male authority now requires, in *Hamlet*, the mixture of comic with *tragic* action.

After *Julius Caesar* relationship to women contributes more and more decisively to the tragic struggle and failure. From the beginning Hamlet is tormented by what he regards as his mother's incestuous union with the murderer Claudius. In *Macbeth* a powerful wife assumes a demonic maternal role in relation to a protagonist who, with her urging, will murder the fatherly king: "Come to my woman's breasts, / And take my milk for gall, you murth'ring ministers" (I.v.47–48). Macbeth hesitates:

> I dare do all that may become a man;
> Who dares do more is none.
> (I.vii.46–47)

Lady Macbeth answers:

> What beast was't then
> That made you break this enterprise to me?
> When you durst do it, then you were a man.
> (I.vii.47–49)

There follows her terrible expression of maternal violence:

> I have given suck, and know
> How tender 'tis to love the babe that milks me;
> I would, while it was smiling in my face,
> Have pluck'd my nipple from his boneless gums,
> And dash'd the brains out, had I so sworn as you
> Have done to this.
> (I.vii.54–59)

Macbeth, at the moment of finally acquiescing to Lady Macbeth's goading, relishes his wife as a mother: "Bring forth men-children only! / For thy undaunted mettle should compose / Nothing but males" (I.vii.72–74). Lady Macbeth for her part extends yet again this tendency to conceive relationships in vertical terms of the family, placing Duncan with "Had he not resembled / My father as he slept, I had done't" (II.ii.12–13).

That Shakespeare postponed for so long a reckoning with such depths of vulnerability and violence—across generations and across gender—is consistent, I think, with the structure of his sensibility. For that sensibility, especially as we can discern it shaping the art before the great tragedies, cherishing is a way of keeping relationship to the maternal presence despite intense anxiety and fear of abandonment. Internalization of maternal modes of relating makes up for the loss of relationship to the feminine by incorporating it into the self and provides a way of achieving identity alternative to confrontation with and subsequent internalization of the male egoism of a strong father. Shakespeare's major use of tragedy departs from the orientation of his earlier work, since it is directed toward imagining encounters with the world by male identity, or more accurately, imagining various heroic attempts to achieve male identity. Beginning with *Hamlet*, the great tragedies are centered in the awareness of the protagonist and dramatize the failure of his struggle. In each there is a crisis of heritage: the problem of the transmission of authority underlies or constitutes the problem of achieving masculine identity. And in each a woman makes a demand on the protagonist (or embodies a need) that is more than can be met. His heroic action is in response to the female presence, however much it is action in the "man's world" of society at large. The tragic extremity of the action can be seen, from one perspective, as the aberrant development of a ritual that normally would serve to assure the transmission of heritage but that is warped to tragic consequences by the intensity of the need at the heart of the relationship to the woman. The relationship is one involving worship or a dependency akin to worship; it regularly embodies an underlying wish to surrender the will, to lose or merge the self.[10]

In the period before the tragedies, men tend to be objects, women subjects (or, where women are excluded, the men are understood in terms of needs they fulfill for other men who cherish them—the

10. For *Timon of Athens* as an exception that, in aborting, proves the rule, see chapter 10, pp. 305–9.

Sonnets poet; Falstaff; the Chorus as spokesman for author, audience, and the play's society in *Henry V*); in the tragedies, men are the subjective centers of awareness, women are objects—but objects in whom, or for whom, the male drive is to lose itself. Shakespeare's turn to tragedy suggests that the mode of relating to the world through the feminine ceases to work for him when, midway in his career, the disruptive potential in the problem of identity as achieved through confrontation with the father appears with overwhelming force. After a sort of moratorium made possible by the separation of genres in the comedies and history plays, Shakespeare enters his major tragic period and begins to deal with the full interplay and conflict of masculine and feminine roles in human development. This moratorium is an interval between the early work up to about 1595, where the full interplay is dealt with under a predominating feminine aegis, and the period of the tragedies after 1600, where the struggle is fully joined to the effort to assert male identity in the face of the needs and demands of relationship to women.

All the problematic stresses in the family constellation come into the major tragedies. What is new is that their crises are centered in the failure of heroic adult male authority. This may sound like a conclusion that Shakespeare's tragedies dramatize the impossibility of adequate manhood, the impossibility of a hero's being anything but a tragic hero, and in a way it is. But the fulfillment Shakespeare envisages in tragedy would be the focus and consummation of a heroic and sacramental society. The manhood whose failure we feel with awe, regret, and something like metaphysical dismay, is one in which the milk of human kindness is as necessary as the ability to assert virile identity. The tragic loss is the loss of something human society can rarely if ever achieve, toward which the fulfillment of both sexes vulnerably reaches.

Of course the change in Shakespeare's work at about 1600 also reflects the change in the mood of his whole society in the last years of Elizabeth: the breakdown of the Elizabethan compromise,[11] the dying-off of the older generation of Elizabethan worthies, the execution of Essex, the radical questioning and disillusionment and satiric irritation that Patrick Cruttwell, among many others,

11. In *Shakespearean Tragedy and the Elizabethan Compromise* (New York: New York University Press, 1957), Paul Siegel sees in Shakespeare's tragedies a reaffirmation of the "Christian humanist world view," which was being subjected to radical questioning as the social order was forced out of balance in the Queen's last years.

has described.[12] To focus on what the shift to tragedy involved in the dynamic relation between the author and his form does not negate the influence of social and intellectual history: "The great poet, in writing himself, writes his time."[13] But we must consider the fact that, even if the major tragedies had not been written, the change in the mood of the times would be apparent in *All's Well That Ends Well*, *Measure for Measure*, and *Troilus and Cressida*. We can see in these problematic plays, as clearly or more clearly than in the tragedies, the breakdown of faith, the questioning of received values, the crisis about heritage. The tragic form comes when the crisis of faith and heritage and values is focused in the problem of achieving male authority and identity.

An artist's power of development may require him to produce partly unsatisfactory works in response to his own growing sense of realities, in his changing world, and in his own developing personality. In *All's Well* and *Measure for Measure*, Shakespeare dramatizes aspects of social reality that had been left out of his earlier work—and would be missing if we had only the masterful tragedies written in the same period. *Measure* confronts disruptive relationships of love and lust, in society and sensibility, in the brothel's low life as well as in high office, which are beyond the poise of *As You Like It*. *All's Well* faces up to problems of femininity in society and sensibility—problems of sexuality and status—which are dealt with delightfully in *Twelfth Night*, along with problems of patronage like those dealt with in *Henry IV*. In *All's Well*, Shakespeare is undertaking—against odds—to make a comedy of the pattern of marriage arranged by the older generation, which was the norm in Shakespeare's society. At the same time he is undertaking to present the union of a heroine from the middle class, under aristocratic patronage, with a great nobleman, Bertram, against the resistance of the young lord to marrying beneath him.

These plays written in comic or mixed form during the period of the tragedies also seem to me to confirm the critical shift away from the confident identification with the feminine, the failure of that cherishing mode of relating to the world through the drama. *All's Well That Ends Well* goes all the way in that direction—and fails to carry us with it. In dealing with Helena's passion for a highborn lord, a dramatic version of the situation between poet and the

12. Patrick Cruttwell, *The Shakespearean Moment and Its Place in the Poetry of the Seventeenth Century* (London: Chatto and Windus, 1954).

13. T. S. Eliot, "Shakespeare and the Stoicism of Seneca," *Selected Essays*, p. 117.

young man of the Sonnets, Shakespeare takes the identification with the feminine beyond the limit of full dramatic control.[14] With *Measure for Measure* the shift into the tragic period has taken place, and we get a comedy where the center of identification is with men for whom women are problematic objects. The Duke's male identity dominates the play, but in special terms: his friar's habit hides his authority (and sexuality) while he plays at being Providence by means of Art, the art of plotting in the manner of a dramatist.[15] Angelo can be seen as a running dog for the Duke in the pursuit of Isabella, with Lucio as a chorus who serves to bring out the sexual potential of the game the "Duke of dark corners" is playing, without acknowledgment until the theatrical finale.[16] Both *All's Well* and *Measure* situate the action of love against the presence of higher authority that must be appeased before the plays' marriages can be validated. The threat of male-to-male violence when sexual desire (or revulsion) conflicts with moral authority hangs over both plays; it shapes the range of feeling throughout and culminates in the final judgment scenes, which yield to mercy and marriage only at the very end.

Troilus and Cressida also deals, obviously, with the problems of achieving and maintaining relationship to women as objects (and as cause). In Shakespeare's handling of the Trojan war, the most prominent development in the complex action centers on the vulnerability of men to women—without, one must add, fully facing the contribution of the men to the failure. In the great tragedies the protagonist's heroic effort looks toward resolution by way of full relationship both to society and to a particular woman to whom he is bound; his tragic stature is measured by the inclusiveness of the crisis he fails to surmount. Unlike Othello, Macbeth, or Antony, the "boy" Troilus, wholly set from the start on self-realization through Cressida, is never shown struggling simultaneously with the problem of achieving a socially validated manhood—hence, perhaps, the much less fully tragic quality of the play, or at least the fit of his limitation with its satiric cast. But the design of the play seems less to explore his limitation than to make Cressida a scapegoat for Troilus's immaturity.

14. *Shakespeare's Development and the Problem Comedies*, pp. 57–91.
15. See Francis Fergusson's chapter on *Measure for Measure* in *The Human Image in Dramatic Literature* (New York: Doubleday Anchor, 1957), pp. 126–43.
16. *Shakespeare's Development and the Problem Comedies*, pp. 130–39.

The fate of Falstaff's descendants in these problematic plays also indicates the reorientation of sensibility that is shaping the drama at the beginning of Shakespeare's tragic period. *All's Well* presents a degraded version of Falstaff (and of the Sonnets poet) in Parolles's effort to live through his relationship to the young manhood of aristocratic Bertram. Lucio extends this line into *Measure for Measure*— in his advocacy of Claudio, in his satiric indifference to the fate of Pompey, in his freewheeling attack on Angelo's authoritarian severity, in his impromptu appropriation for himself of an insider's intimate knowledge of Duke Vincentio. Much more clearly, and disquietingly, the older man who lives vicariously in the young man's sexuality is dramatized in the degrading role of Pandarus in *Troilus and Cressida*.

In both *All's Well* and *Measure for Measure* Shakespeare creates a world managed by one of his people, with his help. The bed-trick in *Measure* is managed from a distance, and from above, by the Duke. In *All's Well* it is managed from below by Helena. But Helena does not have the benefit of Petrarchan idealization of love and desire, which gives the heroines power over their men in the festive comedies, where social status is not in question. And in *Measure*, once the disguised Duke comes forward to cope, by contrivance after contrivance, with the situation engendered by Angelo's lust, Shakespeare's dramatic rhythm is broken. If the comic finale is to work, one has to accept a shift to a different level or mode of meaning, and even so there are few who can stomach the way the Duke at the end stages everyone to the world, with himself in a coup de theatre at the center—he who had opened the play with "I love the people, / But do not like to stage me to their eyes" (I.i.67–68). As with *All's Well*, where Helena's project culminates in the moral aggression expended on Bertram before he accepts marriage to her, we can feel at the end of *Measure for Measure* that the play is being *used*, rather than that its full human implications are worked into the light.

In other plays Shakespeare would fully work through the destructive and creative possibilities of dramatic manipulation—in the roles of Iago and Prospero. But problems that prove intractable to the comic manipulation of Helena and Duke Vincentio can help illuminate Shakespeare's need to make tragedy his primary medium in plays written at about the same time as *All's Well* and *Measure for Measure*. The problematic comedies have lost the confident reliance on a community feeling for sexuality as benign and sanctioned by natural rhythms. Sexuality is either disassociated from family ties and social sanctions and is thus a pernicious degradation, as in *Measure for Measure*, or else it is too closely bound up with the couple's having grown up together and remaining under the aegis of the older generation, as with Helena and Bertram in *All's Well*. Meanwhile, the major tragedies show violence erupting from the pull of family ties that are too close, "more than kin" (*Ham.* I.ii.65). The whole heroic identity is invested in "holy cords . . . too intrinse t' unloose" (*Lr.* II.ii.74–75) that have an incestuous content, direct or displaced. The investment is at once ennobling and ironically destructive.

In the first three late romances Shakespeare recenters his art on the need men have to be validated by feminine presences, now dramatized as achieved in visionary reunions—reunions anticipated within tragedy in *Lear* and *Antony and Cleopatra*. A daughter restored leads to the recovery of a lost wife, Thaisa, Hermione. The finale is a tempest distanced and managed. Prospero gives up the daughter with whom he has been isolated in his cell, as Lear dreamed of being isolated in a prison cell with Cordelia. By his "art" he masters a usurping younger brother as well as the temptation to talion violence: "The rarer action is / In virtue than in vengeance" (*Tmp.* V.i.27–28). "In my end is my beginning."

In the late romances we have symbolic action that, instead of freeing sexuality from the ties of family, works to restore family ties by disassociating them from the threat of degradation by physical incest. The romance mode of presentation insists that the action is *symbolic*, even though the ecstatic reunions are also actual happenings within a play space that has been enfranchised by a new understanding of the way magic *can* work. Murray M. Schwartz has developed the view that the tragedies use up the play space in which the psyche makes the transition from the world as mother to the larger social world.[17] Presences without which "the wine of life is drawn" (*Mac.* II.iii.95) are destroyed by the demand to become or possess them totally. The romances, in Schwartz's splendid formulation, restore the play space. In the reunions of *Pericles* and *The Winter's Tale*, Shakespeare finds his way to his composite version of Dante's "Vergine madre, figlia del tuo figlio."

17. "Shakespeare through Contemporary Psychoanalysis," in *Representing Shakespeare: New Psychoanalytic Essays*, ed. Murray M. Schwartz and Coppélia Kahn (Baltimore: Johns Hopkins University Press, 1980), pp. 21–32.

THE NEW THEATER AND THE OLD
RELIGION

The creation of a new art form puts men in a new relation to their experience. The sudden emergence of the Elizabethan drama was a step in the developing self-consciousness of modern culture, providing a new location for language and gesture, the theater. Human possibilities could be envisaged with the freedom of a place apart, alternative to the church and to courtly situations. The drama in the new theater provided form for the expression and understanding of much that entered into the discipline of worship to which the church was sacred, and the discipline of courtesy and power centered in the royal presence.

The new vantage point of the audience in watching action on a stage made the drama a new organ of culture, a *novum organum*. It was an agency in the historical shift of the Renaissance and Reformation from a ritual and ceremonial view of life, with absolutist assumptions about meaning and reality, toward a psychological and historical view. A continuous, active shifting of perspective is involved in the Elizabethan theater's presenting life as drama. Ritual, ceremony, the language of orthodox or heroic or romantic expectation give expression to energies that drive the action; the action is dramatic as it shows the expected pattern not being realized, going wrong (or right) beyond expectation. In the works of the few great dramatists who could control the medium, the going wrong or going right is opened to understanding as character and history. The new place apart permits the human situation to be envisaged as tragic or comic.

In seeking to understand the special function of Elizabethan tragedy at the moment it was created, one can ask: Why was it possible just then? and what was the need for it just then? Speculation about why it was possible mostly concerns the secularization of culture: humanism; the rediscovery of the classics; the new arts of Italy and France imported and developed by new, secular patrons and proprietors; the new repertory theater, performing independently of seasonal occasions or the church year; the professionalization of actors and eventually authors in this day-by-day joint stock enterprise; the new cosmopolitanism of the city of London, which provided audiences that included, especially before the Jacobean shift to private theaters, a broad range of social types with a corresponding range of interests; the self-conscious, aristocratic literary culture of the court, which provided the audience, on special occasions, for players and plays maintained by "public means which public manners breeds" (Sonnet 111). In short, the drama was possible because of the Renaissance—as more than a hundred years of effective historical scholarship has demonstrated.

My speculations keep coming back to the other question: Why was *tragic* form for the drama needed? what needs did it serve? Such questioning points toward the new religious situation brought on by the Reformation—or more precisely, the transition or break from Catholicism to Protestantism. The new theater permits the expression of impulses, profoundly disruptive both intrapsychically and socially, which in a monolithically religious culture, or for religiously devoted people in a mixed culture, have their "theater" in the traditional place apart, the church. In the new place apart provided by the Elizabethan theater, tragic form has a function analogous to religious discipline and religious worship, though with profound differences in the relation of the auditor to the protagonist, from that of the worshiper to Christ.

Marlowe used tragic form as a means of controlling the envisagement of disruptive heroic impulse. The action of *Doctor Faustus* confronts poetry of magical expectation with ironic contradiction while carrying the heroic striving through to express its ultimate, self-destructive consummation. Because of its directly religious framework (almost unique in the Elizabethan drama), *Doctor Faustus* permits us to see with a special directness relations between three spheres of experience: religious, infantile, and social. In Shakespeare's work we do not find the same central use of religious terms that we get in one great play of Marlowe's, where the constellation of the family as experienced in infancy looms behind aberrant religious and blasphemous imagery and gesture.

Shakespeare's plays bring in formal religion as subject matter chiefly as it was experienced by the secular communicant, for whom participation in worship was a matter of course, significant largely as it validated social life:

> If ever you have look'd on better days,
> If ever been where bells have knoll'd to church,
> If ever sate at any good man's feast,
> If ever from your eyelids wip'd a tear
> And know what 'tis to pity and be pitied,
> Let gentleness my strong enforcement be.
>
> (*AYL* II.vii.113–18)

So speaks Orlando, invoking "civilized standards" in the "desert" of the Forest of Arden. Or again, an invitation to a christening feast (instead of a wedding) concludes *The Comedy of Errors*, when the Abbess has recovered her long-lost sons and husband.

This sense of Christianity, through the church's validating the world, is present in the plays insofar as they are imitations of social life. But if we ask where in the plays are the enormous energies which in a dedicated religious person are taken up into worship, we can note that some part of them is taken up into the creative dynamics of the dramatic and poetic action, in the "worship" of the hero by figures in the play (and by the audience), and in the worship by the hero of the figures who command his allegiance within the play. More fundamentally, the worship in the plays springs from the fact that the heroic (and romantic) in poetic drama draws on the same roots of infantile feeling that religion draws on. Shakespeare's tragic drama presents a heroic society in which it is assumed that the hero can fulfill, by social action, high expectations grounded in the total relationships and wishes of childhood. There is an investment of self by the hero in the large world—"the big wars"—which is felt initially to be consistent with, and to consummate, the nuclear family relationships from which human beings move out into the common life of society. We in the audience make a similar investment in the hero as a social figure. But regularly there is a shift or swerve by which the larger, social investment is diverted, or reduced, to an investment in a family relationship.

Such engagement is total, as with Othello's bond to Desdemona, and is shaped by the deepest family ties of infantile development, "the fountain from the which my current runs / Or else dries up" (*Oth.* IV.ii.59–60). The roots in infancy from which identity grows outward in healthy situations, and which religion taps for its forms of worship, become, in tragic situations, the source of impossible, destructive, and self-destructive demands. The audience shares the emotion of the familial commitment while seeing its ironies. Instead of worshiping a Holy Family, which is divine, and so taking infantile motives up out of secular life while at the same time sustaining them and providing them with stable objects, the tragedies exhibit family relations, or family-like relations, being made sacred or demonic or both.

When one looks at the heroic and romantic in the tragedies as a form of worship, often anguished worship (as well as intoxicating, elevating, life-enhancing), it is natural to blink twice and consider that most of the symbolic actions of the Old Religion had been forbidden in England by the Protestant reformers around Elizabeth. Most of its visible embodiments—Christ on the Rood, the saints and the Virgin Mary in statues, paintings and stained glass—had been swept from the churches on orders from the Privy Council in the years immediately preceding the birth of Marlowe and Shakespeare in 1564. One of the official homilies, in rebuking the people for not faithfully attending the new service, speaks of their "gross fantasy," their "worldly and carnal affections and desires," missing the "gay gazing sights" of the old worship. One homily denounced "our churches . . . full of such great puppets, wondrously decked and adorned. . . . You would believe that the images of our men-saints were some princes of Persia land with their proud apparel, and the idols of our women-saints were nice and well-trimmed harlots."[18]

Soon "gay gazing sights" were drawing unprecedented crowds to the public theaters with living puppets, including Marlowe's Tamburlaine, self-made prince of Persia, and his captured princess bedecked "with precious iuelles of mine owne: / More rich and valurous than Zenocrates" (1 Tamb. 292–93).[19] For the most part, the sights in the theater were secular, of course: the relocation of iconographic interest is a clear example of what we think of as the Renaissance. But the trend was not simply secular. If the Old Religion's holy images had been partly secularized, the new theater's secular personages could be invested with meanings cognate to those that had entered into worship: "Now walk the angels on the walles of heauen, / . . . To entertaine deuine Zenocrate" (2 Tamb. 2983–85). When images are banished from the old established theater of the soul,[20] some of the need to which the holy images

18. *Sermons or Homilies Appointed to be Read in Churches in the Time of Queen Elizabeth*, 4th ed. (Oxford: Clarendon Press, 1816), vol. 2, no. 8, pp. 294, 295; no. 2, p. 219. The first passage is cited by Philip Hughes, *The Reformation in England*, vol. 3 (London: Hollis and Carter, 1954), p. 104.

19. Quotations from Marlowe are from *The Complete Works of Christopher Marlowe*, ed. C. F. Tucker Brooke (Oxford: Clarendon Press, 1910).

20. Protestant attacks on the mass emphasized its theatricality, a service performed, according to Bishop Jewell, "like a masquery or a stage play." In *Th' Overthrow of Stage Plays* (1599), John Rainolds complained of "*Popish Priests*" who "have transformed the celebrating of the Sacrament of the *Lords supper* into a *Masse-game*, and all other partes of the *Ecclesiasticall service* into *theatricall sights*." Both quotes are from Jonas Barish, *The Antitheatrical Prejudice* (Berkeley and Los Angeles: University of California Press, 1981), pp. 162–63.

had ministered comes over into the new place apart, the theater. "Preaching cannot possibly stay idolatry," a homily warned, "if images be set up publicly in temples and churches."[21] If not in the church, then surely not in the theater, as the same people who denounced the remnants of popery in the Anglican service never tired of insisting as they sought to abolish that "School of Abuse" where "the very Pompes of the Divell" were celebrated.[22]

One kind of worship caught up into the new theater was the residual paganism which had coexisted with Catholicism in seasonal sports and pastimes and which provided a paradigm for feeling and awareness in festive comedy. To understand aspects of the worship involved in tragedy, by contrast to comedy, one needs to look, not in village or churchyard, but in the church itself. First one must look for what is *not* there when Shakespeare and Marlowe are growing up. Christ crucified, constantly before the eyes of worshipers in the Old Religion as he hung on the cross on the rood screen in the middle of the church, is not there; instead, the royal arms are there, if instructions have been carried out. Earlier the Virgin Mary, all-forgiving intercessor, stood close by the crucified Christ and in her special chapels; now the Holy Mother is no longer present, in statue or painting or glass, nor are the saints. The Blessed Sacrament is not there; in its place is a board on which the ten commandments are written. The consecrated altar has been replaced with a plain, movable table.

Such changes in the church reflect the fact that society is officially undertaking to do without hallowed things and places, and without a whole range of thinking now regarded as superstitious. "Alas," laments the homily against idolatry, condemning the proliferation of individual saints' images and the localized imaging of universal figures of worship in the Old Religion,

> we seem in thus thinking and doing to have learned our religion, not out of God's word, but out of the Pagan poets. . . . When you hear of our Lady of Walsingham, our Lady of Ipswich, our Lady of Wilsdon, and such other; what is it but an imitation of the Gentiles idol-

---

21. *Homilies*, vol. 2, no. 2, p. 203; quoted in Hughes, vol. 3, p. 103.

22. *The School of Abuse* (1579) is the title of Stephen Gosson's "pleasant invective gainst poets, pipers, players, jesters, and such-like caterpillars of a commonwealth"; William Prynne declares, in his *Histriomastix* (1633), "*That popular Stage-Playes (the very Pompes of the Divell which we renounce in Baptisme*, if we beleeve the Fathers) *are sinfull, heathenish, lewde, ungodly Spectacles*" (quoted in Barish, p. 84).

aters? . . . Whereby is evidently meant, that the saint for the image sake should in those places, yea, in the images themselves, have a dwelling, which is the ground of their idolatry.[23]

On the stage, the image-making power of poetry takes over some of the modes of finding and giving meaning which Protestant polemicists condemned as idolatrous in the Old Religion.

The Protestant reform, in particular, does away with great religious resources for dramatizing, in iconography that demanded belief, the deepest stresses and longings growing out of the family constellation. We can partly understand the centrality of the sacred and demonic in the major tragedies if we recognize how these plays present a search for something like divinity in the family, or in family-like roles and relationships in society. There is a total investment, which is tragic because its objects are human and conditioned by time. The investment goes with the assumption, more or less unconscious and displaced, of omnipotence of mind, expressed in a poetry of magical expectation or command. Tragedy presents, through the ultimately destructive and self-destructive action of the protagonist, the involuntary sacrifice of this assumption. Can the need that tragedy meets in the theater be unrelated to the elimination, in the church, of the image of a supreme voluntary sacrifice, and the elimination of the Mass understood as an actual, present reenactment of that sacrifice?

The preoccupation of Shakespeare's tragedies with struggles to achieve authority and male identity by overcoming a passive or "negative" resolution of the relationship to authority accords with the fact that the plays are written when civilization is moving away from a monolithic traditional Christianity embodied in Catholic worship. For Christianity institutionalized a passive relationship to ultimate authority in the imitation of Christ's sacrifice to God the Father. Looked at psychologically, this is the "negative resolution of the Oedipus complex." Understood as religious truth, it is dedication to the ultimate sources of life and truth. When in John's Gospel Christ repeatedly says that he does nothing for himself but only for his Father in heaven that sent him, one can note that he is avoiding the self-assertion of a worldly hero, the sort of assumption of male authority that would have been consistent with his seeking to overthrow Herod to become the secular king whom many expected in

23. *Homilies*, vol. 2, no. 2, p. 188.

the Messiah. So he *is* passive in relation to the Father—but with how extraordinary a fund of power and courage, "Galilean turbulence"! And though passive, passive to what?—to the All, to the life-giving, life-cherishing, life-enhancing force that is beyond circumscription in any finite kingdom: "It is he that hath made us, and not we ourselves" (Ps. 100:3).

Yet Christ took, also, another attitude: he said he *was* God. The extraordinary power of Christ, his transcendent fearlessness and penetration, goes with "identification with the father" in psychological terms, as does his power to love unconditionally, as parents love, or are perceived to love, from one vantage point of the infantile situation. Only this father is not Joseph, a mild old man, but a Father to whom the son reaches beyond the finite human being who might have begot him in "an instant of blind rut." [24] This is an adequate father—adequate to the idealized conception of early childhood—objectively understood: the "God of our fathers," the God of Abraham, the God of the Psalms and the whole Jewish monotheistic heritage now being extended, or about to be, beyond the tribe or nation into the wide world of many races and nations brought together by Rome. The identification with the Father means fusion with and responsibility to the ultimate force that creates and cherishes life and society, that makes finite fathers possible.

There is a psychological logic visible in the fact that in the synoptic gospels no sooner does Christ assert his identity with God than he reveals that he must suffer death. As Freud implies in *Totem and Taboo*, to undergo this sacrifice is to accept the punishment threatened for taking the father's place. [25] In terms of that paradigm, this is one way past the vigilant jealousy of the band of brothers, determined that no one of their number shall reassume the power of the tyrannic father in the "primal horde." In Jewish tradition this punishment is the penalty for blasphemy. In Christian tradition it becomes the great exception that proves the rule of human limitation. From the vantage point of psychoanalysis, one can see Christ's entry into Jerusalem as ambivalently aggressive and masochistic, or as aggression in the service of a masochistic need for punishment. The crucifixion itself can be regarded as passive sexualized death, the body pierced by the nails and finally the lance in the side, arms

24. So Joyce's Stephen Dedalus understands "what links [father and son] in nature," in *Ulysses* (New York: Modern Library, 1934), p. 205.
25. *Standard Edition*, vol. 13, pp. 153–55.

spread-eagled in a posture of open helplessness, exposed. But again, one can see his accepting the sacrificial, passive death as a decision made in the knowledge that by no other way could men be led to recognize and repent their jealousy of the presence of the divine *in* the world. From the perspective of René Girard's understanding of the generative principle of myth, Christ took the only way out of the remorseless violence between "enemy brothers" from Cain and Abel on down, brothers intent on establishing "difference" where no real difference exists.[26]

The imitation of Christ comes to mean in future generations of Christians, including the martyrs, an imitation of the passive response of which the Cross is prototype, but *without* the supreme and unique assertion of identity with the Father. The discipline of humility is a constant exercise in recognizing that we cannot be as gods, as the Devil would have us believe. The imitation of Christ's suffering, without his claim to divinity, is thus a way of maintaining relationship to God the Father by a passive renunciation of the drive to assume the identity and authority of the Father.[27] In Catholic Christianity, especially in late medieval or Counter-Reformation practice, this relationship to the Father is supplemented and confirmed by relationship with the Virgin or Holy Mother as intercessor with the Son and the Father, and with the Mother Church, the bride of Christ. Because the Virgin is not a sexual object, she can be appealed to safely as the Holy Mother. Infantile levels of dependence are licensed—to the point of several holy men being miraculously refreshed by milk from her breasts—by her virginity's putting out of question a sexual, Oedipal rivalry with God.

If one asks what conditions enabled individual men to realize their virility in this religious situation, one can see, schematically, three obvious outcomes. Many men, those who successfully became monks, priests, the "religious," renounced physical virility. For others, obviously, religious worship was not in fact important,

26. See René Girard, *Violence and the Sacred*, trans. Patrick Gregory (Baltimore: Johns Hopkins University Press, 1977).

27. This emphasis of Christianity would seem to exclude heroic vocation except in the special case of the Christian hero whose triumph is in self-sacrifice rather than self-assertion, receiving suffering rather than inflicting it. Reuben A. Brower points to the double presence in Shakespeare's drama of "the way of suffering and self-denial, and the way of action and self-assertion," and sets both trends in the historical context of Christian transformations of the heroic tradition (*Hero and Saint: Shakespeare and the Graeco-Roman Heroic Tradition* [New York: Oxford University Press, 1971], p. 418).

whatever their beliefs. Most interesting, for the purpose here, would be those temperaments capable of maintaining a separation between the religious and the human by which the "infinite" longings and drives, rooted in infancy and reaching toward the divine, are disciplined by worship, whereas secular adult desires and ambitions are freed of infantile residues and so are able to enjoy finite satisfactions for what they are. Religion, for such secular worshipers, would provide a place apart, sacred to the very tendencies with which we are today so familiar in neurosis,[28] the church being a theater where the needs generated by the first things of infancy would find objects, expression, and control by relation to the last things—to religious worship and truth. This third pattern is, I take it, the norm for the secular faithful who do not undertake to leave the world but whose devotion sustains their humility by ordering their relationship to the divine.

Religious discipline in which such secular persons take part includes a core of experience that is common to the audience of a tragedy. Christ is like a tragic protagonist, with crucial differences. Like a tragic hero, Christ enacts a forbidden motive: he becomes God. As with the tragic hero, the motive's enactment is heroic, gathering up and completing the aspirations of a society as the Messiah, and at the same time socially disruptive, challenging accepted power relationships and accepted attitudes about blasphemy, for instance, or the observance of the Sabbath. As with the double attitude of the audience of a tragedy, caught up in the protagonist's heroic endeavor but also enjoying the ironies which dog the hero's self-assertion and taking obscure satisfaction in his suffering and death, so the Christian, while he identifies with Christ, must acknowledge that by his sin he is guilty, with the Jews, of Christ's death. "Away with this *man*, and release unto us Barabbas" (Luke 23:18). "Let him be crucified" (Matt. 17:22). A happy ending would be utterly wrong and frustrating for *Hamlet* or for *Lear*. If "My God, my God, why hast thou forsaken me?" (Matt. 17:46) and death were the end for Jesus, that terrible question would be the moment of tragic recognition that his assumption of the role of Christ had been an all-too-human illusion. The sacrifice he offers as

---

28. "Neurotics," Freud wrote, "live in a world apart, where . . . they are only affected by what is thought with intensity and pictured with emotion, whereas agreement with external reality is a matter of no importance" (*Totem and Taboo, Standard Edition*, vol. 13, p. 86).

man is complete because he dies not only in body but also, as his outcry testifies, in human hope. Jesus' sacrifice, without Christ's resurrection, *is* a tragedy—the heroic entry and encounter with Jerusalem, then the agon of condemnation and Calvary—engendering the same awe and dismay and loving admiration one experiences with *Oedipus* or *King Lear*.

The great differences between the tragic hero and Christ are that Christ is without sin and that his death is prelude to resurrection; the two are interdependent, for had there not been the resurrection Jesus would have been a man guilty of the sin of assuming divinity, however blameless the life that sprang from the core of that presumption. These differences are crucial. The auditor of tragedy shares in the guilt of the protagonist, kills Duncan with Macbeth, demands with Lear that his daughters love their father all; but the action of tragic ironies and recognitions is a detaching of the audience from the destructive motives in which they participate. This detachment is what makes them an audience, not a congregation. Among those at the foot of the cross, detachment was brutally encouraged by some in ironic taunts: "If thou be the Son of God, come down from the cross"; "He saved others; himself he cannot save" (Matt. 17:40, 42). But the resurrection transformed the audience of a tragedy into a church. "Why seek ye the living among the dead? He is not here, but is risen" (Luke 24:5–6) turns the ironic awareness of human finitude back upon the mockers and calls the faithful to become one body, a new community united by shared access to final meaning through Christ's sacrifice and resurrection.

At the core of tragedy, of the heroic and romantic striving that leads to tragedy, is a struggle for the incarnation of final meaning in immediate, human life. In the Old Religion, Incarnation had hung over the altar in the Blessed Sacrament, to be carried in procession, dispensed from the pyx.[29] With the Reformation, the individual's relationship to incarnation—participation in it through the Lord's Supper—becomes problematic. "As concerning the natural body and blood of our Saviour Christ, they are in heaven and not here.

---

29. In *John Bon and Mast person*, a Protestant satirist of Edward VI's time mocks the idea that Christ can be inside the pyx. When the parson insists that "It is Christe his own selfe . . . We beare hym in procession and thereby knowe it ye maye," John the ploughman responds: "But me thinke it is a mad thinge that ye saye / That it should be a man howe can it come to passe / Because ye maye hym beare with in so smal a glasse." Quoted in C. W. Dugmore, *The Mass and the English Reformers* (London: Macmillan, 1958), p. 118.

For it is against the truth of Christ's natural body, to be in more places than one at one time."[30] Christ is in heaven, his sacrifice is in the remote past; for the more radical Protestant, the Lord's Supper is only a memorial of a past event. Marlowe's *Doctor Faustus* dramatizes the despair, the famished, insatiable spiritual hunger, and the search for alternative incarnation to which this situation could lead. If we turn to Shakespeare and look for dramatic pressure toward the sort of mystery excluded by the Zwinglian (and nominalist) rubric about Christ's natural body being in one place only, one moment in the tragedies springs to mind:

BERNARDO: 'Tis here!
HORATIO: 'Tis here!
MARCELLUS: 'Tis gone!
            We do it wrong, being so majestical,
            To offer it the show of violence;
            For it is as the air, invulnerable,
            And our vain blows malicious mockery.
                       (*Ham.* I.i.141–46)

The enormous need for relationship to a fully adequate father, so long postponed in Shakespeare's drama, is presented as fulfilled in *Hamlet* by the dramatist's use of theatrical magic to create the Ghost—with astonishing, radically disruptive results. Hamlet looks to the Ghost of his father with religious need, the need implicit in the Oedipus complex. In one of its innumerable aspects, the play is a version of the family romance of which Jesus' conviction that he is the son of God, that "My father and I are one," is the ultimate extreme. In the Messianic role Hamlet assumes as "scourge and minister," we can see analogies to the Gospels, especially with the final confrontation in Jerusalem. There is riddling denunciation of "ye hypocrites," like the aggressive parables Christ tells the Pharisees to their faces. The audience can share in the thrust of Hamlet's riddling wit, as the apostles could in Christ's, by knowing, as the established order does not, Christ's relation to God, Hamlet's to the

---

30. *The Two Liturgies . . . of King Edward VI,* ed. Joseph Ketley, Parker Society, no. 29 (Cambridge: Cambridge University Press, 1844), p. 283. So concludes the "Black Rubric" inserted during the printing of the 1552 Book of Common Prayer as assurance that kneeling during communion should not be construed as idolatry. The rubric was dropped from Elizabeth's Prayer Book, but the issue it addressed was at the heart of English liturgical controversy through the whole epoch. See Dugmore, *The Mass and the English Reformers,* and Dom Gregory Dix, *The Shape of the Liturgy* (London: Dacre Press, 1945), pp. 613–734.

Ghost. There is a similar, if far more ambiguous, acquiescence in being destroyed by the establishment, as Hamlet accepts the initiative of the King and Laertes: "If it be now, 'tis not to come" (V.ii.220–21). Horatio's active concern for the danger posed by Claudius is contrasted with Hamlet's, as Peter's is with Christ's. But Hamlet is not a "Christ figure," and the relationship to Christ is not parodic: it comes about by Shakespeare's working with the same or similar problems in terms of the secularizing movement in *his* tradition. The crucial difference is, of course, the absence of a resurrection in *Hamlet*. There *is* a sacredness about Hamlet, however, as the bearer of a potential redemption tragically not realized: "Now cracks a noble heart. Good night, sweet prince, / And flights of angels sing thee to thy rest!" (V.ii.359–60).

From a Christian vantage point, Hamlet's difficulty stems from his total devotion to his dead father; for most of the play he is unable to get past this allegiance, unable to transcend it for an allegiance to the divine. Access to the mystery of the Ghost, with the subsequent effort to identify totally with him, does not resolve Hamlet's predicament as a son struggling for identity through relationship to the father. The Ghost disrupts Hamlet's relation to the world and himself; it also disrupts the play, or makes the play radically disruptive. If Hamlet could stand "in the great hand of God," he could act as "the scourge and minister" of heaven, instead of merely describing himself in these terms. Instead he stands in the shadow of the Ghost. The tragic situation is in the absence of a sanction and support beyond the Ghost, and the irreducible ambiguity of the Ghost itself, either or both "a spirit of health or goblin damned."[31] In its radical ambiguity, the Ghost is what Freud called a "thing presentation"—an object, cathected by desire, that cannot be contained by language and so bound:[32]

HORATIO: What, has this thing appear'd again to-night?

. . . .

In what particular thought to work I know not.
(I.i.21, 67)

---

31. Compare Hamlet's subsequent doubt about the Ghost's identity as the spirit of his father—"The spirit that I have seen / May be a dev'l" (II.ii.598–99)—with the fateful remark offered by Hans Luther to his son Martin, on the occasion of the son's first Mass, regarding young Luther's conversion experience when nearly struck by lightning in a thunderstorm: "God give it that it wasn't a devil's spook" (Erik Erikson, *Young Man Luther* [New York: Norton, 1958], p. 145).

32. See sec. 7 of "The Unconscious," *Standard Edition*, vol. 14, pp. 196–204.

Though the Ghost dominates the play from the first scene, and dominates Hamlet's struggle for identity from their first confrontation, there is no adequate ironic field around this highly charged figure to stabilize its disruptive force. Then abruptly, once Hamlet has been able to say "This is I, / Hamlet the Dane!" (V.i.257–58), he and the play leave behind the whole business of establishing relationship to the Ghost, with no tangible bridge provided to account for the problematic shift from Hamlet's paternal allegiance to his affirmation of "a divinity that shapes our ends" (V.ii.10).

No less problematic is the radical difficulty of judging the son, whom Wilson Knight could see as an "Embassy of Death," only to turn around on such recognition to join the majority who try to come to rest in various vindications of a "sweet prince."[33] Shakespeare is dealing in *Hamlet* with motives cognate to those envisaged as fulfilled in Christian event or worship. Worship is a bridging term by which we move from the symbolic action of religion to that of the drama; as usual with such bridges, it warps as one crosses it. The text of *Hamlet* has almost gained the status of a modern Gospel, with the difference that the news is tragic.[34] Problems that in the church are repressed or triumphed over or institutionalized are made disruptively central in the new theater: the difficulty of full relationship to women, the difficulty of full relationship to the "things which are Caesar's," the destructiveness of messianic energies, which Christ reserved for the money-changers and hypocrites and the fig tree, but which Hamlet expresses much more fully and indiscriminately.

The problem of relationship to the mother and other women, put to one side by Christ but brought into the anguished center of Hamlet's experience, was directly addressed in the forms of worship made available by the Old Religion. That the Virgin and Holy Mother is no longer present in the reformed church has profound

33. Both Knight's original position, in "The Embassy of Death: An Essay on *Hamlet*" (1930), and his "restatement," in "*Hamlet* Reconsidered" (1947), are included in *The Wheel of Fire*, 5th ed. rev. (New York: Meridian, 1957), pp. 17–46, 298–325. The earlier emphasis on a soul-sick, death-obsessed, unhuman Hamlet, "a discordant and destructive thing whose very presence is a poison and a menace to the happiness and health of Denmark" (p. 30), gives way to a Hamlet "on the way to superman status in the Nietzschean sense" (p. 301).

34. In his essays in *The Story of the Night* (London: Routledge and Kegan Paul, 1961), particularly in "Shakespearean Tragedy and the Idea of Human Sacrifice," John Holloway finds in the major tragedies a ritualization of reality that performs many of the functions of directly religious ritual.

consequences, reflected not only in *Hamlet* but in the whole development of Shakespeare's later drama. Hamlet's recoil from his mother's sexuality exacerbates his experience at every level: his relationship to dead father and to living stepfather, to Ophelia, to his own "sullied" body, to a "rank and gross" world that seems to generalize his mother's corruption. In traditional Catholicism, not only did the Holy Mother provide intercession between man and God, son and father; her worship could help meet the profound need for relationship to an ideal feminine figure, unsullied either by her own sexuality or by the sexual insecurities of men and unlimited in maternal solace and generosity. The prayers to the Virgin that had been in the Catholic liturgy, translated into English for the benefit of lay folk in pre-Reformation prayer books, are eloquent. "Saint Mary, maid of maidens, mother and daughter of the king of kings." [35] Dante salutes her in these terms at the summit of the *Divine Comedy*. That she is both mother and daughter conforms with the vertical structure of feeling at the core of family. "Holy gate of heaven, set us all at peace, changing the name of Eve." The Elizabethan drama is haunted by the fear that all women may be betrayers, like our first mother, Eve. The root of this fear in the earliest child-mother relationship is urgently present as the worshiper pleads: "Show that thou art our mother." The abolition of the cult of the Virgin Mary meant the loss of ritual resource for dealing with internal residues of the once all-powerful, all-inclusive mother, present in all of us.

That the tragic heroes are vulnerable to the feminine can remind us not only that Mary was no longer present as object of worship in the Elizabethan settlement, but that the church ceased to be "Our Holy Mother the Church." Instead, at the head of the English church as well as the state was our Lady Elizabeth, in her later years imaged constantly as a virgin of all but magical powers. And on the other side of the channel was "the idolatrous church . . . being indeed not only an harlot, (as the Scripture calleth her,) but also a foul, filthy, old, withered harlot, (for she is indeed of ancient years,) . . . the great strumpet of all strumpets, the Mother of Whoredom set forth by St. John in his Revelation." [36] The absence

---

35. I have modernized this and the immediately following quotations from several prayers to the Virgin Mary in *The Prymer or Lay Folks' Prayer Book*, ed. Henry Littlehales, EETS original series, no. 105 (London: Kegan Paul, 1895).

36. *Homilies*, vol. 2, no. 2, p. 216; quoted in Hughes, vol. 3, p. 102.

of Mother Church in England, and the presence of this imagery of whoredom and the mother of whoredom (in which one often senses that Protestant polemicists are enjoying, through the negative, a "common form of object choice with men"!), must bear some relation to the fact that the heroes of the major tragedies regularly struggle toward an absolute fulfillment, which proves to be destructive and self-destructive, under pressure of a demand, from a woman or on a woman, with which they cannot cope. And the women tend to be—or to be regarded as—either figures "enskied and sainted" (*MM* I.iv.34) or else strumpets.

Although Protestantism did away with the cult of the Virgin Mary and played down the maternal role of the church, the threatening mother survived as an immediate, physical supernatural presence in Protestant countries. After the benign Holy Mother had been drastically reduced in scope and presence, the terrible mother was still conjured up and pursued with persecution in the witch manias well into the seventeenth century. Keith Thomas notes that the belief in witches survived in England after many Catholic resources of exorcism had been dispensed with.[37] Witches proper are of course among Shakespeare's repertory of overpowering women: Joan de Pucelle in a history at the outset, the Weird Sisters in the most intense of all the tragedies. The witches in *Macbeth* lure the hero on through the expectation of a magical omnipotence of mind by which what is envisaged must come true, a child's assumption. Macbeth expects the achievement of some absolute, total state of being by being crowned, yet in the process he is unmanned. Banquo, by contrast, has always a sense of his human limits: he can say "In the great hand of God I stand" (II.iii.130), and the play invests the future of Scotland in the heirs of his manhood. To expect and seek the absolute as Macbeth does is heroic, and at the same time childlike. *Macbeth*, in its complex way, is an exorcism, for it presents the witches as the outstretched shadows of Lady Macbeth as Macbeth relates to them in the dependent, childlike side of his nature. Their power is understood as depending on masculine insecurity. But they are also objectively supernatural beings.

After the Reformation, the benign supernatural figure of the Holy Mother could not be present in a comparable way. The elim-

37. Keith Thomas, *Religion and the Decline of Magic* (London: Weidenfeld and Nicolson, 1971), pp. 493–501.

ination of the Blessed Virgin is particularly significant for the sensibility we find in Shakespeare, which achieves increasingly profound expression in the great tragedies and the romances to follow. In *Othello*, for example, the sacred and the secular, the maternal and the sexual, converge in the hero's regard for a single human figure. In Othello's worshipful love for Desdemona, we can see the relationship of family ties to the search for the divine or supernatural by considering the famous handkerchief. The "magic in the web of it" connects Othello's relation with Desdemona to an earlier relation with the mother:

> That handkerchief
> Did an Egyptian to my mother give;
> She was a charmer, and could almost read
> The thoughts of people. She told her, while she
> kept it
> 'Twould make her amiable, and subdue my father
> Entirely to her love; but if she lost it,
> Or made a gift of it, my father's eye
> Should hold her loathed, and his spirits should hunt
> After new fancies. She, dying, gave it me,
> And bid me, when my fate would have me wiv'd,
> To give it her. I did so; and take heed on't,
> Make it a darling like your precious eye.
> To lose't or give't away were such perdition
> As nothing else could match.

DESDEMONA: Is't possible?
OTHELLO: 'Tis true; there's magic in the web of it.

> A sibyl, that had numb'red in the world
> The sun to course two hundred compasses,
> In her prophetic fury sew'd the work;
> The worms were hallowed that did breed the silk,
> And it was dy'd in mummy which the skillful
> Conserv'd of maidens' hearts.

(III.iv.55–75)

This is surely one of the most astonishing passages in Shakespeare for sheer reach of imagination, opening a window on a whole exotic world that Othello has brought with him to Venice—along with the basic insecurity that makes him need such a talisman to magically secure his ability to love as his father loved. The intensity reaches to religious language: "to lose't . . . were such perdition," while the whole passage is shot through with sexual suggestion: the hallowed breeding worms, "your precious eye"—yet at the same time with suggestions of danger associated with women: reading the thoughts of people, prophetic fury, "mummy . . . / Conserv'd of maidens' hearts." The infantile search for the divine tends toward the grotesque, and Shakespeare's art is fully in control of that dimension. But his art also keeps in touch with the humanly heroic dimension. What makes the tragedy moving instead of merely horrifying and clinical is Shakespeare's realization for us of the value of the relationship, its spiritual reality, even though this is presented as what makes it vulnerable. Othello's expectations and demands are absolutes: "My soul hath her content so absolute / That not another comfort like to this / Succeeds in unknown fate" (II.i.191–93). It is the completeness of the expectation that makes impossible the equanimity that would so easily permit a less religious lover—or, we could say, a less childlike lover—to see through Iago.

In a split that is characteristic of the whole modern epoch, Othello must struggle so violently to separate ideal woman from woman as sexual object precisely because he is unable, at deep levels of feeling, to undo the identification of wife and mother. Othello's love for Desdemona, in René Girard's terms, makes no difference where acknowledgment of difference is what is demanded to make relationship possible.[38] Othello makes no difference between the mother and the wife; he holds Desdemona sacred in this way and then destroys her, with Iago's diabolical prompting, on the assumption that if she is a secular woman she will make no difference between him and Cassio. The final "ocular proof" comes when he sees the mother's handkerchief in the hands of Cassio's whore. Part of the logic of his seduction by Iago—"that demi-devil" who "thus ensnar'd my soul and body" (V.ii.301–302)—is that it enables Othello to envisage Desdemona sexually: following Iago's clues, Othello is fascinated by his otherwise inhibited access to his wife's sexuality, at the same time that it devastates him. What engenders the sense of sacredness about Desdemona is also what calls for her destruction, and his.

Hamlet, *Lear*, and *Coriolanus* center directly on intensely conflictual relationships between parents and children. But in the tragedies that are not centered in the nuclear family, relations between child and parents are usually in the background, as we have seen in *Othello*, or present by implication and analogy. So in *Julius*

---

38. The thesis that "it is not difference but the loss of it that gives rise to violence" (p. 151) is central to Girard's *Violence and the Sacred*. He recasts Freud's conception of the Oedipus complex to emphasize the function of "mimetic desire" by which the son endeavors to make no difference between himself and his father in the choice of his love object.

Caesar there is a violent negation of the worship of Caesar by the conspirators:

> And this man
> Is now become a god, and Cassius is
> A wretched creature, and must bend his body.
>   (I.ii.115–17)

The conspirators are explicitly a band of brothers; they submerge their mutual rivalry to destroy a paternal figure—in some respects very much like the band of brothers who commit the father murder in Freud's *Totem and Taboo*, that Just-So story about the origin of guilt. With Caesar dead, rivalry erupts between Brutus and Cassius, to be reconciled only in their common recognition that they are both bereft, lost inwardly without the center that Caesar gave their lives. One way to understand the whole tragedy is to see it as the exhibition of a failure to separate the divine from the human. The conspirators' attempt to prevent the man Caesar from becoming a god results in a hideous parody of blood sacrifice, from which the Ghost of Caesar emerges as a demonic power.

Julius Caesar, the overture to the sequence of great tragedies that begins with *Hamlet* and extends through *Othello, Lear,* and *Macbeth,* introduces many of the great themes that dominate these plays: crisis in the transmission of heritage, the desperate struggle to achieve or maintain male identity, the collapse of authority in the state. It is striking that in the tragedies written after *Lear* and *Macbeth* and before the late romances—*Antony and Cleopatra, Coriolanus,* and *Timon of Athens*—we do not find the sort of sacred-in-the-human investments of feeling I have been describing, though these plays extend the preoccupation with male-female conflict characteristic of the tragedies that precede them. That these last three tragedies are set in the classical world is, of course, consistent with the relative absence of Christian adumbration. But their different quality can also be attributed to the fact that they deal with their heroes' relationships to women without looking for the sort of "absolute" Othello seeks in Desdemona.

The movement into the late romances is the final swing in a large rhythmic alternation within Shakespeare's development between emphasis on or recourse to the secular and emphasis on feelings of the sacredness in life. Earlier, the predominance of secular concerns in the period of the mature histories and comedies is followed by the attempt in the major tragedies to reach the sacred-in-the-human. Then comes the celebration of exotic secular passion in *Antony and Cleopatra*, and the tragedy of overwhelming maternal power in *Coriolanus*—with the sacred and beneficient female power out of range, so that in *Timon* we have the protagonist's futile attempt to be that power in his own person. *Pericles* and the romances that follow it are in a fundamental way a return to areas of feeling that Shakespeare dealt with most deeply in the greatest tragedies, after the three late tragedies present what I can call a more secular range of feeling: heroic and poetic beyond anything else in *Antony and Cleopatra*, almost clinically psychological and sociological in *Coriolanus*, abortively regressive under the thinly realized social surface in *Timon of Athens*. In their several ways, the first three romances, particularly *Pericles* and *The Winter's Tale*, are symbolic actions that move through loss to recovery of relationships to nurturant, validating, feminine presences. They do so by dramatizing the power of art to shape and transform human attitudes and so restore access to those presences, endowed with the quality of the sacred, without which the grace of life is lost.

In *The Tempest*, a father's feeling of loss accompanies, and almost overshadows, the renewal Prospero arranges, using all the resources of his magical powers, in the marriage to which he surrenders his precious daughter, Miranda. Prospero resigns himself to that loss under conditions which, without such resignation, could lead to tragedy. He can do so, in part, because of the compensation he finds in the aggressive magic of the self-consciously theatrical role he assumes throughout the play. In the epilogue, his "rough magic" abjured, its limits within the larger rhythms of nature recognized, Prospero steps partly outside the frame of the action to address his theater audience directly. His "prayer" both appeals to the spectators for their mercy and identifies him with them in shared dependence on powers beyond the reach of the magic he has exercised: "As you from crimes would pardon'd be, / Let your indulgence set me free."

In Shakespeare's greatest tragedy, Lear's preferred audience, when he turns away in anguish from the human reality on the stage, is not, like Prospero's, made up of the spectators in the theater:

> You heavens, give me that patience, patience I need!
> You see me here, you gods, a poor old man,
> As full of grief as age, wretched in both.
>
> (II.iv.271–73)

But Shakespeare will not locate within the "heavens" to which Lear appeals either responsibility for his sufferings or consolation for them. His audience does not free him, grant him an indulgence, does not, indeed, respond at all or provide any indication that it is listening, receiving Lear's plea. Christian expectations for what a transcendent frame of meaning could provide, repeatedly invoked by the play's language, are not fulfilled by the resolution of the action.

King Lear, like *The Tempest*, is centered in a father's love for a daughter who has become a woman. But Lear never relinquishes his longing for Cordelia "to love [her] father all." The "holy cords" of family bonds, made sacred by the intensity of the need Lear seeks to fulfill in Cordelia (and made diabolical in response to his demand on them by Regan and Goneril), do prove "too intrinse t' unloose." What Lear seeks in Cordelia is from the beginning a fulfillment that can only be achieved, as it eventually is, by the sacrifice of her womanhood to his need for her. Poetry that reaches toward the sacred in the human leads not to religious fulfillment but to tragedy. Instead of intimations of a Christian resolution, Shakespearean tragedy, as I see it, presents versions of the Oedipus complex tragically unresolved. His tragedies dramatize the post-Christian situation, shaped by some of the expectations and values of Christianity, but without God and the Holy Family, with only the human family. Individual protagonists make a demand on life, or on *a* life, which life cannot yield, and without which the protagonist's self cannot endure.

Shakespeare in the Rising Middle Class

Shakespeare was so perfect an artist, so completely engaged by and fulfilled by his creation, that it is notoriously difficult to talk about the man apart from his work. His separate humanity seems invisible, a transparent medium we see *through* but cannot see. One way of avoiding the embarrassments of the effort to understand the man working in the work is to insist that he was simply a good workman who made productions that would appeal to his public. "He was a great artist, which means a great craftsman— damn the thing else!" This response is often animated by irritation with the subjective follies of those who, looking for Shakespeare behind his art, see themselves. In *Shakespeare's Lives*, a monumental study of the painstaking recovery of the facts about Shakespeare, Samuel Schoenbaum makes a dryly humane story of three centuries of credulous and wishful speculation, oblique self-portraiture, bardolaters, Baconians, compulsive forgers.[1] In surveying the proliferation of legends and theories, fancies and forgeries, Schoenbaum makes clear the temptation of self-projection to which the authors of biographies have given way. Yet one has, finally, no other instrument to work with than one's own sensibility, corrected as much as possible by the reports of others about their encounters with the work.

I must in candor add that in my experience the animus against "subjective" interpretations is also frequently a response to Shakespeare's work itself—a way to avoid seeing the strangeness of it, the frightening things in it. His art is tactful: it makes troubling things acceptable, indeed enjoyable (with a few exceptions); it provides many kinds and levels of interest to hold attention. There is no *necessity* to look at what points back to the author in the individual play or in the succession of plays. Some feel that to do so involves disrespect or a violation of privacy, and buttress their objection

---

1. Samuel Schoenbaum, *Shakespeare's Lives* (Oxford: Clarendon Press, 1970).

with an "impersonal theory of poetry," such as T. S. Eliot's in "Tradition and the Individual Talent." [2] Eliot's insistence in that essay on
the importance of tradition for the individual talent is crucial. But
the almost total separation he asserted there between the man who
suffers and the mind that creates—though a useful corrective to
Georgian notions of poetry as simply the expression of personality,
and perhaps a necessary screen for Eliot at that stage—is simply
false, as his own later poetry and criticism testify. Eliot effectually
abandoned the impersonal theory in his later criticism, when in his
own poetry he had become able to speak more directly in his own
voice, and when he became concerned with understanding the
whole oeuvre of various writers, notably Dante and Shakespeare.

The purpose of setting Shakespeare's works against what we do
know about his life is not, of course, to derive his creative achievement from, or reduce it to, such facts as we have. The bare facts
suggest a pattern that could have many other outcomes, and the
odds against any circumstances having led to the development of
Shakespeare's genius are incalculable. But that Shakespeare came
from a family where the father rose from humble origins to become
bailiff (mayor) of a prosperous market town, having married the
heiress of an affluent yeoman, and then when his eldest son was
twelve withdrew from civic life and fell into debt; that Shakespeare
worked and prospered in the social and financial situation of a
booming joint stock company, the most successful company of
players, who owned their own theater, of which Shakespeare owned
a share—these are circumstances which clearly helped to shape the
attitudes and values expressed in his plays. The circumstances
of his working life provided support for the poet's role as a man
among men. The particular constellation of the burgher family he
grew up in is consistent with the thematic preoccupations visible in
his works.

Here the relative scarcity of information is less an impediment
than it might at first appear to be. We cannot know just how Shakespeare's working life and the works he produced were conditioned
by the experiences of infancy, childhood, and youth, but we could
not derive such inward matters simply from external data even if
we had far more of them than we have. In the psychoanalysis of
adults, the key early situations and the events occasioning them

2. T. S. Eliot, *Selected Essays*, new ed. (Harcourt, Brace and World, 1950),
pp. 3–11.

usually emerge gradually from the patient's fantasies and dreams and from his or her reenactment of the earlier situations transferred to the relationship with the analyst. Biographical information is read inferentially, in terms of this later material. Similarly, Shakespeare's supremely resonant adult works permit inferences, some tentative, about the way the known circumstances of his early life shaped his sensibility. In this chapter we shall look first at these circumstances in relation to some aspects of Shakespeare's development, then consider his adult working situation and its implications about his temperament and its equilibrium.

"THIS MOST BALMY TIME"

In Samuel Schoenbaum's excellent *William Shakespeare: A Documentary Life* the facts we have about the poet's family and civic origins are presented by a skeptical scholar who has mastered the full range of evidence and the complex life of the times in which it is embedded.[3] There is much more factual evidence about Shakespeare's life in the mundane world than people usually assume; there is a great deal of evidence about Shakespeare's father's rapid rise from humble beginnings and his abrupt withdrawal in mid-career and subsequent financial and legal reverses. Two important areas are blank: what Shakespeare did from the time of his marriage at eighteen in Stratford until we encounter him as a London playwright, and what the reasons were for his father's withdrawal.

John Shakespeare set his son an example for rising in the middle-class world. In the middle of the century, he moved from a tenant farmer's household to apprenticeship as a glover in a prospering town which had just received its charter of incorporation providing for its government by a common council of burgesses and aldermen, with a bailiff elected annually from among the latter by majority vote. The Earl of Warwick, as "lord of the manor, retained the nomination of the vicar and the schoolmaster, and could, if he wished, veto the corporation's choice of a bailiff."[4] But the borough had a great deal of autonomy and a tough-fibered, legally defined structure of relationships among its citizens. Shakespeare's father rose rapidly within this new establishment: ale-taster in 1556; con-

---

3. Samuel Schoenbaum, *William Shakespeare: A Documentary Life* (Oxford: Clarendon Press, 1975).
4. Ibid., p. 29.

stable in '58; afeeror of the Leet court in '59, assessing fines; burgess soon after, with the duties from '61 to '63 of administering the borough property as one of two chamberlains; alderman in '65, henceforth to be addressed as Master Shakespeare; then elected bailiff in '68, "exchanging his black gown for one of scarlet." He and his deputy "wore their furred gowns in public, were escorted from their houses to the Gild Hall by serjeants bearing their maces before them. They were waited on by these buff-uniformed officers once a week to receive instructions, and accompanied by them through the market on Thursdays, through the fair on fair-days, about the parish-bounds at Rogation, and to and from church on Sundays. At church they sat with their wives in the front pew on the north side of the nave."[5] The bailiff was a justice of the peace, presided over the Court of Record and council meetings, and dealt for the borough with the lord of the manor.

Civic rituals were small affairs compared with the great ceremonials of court or noble magnate's household. But they must have been great in the eyes of a four-year-old boy accompanying or watching his scarlet-robed father. When William was seven, John Shakespeare was appointed deputy to his friend and neighbor Adrian Quiney, riding with him in January to London on borough business. At this time he contemplated applying to the Heralds' College for a coat of arms, to which his municipal offices "of dignity and worship" (and his wife's connections) entitled him, but did not follow through after furnishing "a 'pattern,' or sketch, for his arms." It remained for Shakespeare to apply in his father's behalf in 1596, when "the Clarenceux King-of-Arms noted: 'And the man was A magestrat in Stratford upon Avon. A Justice of peace he maryed A Daughter and heyre of Ardern. and was of good substance and habelite.'"[6]

I quote and paraphrase at such length from Schoenbaum, because his massed detail demonstrates that Shakespeare's father was a considerable person in a considerable world, a world all too frequently patronized by critics who adopt, half-unconsciously, the aristocratic perspective for which Shakespeare himself gave the cue in presenting such figures as Justice Shallow or the merry wives. Shakespeare undoubtedly attended the good grammar school to which his father's offices entitled his son. Until William was twelve

5. Ibid., p. 34 (quoted from Edgar Fripp, *Shakespeare: Man and Artist*, 1935).
6. Ibid., p. 36.

his father was a leading citizen, faithfully attending the council as alderman, buying two houses, dealing in wool and probably other commodities in his trade as a maker of soft leather goods.

John Shakespeare's fortunes had been enhanced considerably when, at about the age of thirty, he married Mary Arden, the daughter of his father's landlord, a well-to-do farmer with connections to the long-established minor gentry. The youngest child among ten daughters (eight by an earlier marriage) and two sons, she was clearly her father's favorite. In his will, made as he lay dying in 1556, he left her all his principal property, after making modest provision for a widow whom he had married late in life. In Schoenbaum we get the inventory of the property, of which Mary Arden was one of the executors, from eleven painted cloths through ample furnishings in the house (which may or may not be the one now identified as the Arden homestead) to "a barn filled with wheat and barley, store of livestock, . . . wood in the yard and bacon in the roof." Shortly after her elderly father's death, Mary Arden married his tenant's son, who was considerably older than she was.[7] John Shakespeare was already prospering, living in the house that became Shakespeare's birthplace, and buying, in 1556, the adjacent house, which became known as the Woolshop. In September of 1558 the couple had a girl, christened Joan; in 1562, another girl, Margaret, who was buried five months later. Then William Shakespeare was christened on April 26, 1564. He was the eldest male child, and the eldest to survive, for the next girl to be born, in 1569, was christened Joan like the firstborn girl. Thus the first Joan was dead, but her death is unrecorded, and may have happened any time before 1569; she may or may not have been alive at Shakespeare's birth.

So Shakespeare is born and grows up in a home that is also a prospering business. His busy, enterprising father is a man to whom his fellow citizens looked with admiration and confidence—obvious from the trusts he was given by the community—and with compassion, as is later made clear by their forbearance when he ceased to participate and got heavily into debt. In legal matters, of which we have records, the role of women was so subordinate to that of men that all the evidence surviving about the mother concerns her inheritance, the christenings of her children, the dissipation of her inheritance by borrowing, and her death in 1608. But, as

7. Ibid., p. 19.

we have seen, she was the youngest daughter of a father who gave
her, not "a third more opulent than your sisters'," but virtually *all*.
She marries an exceptionally able, older man of lower social origins, and after the disappointment of one girl-child's death, perhaps two, she gives birth to her first son. For two years and five
months, until the birth of Gilbert in October of 1566, William
Shakespeare is her only child, or only male child, at a time when
her very successful husband is extremely busy.

Shakespeare's enormous resonance to life and capacity for play,
his set toward generous cherishing, must have roots in this very
early experience. The sort of timeless, blissful moment some of the
Sonnets to the friend function to recover would find an active, enduring prototype in "this most balmy time":

> Not mine own fears nor the prophetic soul
> Of the wide world dreaming on things to come
> Can yet the lease of my true love control,
> Supposed as forfeit to a cónfined doom.
> The mortal moon hath her eclipse endured,
> And the sad augurs mock their own preságe,
> Incertainties now crown themselves assured,
> And peace proclaims olives of endless age.
> Now with the drops of this most balmy time
> My love looks fresh, and death to me subscribes,
> Since spite of him I'll live in this poor rhyme,
> While he insults o'er dull and speechless tribes.
>   And thou in this shalt find thy monument,
>   When tyrants' crests and tombs of brass are spent.

One can certainly read Sonnet 107 without reference to infancy,
as the recovery of a private feeling of omnipotence through confident love, in an auspicious moment of renewed public confidence. The poem swings around the experience of a threat overcome—understandable as the threat of a sibling, expected and
feared, but not after all finally decisive, because through the love of
the young man the original situation has been restored, almost
beyond belief, and whole tribes of rivals can do nothing about it.
To see this in the poem depends on its exquisite generalization by
concrete suggestion, its openness to a multiplicity of readings.
Through the cryptic reference to a "time" in which it is being written, it is open to or conveys feelings from an earlier time, like those
adumbrated in the absences lamented in Sonnets 97 ("How like a
winter hath my absence been") and 98 ("From you I have been absent in the spring"), when a child's fears are animated "by the prophetic soul" of his whole "world," "dreaming," not of him, but of

"things to come."[8] Sonnet 107 evokes these "incertainties" as overcome: the maternal moon, whose loss was presaged by the sad au-
guries, has only been eclipsed. Now, in this new time, moist and
"balmy," without conflict, the "death" of separation is overcome.

As elsewhere in the Sonnets, it is impossible in 107 to separate
the poet's love as his act of loving from his love as his object: "My
love looks fresh, and death to me subscribes." The whole thing is
made possible by the poem, by "this poor rhyme," which holds,
out of ordinary time, the loving and the beloved. The gesture abjuring conflict, the modesty in "this *poor* rhyme," in keeping with the
peace proclaimed by "olives of endless age," is belied by the aggression that "insults o'er dull and speechless tribes," while the
poet will "live in this poor rhyme." The couplet returns simply to
the friend and the "rhyme"; the idea of death returns with "monument," but there is a final balancing aggression, which asserts victory for the poetry of the private love over the pride of the mighty
of this world.

The public event is made part of the private, but to assume that it
is the sufficient cause of the exultant affirmation is utterly implausible. Quite probably, the "mortal moon" refers to Elizabeth, surviving the "eclipse" of a political or, more likely, an astrological
danger.[9] Shakespeare shared, of course, in the cult of "the imperial
vot'ress" (*MND*, II.i.163).[10] Courtly worship of her obviously drew

8. See the discussion of Sonnets 97 and 98 in chapter 6, pp. 176–78.
9. The interpretation of the crisis passed as Elizabeth's passing her astrological
climacteric seems intrinsically an acceptable construction. But the date it involves,
1601, seems too late in view of Shakespeare's emotional development. It puts the
composition of Sonnet 107, with its exultation in a secure love, based in the way we
have seen, into the period of *Hamlet*! It is possible that Shakespeare returned to writing the latest sonnets in that period, in connection with a new or renewed love of a
confident, mutual kind, not vulnerable, as it seemed, to difference in rank—not to
be confused with the sort of love inspired by court adulation ("If my dear love were
but the child of state, / It might for Fortune's bastard be unfathered," as Sonnet 124
puts it). But the plays of that period dramatize the roots of such love being disrupted, by contrast to the period of *Henry IV–Henry V*, with which a love that "all
alone stands hugely politic" is congruent. The three years "since first I saw you
fresh, which yet are green" (Sonnet 104) are consistent with the interval between
Henry IV and the earlier comedies, where sonnets are in vogue and echoes across to
the Sonnets are frequent. There were other crises which the Queen weathered.
The notion that "the mortal moon" is the Armada is utterly implausible, both
because of the positive attitude expressed toward the moon's surviving the crisis,
and because the consequent dating of the later-numbered sonnets in 1588 or 1589
could not conceivably fit with their repeated references to the poet's achieved theatrical role.
10. Cf. Frances A. Yates, *Astrea: The Imperial Theme in the Sixteenth Century* (London: Routledge and Kegan Paul, 1975), pp. 29–87.

on roots of feeling going back, often explicitly, to childhood; it included many adaptations of ceremonial adoration of the Virgin Mary, whose place Elizabeth in some ways took over. Sir Walter Ralegh, expressing in "The Ocean to Cynthia" his anguish, insecurity, and frustration after his marriage temporarily lost him the Queen's favor and love, at one point compares his loss to the loss of a mother's breast. But Ralegh's relationship was personal, as well as the whole basis of his career. His love was indeed "the child of state"; Shakespeare describes such courtly loves in Sonnet 124, by contrast with his disinterested love, which "suffers not in smiling pomp, nor falls / Under the blow of thrallèd discontent." In Sonnet 107, clearly, the public situation is merely the occasion for the private renewal, and becomes a trope for it as the poem turns from vehicle to tenor with the new surge of the third quatrain, "Now . . . My love looks fresh."

In the earlier work, as was noted in the last chapter, identification with the maternal predominates, partly in compensation for fears of abandonment or of being overwhelmed. The whole structure of Shakespeare's sensibility is deeply responsive to the "lines of life" that extend vertically across generations through the node of infancy and childhood; horizontal relationships in the same generation are decisively shaped by residues of the family constellation. The triumph of Sonnet 107, over fears of isolation within a "confined doom," recapitulates the recovery of the initial union with the mother as it opens out onto riches of sensuous and verbal experience. This recovery can be realized, in the period of the Sonnets, in poetry about adult human relationships and about the power of his art. But the need to enact such recovery conditions all phases of Shakespeare's work.

From first to last, Shakespeare in his art responds to life most deeply according to patterns of relating grounded in the bond to a mother—fulfillment through the cherishing of another, loss of self by abandonment or betrayal. The cherishing sympathy is rooted in a rich narcissism which extends outward by empathy, putting the self in others' places. But on practical levels, Shakespeare clearly has a firm sense of mine or thine, and the cherishing can move toward possessing others as confirmation of an egoism. So the temperament is richly sociable, centered in kinship extended outward by a high valuation of kindness; evil is most intensely felt as violation of kinship, as "unkindness" in the sense of "unnatural" where natural means kinship. This temperament has its own kind of selfishness and detachment: others are extensions of self, and all relationships are provisional, contingent because they replace others. At the core is the original loss of the parental objects and the possibility of its recurrence; when, in the later work, this threat is fully explored, "everything" reached by a cherishing possession may suddenly become the "nothing" that echoes in *King Lear*.

Keats, in exploring his own nature, illuminated the receptive side of Shakespeare in speaking of him as the supreme example of "negative capability." This power to be "in for" other beings accounts for Shakespeare's being able, next after God or Nature, to create most—to fill even the wings of the theater with human spirits bursting with life, to be the boy in act one and the old man in act five, to be Othello and also Iago, as Stephen Dedalus says in *Ulysses*. Keats also observed in himself, and guessed in Shakespeare, that this poetic capacity for "humility before life" went with a lack of self, with being almost without a determinate identity—as we can see in those sonnets where the poet's selfless cherishing of the friend leaves him in the lurch. Genius, working with the resources of poetry and theater, was crucial in enabling Shakespeare to live so fully in this mode. But his root sense of self and self-enjoyment ("No, I am that I am"), together with his "deepest sense, how hard true sorrow hits," must reach back to the buoyant time when he was the only male child of a young mother, and to the inevitable discovery that such a time, despite its infinite promise, is "but a little moment" (Sonnets 121, 120, 15).

"HIS VIRTUES ELSE"

The birth of a brother, with the inevitable dethronement of his majesty the baby, is the initial shock suggested by the biographical record; the second, much more striking, is his father's failure, obvious to all by the time the boy is twelve. The familiar eldest child's experience of dethronement and fear of abandonment in infancy seems to have fused in Shakespeare's imagination with sympathetic preoccupation with his amiable father's failure, shaping the tendency to incorporate maternal qualities and powers into his own sensibility toward an ideal of a cherishing fatherhood. In the plays, especially those from the early phases of Shakespeare's development as an artist, we find fear for and sympathy with generous, vulnerable men dramatized with full understanding of the weakness of such men and its provocation to their women.

John Shakespeare's rise was obviously helped materially by his marriage; how his decline was related to it we can never know with certainty. But his younger, better-born wife can scarcely have failed to feel deep resentment as she saw her inheritance dissipated, whatever likable qualities her husband possessed for the community. Soon after the death of her affluent father she had married another older, substantial man, the John Shakespeare of 1556 or 1557, who, after years of prosperity and civic responsibility, turned into something else. From the later 1570s he is repeatedly in financial trouble. He borrows £40 in 1578 on the security of his wife's inheritance, allegedly fails to repay it on time in 1580, and never recovers the disputed house and land, despite repeated legal efforts. Other property which came to him from Mary Arden is rented or sold in the late 1570s. In 1580 failure to appear in court results in a £20 fine. Another £20 fine was imposed on John Shakespeare when a hatmaker for whom he had stood surety failed to appear in court. Two other forfeits of £10 each for those for whom he had stood surety, a tinker and his brother Henry, suggest bad judgment and generosity—or need for ready cash, since by standing surety one could collect a small fee, as for a bail bond now.[11]

After 1576 John Shakespeare abruptly stopped attending council meetings and going to church. He was, however, kept on the council for ten years, despite attendance at only one recorded session in that period; fines for nonattendance were forgiven him, as well as contributions toward poor relief. He was never ruined, quite possibly thanks to help from his successful son, who joined in the long, heartbreaking legal struggle to recover his mother's inheritance, and who was in the later 1590s still involved in legal action in Chancery. Near the end of his life John Shakespeare was still living in the house where his children were born. In the last year of his life, when "he must have been in his early seventies,"[12] he was listed in a petition to London as one of those who could testify to the economic difficulties Stratford was experiencing.

It is almost certain that John Shakespeare had Catholic sympathies, at least briefly. There is strong evidence that he executed, presumably under the influence of a secret Jesuit missionary, a Catholic "spiritual testament" (a translation of a formulary by Cardinal Borromeo), which such missionaries carried to England in 1580–81.

11. Schoenbaum, *Documentary Life*, pp. 36–38.
12. Ibid., p. 40.

The document was found in the roof of his house in the middle of the eighteenth century; maddeningly, only a transcript, lacking the first page, has survived, but Schoenbaum and other archival scholars now regard it as genuine. John Shakespeare may have executed the testament in a moment of enthusiasm and then hidden the little manuscript booklet when persecution intensified.[13] But his fellow townsmen, among whom on the council there were Catholics, did not regard him as one; in 1592, when commissioners ordered to ferret out recusants filed two reports, John Shakespeare is listed among nine nonattenders who "coom not to Churche for feare of processe of Debtte."[14]

Some inferences, speculative but consistent with the record, can be made about the poet's relation to his father's failure, and about consequences for Shakespeare of the episode of the Catholic testament. The British psychoanalyst John Padel has suggested that the self-disabling of the Sonnets could have been shaped by identification with the father when "in disgrace with fortune and men's eyes."[15] Such "transference feeling" in the relationship to the young man would be natural in those moments when a different identity, maternally derived and based on the experience of being cherished, does not sustain the poet—when "all alone" he beweeps his "outcast state" (Sonnet 29). The degree to which parents' identities subsist at deep levels is more familiar to an analyst than to most of us; his experience of the fluid, protected analytical process dramatizes such internalized presences in the transference to him. Parents are also omens for us all, often ill omens from which we struggle, consciously or unconsciously, to disassociate ourselves. There is no inconsistency in John Shakespeare's having been also a cherishing father. The "decrepit father" of Sonnet 37 "takes delight" in "his active child." One of Shakespeare's first great portraits is Henry VI, cherishing his realm even as his weakness lets his

13. Ibid., pp. 41–46.
14. Ibid., p. 38.
15. J. H. Padel, "'That the thought of hearts can mend': An Introduction to Shakespeare's Sonnets for Psychotherapists and Others," *Times Literary Supplement*, December 19, 1975, pp. 1519–21. For Padel, Shakespeare's response to his "depressed" father and to the death of his son Hamnet, as well as the relationship of the aging John Shakespeare to both his son and his grandson, lead to multiple identifications transferred into and elaborated by the poems that address the friend of the Sonnets. Padel has since given his reading of the Sonnets book-length treatment in *New Poems by Shakespeare: Order and Meaning Restored to the Sonnets* (London: The Herbert Press, 1981).

nobles and his queen tear it to pieces. If John Shakespeare came to combine weakness and generous love, he would have been both a poor model for manhood and a parent difficult to reject wholly.

Henry VI's credulity is heavily stressed, along with his religious devotion, as in the scene, not required at all by the plot, where he superstitiously believes the "miracle" of a poor man's sight restored—a fraud that his uncle Gloucester handily exposes. Conceivably, the connection between Henry's weakness and his gullible piety is partly shaped by recollections of John Shakespeare's Catholic profession of faith—though the "miracle" episode in *Henry VI* (which comes from the chronicles) was calculated as drama to appeal to Protestant sentiment, and the religious preoccupation that goes with Henry's weakness is also historically derived. The son's response to John Shakespeare's Spiritual Last Will may be writ large, however, in the almost complete absence, from all the works, of religious resolutions of central dynamic stresses. Pious gestures at the moment of death, or in oaths and appeals to ultimate authority, are dramatic renderings of behavior in a Christian culture. Arguments have been mounted on the basis of Shakespeare's *sensibility* that he was either Catholic or a devoted high Anglican. But the point of view his drama adopts never, in my judgment, involves religious eschatology. Such this-world perspective fitted of course with the prohibition of religious themes in the theater, including the ban (which he frequently violates) on using the Lord's name. But it is in human beings and society that Shakespeare invests himself. To have watched, at age sixteen or seventeen, a precarious father make and then take back an extreme religious gesture, might well have contributed to Shakespeare's resolute secularism, despite the religious need in his temperament.

Lawrence Stone has described the extreme patriarchal authority exercised by parents, especially fathers, in the sixteenth and the earlier seventeenth century, which went with the rise of the nuclear family—a domination over children, and ritual subservience yielded by them, often astonishing to our modern sensibilities.[16] It seems highly unlikely that Shakespeare's father can have maintained such authority within his own house, from the time when

16. "The Rise of the Nuclear Family in Early Modern England: The Patriarchal Stage," in *The Family in History*, ed. C. E. Rosenberg (Philadelphia: University of Pennsylvania Press, 1975), pp. 13–57. Stone has published a revised and expanded version of this article as chap. 4 in *The Family, Sex and Marriage in England 1500–1800* (New York: Harper and Row, 1977), pp. 123–50.

he abdicated public authority, if not some time before. So we encounter extreme contrast between the father of infancy and early childhood and the precarious figure implied by the public record after Shakespeare was twelve, an objective contrast much more drastic, involving more for a son to deal with, than the usual dismantling of infantile overestimation, which is part of growing up.

Heinz Kohut stresses the importance of the child's gradual disillusionment in dealing with idealized figures upon whom parts of the self are patterned. "Under optimal circumstances," Kohut writes, the "child's evaluation of the idealized object becomes increasingly realistic"; a process of "gradual disappointment" permits the secure internalization of parental objects as structures of the self.[17] A sudden intensification of the disillusioning process forced by the abrupt failure of the idealized figure can lead to "what seems to be an intense form of object hunger. The intensity of the search for and of the dependency on these objects is due to the fact that they are striven for as a substitute for the missing segment of the psychic structure" (p. 45). Of course, John Shakespeare's decline, which seems to have coincided with his son's early adolescent years, would not have presented the kind of "very early traumatic disturbances" with which Kohut is most concerned, and which can lead to severely disabling disorders, as with "personalities who become addicts" (p. 46). But the father's failure would have corresponded to years in which, in "optimal circumstances," the son's gradually dismantled idealization of the father leads into and becomes the basis for a boy's preoccupation with manhood—as ideal and identity. Shakespeare puts to creative use potentially disruptive trends such as Kohut describes: an "intense form of object hunger" is fulfilled in the dramatist's power to create others.[18] Many

17. Heinz Kohut, *The Analysis of the Self* (New York: International Universities Press, 1971), p. 45.

18. There are, of course, difficulties about "applying" Kohut's account to Shakespeare. Common sense (and common prejudice) rejects making Shakespeare a "case." "It must have been something *psychological* that made him write all those things," would be the vulgar way of accepting such an explanation, from which common sense recoils. The process of taking new objects for old needs is, after all, nearly universal. An expression such as a "missing segment of the psychic structure" assumes as a psychological norm what in fact must be an achievement of culture. Yet there is surely evidence in the creative achievement for an exceptional need, along with exceptional mastery of it by means of heroic and romantic imagination—balanced by the sense of reality that controls ironic awareness about the heroic and romantic. And that need is itself consistent with the dominant concerns of the culture Shakespeare knew. In that culture, the tension between received ideas of

of these created persons carry on the search for ideal embodiment in the art. The Sonnets poet conducts such a search in his effort to live through the aristocratic manhood of his friend. Hamlet's effort to identify himself with the heroic manhood of his dead father will launch the series of plays in which the protagonist's search for self-fulfillment in or through another ends in tragedy.

The action in *Hamlet* is determined by the violent dethronement and death of a father. But for the first time he is a father apprehended as "a goodly king" (I.ii.186), strong, majestical. As Shakespeare moves up, in social terms, past caste difference, to invest his powers in the son who might inherit from such a figure, he moves back, in terms of individual development, to derivatives of the world of childhood, where such a figure would have been known and then lost. Not lost, however, as is Hamlet's father, in the full vigor of his active manhood, but lost behind the abruptly and unaccountably diminished figure of a father whose failure makes him an object of pity, not open confrontation. That Hamlet is not an adolescent but a grown man (thirty, if we take the gravedigger as calendar), fits with the long delay and incomplete accomplishment in Shakespeare's own development of a process that in simpler or different natures, in different family situations, takes place earlier—if perhaps never completely. The situation in *Hamlet*, centered on the son's all-or-nothing struggle with a beloved father who commands his loyalty and with a hated stepfather who must be destroyed, seems to offer the son a second chance for confrontation and internalization.

When we consider Shakespeare's long delay in turning to the tragic exploration of such confrontation, it seems significant that his own father was likely a man not easy for a son to hate. On this point, at least with regard to John Shakespeare's sociable and civic relations, we have seen that the external evidence is very strong—his being kept on the town council despite nonattendance, the forgiving of his fines and assessments for poor relief, his own standing surety for others even after extensive losses have cut deeply into his wife's inheritance. It is hard to hit a man who is down, to release into the filial bond the aggression by which a son can assert his own independent identity, especially if the father is a kind man

---

static, hierarchical society and the increasing social mobility, along with the loosening of earlier communal structures and their traditional religious reinforcements, put a new emphasis on reverential attitudes toward patriarchial authority and on the nuclear family and its survival through generations.

and the son is understanding; it is harder still if the father's being down has made him an object of disappointment—whether expressed as hostility or as pity—for a mother whose fortune he has brought down with him.

In the situation of Hamlet, however, there is Claudius, who is very much up, a thoroughly hateable figure who is a mighty opposite. The splitting of the father figure *seems* to give license for that passage through hatred that can lead to atonement. Shakespeare brings Claudius, with the sound of cannon and the trumpets that "bray out / The triumph of his pledge" (I.iv.11–12), into the beginning of the great scene on the battlements in which Hamlet will finally encounter the Ghost. Hamlet's clear-headed description, in the "nipping and . . . eager air" (line 2), of what is going on below, is icy with scorn:

> The King doth wake to-night and takes his rouse,
> Keeps wassail, and the swagg'ring up-spring reels.
> (lines 8–9)

But as Claudius "drains his draughts of Rhenish down," Hamlet feels himself involved, shamed, by the wassailing custom he regrets, "though to the manner born" (lines 10, 15):

> This heavy-headed revel east and west
> Makes us traduced, and tax'd of other nations,
> They clip us drunkards, and with swinish phrase
> Soil our addition, and indeed it takes
> From our achievements, though perform'd at height,
> The pith and marrow of our attribute,
> So oft it chances in particular men,
> That for some vicious mole of nature in them
> As in their birth wherein they are not guilty,
> (Since nature cannot choose his origin)
> By their o'ergrowth of some complexion
> Oft breaking down the pales and forts of reason,
> Or by some habit, that too much o'er-leavens
> The form of plausive manners, that these men
> Carrying I say the stamp of one defect
> Being nature's livery, or fortune's star,
> His virtues else . . .[19]
> (lines 17–33; punctuation as in Q2)

19. E. Nicholas Knight, in his study of *Shakespeare's Hidden Life: Shakespeare at the Law* (New York: Mason and Lipscomb, 1973), quotes the famous generalizing lines beginning with "So oft it chances in particular men" in the course of an exhaustive and moving account of John Shakespeare's legal difficulties in decline, taking them

As Hamlet shifts from scorn for those who perpetuate a national disgrace to compassion for those afflicted with an inescapable "defect," Claudius is left behind as the object of his meditation. This passage is often taken as a description of Hamlet himself and more generally of Shakespeare's tragic heroes, with support from "Oft breaking down the pales and forts of reason."

But the passage describes private persons, what often "chances in particular men," and the first instance of a disabling "mole of nature" is "in their birth, wherein they are not guilty, / (Since nature cannot choose his origin)." None of Shakespeare's heroes, least of all Hamlet, is lowborn. "By their o'ergrowth of some complexion" describes a developing character defect, not rapid crisis such as we get in the tragedies: it is a long-term process that is spoken of as breaking down rational control. "Or by some habit which too much o'er-leavens / The form of plausive manners" specifies a character defect that is sociable; the description would fit a sociable drinker who becomes an alcoholic: "plausive" suggests manners that are pleasing but lose their pith and become merely plausible. Too much yeast, too much ferment, is suggested by "o'er-leavens," a suggestion picked up in the final summary drink image: "the dram of eale / Doth all the noble substance of a doubt / To his own scandal" (lines 36–38).[20] "Yeast" is probably the first meaning of "eale," with a punning suggestion only of "evil." The small "dram" contrasts with the "draughts of Rhenish" Claudius "drains," even while it develops the theme. The result, for such "particular men," is not final, tragic destruction, but "scandal": they "in the general censure take corruption / From the particular fault" (lines 35–36).

The oblique language, hovering between technical terms and exquisitely suggestive metaphor, with the poised enumeration of alternatives, suggests an impulse to keep a distance. But for all the distance, the emphatically objective tone, a gathering intensity of regret takes over as the reflections accelerate (through a doubling syntax that modern punctuation spoils):

---

to be a description of the dramatist's own father (p. 28). I find very compelling the idea that the text moves into an account of men manqué, such men as Shakespeare's father. I have preserved the punctuation of the second quarto to keep the huddled, sliding quality of the movement of thought, which is broken up by modern punctuation; the comma after "attribute" (line 22) may not be a printer's error.

20. Q2's "eale" (yeast), often emended, as in *The Riverside Shakespeare*, to "ev'l" (evil), is here retained.

                                    that these men
                Carrying I say the stamp of one defect
                Being nature's livery or fortune's star,
                His virtues else be they as pure as grace,
                As infinite as man may undergo,
                Shall in the general censure take corruption
                From the particular fault: the dram of eale
                Doth all the noble substance of a doubt
                To his own scandal.
                            Enter Ghost.
HORATIO: Look my lord it comes.
HAMLET: Angels and ministers of grace defend us.
                    (lines 30–39; punctuation as in Q2)

The abruptness of the final lines of the long passage emphasizes a finality about the result of the process. Even as he recognizes sadly how the virtues are vitiated, Hamlet's regret pays tribute to them in the strongest terms. The subject shifts significantly from plural ("these men") to singular as a new start is made; "His virtues else be they as pure as grace" is high praise indeed, topped by "as infinite as man may undergo." The emphasis on "*one* defect" stresses what might have been, what was promised—and lost.

The lines serve the dramatic purpose of diverting the audience— and Hamlet—so that the sudden apparition of the Ghost takes them by surprise.[21] The omission of these lines from the Folio version (and from the quite full version of the first act in the first quarto) shows that they are not a "necessary business of the play." But in Shakespeare's own development, if this way of reading them is correct, they are a characteristically generous business of the play's author. Between Claudius, made present by braying trumpets and ordnance, and the appearance of the awesome Ghost, two potent father figures rooted in early childhood, Shakespeare puts Hamlet into relationship with a third father, neither villainous nor majestic. As he moves his hero toward encounter with a most powerful, indeed overpowering, paternal presence, and so into high tragedy, Shakespeare writes a poignant valediction to the kind of flawed figure his own father had become. In the process, with marvelous associative freedom and resonance, the Prince moves from despising the heroically evil stepfather, Claudius, in his drink, through reflections on the shame of a disabling weak-

---

21. See Kenneth Burke's illuminating commentary on this scene in *Counter-Statement*, 2nd ed. (Los Altos, California: Hermes Publications, 1953), pp. 29–30.

ness in quotidian life associated by imagery with drink, to regret for the noble substance so vitiated—and then comes the ghostly return of a father whose noble substance is intact, though robbed of life.

That Claudius's drunkenness provides the link between Hamlet's scorn for the usurper and his compassion for particular men may further reflect conditions in the Stratford home, though there is no evidence, beyond congruence with other circumstances, and one belated anecdote of a merry-cheeked, Falstaffian old man, to make it certain that John Shakespeare's problem was drink, and one's sense of the whole situation does not depend on that specification. It is worth remarking that the lines about the private men refer to a decline ending not in death but in "general censure." Such an assessment of a life or lives still present is consistent with the likelihood that Shakespeare's father was still alive when *Hamlet* was written, or at least first written. John Shakespeare was buried in September of 1601; if, as most scholars judge, Gabriel Harvey's marginalia note—that Shakespeare's "*Lucrece*, and his tragedy of Hamlet, Prince of Denmark, have it in them to please the wiser sort"[22]—was not later than early 1601, then a version of the tragedy that could command such respect must have been written at the latest in 1600. It is not the actual father who is dramatized as returning from the grave. But the apparition of past greatness may have something to do with half-buried recollections of the dramatist's father in his red, furred gown escorted to church by constables, as awesome for a four-year-old son as, in heroic iconography, "that fair and warlike form / In which the majesty of buried Denmark / Did sometimes march" (I.i.47–49). "We do it wrong, being so majestical / To offer it the show of violence" (lines 143–44).

"AN ABSOLUTE *IOHANNES FAC TOTUM*"

That Shakespeare at eighteen should have married a woman eight years older accords with the dominance of the vertical axis of family relationships in his sensibility. That it was something that happened rather than something planned seems evident, precontract or no precontract, from the fact that the marriage was performed less than six months before the birth of their first child. An ecclesiastical license was sought and paid for to allow only one asking of

22. *Riverside Shakespeare*, p. 1840.

the banns, instead of three on successive Sundays, so that the ceremony could take place before the Christmas season, when marriages were prohibited.[23] The responses of commentators have varied, from explanations making it all respectable for the nineteenth century, to beating pots and pans in charivari, versions of that old ritual gesture against the confusion of sexuality by verticality, citing passages from the plays, such as:

LYSANDER: Or else misgraffed in respect of years—
HERMIA: O spite! too old to be engag'd to young.
(*MND* I.i.137–38)

The comment of Stephen Dedalus is exceptional in that Joyce, controlling the whole, makes Stephen's own involvement part of his interpretation:

He chose badly? He was chosen, it seems to me. If others have their will Ann hath a way. By cock, she was to blame. She put the comether on him, sweet and twenty-six. The greyeyed goddess who bends over the boy Adonis, stooping to conquer, as prologue to the swelling act, is a boldfaced Stratford wench who tumbles in a cornfield a lover younger than herself.
And my turn? When?[24]

23. Schoenbaum, *Documentary Life*, pp. 62–65.
24. James Joyce, *Ulysses* (New York: Modern Library, 1934), p. 189. Norman Holland, in *Psychoanalysis and Shakespeare* (New York: McGraw-Hill, 1966), has a subtly and carefully built-up hypothetical portrait, which, "not unsurprisingly, turns out rather like the one Stephen Dedalus drew in the library scene of *Ulysses*." Holland conjectures that "one's first impression would be of a sort of Enobarbus, a man's man, aggressive, competitive, at home in the world of men, the kind of man one thinks of as rather puzzled by and a little afraid of women whom he tends to see either as ideal figures . . . or as mere amusements put on earth for man's convenience." Holland infers, on the basis of Shakespeare's active role in his company, in lawsuits, and in business, and the abounding imagery in the plays of "sports and violent action, particularly the explicit acting out of parricide and fratricide," that such "aggressive masculinity served Shakespeare as a defense against passive feminine needs." But somewhere within the man's man "there is a very tender, gentle person, even weak and wavering, someone who could cry easily, who dislikes violence and cruelty, who submits easily to others, particularly if they impose interest or tenderness on him. His own interest in other people is intense; he seems quite uncannily able to see things from their point of view and to sympathize, even to fuse with them. At times he becomes almost motherly, particularly toward younger men" (pp. 140–42). Holland's whole account is well worth reading; without contradicting the basic dual structure he posits, I feel that it is necessary to emphasize, more than he does, the vulnerability of the poet's negative capability, a vulnerability reflected most directly in the sonnets to the friend. Shakespeare is capable of opening up, in his art, staggeringly disruptive motives, and of giving himself to the realization of other identities with a fullness that in other temperaments and situations would require drastic defenses against passivity. Clearly, his art not only permitted the opening-up, but also provided resources of control.

That Shakespeare left Stratford for London but did not leave the marriage, begetting in its early years the first daughter and then twins, a daughter and the son who was to die when eleven and a half years old—these are crucial facts, however bare. We do not know whether he joined a company traveling through Stratford, was for a period "a schoolmaster in the country," or became a noverint, a legal secretary, as Nicholas Knight has argued plausibly but not compellingly.[25] What is clear is that in making this move, as so many were doing, he brought to London a rich local heritage, shaped both by civic experience and by the agricultural life surrounding his market town and lived by some of his kindred nearby. What he encountered there, in the professional theater, was an institution in the process of establishing its economic independence, a vocation that made it possible for a gifted writer to exist apart from aristocratic patronage.

With his usual multiple ironies, Shakespeare addresses the prospect of permanent financial patronage in *A Midsummer Night's Dream*, where the artisans lament Bottom's absence just before their play is scheduled to be put on:

> O sweet bully Bottom! Thus hath he lost sixpence a day during his life; he could not have scap'd sixpence a day. And the Duke had not given him sixpence a day for playing Pyramus, I'll be hang'd. He would have deserv'd it. Sixpence a day in Pyramus, or nothing.
>
> (IV.ii.19–24)

The noble persons for whom Shakespeare's marriage play may have first been written could scarcely miss this damnable iteration. Though it can pass off as a joke about the palpable-gross play that follows, Shakespeare at this early stage of his career seems to be glancing, at least, at the possibility of steady financial patronage— though he may already be enjoying a glance back at a situation from which his successes in the commercial theater have released him, or promise to release him. A little earlier, in 1593 and 1594, there are the dedications of the poems to Southampton; though they are in the mode of devoted compliment customary in the age, they seem to point hopefully in the direction of acquiring patronage, especially the second: "What I have done is yours, what I have to do is yours, being part in all I have, devoted yours." But by the time *Hamlet* is written, in about 1600, the Prince, elated by the success of the play within the play, exclaims:

25. *Shakespeare's Hidden Life.*

> Would not this, sir, and a forest of feathers—if the rest of
> my fortunes turn Turk with me—with two Provincial
> roses on my raz'd shoes, get me a fellowship in a cry of
> players?
> HORATIO: Half a share.
> HAMLET: A whole one, I.

(III.ii.275–80)

For all his enthusiasm about the traveling company, Hamlet thinks of them as self-supporting, sharing ownership won by their talents.

This financial independence, along with aristocratic sponsorship and intermittent performances with rewards at court, provided a relatively secure working situation and a measure of independence crucial for Shakespeare's productivity and the critical perspectives of his productions. Robert Greene's deathbed attack in 1592, and its publisher Henry Chettle's subsequent apology, speak volumes here and are worth dwelling on despite their familiarity. Greene, one of the University Wits who first gave educated voice to the burgeoning acting profession, warns Marlowe, Nashe, and Peele, "*those Gentlemen his Quondom acquaintance, that spend their wits in making plaies,*" to take a lesson from his own miserable state, brought on by "those Puppets . . . that spake from our mouths, those Anticks garnisht in our colours."[26] If Greene, to whom such "burres" have sought "to cleave," has been forsaken by actors turned base imitators, shall not these three, "to whome they all have beene beholding," be forsaken as well?

> Yes trust them not: for there is an vpstart Crow, beautified with our feathers, that with his *Tygers hart wrapt in a Players hyde*, supposes he is as well able to bombast out a blank verse as the best of you: and beeing an absolute *Iohannes fac totum*, is in his owne conceit the onely Shake-scene in a countrey. O that I might intreat your rare wits to be imploied in more profitable courses: & let those Apes imitate your past excellence, and neuer more acquaint them with your admired inuentions. I knowe the best husband of you all will neuer proue an Vsurer, and the kindest of them all will neuer proue a kind nurse: yet whilest you may, seeke you better Maisters; for it is pittie men of such rare wits, should be subiect to the pleasure of such rude groomes.

When one thinks of the stress to which the need for patronage subjected even such a well-derived poet as John Donne, despite the early recognition of his genius, once his marriage had alienated his patron, one is grateful that Shakespeare could provide for his life

---

26. *The Riverside Shakespeare*, p. 1835.

by "public means." He could feel, in relation to the world of his highborn friend, uncomfortable about his profession—"almost thence my nature is subdued / To what it works in, like the dyer's hand" (Sonnet 111). But if Shakespeare is associated with "rude groomes," the rude grooms have money—that is the root of the animus of poor Pierce Penniless Greene. In a time before theatrical copyright, to be the players' in-house playmaker was a secure way to make a solid living. Greene, at the end of the road of hand-to-mouth insecurity to which the University Wits were subject, speaks with a dilapidated gentleman's scorn of anyone who could "proue an Vsurer." But to put some of his money out at interest was just what Shakespeare in fact did do, as did many members of the rising mercantile class, along with alert members of the aristocracy.

Before the year 1592 was out, Henry Chettle responded to the stir caused by his posthumous publication of Greene's letter "to diuers play-makers," which had been "offensively by one or two of them taken." After defending his own reputation as a printer who has long "hindred the bitter inueying against schollers," Chettle goes on to apologize for not deleting the remarks about Shakespeare:

> With neither of them that take offence was I acquainted, and with one of them [Marlowe] I care not if I neuer be: The other [Shakespeare], whome at that time I did not so much spare, as since I wish I had, for that as I haue moderated the heate of liuing writers, and might haue vsde my owne discretion (especially in such a case) the Author beeing dead, that I did not, I am as sory, as if the originall fault had beene my fault, because my selfe haue seene his demeanor no lesse ciuill than he excelent in the qualitie he professes: Besides, diuers of worship haue reported, his vprightnes of dealing, which argues his honesty, and his facetious grace in writting, that aprooues his Art.[27]

It is striking that in many of the Sonnets, even as Shakespeare expresses his adulation of aristocratic heritage, he does so in prudential monetary and legal terms of middle-class provenance, terms used in "upright dealing"—or sharp practice (compare Sonnet 134). He feels his heritage as a stain in the situation of writing them, perhaps referring to his father's trade as a glover in "the dyer's hand." But from within the nascent middle class, in the dipolar society of the time, Chettle's praise defines his professional situation in complimentary, positive terms. His "facetious grace" in writing, Shakespeare would have learned and polished in London, but the status Chettle describes with middle-class admiration extended

27. Ibid., pp. 1835–36.

what the dramatist brought with him from Stratford. If on one side Shakespeare's tough business success reflects determination not to be like the father who failed to carry through, the young playwright's model for "vprightness of dealing," which "diuers of worship haue reported," must also have been that father and the firm-textured society in which he had earlier succeeded.

Greene's belittling turns inside out as one thinks of what it implies about Shakespeare's roles, besides what it says of his financial independence. The *fac totum*, as he makes and "shakes" scenes and writes parts for everybody, is in the position, if he has the sense of form that Shakespeare had, to dominate the whole, to be *dominus factotum*—not a mere jack-of-all-trades but master. It is ironic that Greene's attack on Shakespeare, "his *Tygers hart wrapt in a Players hyde*," suggests this dominance by likening the enterprising playwright to one of the domineering women prominent in his early work—Queen Margaret, as she violently usurps the power of British royalty. Having captured York, her great dynastic rival, Margaret taunts him fiendishly by wiping his face with a napkin soaked in the blood of his youngest son. York, about to die on her dagger and Clifford's, cries out:

> O tiger's heart wrapp'd in a woman's hide!
> How couldst thou drain the life-blood of the child,
> To bid his father wipe his eyes withal.
> (3H6 I.iv.137–39)

But Shakespeare's actual role in the theater—to be constantly giving, working within a team, creating parts to realize and nurture the talents of his fellows—is directly counter to Greene's jibe. It is a cherishing role, the very opposite to the dread maternal destructiveness portrayed—and so distanced—in Margaret.

Apart from Greene, his contemporaries speak of "gentle" Shakespeare; he has a supremely generous imagination. Identification with the cherishing role of the parents is built into Shakespeare's genius as he functions as player and playwright. In the Sonnets, such cherishing goes with an inhibition on the middle-class poet's characterizing and so limiting the aristocratic young man. If we considered only the self-disabling adulation in the Sonnets, we might well ask: what did Shakespeare, by contrast with quarrelsome Marlowe and Jonson, do with his aggression? How was he spared the destructive effects where aggression not directed outward turns inward, back against the self?

It seems clear that he puts aggression fully in the service of his dramatic art. He uses it in creating aggressive characters: Richard III, in his first great public hit, is utterly captivating as he plays ruthlessly and humorously for the crown. But the dramatist also, crucially, uses aggression to shape and limit the characters he creates, subduing each to the mastery of the whole production:

> And let those that play your clowns speak no more than is set down for them, for there be of them that will themselves laugh to set on some quantity of barren spectators to laugh too, though in the mean time some necessary question of the play be then to be consider'd.
> (*Ham.* III.ii.38–45)

The royal amateur of the theater who says this is about to use a play from the repertory of the visiting common players for extremely aggressive purposes, to show royal crime its own image. Hamlet speaks patronizingly of "a fellowship in a cry of players," but the whole situation suggests the remarkable role the players had in their relationship to the world of court and kings.

Leo Salingar has made the point that, as a way of expressing their special, new, undefined status, the poets of the common players "found the equivalent of a professional emblem in the novel device of inserting a play within the play,"[28] often with royal or noble spectators. We can see Kyd doing this, with aggressive protest, in *The Spanish Tragedy*, where a court official, unable to obtain justice for the murder of his son, turns the play he is staging into a brutal attack on his royal audience, destroying a whole dynastic line. Salingar sees Shakespeare, in his comedies, balancing prerogatives, political and artistic: "the real influence of the monarch" and "the idea of play-acting." These polarized preoccupations reflect Shakespeare's "historically novel situation, as a professional playwright in a mainly commercial theatre, writing for, and even in a sense creating, a national public, but depending first and last on aristocratic favour. At one pole of his comic world is the actor-poet, at the other, his ultimate patron, the prince" (p. 256).

The two poles, with their class or caste difference, are implicit in the interplay between admiration and irony in history and tragedy as well as in comedy. Shakespeare's art shares the assumption of most Englishmen of the age that the fullness of life could be realized only by the nobility and gentry, with the royal family at what should be the pinnacle. On occasion he could give the merry wives of Windsor and other neighbors their due, but as Salingar observes:

28. Leo Salingar, *Shakespeare and the Traditions of Comedy* (Cambridge: Cambridge University Press, 1974), p. 267.

"His stage world gravitates to the great house or the court. He depicts the gentry from outside, but they stand at the centre" (p. 255). The stage itself, however, was a middle-class property and point of vantage. In the commercial theater, Shakespeare could use the power of dramatic form to develop aggressive, ironic understanding of the court world—its ideals and iconography, with the magical expectations they could foster.

The Elizabethan theater was very much open to life shaped by aristocratic expectations and values, generous in the sympathies it extends toward that life, but also ruthless. The lesser dramatists reveled in ruthlessness or sympathy as opportunity and convention offered. Marlowe's plays are often, in effect, acts of aggression in which the audience is invited to participate. But in Shakespeare the range of sympathy and the range of ruthlessness are perfectly matched and balanced, transforming aggression into dramatic irony. Irony is a form of aggression where the ironist does nothing to his object except as his auditors join with him. An ironic attack depends on somebody *else*'s seeing the point. When such dramatic irony is present, the audience gives the aggression social validation, taking the burden off their dramatist's shoulders. So the ironist's aggression is also his audience's and is validated by the audience. This is as true of the large, tragic ironies implicit in *King Lear* as it is of a thrust of ironic wit or a satiric sally. The art puts aggression in the service of a common recognition of the ludicrous and tragic potentials of aristocratic values accepted, but only prima facie, by Shakespeare's art.

Shakespeare's remarkable unassertiveness in his own person as an author fits, I think, with his ability to transform aggression into the mirth of comedy or into the ruthless ironic knowledge which accompanies the ruth of tragedy. Shakespeare conducts something like a public execution in a tragedy, something like a saturnalian public holiday in a comedy. With the rhythms of comedy and tragedy, he is able to realize aristocratic and royal identities and at the same time limit them—by dramatizing an understanding of them. In his role as unseen judge and executioner—or lord of misrule—Shakespeare follows, in his most fully achieved works, the ironic logic of the very motives he is liberating and cherishing; the audience, in recognizing the irony, shares in the ruthlessness of his art.[29] The whole play, not only as a composition of utterances but

29. The analogy with the public execution was developed by Wyndham Lewis in *The Lion and the Fox* (London: G. Richards, 1927) and John Holloway in *The Story of*

also as an event in the theater, provides a mode of self-assertion to balance Shakespeare's giving himself to the realization of other identities. Perhaps it was only possible for Shakespeare's personality, with its intense responsiveness, its negative capability and lack of ordinary self, to achieve domination through his art and in this social way.

We noted in chapter 1 that Shakespeare does not use his art to dramatize tragic male-to-male confrontation until more than half of his plays have been written. In relation to the concerns of this chapter, we can add that by the time Shakespeare comes to write *Hamlet* he has succeeded wonderfully, in middle-class terms, by his own role in a joint stock company; followed through with his father's earlier application for a coat of arms to make his father and himself gentry; and invested a large part of his earnings in his native Stratford, including the purchase of New Place. In short, he does not make tragedy, with its dominant concerns of heritage and authority organized by the stresses of Oedipal conflict, his central form of expression until he has outdone his father in the rising middle class. From his own fully established place in the independent, commercial theater, Shakespeare could use his drama to risk testing the possibility of becoming the ideal, omnipotent father of infancy: he could begin to express, in the major tragedies, the longing for that figure of authority, with the parricidal rage, the immense anxiety, and the feared destruction that accompany it.

The shift into the preoccupations of the major tragedies can be summarized by the change from a special investment of self in Falstaff to such an investment in Hamlet. Falstaff, as William Empson long ago suggested, relates to Prince Hal somewhat as the speaker of the Sonnets relates to the highborn young man, but with "a savage and joyous externalisation of self-contempt."[30] When one asks what happened in *Hamlet* to the gulf of caste or class differ-

---

the Night (London: Routledge and Kegan Paul, 1961). Both books, Holloway's more extensively, show attitudes in characters within the drama, and attitudes in the audience's perspective, congruous with the Renaissance acceptance of men's suffering death (by contrast to our humanitarian avoidances). Not only the audience at a public execution, but also, in many cases, the condemned man participated in the process which we prefer not to see except on film and television. The analogy between comedy and saturnalian ritual is developed in the first chapter of C. L. Barber, *Shakespeare's Festive Comedy* (Princeton: Princeton University Press, 1959).

30. William Empson, *Some Versions of Pastoral* (London: Chatto and Windus, 1935), p. 100.

ence which in part animates the Sonnets and the role of Falstaff, one seems to see a further contribution made to his art by Shakespeare's origins and his way of handling them. Hamlet can be gracious with the players or his old school fellows, but when the chips are down the Prince puts them in their place: "Besides, to be demanded of a spunge, what replication should be made by the son of a king?" (IV.ii.12–13). Why is there not an element of wish fulfillment, a vicarious enjoyment making for sentimental or snobbish distortion in the player/dramatist's realizing the sense of self of a higher caste? Is not the answer, in part at least, that the whole spectacle is presented in the commercial theater, an independent place from which Shakespeare could stand and look with his awesome ironic understanding at the great world and its secular magic? There is no such control in the Jacobean court masques, which dramatize "expressions of royal power," as Stephen Orgel observes, not ironic explorations of it.[31] The caste difference separating middle-class author, players, and much of the audience from the play's royal subject matter in Shakespearean tragedy contributes to the awe with which figures of authority and the struggle for it are invested, in accord with the worshipful patterns of the secular hierarchy that shape expression in the Sonnets. But Shakespeare's middle-class difference and sense of tough realities simultaneously contribute to the increasing ironic clarity with which he makes us see that a social order, whose structure as such he does not question, fails to work. Moreover, the whole dramatization of aristocratic heroic struggles is made within the matrix of the early-based, cherishing sensibility, with its deep commitment to kinship and kindness, shaped too in the family in middle-class Stratford.

The London in which Shakespeare practiced his dramatic art was the nerve and power center of England, open to foreign influence by commerce, travel, and foreign residents, including the Huguenots among whom he lived for a time. The four great dramatists of Athens all came from rural demes; in their work traditional attitudes, beliefs, and values are articulated (and put to tragic or comic test) by the cosmopolitan consciousness of a city that had become the crossroads of Greece and an imperial power. A great nascent moment seems to involve such interplay regularly. The English Renaissance, especially in Shakespeare's supreme example,

---

31. Stephen Orgel, *The Illusion of Power: Political Theater in the English Renaissance* (Berkeley and Los Angeles: University of California Press, 1975), p. 45.

is not primarily the recovery of classical resources so reborn—though it includes that. More fundamentally, it is the articulation of tradition-directed ways of living and thinking as these are brought into the field of developing metropolitan consciousness. The interplay of Stratford and London was crucial, even though the Stratford kind of experience is not a major subject, as such, in Shakespeare's works. The fact that he used his London winnings to establish himself in Stratford by the purchase of New Place in 1598 and returned to live there when his London career came to an end is in line with the characteristically English country-city polarity, crossed by the polarity between his own middle-class heritage and his court-centered art, fundamental in his achievement.

3

Domestic Comedy

Family-centered energies that animate the action are made enjoyable by dramatic form in the first two plays that have held the stage, *The Comedy of Errors* and *Richard III*. In this chapter and the next we will explore the importance of family-based conflicts in the vividly realized social worlds of these plays. We will then turn in chapter 5 to what can be seen as abortive domestic tragedy in *Titus Andronicus*, another early play that clearly succeeded on the Elizabethan stage. But Shakespeare's first essay in tragedy, since the success that Ben Jonson recalled in linking it with *The Spanish Tragedy*, has been very rarely seen; disowned on behalf of Shakespeare by early critics, *Titus* has been only recently recognized as indubitably all his work and revived in highly stylized performances. Shakespeare goes beyond Kyd to make a revenge play where horrors of family and sexual violence are realized imaginatively in such drastic ways that we are virtually forced to find psychological motives beyond the fictive social situation. To look first at the success of dramatic form in *The Comedy of Errors* and *Richard III*, then at its partial failure in *Titus*, will help to avoid psychological reduction of his art's crucially social achievement. For Shakespeare obviously did not set out to "express himself"—or to project "his internalized family situation." He set out to make plays for his fellows to perform and their audiences to enjoy. Ways of playing were already, of course, current—in the case of *The Comedy of Errors*, Plautus's way, in original, Italian, and academic versions. And Leo Salingar has noted the play's indebtedness to the dramatized romance, a popular theatrical mode in Shakespeare's youth, which included the tradition of the "saints' plays" as well as secular romance.[1]

---

1. In *Shakespeare and the Traditions of Comedy* (Cambridge: Cambridge University Press, 1974), Leo Salingar argues that in "the first half of Elizabeth's reign . . . roughly a third, perhaps more, of the actors' repertoire must have consisted of plays of this type." They extend a "tradition of romantic plays, religious and secular, . . . unbroken from the fourteenth and fifteenth centuries" (p. 67).

"THIS SYMPATHIZED ONE DAY'S ERROR"

R. A. Foakes, introducing his excellent Arden edition of *The Comedy of Errors*, remarks that producers of the play have too often regarded it "as a short apprentice work in need of improvement, or as a mere farce, 'shamelessly trivial' as one reviewer in *The Times* put it."[2] Accordingly they have usually adapted it, added to it, fancied it up. But in its own right, as its stage popularity attests, it is a delightful play. Shakespeare outdoes Plautus in brilliant, hilarious complication. He makes the arbitrary reign of universal misapprehension the occasion for a dazzling display of his dramatic control of his characters' separate perspectives, keeping track for our benefit of just what each participant has experienced and the conclusions he or she draws from it. One must admit that the way the confusion is elaborated by wrangling with words is sometimes tedious, especially on the stage, where the eye cannot assist the ear in following the young poet's fascination with the manipulation of language. But most of the time one can enjoy the wonderful verbal energy with which he endows his characters as they severally struggle to put together and express their baffling encounters.

Shakespeare feeds Elizabethan life into the mill of Roman farce, life realized with his distinctively generous creativity, very different from Plautus's tough, narrow, resinous genius. And, although the mill grinds a good deal of chaff as well as wheat, he frequently makes the errors reveal fundamental human nature, especially human nature under the stress and tug of marriage. The tensions of marriage dramatized through Antipholus of Ephesus and his wife are related to the tensions in the romantic tale of Egeon and Aemilia with which he frames the Ephesian mix-ups. In this framing, Shakespeare's distinctive sense of life in its family matrix asserts itself.

There is more of daily, ordinary life in *The Comedy of Errors* than in any other of the comedies except *The Merry Wives of Windsor*. A mere machinery of mistakes is never enough even for the most mechanical comedy; the dramatist must be able to present particular lives being caught up in mistakes and carrying them onward. Something must be going on already—Antipholus of Ephesus late for dinner again, his wife in her usual rage ("Fie, how impatience low'reth in your face!" [II.i.86]). Shakespeare is marvelous at conveying a sense of a world already there, with its routine tensions:

2. (London: Methuen, 1962), p. lii.

The capon burns, the pig falls from the spit;
The clock hath strucken twelve upon the bell:
My mistress made it one upon my cheek:
She is so hot because the meat is cold.

(I.ii.44–47)

He creates a prosperous commercial town outside the domestic world of the jealous wife's household: its merchant-citizens are going about their individual business, well known to one another and comfortably combining business with pleasure—until the errors catch up with them.

To keep farce going requires that each person involved be shown making *some* sort of sense out of it while failing to see through it—as the audience can. It would be fatal for one twin to conclude, "Why, I must have been mistaken for my long-lost brother!" So the dramatist must show each of his people taking what happens according to his own bent, explaining to himself as best he can what occurs, as when, for example, one of the twin masters meets the wrong slave and finds the fellow denying that he ever heard instructions received by the other slave a few moments before. Too often the master concludes simply that the slave is lazy or impudent and beats him; this constant thumping of the Dromios grows tedious and is out of key with their winning wit and humor when they speak out as Elizabethan stage clowns.

The idea that the mistakes must be sorcery opens out onto fine extravagance. The traveling brothers have heard that Ephesus is full of "Dark-working sorcerers that change the mind" (I.ii.99). (The town was identified with sorcerers by Saint Paul's reference to their "curious arts" in his *Epistle to the Ephesians*, one reason perhaps for Shakespeare's choice of the town as a locale, as Geoffrey Bullough has suggested.)[3] The visitors decide that "this is the fairy land. O spite of spites! / We talk with goblins, owls and sprites" (II.ii.189–90). As the errors are wound up tighter and tighter, the wife and sister conclude that husband and slave must be mad and bring on a real, live exorcist, the absurd schoolmaster, Dr. Pinch, in a huge red wig and beard, to conjure the devil out of them. By the end, Adriana is calling on the whole company to witness that her husband "is borne about invisible" (V.i.187). We relish the elaboration of these factitious notions of magic to explain events that do indeed seem to "change the mind"; at the same time we enjoy the final return of all hands to the level of fact, where we have

3. *Sources*, vol. 1, p. 10.

been situated all along. The end of the delusions is heralded by Dr. Pinch's being all but burned up by his outraged "patients." The Ephesian husband stubbornly hangs onto his senses and his sense of outrage; he sets fire to the "doctor" as a comic effigy on whom to take vengeance for the notions of madness and magic to which almost everyone has given way.

The most interesting misinterpretations of the mistakes about identity are of course those where error feeds already existing passions—Adriana's jealousy, her husband's irritation—and leads to a kind of rhapsody exploding just before the final resolution. Particularly, Adriana's self-defeating rage at her husband is finely treated, especially in the moment when the traveling brother seems to provide her with the ultimate provocation—her husband's making love to her sister! (Shakespeare added the charming, sensible sister, not in Plautus, as a foil and confidante for the shrewish wife.) After listening to a frenzy of railing, the sister brings the wife up short by asking why she cares about her husband if he is so despicable, and she answers "Ah, but I think him better than I say, / . . . My heart prays for him; though my tongue do curse" (IV.ii.25, 28). She is brought up short again, in a final tableau, when the Abbess traps her into betraying how she has made her husband's life miserable. The older woman delivers a splendid, formal rebuke:

ADRIANA: Still did I tell him it was vild and bad.
ABBESS: And thereof came it that the man was mad.
          The venom clamors of a jealous woman
          Poisons more deadly than a mad dog's tooth.
                                              (V.i.67–70)

Adriana is chastened: "She did betray me to my own reproof" (V.i.90). But her domineering bent is still there; she goes on insisting on her right to manage her own husband's madness: "I will attend my husband, be his nurse, / Diet his sickness, for it is my office, / And will have no attorney but myself" (V.i.98–100).

We can see a revealing contrast with Plautus in the handling of the Ephesian couple's relations. Shakespeare's husband and wife are more complex; they are also more decent. At the opening of *Menaechmi* the husband is making off with a fine cloak of his wife's to give it to Erotium, the courtesan; he has already stolen for her his wife's gold chain. Shakespeare's Antipholus only decides to go elsewhere to dine in response to the incomprehensibly outrageous behavior of his wife in locking the doors (while *she* thinks she has at last got him home). It is in revenge for this that he decides to give the young "hostess" the necklace originally ordered for his wife. His eye has strayed, to be sure—"I know a wench of excellent discourse, / Pretty and witty; wild, and yet, too, gentle; / . . . My wife (but I protest, without desert) / Has oftentimes upbraided me withal" (III.i.109–10, 112–13). In Plautus there is no ambiguity and no mixture of attitudes: from the outset it is "To hell with my wife, I'm going to have my fun." When in Plautus the visiting twin comes along, he has his unknown brother's good time with Erotium, gets the cloak and chain, and rejoices that it was all free. Shakespeare's twin, by contrast, falls romantically in love with the modest sister Shakespeare has provided, speaking some lovely poetry as he does so.

The difference in the two plays reflects the difference in the two cultures, Roman and Elizabethan. It also reflects the different form of comedy which Shakespeare was beginning to work out, a comedy appropriate to the fullest potentialities of his culture. Roman comedy functioned as a special field day for outrageousness; by and large, it fitted Aristotle's formula that comedy deals with characters who are worse than we are. Though there are some conventional, stock heroes and heroines, most of the stage people are meant to be fractions of human nature on its aggressive, libidinal side. The central characters in Shakespeare's comedies, on the other hand, whatever their faults, are conceived as whole people. His comedy dramatizes outrageousness, which usually is presented, however, as the product of special circumstances, or at least it is abetted by circumstances. Often the occasion is festivity, or a special situation like a holiday, a moment felt as a saturnalian exception to ordinary life, as I stressed in *Shakespeare's Festive Comedy*. Here in *The Comedy of Errors*, with its central domestic focus, the mistakes of identity bring the husband and wife to extremities on a day that is otherwise very much an "everyday." But unlike Plautus, Shakespeare frames the release begot of error with presentations of the normal and the ideal. Roman comedy had its recognized place in the whole of life, its accepted fescennine function; but this was so firmly institutional that it could be implicit, understood by author, actors, and audience. Shakespeare even in this early play makes the *placing* of the comic extremes part of the comedy itself.

The headlong day is begun and ended with the story of Egeon, the bereft father of the twins, condemned to die in the morning, pardoned at evening and reunited with his long-lost wife and sons.

In the final scenes of farce, feelings break loose, people are beside themselves; extras rush on the stage to bind struggling Antipholus and Dromio; a moment later the two are loose again, as it seems, with swords drawn, driving away all comers. Then suddenly, after this release, the tone changes: the Abbess and the Duke, with aged Egeon, take over the stage, figures of authority and reverence. We hear poignant accents of family feeling in Egeon's

> Not know my voice! O time's extremity,
> Hast thou so crack'd and splitted my poor tongue
> In seven short years, that here my only son
> Knows not my feeble key of untun'd cares? . . .
> Tell me thou art my son Antipholus.
>
> (V.i.308–11, 319)

A moment later the Syracusan Antipholus, who does know his father, comes on stage; the doubles are visible together at last, and the plot is unsprung. But instead of ending there, we are lifted into a curiously serious final moment. The Abbess, now discovered as the wife, speaks of the moment as a new birth of her children:

> Thirty-three years have I but gone in travail
> Of you, my sons, and till this present hour
> My heavy burthen ne'er delivered.
>
> (V.i.401–3)

She invites all to "a gossips' feast"—a christening party, "gossips" here being the old, Prayer Book word for godparents, "god-sybs," brothers and sisters in God of the parents. "After so long grief, such nativity!" the Abbess-wife exclaims. As all go out except the four brothers, the Duke sets his seal on the renewal of community, centered in the family: he uses the word gossip in both its ceremonial sense of "sponsor" and its ordinary, neighborly sense: "With all my heart, I'll gossip at this feast" (V.i.408).

Shakespeare's sense of comedy as a moment in a larger cycle leads him, right at the outset, to frame farce with action that presents the weight of age and the threat of death, and to make the comic resolution a renewal of life in both generations, indeed explicitly a rebirth. He seems to go rather far out of the way to do it: Egeon and Aemilia are offstage and almost entirely out of mind in all but the first and last scenes. But there are meaningful connections between the two actions at many levels, as we shall see. We can notice, first, that the bonds of marriage, broken in the parents' case by romantic accident, are also much at issue in the intervening scenes, where marriage is subjected to the unromantic strains of temperament grinding on temperament in the setting of daily life. Moreover, Adriana and her Antipholus are both *in* their marriage (though not as wooing couples are in love); its hold on them comes out under the special stress of the presence of the twin doubles. The seriousness of the marriage, however trying, appears in Adriana's long speech rebuking and pleading with her husband when he seems at last to have come home to dinner (it is, of course, the wrong brother):

> Ah, do not tear away thyself from me;
> For know, my love, as easy mayst thou fall
> A drop of water in the breaking gulf,
> And take unmingled thence that drop again, . . .
> As take from me thyself and not me too.
> How dearly would it touch thee to the quick,
> Shouldst thou but hear I were licentious.
> (II.ii.124–27, 129–31)

That for her husband home and wife are really primary is made explicit even when he is most angry:

> Since mine own doors refuse to entertain me,
> I'll knock elsewhere, to see if they'll disdain me.
> (III.i.120–21)

Shakespeare nowhere else deals with the daily substance of marriage, its irritations, and its strong holding power (*The Merry Wives of Windsor* touches some of this, at a later stage of married life; the rest of the comedies are wooing and wedding). There *is* a deep logic, therefore, to merging, in the ending, the fulfillment of a long-stretched, romantic longing of husband and wife with the conclusion, in the household of Antipholus, of domestic peace after domestic frenzy. No doubt their peace is temporary, but for the moment all vexation is spent; and Adriana *may* have learned something from the Abbess's lecture, even though the Abbess turns out to be her mother-in-law!

"ONE FACE, ONE VOICE, ONE HABIT, AND TWO PERSONS"

The Comedy of Errors can bring home how outgoing Shakespeare's genius is from the beginning, and how inclusive, in bringing together dramatized romance and Plautus's farce, medieval and classical heritage, popular and academic stage traditions. But there is nothing in the piece that requires our looking to special preoccupations in its author—until we set it in relationship to circumstances in his life and to other works. Then what he chooses to play with becomes significant, just as a child's play, outward-directed as it uses toys imitating or drawn from the larger world, gradually reveals themes loaded with his immediate concerns. The act of choice is beyond articulation, reflecting a global situation. But by pursuing such themes we can catch a glimpse of how the dramatist, in an early, masterful comedy, is using the theater in ways that reflect circumstances of his own life and of his age.

With an eye to Shakespeare's other works, notably *Richard III*, we can notice that Antipholus of Syracuse and Antipholus of Ephesus are brothers who, through no fault of their own, are getting drastically in each other's way. The fun, the repeated détentes for the audience, go with the *absence* of fraternal hostility, indeed of any motive for causing trouble: each brother is well-bred and reasonable in his responses until provoked beyond endurance and seemingly plunged into an abyss of irrational claims and wrongs and threats. Resentment or fear of a doppelgänger is excluded by the plot's requirement that neither brother suspect the other's involvement. As if to provide a final reminder of how consistently the mishaps endured by the play's two pairs of brothers have *not* been linked to fraternal enmity, the Dromios conclude the play by abjuring rivalry over who is the elder: "We came into the world like brother and brother; / And now let's go hand in hand, not one before another" (V.i.425–26). A few lines earlier, the Ephesian Dromio had expressed his delight in an image frequently used in the Sonnets: "Methinks you are my glass, and not my brother; / I see by you I am a sweet-fac'd youth" (lines 418–19).

Instead of the fraternal resentment or rivalry central to *Henry VI* and *Richard III*, *The Comedy of Errors* emphasizes the Syracusan's longing for his brother. At his first entrance, after he is warned of his perils in Ephesus, the wandering twin tells his Ephesian friend:

> Farewell till then. I will go *lose myself*,
> And wander up and down to view the city.
> MERCHANT: Sir, I commend you to your own content. *Exit*.
> S. ANTIPHOLUS: He that commends me to mine own content,
> Commends me to the thing I cannot get:
> I to the world am like a drop of water
> That in the ocean seeks another drop,

Who, falling there to find his fellow forth
(Unseen, inquisitive), confounds himself.
So I, to find a mother and a brother,
In quest of them (unhappy), ah, *lose myself.*
(I.ii.30–40; my italics)

This is the same imagery for family feeling and loss as Adriana's for fusion in married love; Antipholus S. will use a version of this imagery again when he falls in love with Luciana.[4] But the Syracusan brother's lost self will be restored to him, he will be given his place in a family and a marriage, and marital harmony will return to his Ephesian twin and Adriana, only when the lost mother is recovered in the final scene.

Anne Barton observes that the Syracusan twin loses himself "in ways that neither he nor the writers of classical comedy could possibly have anticipated." In contrast to the characters of New Comedy, for whom identity "is principally a matter of establishing parentage and social class," Antipholus S. "has voluntarily left a father and a defined and satisfactory social role in order to find a missing mother and twin brother without whom he feels psychologically incomplete."[5] As she picks up the two levels on which the questing Antipholus speaks of losing himself, in the oceanic imagery and in the temporary disturbance of viewing the town, Barton rightly does not force on the play full Christian meanings like "losing himself to find himself." The shape of the dramatic action as it runs its secular course right up to the end brings out the factitiousness of supernatural or demonic explanation. But in getting at what distinguishes the wandering twin's predicament from those of his New Comedy prototypes, Barton appropriately emphasizes that between Menander and Shakespeare "there stretches not only an immense gulf of space and time but also the fact of Christianity with its stress on the inner life" (p. 81).

The relationship to Christian culture also shapes the quality of the final reunion differently from those typical of Hellenistic New Comedy (and missing in Plautus's *Menaechmi*). Barton underscores the fact that the presence in the Abbess of the lost wife and mother,

---

4. Harry Levin points to the importance of this imagery for the theme of lost and found identity in his introduction to *Errors* for the *Complete Signet Classic Shakespeare*, gen. ed. Sylvan Barnet (New York: Harcourt Brace Jovanovich, 1972), p. 77.

5. Anne Barton, Introduction to *The Comedy of Errors*, *The Riverside Shakespeare*, p. 81.

Aemilia, is a complete surprise to the audience. She catches beautifully the sort of reality and unreality the drama gives to the final discovery of the mother, "comical in the fullest sense of the word":

> At its ending *The Comedy of Errors* admits its own artificiality, its participation in that special realm of fairy tale where the lost are always found, while reminding the theatre audience that it has not been in complete control of the situation after all. This last scene is consciously contrived but also moving in a way that seems to anticipate the marvelous discoveries of *Cymbeline* and *The Winter's Tale*. Certainly the emotions liberated look forward to the last plays. (P. 82)

One can of course include *Pericles* among the last plays, where the oceanic imagery adumbrated in *The Comedy of Errors* is given an enveloping resonance with the loss and recovery of fortune and family. The early comedy is an overture for so much that comes later because its handling of commerce and marriage is placed in an emotional field shaped by the family as a whole—siblings, wife and prospective bride, and parents—but here from the son's vantage rather than, as in the late romances, that of a bereft father.[6] Reunion after sundering is consummated in a Christian rite of passage; but the objects of feeling are secular, a vulnerable father and a mother both sanctified and managerial.

When Shakespeare wrote *The Comedy of Errors*, he had left a wife in Stratford for the commercial metropolis of London. In this situation, how could he write such affecting lines about a wife's abandonment as those he gives to Adriana?

> Ay, ay, Antipholus, look strange and frown,
> Some other mistress hath thy sweet aspects:
> I am not Adriana, nor thy wife.
> The time was once, when thou unurg'd wouldst vow
> That never words were music to thine ear,
> That never objects pleasing in thine eye,
> That never touch well welcome to thy hand,
> That never meat sweet-savor'd in thy taste,
> Unless I spake, or look'd, or touch'd, or carv'd to thee.
> How comes it now, my husband, O, how comes it,

---

6. Coppélia Kahn groups *The Comedy of Errors* with *Twelfth Night, Pericles, The Winter's Tale,* and *The Tempest* in her chapter "The Providential Tempest and the Shakespearean Family" in *Man's Estate: Masculine Identity in Shakespeare* (Berkeley and Los Angeles: University of California Press, 1981), pp. 193–225. These plays "depict the separation of family members in a literal or metaphorical tempest, the resulting sorrow and confusion, and the ultimate reunion of the family, with a renewed sense of identity or 'rebirth' for its members" (p. 194).

> That thou art then estranged from thyself?
> Thyself I call it, being strange to me,
> That, undividable incorporate,
> Am better than thy dear self's better part.
> Ah, do not tear thyself away from me.
>   (II.ii.110–24)

Part of the answer is that she is talking to the wrong Antipholus; *he* need feel no guilt. Norman Holland has observed that splitting is a basic Shakespearean strategy for managing conflict.[7] Here the young dramatist has split himself into a stay-at-home twin, married, and carrying on in a commercial world (as Shakespeare might have, had he followed his father in "uprightness of dealing" as a successful merchant in Stratford), and into a wandering, searching twin for whom the world of Ephesus, including the situation of marriage, is strange.

There is a core of surprise in all of us from which we may look out on even our most settled relationships, like the feelings Antipholus S. expresses as he acquiesces in going off to dinner at the end of his first encounter with his brother's wife: How did it happen that I am here, in this marriage?

> Am I in earth, in heaven, or in hell?
> Sleeping or waking, mad or well-advis'd?
> Known unto these, and to myself disguis'd?
> I'll say as they say, and persever so,
> And in this mist at all adventures go.
>   (II.ii.212–16)

All the while the absurdity of what keeps happening—"There's not a man I meet but doth salute me / As if I were their well-acquainted friend"—keeps insisting that this *is* all fantasy—or more disquietingly, witchcraft: "Sure these are but imaginary wiles, / And Lapland sorcerers inhabit here" (IV.iii.1–2, 10–11).

As Anne Barton observes, Shakespeare shows less interest in the stay-at-home twin than "in the more extreme situation of the traveller, especially vulnerable because far from home, who finds himself losing his own sense of self in an alien city of reputed sorcery and spells."[8] It should be noted, however, that the wandering brother, unlike his more insistently exasperated Ephesian twin,

7. Norman Holland, *Psychoanalysis and Shakespeare* (New York: McGraw-Hill, 1966), pp. 134–35, 285–86, 338.
8. Introduction to *The Comedy of Errors*, *Riverside Shakespeare*, p. 81.

suffers very little except disorientation and a gathering fear of the irrational. Although he has to experience Adriana's rebukes and clinging-vine appeals, Antipholus S. can make love in good conscience to charming Luciana, however shocking it is to her. Echoing the language that earlier expressed his imperiled sense of self in search of his lost brother, he uses oceanic imagery, with a submerged pun on "die"—to lose himself by this kind of metaphorical drowning would not "confound himself":

> O, train me not, sweet mermaid, with thy note,
> To drown me in thy sister's flood of tears.
> Sing, siren, for thyself, and I will dote;
> Spread o'er the silver waves thy golden hairs,
> And as a bed I'll take them, and there lie,
> And in that glorious supposition think
> He gains by death that hath such means to die.
>   (III.ii.45–51)

One can see a fantasy splitting off through the wandering brother, which could fit one pole of Shakespeare's feeling as the London world opened out to him. He still had and would keep his ties in Stratford, by marriage and children and legally tangled inheritance. If only there were an alter ego obligated to the marriage back home, with its legitimate claims as well as vexations!

Shakespeare left in Stratford not only a wife but a once-prospering father who had fallen on bad times. As was noted in chapter 2, in 1591 Shakespeare's father was listed by a commission of inquiry as one of nine persons who "coom not to Churche for feare of processe of Debtte."[9] When we consider the father recovered by the *Errors*, the striking thing, of course, is that he is in danger of forfeiting his life "Unless a thousand marks be levied / To quit the penalty and to ransom him." His "substance, valued at the highest rate, / Cannot amount unto a hundred marks" (I.i.21–24). Egeon's economic plight suggests that of John Shakespeare, although lack of money is not the cause of his arrest. What was feared in the Stratford home does happen in the play. It happens, however, not to the father, but to his prosperous Ephesian son.

Antipholus of Ephesus, arrested in the street by the goldsmith, has no problem about sending home (by the wrong Dromio) for five hundred ducats in a purse in his desk. But the event is very

---

9. Samuel Schoenbaum, *Shakespeare: A Documentary Life* (Oxford: Clarendon Press, 1975), p. 38.

elaborately staged, with the goldsmith's surprise at the unwillingness of his trusted friend and customer to pay for the gold chain
the other twin has received, and the Ephesian twin's indignation:

> E. ANTIPHOLUS: Arrest me, foolish fellow, if thou dar'st. . . .
> ANGELO: I would not spare my brother in this case,
> If he should scorn me so apparently. . . .
> E. ANTIPHOLUS: But, sirrah, you shall buy this sport as dear
> As all the metal in your shop will answer.
> (IV.i.75, 77–78, 81–82)

There is heavy emphasis on the connection of solvency and reputation; the goldsmith owes a debt in his turn, urgently claimed:
"This touches me in reputation" (IV.i.71). Adriana, like John Shakespeare's wife, is an heiress (the Duke arranged the marriage out of
gratitude for Antipholus E.'s rescue of him in the wars), and the
husband is concerned about her response to his public humiliation:
"That I should be attach'd in Ephesus; / I tell you, 'twill sound
harshly in her ears" (IV.iv.6–7). She on her side is surprised: "This I
wonder at, / That he unknown to me should be in debt" (IV.ii.-
47–48). "Tell me," she asks Dromio, "was he arrested on a band?"
(IV.ii.49)—a bond involved in standing surety for some acquaintance out there in the streets? We can recall that among John Shakespeare's troubles were instances of standing surety for others when
the bail money was forfeited; one such occasion, when he stood
surety for a debt run up by his brother, nearly landed him in jail.[10]

Dromio S. brings home to Adriana the news of her husband's arrest, and it is he who expresses the perturbation that might be involved for a less well provided household. He riddles about the terrors of arrest for some twenty lines in response to "Where is thy
master, Dromio? Is he well?" "No, he's in Tartar limbo, worse than
hell: / A devil in an everlasting garment hath him" (IV.ii.31–33).
The wife can only make out what has happened after ten lines of
such extravagant burlesque. Dromio mimes a debtor's fear of the
"fellow all in buff . . . that countermands . . . passages" and "before the judgment carries poor souls to hell" (lines 36–38, 40).
Adriana gets no full account because he is so full of haste—which
permits a farfetched conceit to arrive at *bankrupt*: "Time is a very
bankrout and owes more than he's worth to season" (line 58). Although it is the son who incurs the debt, "*feare* of processe of Debtte"

10. Ibid.

is thus further displaced onto the clown, indeed, the wrong clown, whose actual master has not in fact been imprisoned, while the re-action of a chronic debtor's household is represented through its opposite—a prosperous household accidentally involved.

If we look at the play against the backdrop of the troubled family situation in Stratford, we can begin to see a pattern in these dis-placements that suggests the purposes they serve. In one direction, the wandering twin is cleared of the claims energetically made on him by the woman who considers him to be her husband. In an-other direction, centered in the Ephesian twin's marital and eco-nomic discord, the father's debt is transferred to the son; the dismay engendered at the prospect of prosecution for debt is made laugh-able by the clown's exaggerated panic; and the whole troubled do-mestic situation of an enterprising husband and his wellborn wife becomes a matter, not of irreversible decline, but of farcical mis-takes. The mockery that in New Comedy would typically take as one of its objects an aging, obstructive, paternal figure is displaced onto the separated twins as each unwittingly stands in for the other, and onto the Ephesian couple whose marital discord and brush with debt make their discomfiture the object of our laughter. One result of all this is that, in a play dominated by family bonds, there is no expression of conflict across generations. The father dramatized as Egeon can accordingly remain "a reverent Syracu-sian merchant, / Who put unluckily into this bay" (V.i.124–25). One can see that the son who is arrested for debt in the play takes the father's punishment for him, as, indeed, the son is well able to do—being as he is at the same earlier stage of life when John Shake-speare in his time was riding high.

Egeon is himself presented as the helpless but blameless victim of the arbitrary law that condemns him when, in the opening scene, he tells his story of his physical estrangement from his wife. His account of the wreck at sea is the occasion for "griefs unspeak-able": "Nay, forward, old man, . . . / For we may pity, though not pardon thee" (I.i.32, 96–97). That account is also notably implau-sible. The mast holding the castaway family, strung out so sym-metrically, breaks all too neatly *after* the "seas wax'd calm" (line 91). Shakespeare, we have seen, is adapting the mode of dramatized ro-mance in which implausibility may be gathered up into a sense of the wonderful or the miraculous. Anne Barton has noted that the unprepared discovery of the lost wife at the close verges on the comedy of recognized artifice. But Egeon's opening tale does not seem to dramatize self-conscious recognition of its artificiality in this way. Instead, its implausibility suggests something like the sort of fantastic exaggeration that, in infantile or neurotic lying, distorts and replaces the actuality the lie conceals. In such instances, Otto Fenichel observes, implausibilities deny conflictual realities with which they are symbolically identified by conveying tacitly: "Just as *this* is only a fantasy, *that* (occurrence) was not true."[11] Egeon, of course, is not lying; his account describes the fictional truth about a past from which the events of the play spring. And the dramatist is not lying either; he is making a play. But perhaps Egeon's strange account of a family separated, not through fault or action of any of its members but purely by the intervention of impersonal chance, serves for the dramatist who invents the fiction a purpose analogous to that served for the liar in Fenichel's account—by averting recognition of what can (or did) go on within a family to disrupt its unity.

In dreams, psychoanalysis has shown, absurdity often functions to distort and conceal "a mocking or malicious intention of the dreamer."[12] Perhaps Egeon's implausible tale is being put to comparable use, its absurdity blurring a connection between the pathetic plight of the father and the aggressive energy mockingly expended on the brothers in the farce action. In the perspective proposed here, the conflictual aggressive motive denied by the apparently unmotivated rupturing of Egeon's family amid becalmed seas would have taken shape in landlocked Stratford, in the life Shakespeare left behind him to pursue his own business ventures by writing plays for the London audience. On this point, an essay by Barbara Freedman has proved very helpful; she reads the play without reference to Shakespeare, though in a way that is open to the construction put on it here in relation to the dramatist's own exigencies.[13]

Freedman makes the familiar points that "the key to farce . . . is that we laugh at violence," and that it is precisely "the denial of the cause and effect of farce's violence that enables its expression and renders it safe" (pp. 235, 236). But she adds that "were some initial,

11. Otto Fenichel, *The Psychoanalytic Theory of Neurosis* (New York: Norton, 1945), p. 291.

12. Ibid., p. 529.

13. Barbara Freedman, "Errors in Comedy: A Psychoanalytic Theory of Farce," in *Shakespearean Comedy*, ed. Maurice Charney (New York: New York Literary Forum, 1980), pp. 233–43.

meaningful aggression not present to be disowned or denied, farce
would lack both pleasure and humor" (p. 236). Freedman seeks to
explain "why the more the characters seek gratification, the more
the play punishes them for it," and concludes: "The lawless plot aggression in farce is, paradoxically enough, punitive superego aggression" (p. 237). She offers as the "perfect psychoanalytic description of farce" Charles Brenner's account of the punishment
dream, in which the manifest dream, "instead of expressing a more
or less disguised fantasy of a repressed wish expresses a more or
less disguised fantasy of punishment for the wish in question." [14]

To get at the "meaningful aggression" animating the farce in *Errors*, Freedman pursues the theme of monetary and marital indebtedness that connects Egeon's arrest and the subsequent arrest of
the Ephesian twin. She emphasizes that "Egeon's debt is actual, obscure, and monetary, whereas his son's debts are mistaken, meaningful, and marital." [15] But textual links between the two kinds
of debts suggest a symbolic equivalence that blurs such distinctions. The scene preceding the husband's arrest in the street begins
with the wife's sister, Luciana, pleading with the other Antipholus:
"And may it be that you have quite forgot / A husband's office?"
(III.ii.1–2). Egeon, in his opening story, mentions frequent separations "from kind embracements of my spouse" (I.i.43) before the
shipwreck, the "husband's office" neglected in the pursuit of his
prospering business. Freedman notes that just as Antipholus E.
fails to return home (however innocently in fact: he was buying the
gold chain to take back to his wife!), "the highlight of Egeon's story
is equally a failure to return home" (p. 240). The aborted voyage is

---

14. Charles Brenner, *An Introductory Textbook of Psychoanalysis* (1955: reprint,
Garden City, N.Y.: Doubleday-Anchor, 1957), p. 184; quoted in "Errors in Comedy,"
p. 238. Of course, as Freud notes, punishment dreams are "distressing" for the person who dreams them, sources of "unpleasure" and thus kin to anxiety dreams and
even nightmares (*The Interpretation of Dreams, Standard Edition*, vol. 5, pp. 556–60).
Farce, however, suppresses identification with the victims of what might seem like
nightmarish disorientation and makes it possible for author and audience to identify
with aggression stripped of its moral significance and released as laughter. These
victims are themselves protected by the overriding rule—"it's only a farce"—which
in turn protects author and audience from the anxiety that might otherwise be generated by such aggression. Although the actual resolution surprisingly introduces
the lost wife and mother to complete the family reunion beyond expectations, the
key to making the dramatized mistakes disappear is always visible to the audience—
the presence of two identical brothers. The play permits the confusions of the wandering twin and the troubles of the Ephesian couple to proliferate within a firmly
established comic contract that promises to clear them up and make everything right
once the mistakes are corrected.

15. Freedman, "Errors in Comedy," p. 239.

"melodramatically presented to us as the result of 'cruel fate,'" but Egeon also admits that he undertook the journey home unwillingly, at his wife's insistent urging: "My wife . . . / Made daily motions for our home return: / Unwilling I agreed" (lines 58–60). In Freedman's analysis, the marital debt of the father, hinted at in his story of the shipwreck, constitutes the crucial motive: denied direct expression, it is displaced onto the Ephesian son, whose vexations work out and work off the guilt the father is thus spared.

There is a seeming incongruity in Freedman's construction: it is the father's unpaid marital debt for which the twins farcically suffer, but Egeon is presented as so old and impotent—his "grained face . . . hid / In sap-consuming winter's drizzled snow, / And all the conduits of my blood froze up" (V.i.312–14)—that a sexual relationship to his wife seems scarcely an issue. But it is the father at a much earlier stage of life who is the source of the guilt that animates the farcical punishments and creates the need, finally enacted, to reconcile parents. Such guilt originates in early wishes for the mother's whole affection and in hostility toward a paternal figure who is far from impotent. Infantile wishes, unconscious or having become unconscious, are as good as deeds; to find the father weak and helpless and estranged from his wife can seem like the unwelcome fulfillment of wishes that have long been repressed. And there may be a basis for guilt in fact, if the mother makes the son her object, perhaps in place of her husband, in various ways or degrees. Reckoning with this Oedipal pattern, as such, is postponed until much later in Shakespeare's development. Here it is present only in the absurd "punishments" inflicted upon the sons and in the benign wish to undo Oedipal guilt by ending the parents' estrangement and redeeming the father from monetary debt. The displacements of the play at once deny Oedipal hostility and punish the doubled son for stresses forced onto the parents' marital bond by Oedipal competition. But after the farce action has completed its punitive function, the father's aged impotence makes compassion and reverence easy. Egeon is perfectly characterized to make him a father fit for rescue without male-to-male rivalry coming directly into question.

From this vantage point the "superego aggression" active in the play deals with the guilt that a son may feel about not bringing about a reconciliation between his parents, or more broadly, making everything right for them and so between them. We can, of course, know nothing of what went on between John and Mary Shakespeare in the years of the father's decline. But kindly Egeon's

indebtedness and melancholy condition at the play's beginning—
"Hopeless and helpless doth Egeon wend, / But to procrastinate
his liveless end" (I.i.157–58)—are suggestive of what we do know
about John Shakespeare's monetary difficulties and his withdrawal
from his earlier enterprising activity as a thriving Stratford merchant and public official. And the effect of the father's fall from
prominence and prosperity must certainly have been felt throughout the household of the former alderman, council member, and
bailiff. To have left one's parents behind, either by going away or by
succeeding beyond the father, leaves a son open to just such an accusation as is leveled by Egeon at the Ephesian twin in the extremity of his need: "my only son, / Knows not my feeble key of
untun'd cares?" ". . . perhaps, my son, / Thou sham'st to acknowledge me in misery" (V.i.310–11, 322–23). But once the recognition
has taken place, "These ducats pawn I for my father here" (line 390)
both makes up for blameless neglect and obviates the shame a son
may come to feel for (and with) a father who has failed to sustain an
image of manhood that could make open confrontation possible.

When the mother finally comes forward to resolve the complica-
tions of the plot, with a mastery that contrasts sharply with the
passive suffering of Egeon, she is primarily preoccupied with her
sons. She takes charge as she recognizes Egeon in the bound prisoner awaiting execution—and turns at once to the sons:

> Whoever bound him, I will loose his bonds,
> And gain a husband by his liberty.
> Speak, old Egeon, if thou be'st the man
> That had a wife once call'd Aemilia,
> That bore thee at a burthen two fair sons.
>
> (V.i.340–44)

It is not Egeon but the Duke who first responds: "Why, here begins
his morning story right" (V.i.357).[16] Egeon speaks only three more
lines in the play, and two are about the lost son:

---

16. The *Riverside Shakespeare* text, from which these quotations and line numbers
are taken, follows a transposition of the Folio text, introduced by Capell (1768),
which places the Duke's speech, beginning with this line, after Aemilia's next speech
and hence after Egeon's response to his wife. But R. A. Foakes, who retains the Folio
order, points out that the reasoning behind the transposition is not compelling
(Arden ed., pp. 103–4n). From the perspective developed in this chapter, that the
Duke should respond first, while Egeon stands silent, is consistent with the small
role Egeon takes, and the more authoritarian position the Duke assumes, in the
final reunion.

If I dream not, thou art Aemilia.
If thou art she, tell me, where is that son
That floated with thee on the fatal raft?
(V.i.347–49)

Of course Shakespeare is unwinding the confusions of a plot that has primarily concerned the sons. But the absence of any moment for a flow of feeling into an embrace of the parents accords with feeling flowing instead into the mother's moving celebration of the new begetting of her children: the gossips' feast is under *her* aegis, sealed by the Duke as the figure of authority.

The two lives tugging at Shakespeare when he writes *The Comedy of Errors*—the married man with a wife and family in Stratford, the London playwright who leaves family and marriage behind (but who puts familial bonds at the center of his art)—in effect merge as the whole family is reunited. As within the fiction the twins refind the intact family, Shakespeare refinds it by having made the fiction. If farce has served to protect the father by displacing aggression onto those mocked for faults that are, subtextually, associated with him or with his prototype, it is through the figure of the generous, masterful mother, giving new unity to the long-dispersed family, that the play moves out of its dimension as farce. As we have noted, Shakespeare will much later make the recovery of the maternal the guiding motif of *Pericles* and *The Winter's Tale*. In the history plays from the early period, however, strong women are characteristically not redemptive but menacing. Like *Errors*, these plays avert father and son conflict; only with the great tragedies will such confrontation become central to Shakespeare's art. But the fraternal enmity that is denied direct expression in *Errors*, despite the troubles the twin brothers create for one another, provides the chief form of male-to-male violence in the early histories, culminating in *Richard III*. In the next two chapters we will look at how fraternal rivalry and the disruptive potential in relations to figures of maternal power shape the action in these early histories and in the earliest tragedy.

4

Savage Play and the Web of Curses in
Richard III

Instead of two brothers indistinguishable, Richard III's manifesto is
"I have no brother, I am like no brother" (*3H6* V.vi.80). Richard's
brilliant playing-within-the-play is often farcical, but savage motivation for it is emphatically explicit. So are the consequences—and
dread of them. Instead of the final maternal blessing of *The Comedy
of Errors*, we have the outraged and outrageous curses of Margaret and the chorus of bereft maternal figures, including Richard's
mother, who finally also curses him. The tragical history is the ob-
verse of the comedy in its handling of the ties between brother and
brother, son and mother. In his exploration of fratricidal violence
and mother-son structures of fear and hate, Shakespeare goes far
down, or far back, in dramatic understanding of motives growing
from the family constellation, with more explicit reference to infancy and childhood than we get in any other play. He licenses theatrical aggression in a way that is new for him, and at the same time
builds a complex formal structure to contain it. His extrapolation of
family motives, far beyond suggestions in his sources, skillfully
makes these motives part of the social pathology, though, as we
shall see, his dramatization of the political resolution lacks the
cogency of the play's dreadful logic of family violence.

"INDUCTIONS DANGEROUS"

As games may do in life when one of the players breaks the social
compact on which playfulness depends, the games Richard plays
move beyond play to actual hurting. A player who keeps doing this
is soon likely to be isolated—unless the whole gang joins in and
makes the game into hurting, as with street gangs. Richard has
been brought up in such a gang, the house of York in the conten-
tion of the two noble houses of York and Lancaster. The broad-

gauged chronicle history of the Henry VI plays shifts to a highly formalized drama built around a single protagonist as Richard decides to go it alone after being the most savage partisan of a savage lot.

Already in the middle of 3 *Henry VI* he announces his covert intentions in a long self-revelatory soliloquy; the scenario and the character to animate it are presented with unprecedented explicitness. The shift to solitary villainy takes place after Richard kills sainted King Henry in the last act. First he speaks as a partisan: "What? will the aspiring blood of Lancaster / Sink in the ground? I thought it would have mounted" (V.vi.61–62). Then he responds to Henry's execrations about his loathsome birth, legs forward, body hunched, his teeth already in:

> And so I was, which plainly signified
> That I should snarl, and bite, and play the dog.
> Then since the heavens have shap'd my body so,
> Let hell make crook'd my mind to answer it.
> I have no brother, I am like no brother;
> And this word "love," which greybeards call divine,
> Be resident in men like one another,
> And not in me: I am myself alone.
> Clarence, beware! thou keep'st me from the light.
> (lines 76–84)

"I am myself alone"—and yet Richard is gamesome. He can play, with a zest realized here for the first time, because in fact he is not alone: he has the theater audience, whom he now addresses, to play with—"Had I not reason, *think ye*, to make haste" (line 72). A playful stage villain depends on the fact that "men like one another" are similar, not only in their susceptibility to "this word 'love'" but also to the pleasure of rejecting social and moral restraints.

Villainous wit, and hypocrisy that we can see through as it pays a specious tribute to virtue, both involve the tendentious manipulation of a verbal and social surface. As *Richard III* begins the audience is elaborately cued to see through to what is under Richard's hypocrisy:

> Plots have I laid, inductions dangerous, . . .
> And if King Edward be as true and just
> As I am subtle, false, and treacherous,
> This day should Clarence closely be mew'd up
> About a prophecy which says that G
> Of Edward's heirs the murtherer shall be.

> Dive, thoughts, down to my soul, here Clarence
> comes!
> *Enter Clarence, guarded, and Brakenbury, [Lieutenant of the*
> *Tower].*
> Brother, good day. What means this armed guard
> That waits upon your Grace?
> CLARENCE: His Majesty,
> Tend'ring my person's safety, hath appointed
> This conduct to convey me to the Tower.
> RICHARD: Upon what cause?
> CLARENCE: Because my name is George.
> RICHARD: Alack, my lord, that fault is none of yours;
> He should for that commit your godfathers.
>   (*R3* I.i.32, 36–48)

Richard takes up Clarence's bitter irony about his name and winds the fancy around to allude to the butt of malmsey wine in which Clarence is to be drowned, a circumstance so familiar from the chronicles that many first-time auditors would be able to share his private joke: "O, belike his Majesty hath some intent / That you should be new christ'ned in the Tower" (lines 49–50). Then comes a characteristic shift into his plausible "plain man" (I.iii.51) vein to express brotherly concern—"But what's the matter, Clarence, may I know?" (I.i.51)—which Clarence takes at face value.

After his brother has retailed the king's superstitious fears of the letter G, Richard displaces the blame to Edward's common-born queen, with scorn that speaks solidarity with his royal brother:

> Why, this it is, when men are rul'd by women:
> 'Tis not the King that sends you to the Tower;
> My Lady Grey his wife, Clarence, 'tis she
> That tempers him to this extremity. . . .
> We are not safe, Clarence, we are not safe.
>   (I.i.62–65, 70)

Richard is a virtuoso with displacement, representation through the opposite, allusion, all the "wit mechanisms" that Freud saw to be active also in the dream work and that transform latent content into the manifest dream. His wit gives the play the quality of a bad dream, one where for the audience the latent content has been made manifest, in contrast to *The Comedy of Errors*.

Richard is expert, indeed inspired, in the kind of thinking that moves through the corporeality of a word from one of its senses to another, as when Rivers takes up Queen Elizabeth's protest that she has been falsely accused:

RICHARD: You may deny that you were not the mean
Of my Lord Hastings' late imprisonment.
RIVERS: She may, my lord, for—
RICHARD: She may, Lord Rivers! Why, who knows not so?
She may do more, sir, than denying that:
She may help you to many fair preferments,
And then deny her aiding hand therein
And lay those honors on your high desert.
What may she not, she may, ay, marry, may she.
RIVERS: What, marry, may she?
RICHARD: What, marry, may she! Marry with a king,
A bachelor, and a handsome stripling too:
Iwis your grandam had a worser match.
(I.iii.89–101)

A manic energy animates such aggressive wit, like the manic physical energy with which an accomplished actor can move Richard's
deformed body. Richard's artful management of the social surface is
conducted with wonderful plausibility—"We are not safe, Clarence, we are not safe." We in the audience can hear: "You are not
safe, Clarence, you are not safe." The relation between the two levels is expressed spatially in "Dive, thoughts, down to my soul, here
Clarence comes!"

The menace complicates or interrupts simple amusement. That
people in the play take Richard's hypocrisy at face value often depends as much on a conventional theatrical compact as does our
accepting that no one on stage in *The Comedy of Errors* should realize he is dealing with identical twins. One of the formal conventions Shakespeare is adapting is explicit in "Thus, like the formal
Vice, Iniquity, / I moralize two meanings in one word" (III.i.82–83).
The Vice's role gives scope for representation through the opposite
in the guise of pious charades:

Poor Clarence did forsake his father, Warwick,
Ay, and forswore himself—which Jesu pardon!—. . .
To fight on Edward's party for the crown,
And for his meed, poor lord, he is mewed up.
I would to God my heart were flint, like Edward's,
Or Edward's soft and pitiful, like mine:
I am too childish-foolish for this world.
(I.iii.134–35, 137–41)

We are invited to hoot at such transparent flummery. Or Richard
himself breaks up the social surface. After the reconciliation the
dying King Edward thinks he has brought about, his poor queen
wants to believe in it:

> My sovereign lord, I do beseech your Highness
> To take our brother Clarence to your grace.
> RICHARD: Why, madam, have I off'red love for this,
> To be so flouted in this royal presence?
> Who knows not that the gentle Duke is dead?
> *They all start.*
> (II.i.76–80)

Richard repeatedly disrupts scenes in this way. Besides double entendres and asides, he uses abrupt, naked ruthlessness, the "sudden stab of rancor" (III.ii.87).

> BUCKINGHAM: Now, my lord, what shall we do if we perceive
> Lord Hastings will not yield to our complots?
> RICHARD: Chop off his head!
> (III.i.191–93)

Richard here is Punch throwing the troublesome baby out the window, simplifying the problem of government as Punch simplifies the problem of child care. We cannot resist something like glee at such a moment, with a laugh close to a gasp.

The difference from Punch of course is that the serious consequences of this savage farce are kept before us. In the scene that immediately follows, we are caught up in anxiety for Hastings as he ignores the warning of Stanley's ominous dream that "the boar had rased off his helm" (III.ii.11). Our concern is then complicated by Hastings's own cruelty about the sudden execution of the Queen's kindred. Richard's strategy of playing the old nobility off against the new, explicitly described in the sources, works as Catesby brings the news that the Queen's kindred are to die. The aristocrat is as ruthless in his bland way as the future usurper, even though he will not go along with usurpation:

> HASTINGS: Well, Catesby, ere a fortnight make me older,
> I'll send some packing that yet think not on't.
> CATESBY: 'Tis a vile thing to die, my gracious lord,
> When men are unprepar'd and look not
> for it.
> HASTINGS: O monstrous, monstrous! and so falls it out
> With Rivers, Vaughan, Grey; and so 'twill do
> With some men else, that think themselves
> as safe
> As thou and I, who (as thou know'st) are
> dear
> To princely Richard and to Buckingham.

CATESBY: The princes both make high account of you—
[*Aside.*] For they account his head upon the bridge.
(III.ii.60–70)

The play combines the appeals of stage villainy with clear-eyed presentation of a whole complex world of court intrigue, its bad faith and callous cruelty. After pious protestation about the sanctity of sanctuary, the Archbishop complies in getting the child Duke of York out of sanctuary. The Lord Mayor connives. Shakespeare underlines how moral weakness and failure of nerve contribute to the political maneuvers recorded in Sir Thomas More's *History of Richard III* as transcribed in the chronicles. Our flesh creeps as we watch victims being ensnared in Richard's web, especially with Clarence and the little princes. Yet at the same time, in the first three acts, until the crown is won the villain fascinates us and even delights us. Richard is the first of the line of figures, all in one way or another either alienated or outsiders, whom Shakespeare endows with some of his own dramatic powers, most notably Falstaff, Hamlet, and Iago. He is also Shakespeare's first great exploitation of theatrical aggression, the turning of acting into action, fundamental to Marlowe's and Kyd's radically disruptive use of the new dramatic medium. Richard's alliance with the audience is similar in some ways to Tamburlaine's, in that it works to free aggressive energies from conscience.

Yet unlike *Tamburlaine, Richard III* is emphatically designed to contain the theatrical aggression within a larger pattern. Richard has to do his savage playing within the net of retributory curses initiated by Margaret; he is their agent, only finally to be subject to them himself. His disruptive energy is also contained by being understood, both as the product of the great family feud Shakespeare has dramatized and as an individual psychology shaped by his physical deformity and the rejection it comes to embody.

The contrast with Marlowe's radical theatrical aggression is clearest in *The Jew of Malta*. Marlowe's Punch-like figure, with his enormous "*Halcions* bill," is an alienated alien; Shakespeare's alienated villain is at the very center of established society. Barabas is as ruthless as Richard in disposing of family ties, but he has only one, to his daughter—no mother or father or childhood. Both are self-proclaimed Machiavels, and both bring out and show up the venal ruthlessness beneath moral hypocrisy, of people around them, enlisting us in the enterprise. But Marlowe's savage farce exhibits his hero as the epitome of motives animating the *whole* society; there is nothing but aggressive greed and hypocritical cover:[1] "Welcome, great *Bashaws*, how fares *Callymath*, / What wind drives you thus into *Malta* rhode?" The answer summarizes the play's whole society: "The wind that bloweth all the world besides, / Desire of gold" (lines 1420–24). The radical perspective and terse scorn of Marlowe's play depend on a devastating rejection of social values, including their roots in relationship to the feminine, utterly different from Shakespeare's embrace of the whole society even as he exhibits it being subverted. Like Richard, Barabas makes an appeal to honesty about ruthlessness: "As good dissemble that thou neuer mean'st / As first mean truth and then dissemble it" (lines 528–29). But Marlowe engages us in seeing through morality. The whole construction in *The Jew of Malta*, like the hero, forces radical awareness on us. As the Governor ends the play with a blatantly conventional concluding couplet, there can be nothing but a jeering response: "So march away, and let due praise be giuen / Neither to Fate nor Fortune, but to Heauen" (lines 2409–10).

"AND AM I THEN A MAN TO BE BELOV'D?"

In presenting given historical events in *Richard III*, Shakespeare molds them and supplements them in ways characteristic of the shaping influence of his sensibility in his early works. Along with the incarnation of specifically theatrical power in Richard, the most striking thing is the way the dramatist defines Richard in domestic and sexual terms, pitting his power against women as well as a brother. There are suggestions for some of this, as we shall see, in the chronicles; but most of it is Shakespeare's adaptation or purely fictive extrapolation. The murder of Clarence, which in the play is contemporary with King Edward's final illness and is all Richard's doing, in fact occurred years earlier and by Edward's orders. There is only a suggestion in the chronicles that Richard's hostility contributed to the king's action. Queen Margaret, Henry VI's widow,

---

1. One must except poor Abigail's love for Mathias, but it is really there to provide the occasion for Barabas to turn her lover and his rival into mutually destructive puppets: "O brauely fought, and yet they thrust not home. / Now *Lodowicke*, now *Mathias*, so; / So now they haue shew'd themselues to be tall fellowes" (lines 1186–88). By contrast with the vitality of this, Abigail's grief is perfunctorily dealt with as she leaves for the convent—and her share of the poisoned pot of porridge. Quotations from Marlowe are from *The Complete Works of Christopher Marlowe*, ed. C. F. Tucker Brooke (Oxford: Clarendon Press, 1910).

had died in France well before King Edward's death. Our familiarity with the play as it stands can obscure the drastic originality of Shakespeare's bringing her back to serve as maleficent chorus and Richard's principal emotional antagonist—a figure almost equal to him in dramatic and poetic energy.

If one regards *Richard III* as the finale of the Henry VI plays, Margaret's role is less surprising than it would otherwise be, not only because she serves so beautifully as a channel through which that past is brought to bear on the present, but because on a deeper level she continues the series of overweening or overpowering women in those plays, being herself their most extreme instance.[2] Until Shakespeare arrives at his conception of Richard, none of the men can match these women, with one entirely invented exception—Talbot's turning the tables on the Countess of Auvergne. Joan de Pucelle takes over the Dauphin, after defeating him in a trial of strength; even Talbot cannot overcome her in single combat! Only after her fiends melodramatically forsake her is the captured witch led in, spitting curses—and immediately we see Suffolk bewitched by the beauty of his captive, Margaret of Navarre. His ambiguously motivated project of marrying her to weak King Henry is set up before we see Joan exposed as a vainglorious upstart. Joan denies her own father and is proved to be a mere woman after all, sexually promiscuous and ready to plead "the fruit within my womb" (*1H6* V.iv.63) in a vain effort to avoid the stake. Male superiority is restored with York's taunt, "Why, here's a girl! I think she knows not well / (There were so many) whom she may accuse" (V.iv.80–81). But the final scene shows King Henry consenting to the marriage with the woman who is to dominate him in the two following plays, becoming in time the murderous virago with a "tiger's heart wrapp'd in a woman's hide" (*3H6* I.iv.137). As her role develops we also watch the Lord Protector, the Good Duke Humphrey, prove helpless to cope with his overweening wife; then he is murdered, partly in consequence, by the Queen and Suffolk's faction.

2. David Bevington has pointed out that in *1 Henry VI* not only is Joan de Pucelle's part extended and elaborated beyond the sources, but Shakespeare invents out of whole cloth the Countess of Auvergne's abortive attempt to entrap brave Talbot by hospitality, and brings Queen Margaret on stage immediately after Joan is captured, discredited, and dragged off to the stake. So one sort of overpowering woman is made to succeed another; Margaret's beauty captivates her captor Suffolk and sets him to making his fatal plan to marry her to the young Henry and so dominate both. "The Domineering Female in *1 Henry VI*," *Shakespeare Studies* 2 (1966): 51–58.

Much of this was taken over from Shakespeare's chronicle sources, if often rearranged, and of course focused on selected persons and moments. Shakespeare shapes his materials in the direction of the domestic patterns here described, but he does so in the course of pioneering the dramatization of history. He is interested in the whole life of England, his England, as Marlowe's alienated genius never was, even when he too pioneered the use of English historical materials in *Edward II*. The focus in *1 Henry VI* is on patriotic heroics and lament as Henry V's conquests in France are lost despite Talbot's heroism. The dramatization of Joan's power is balanced by chauvinistic celebration of the male bond of battle. The emotional climax is the death of Talbot with his dead son in his arms, after the son has refused to escape the encircling French and has proved his fledgling honor. When one sees the play performed one realizes how effectively the company were serving interests now catered to by popular films of patriotic violence. Nashe's familiar account of Talbot's "bones newe embalmed with the teares of ten thousand spectators at least"[3] makes vivid its Elizabethan public appeal. Such battle heroics are never dropped from Shakespeare's histories, which all reach climax in them, often with emotional atonements of dying heroes: at Agincourt in *Henry V*, Suffolk and York are together lovingly "espous'd to death" (IV.vi.26). But even in *Henry VI: Part One* vital public issues of authority and loyalty, faction and subversion, are brought out, and these come into clearer and clearer focus in *Part Two* and *Part Three*. The murder of good Duke Humphrey opens the way for the Wars of the Roses, with the telling study of the social consequences of King Henry's weakness despite his spirituality. The exemplary function of history becomes particularly prominent in the last play, in the choric scene during the battle of Towton where King Henry's meditations on the happy life of the homely swain are interrupted by "a Son that hath kill'd his father," and "a Father that hath kill'd his son" (II.v.54s.d., 78s.d.).

The Henry VI plays are conducted so as to exhibit "what mischiefe hath insurged in realmes by intestine devision,"[4] with relatively little aggressive use of the theatrical medium as such. There is a moment of almost egregious imitation of Marlowe in *Part Two* as York returns to England with "his army of Irish" (s.d.):

3. *Pierce Penilesse* (1592); quoted from *The Riverside Shakespeare*, p. 1837.
4. Edward Hall, *The Union of the Two Noble and Illustre Famelies of Lancastre and Yorke*, *Sources*, vol. 3, p. 16.

From Ireland thus comes York to claim his right,
And pluck the crown from feeble Henry's head.
Ring bells, aloud, burn bonfires clear and bright
To entertain great England's lawful king!
Ah, *sancta majestas!* who would not buy thee dear?
Let them obey that knows not how to rule;
This hand was made to handle nought but gold.
                                        (2H6 V.i.1–7)

But this echo of Tamburlaine on heaven entertaining Zenocrate is
not typical, and its effect on the audience cannot be mesmeric: too
much else is in action. So too with Richard's momentary rise into
Marlowe's idiom as he urges his father, York, to break his covenant:

How sweet a thing it is to wear a crown,
Within whose circuit is Elysium
And all that poets feign of bliss and joy.
                        (3H6 I.ii.29–31)

The whole pattern by which "Measure for measure must be answered" (3H6 II.vi.54) is much too strongly realized to be taken
over by any such one-way visions of omnipotence. Richard's talk of
Elysium persuades his father to make the fatal sortie from Sandal
Castle. It will put him, captive, at Margaret's mercy:

Where are your mess of sons to back you now,
The wanton Edward, and the lusty George?
And where's that valiant crook-back prodigy,
Dicky, your boy, that with his grumbling voice
Was wont to cheer his dad in mutinies?
Or with the rest, where is your darling, Rutland?
Look, York, I stain'd this napkin with [his] blood.
                        (3H6 I.iv.73–79)

—and so on to the paper crown and her joining in stabbing York to
death. (In the chronicles his head is brought to her in the camp.)
    So long as his strong father is alive, Richard's violence is dedi-
cated to his support. The sudden new development of theatrical
power in his role accords with his decision to seek the crown for
himself. The long soliloquy that first announces Richard's ruthless
ambition comes immediately after his brother has used newly acquired royal power to make Lady Grey his wife. In the historical
sources the onset of Richard's determination to usurp the crown did
not become manifest until years later. There is a dynamic coherence, however, in Shakespeare's putting it soon after the loss of the
father who has focused the sons' loyalty and sanctioned their ag-

gression against others—and immediately after the older brother's emphatically sexual commitment to marriage.

Taunts by Richard and Clarence about Edward's sexual appetite precede Richard's account of his own sexual unfitness. Edward has made Lady Grey's silence do for her consent: "Widow, go you along. Lords, use her honorably."

> Ay, Edward will use women honorably.
> Would he were wasted, marrow, bones, and all,
> That from his loins no hopeful branch may spring,
> To cross me from the golden time I look for!
> (3H6 III.ii.123–27)

Richard's "soul's desire" blocked not only by "lustful Edward's title" but by another older brother and the "unlooked for issue of their bodies," he pauses momentarily to consider the alternative: "What other pleasure can the world afford?" He dismisses as "miserable" and "unlikely" the prospect of narcissistically rewarding sexual conquest with his stunning account of the history and implications of his deformity:

> Why, love forswore me in my mother's womb;
> And for I should not deal in her soft laws,
> She did corrupt frail nature with some bribe,
> To shrink mine arm up like a wither'd shrub,
> To make an envious mountain on my back,
> Where sits deformity to mock my body;
> To shape my legs of an unequal size,
> To disproportion me in every part,
> Like to a chaos, or an unlick'd bear-whelp
> That carries no impression like the dam.
> (lines 153–62)

Finding himself no "man to be belov'd," Richard returns to his overriding desire:

> Then since this earth affords no joy to me
> But to command, to check, to o'erbear such
> As are of better person than myself,
> I'll make my heaven to dream upon the crown.
> (lines 165–68)

Richard's deformity and the rumor about his unnatural birth were in the chronicles.[5] But sexual frustration as a consequence, and so

---

5. In More's account, as given by Hall (Sources, vol. 3, p. 253), Richard was "in witte and courage egall" to his elder brothers,

the motive for compensatory villainy, is entirely from Shakespeare. The opening soliloquy of *Richard III* is so familiar that it is easy to overlook the fact that there is no historical basis for its neat antithesis:

> And therefore, since I cannot prove a lover
> To entertain these fair well-spoken days,
> I am determined to prove a villain
> And hate the idle pleasures of these days.
>
> (I.i.28–31)

The chronicles do contain a circumstantial narrative of Richard's astonishing outburst about being bewitched, in the council meeting over the coronation, at which he turned on Hastings and sprang his coup d'etat. In Edward Hall's transcription of Thomas More, Richard arrives late because "he had been a sleper that daye." As in the play, he sends the Bishop of Ely to fetch strawberries, then leaves the chamber. He returns "all chaunged with a sowre angry countenaunce knittyng the browes, frowynng and fretyng and gnawyng on his lips" as the dismayed lords marvel at "what thyng should hym ayle." Richard sits silent for a time, then asks: "What were they worthy to have that compasse and ymagine the destruccion of me beyng so neare of bloud to the kyng & protectour of this his royall realme: At which question, all the lordes sate sore astonyed, musyng muche by whom the question should be ment, of which every man knew him self clere." Hastings answers that "they were worthy to be punished as heynous traytors," and when the others agree, Richard accuses "yonder sorceres my brothers wife and other with her, menyng the quene. At these woordes many of the lordes were sore abashed which favoured her," though Hastings's only regret is that "he was not afore made of counsail of this matter":

---

but in beautee and liniamentes of nature far underneth bothe, for he was litle of stature, eivill featured of limnes, croke backed, the left shulder muche higher than the righte, harde favoured of visage, such as in estates is called a warlike visage, and emonge commen persones a crabbed face. He was malicious, wrothfull and envious, and as it is reported, his mother the duches had muche a dooe in her travaill, that she could not be delivered of hym uncut, and that he came into the worlde the fete forwarde, as menne be borne outwarde, and as the fame ranne, not untothed: whether that menne of hatred reported above the truthe, or that nature chaunged his course in the beginnynge, whiche in his life many thynges unnaturally committed, this I leve to God his judgemente.

> Then sayed the protectour in what wyse that sorceresse and other of
> her counsayle, as Shores wyfe with her affinitie have by their sorcery
> and witchecrafte this wasted my body, and therwith plucked up his
> doublet sleve to his elbowe on hys left arme, where he shewed a
> weryshe wythered arme & smalle as it was never other.

More then describes the misgivings Richard's accusation produces
in "every mannes mynde, . . . well perceyvyng that this matter was
but a quarell," for the queen was "too wyse to go about any such
folye," and would in any case scarcely have turned to Shore's wife,
"whom of all women she most hated as that concubine whom the
kyng her husband most loved." "Also, there was no manne there
but knewe that hys arme was ever such sith the day of his birth."
Hastings, whose "hart somewhat grudged to have her whom
he loved so highly accused, . . . aunswered and sayed, certaynly
my lorde, yf they have so done, they be worthy of heynous pun-
ishement." In More's account, the particular vehemence against
Hastings is compounded by the arrest of the other lords by armed
men summoned by Richard's signal:

> What quod the protectour, thou servest me I wene with yf and with
> and, I tell the they have done it, and that wyll I make good on thy
> bodye, traytour. And therewith (as in a great anger) he clapped hys
> fyste on the borde a great rappe, at whiche token geven, one cried
> treason without the chamber, and therewith a doore clapped, and in
> came rushyng men in harneyes as many as the chamber could hold.
> And anone the protectoure sayed to the lorde Hastynges, I arrest
> thee traytoure, what me my lorde quod he: yea thee traytoure quod
> the protectour. And one let flye at the lorde Stanley, which shroncke
> at the stroacke and fell under the table, or els hys head had bene cleft
> to the teth, for as shortly as he shrancke, yet ranne the bloud aboute
> hys eares. Then was the Archebishop of Yorke and the doctour Mor-
> ton bishopp of Ely & the lorde Stanley taken and divers other whiche
> were bestowed in dyvers chambers, save the lorde Hastynges (whom
> the protectour commaunded to spede and shryve him apace) for by
> sainct Poule (quod he) I wyll not dyne tyll I se thy head off.[6]

The event is unforgettable as Shakespeare compresses it into a
coup de theatre:

> Look how I am bewitch'd; behold, mine arm
> Is like a blasted sapling, wither'd up;
> And this is Edward's wife, that monstrous witch,
> Consorted with that harlot, strumpet Shore,
> That by their witchcraft thus have marked me.

6. *Sources*, vol. 3, pp. 263–65.

HASTINGS: If they have done this deed, my noble lord—
RICHARD: If? Thou protector of this damned strumpet,
          Talk'st thou to me of "ifs"? Thou art a traitor.
          Off with his head! Now by Saint Paul I swear
          I will not dine until I see the same.

                                        (III.iv.68–77)

It is a good corrective for a venture such as mine that this strange behavior of Richard is not invented by Shakespeare, but is in his source. Indeed something like the scene may actually have occurred; it seems scarcely possible that "doctour Morton bishopp of Ely," who is recorded as present and who was More's source, can have made up something so bizarre from whole cloth. Life can be as strange as art! The historical Richard may well have externalized his suffering over his deformity by accusations of witchcraft. To eliminate Hastings was part of the practical strategy of the coup— recorded in the sources at length, with emphasis on Hastings's ignoring of portents. But no practical motive can account for doing it through accusations of witchcraft against Richard's brother's wife and his former mistress, least likely of allies, as More's account notes. A projection which everyone can see through conveys a sense of injury by a woman or women who have "wasted my body." Jealous rage at the sexuality of more fortunate men finds a present object in Hastings, who is enjoying the hand-me-down mistress. "I wyll not dyne tyll I se thy head off" seems to fit, as does "make good on thy bodye," with a sense of deprivation that seeks resolution by eliminating a sexually competent and satisfied man.

Shakespeare's remarkable elaboration of Richard's relationship to women is extrapolated from this account, along with the rumors reported about his birth. At the same time it carries on the subject of overpowering women, which has occupied so much of the three earlier histories. There is a striking similarity, almost uncanny, between the council scene in the historical source of *Richard III* and the entirely invented scene between Talbot and the Countess of Auvergne near the beginning of the *Henry VI* series. The Countess tries to entrap the martial hero by luring him to dinner. Talbot takes the precaution of secretly infiltrating his soldiers into her castle. When he appears, alone, she mocks him; having expected a "second Hector," she claims to find him instead

          a child, a silly dwarf!
     It cannot be this weak and writhled shrimp
     Should strike such terror to his enemies.

                                   (1H6 II.iii.20, 22–24)

She thinks she has closed the trap:

> COUNTESS: Long time thy shadow hath been thrall to me,
> For in my gallery thy picture hangs;
> But now thy substance shall endure the like, . . .
> TALBOT: I laugh to see your ladyship so fond
> To think that you have ought but Talbot's shadow
> Whereon to practice your severity. . . .
> No, no, I am but shadow of myself.
> You are deceiv'd, my substance is not here; . . .
> *Winds his horn. Drums strike up; a peal of ordnance.*
> *Enter soldiers.*
> How say you, madam? Are you now persuaded
> That Talbot is but shadow of himself?
> There are his substance, sinews, arms, and strength.
>   (lines 36–38, 45–47, 50–51, 61–63)

Here the disabling body imagery is cast upon the man, not as a spell but in scorn, by a woman who "compasses and imagines" his destruction, and who would "chain these arms and legs of thine" (line 39). But she is baffled when he summons military force— much as in More's account of Richard with the council, where "in came rushyng men in harneyes as many as the chamber could hold." It may be mere coincidence, but the Countess's picturesque phrase, "weak and writhled [withered] shrimp" fits with More's description of the "weryshe wythered arme and small" that Richard displays as proof of his being bewitched. It seems possible that Shakespeare, in designing this scene early in his sequence of histories, shaped it, consciously or unconsciously, from recollection of reading the account of Richard's coup in the chronicle. Be that as it may, what is manifest is that he invents an episode where a virtuous hero, dedicated to his country's service, turns the tables on a scheming, scornfully disabling woman, proving he is no "child" or "silly dwarf." Talbot's mastery is clinched when he chivalrously forgoes retaliation: "Be not dismay'd, fair lady, . . . / What you have done hath not offended me; / Nor other satisfaction do I crave"—but the wine and cates of the original dinner, "For soldiers' stomachs always serve them well" (lines 73, 76–77, 80). He does not require her head before he dines! She does not have a "head" in the subliminal sense that is present as Richard takes vengeance on Hastings's sexuality along with his political intransigence. It is enough for Talbot's assertion of his manhood to use his male solidarity in war to force the French amazon back to her woman's role of providing food.

Talbot confidently relies on his troops to evade the snare set for him by the Countess; Richard isolates himself from his own astonished council with the charge that Mistress Grey has ensnared him with her witchcraft. Set beside each other, these two scenes highlight both similarities and differences in the dramatic and psychological circumstances of the two plays. Beneath the male bonding in chivalric aggression of the earlier play, there is the potential of naked brother-to-brother aggression, which Shakespeare dramatizes as the fruit of the civil strife that undoes Talbot's achievements.[7] Richard, instead of having command of chivalric and patriotic male solidarity to baffle threatening women felt as "strangers," must try to cope with those women who are closest to a child—or "the child in the man." Male solidarity in war and more generally in patriarchal institutions can serve as defense—one Richard does not have—against the child in the man. There is a sense in which Richard, trapped in his body and the fixation on rejection by women it symbolizes, is indeed "too childish-foolish for this world" (*R3* I.iii.141). His violent pursuit of the crown seeks something like infantile omnipotence—and is ultimately foolish. But moment by moment, through his wit and his ruthlessness, he has tastes of such uncircumscribable power. His special role as a stage villain, by its alliance with the audience, also has power as an incarnation of plot; he shares with us a superior awareness of what will happen, which the other characters do not have.

Talbot also shares his plot with us as he whispers directions to a captain. But he is the very opposite of the lone stage villain. He turns the tables by his *social* role, emphasizing that he has power only through others: "I am but shadow of myself." Sigurd Burckhardt, in *Shakespearean Meanings*, uses that line as title of a chapter in which he suggests that we can see Talbot's expression of his relationship to his soldiers as a type of Shakespeare's relation to his dramatis personae. His actors are his "substance, sinews, arms, and strength" as the young dramatist takes over full control, "the only Shake-scene," after working on individual scenes in collaboration with more established playwrights. In developing this construction, Burckhardt emphasizes that the scene is entirely invented, and that Talbot is not in character with his role of chivalric

---

7. See Coppélia Kahn's account of Talbot as "the tetralogy's great exemplar of chivalric masculinity based on devotion to the father," in *Man's Estate: Masculine Identity in Shakespeare* (Berkeley and Los Angeles: University of California Press, 1981), p. 52.

derring-do everywhere else: "His strength lies precisely in his 'negative capability,' his having learned the secret of self-effacement, of assertion only through the larger design."[8] Whether or not Burckhardt's equation of Talbot with Shakespeare was conscious for the author, it can stand for Shakespeare's relationship to his drama in the Henry VI plays. A very different relationship obtains when in *Richard III* he endows the isolated and obsessed king of the chronicles with his own verbal and dramatic powers. An explosion of creative energy accompanies the dramatization of the release of violent libidinal energy.

"SOME CERTAIN DREGS OF CONSCIENCE"

Shakespeare's exhaustive exposition of Richard's relationship to women emphasizes hostility to their sexuality. A cue for this was the chronicle's account of his public humiliation of Mistress Shore. Although Shakespeare leaves this out, he exhibits the motive in Richard's mocking asides about her, his attacks on his brother's queen, and most extensively in his pseudo-moral castigations of his brother's "bestial appetite in change of lust" (III.v.81). This tendentious strain fits with the mummery oration's goal of disinheriting Edward's children—and of casting doubt on the legitimacy of Edward himself, who was conceived, Buckingham is instructed to suggest, when Richard's father "had wars in France": "Yet touch this sparingly, as 'twere far off, / Because, my lord, you know my mother lives" (III.v.88, 93–94).

The wooing of Anne is of course no exception to this hostility; Richard wins her by histrionic "o'erbearing." The wooing mimes Petrarchan hyperbole in a sadomasochistic way: his life depends on her, his crimes were done for her—the charade is carried through by his kneeling, handing her his sword, and baring his breast. We feel the unwholesomeness of the motives along with amusement at Richard's zest and revulsion at the way his schemes succeed. He pretends to find her an overwhelming woman, as the way to overwhelm her. Her motives as "She falls the sword" (s.d.) are not articulated. Someone has observed that when she spits on him, she has become physically involved, despite what she says: "Would it were mortal poison for thy sake!" "Never came poison from so sweet a place." "Never hung poison on a fouler toad" (I.ii.145–47).

8. Sigurd Burckhardt, *Shakespearean Meanings* (Princeton: Princeton University Press, 1968), p. 70.

Her final yielding can be played as the response of a helpless woman to sheer male force. Richard's response is contempt: "I'll have her, but I will not keep her long. / What? I, that kill'd her husband and his father" (lines 229–30).

All this hostility to sexuality has political as well as purely expressive purpose, expressive though it is. The historical Richard did indeed marry Anne, the daughter of Warwick the king-maker, after destroying her father and King Henry. Choices were limited at the dangerous confluence of dynastic interests. Shakespeare follows orthodox Tudor history by duly celebrating the marriage of Elizabeth of York with virtuous, victorious Richmond at play's end: "The true succeeders of each royal house, / By God's fair ordinance conjoin together" (V.v.30–31). But he also shows the falseness of romantic pretense in such matches by his handling of Richard's attempt to marry Elizabeth:

> Now for I know the Britain Richmond aims
> At young Elizabeth, my brother's daughter,
> And by that knot looks proudly on the crown,
> To her I go, a jolly thriving wooer.
>
> (IV.iii.40–43)

News of Buckingham's revolt and Bishop Morton's defection to Richmond interrupts this jolly project. In the next scene, Richard's mother, intercepting him on his way to war, identifies herself as "she that might have intercepted thee, / By strangling thee in her accursed womb" (IV.iv.137–38). She is part of the chorus of grieving, cursing women whose kin Richard has destroyed:

> QUEEN ELIZABETH: Tell me, thou villain-slave, where are my
>   children?
> DUCHESS OF YORK: Thou toad, thou toad, where is thy brother
>   Clarence?
>   And little Ned Plantagenet, his son?
> QUEEN ELIZABETH: Where is the gentle Rivers, Vaughan, Grey?
> DUCHESS OF YORK: Where is kind Hastings?
>   RICHARD: A flourish, trumpets! Strike alarum, drums!
>   Let not the heavens hear these tell-tale women
>   Rail on the Lord's annointed. Strike, I say!
>   *Flourish. Alarums.*
>
> (lines 144–51)

Richard here tries to deal with the women the way Talbot dealt with the Countess! All the right is on their side, however—or better, all the wrongs—and his martial countermove verges on comedy.

Nevertheless, after receiving his mother's final curse, he still has the buoyancy to woo young Elizabeth through her mother, despite the Queen's devastating demonstrations of his moral bankruptcy. Her recapitulation of his outrages and his mobilization in return of prudential and political considerations, along with specious repentance, are almost tediously shocking. But the final turn makes one shiver:

> QUEEN ELIZABETH: Yet thou didst kill my children.
> KING RICHARD: But in your daughter's womb I bury them;
> Where in that nest of spicery they will breed
> Selves of themselves, to your recomforture.
> QUEEN ELIZABETH: Shall I go win my daughter to thy will?
> KING RICHARD: And be a happy mother by the deed.
> QUEEN ELIZABETH: I go. Write to me very shortly,
> And you shall understand from me her mind.
> KING RICHARD: Bear her my true love's kiss; and so farewell.
> *Exit Queen.*
> Relenting fool, and shallow, changing woman!
> (IV.iv.422–31)

Whether the Queen is acquiescing or merely temporizing, this scene is characteristically Shakespearean in its multiple perspectives. The women's curses exemplify the fearful power of women as mothers; but their laments and maledictions issue from their helplessness in the patriarchal society gone wrong. Their whole relationship to life is through the men who take them in marriage and through their role as mothers. They can only suffer the male-determined developments of dynastic struggle. Richard's lines about "that nest of spicery" focus these relations sensuously in a disquietingly obscene way. Woman's genital sexuality is relished because it can make up for male destruction buried in it! That the Queen accedes to this role for her daughter then is made matter for Richard's contempt. As with the wooing of Anne, we can only recoil from Richard's ruthlessness. But we cannot altogether dismiss his contempt for the weakness of the two women, even though the dramatist's presentation of the social constraints on them makes it comprehensible. Yet it is through the women that we chiefly feel the human consequences of "intestine division," as when the Duchess of York, craving death's release from the "preposterous / And frantic outrage" that has marked her "Accursed and unquiet wrangling days," summarizes her dependent experience:

> My husband lost his life to get the crown,
> And often up and down my sons were toss'd
> For me to joy and weep their gain and loss;

And being seated, and domestic broils
Clean overblown, themselves, the conquerors,
Make war upon themselves, brother to brother,
Blood to blood, self against self.

(II.iv.55–63)

The naturalistic if formalized handling of the woman's responses is extended onto another plane in the curses of Queen Margaret. We have seen the historical Richard inventing witches in fastening on the Queen and Mistress Shore his sense that he is bewitched. Shakespeare invents Margaret as a real woman to play this witch's role. Richard's own mother is relatively restrained with her son, until the very end, when she sends him off to battle with "take with thee my most grievous curse" (IV.iv.188). Only then does she herself throw at him the circumstances of his birth, which so many others have dwelled on, including Richard himself:

Thou cam'st on earth to make the earth my hell.
A grievous burden was thy birth to me,
Techy and wayward was thy infancy;
Thy school-days wayward, desp'rate, wild, and furious,
Thy prime of manhood daring, bold, and venturous;
Thy age confirm'd, proud, subtle, sly, and bloody,
More mild, but yet more harmful—kind in hatred.
What comfortable hour canst thou name
That ever grac'd me with thy company?

(IV.iv.167–75)

Even here, her account leaves out—what in life might well be left out—the mother's active hatred and rejection of such a child, under the surface of her efforts to cope with him. What is left out also is the child's fear of violent retaliation by the mother on the pattern of his own violent feelings toward her.

Shakespeare provides the embodiment of this terrible mother, not in Richard's actual mother but in Margaret, whom he retrieves from historical exile and death to serve this displaced purpose. Infantile fear that the angry mother is omnipotent, at the root of the later irrational conviction animating the discovery and persecution of witches, is dramatized as the preternatural efficacy of Margaret's curses. On one side, her role—despite the fact that it has no historical basis—is humanly understandable because her curses are motivated by what she has suffered in the dynastic wars that led to her final defeat and exile. Because of her active role in those wars— a woman who would not accept a woman's role and who engaged in the violence traditionally reserved for men—her resort to the witchcraft of the curses seems natural now that she is reduced to impotence except for curses.

But these naturalistic and historical elements are so handled that we feel her presence and her powers as uncanny. To have her enter, unseen, to comment in asides on the recriminations of those who have displaced her, gives her a special aura; she is a presence in another dimension, the embodiment of the past they are neglecting and that will shape their future:

> *Enter old Queen Margaret [behind].*
> QUEEN ELIZABETH: Small joy have I in being England's queen.
> QUEEN MARGARET: [*Aside*] And less'ned be that small, God I
>   beseech him!
>   Thy honor, state, and seat is due to me.
> (I.iii.109–11)

Her asides, picking up and turning words and syntax, are like wit in moving attention to a latent stream of feeling, as Richard's asides so often do. She hoots for us, in effect, at Richard's hypocrisy:

> I am too childish-foolish for this world.
> QUEEN MARGARET: [*Aside*] Hie thee to hell for shame, and leave
>   this world,
>   Thou cacodemon, there thy kingdom is.
> (lines 141–43)

When she comes forward—a stunning coup de theatre we wait for— she abruptly halts the ongoing action, as Richard so often does:

> Hear me, you wrangling pirates, that fall out
> In sharing that which you have pill'd from me!
> Which of you trembles not that looks on me?
> (lines 157–59)

In actual life the malevolence dramatized in witchcraft must have frequently been the last resort of old, destitute, isolated women, all they once had lost. Even as Shakespeare lays out this human basis for Margaret's role, her preternatural role is labeled by Richard: "Foul wrinkled witch, what mak'st thou in my sight?" (I.iii.163).

Her 100-odd lines of curses, here at the outset, with Richard's ripostes, recapitulate the violence done in 3 *Henry VI*. Simply as a resource in dramatic structure, the curses work beautifully to make past outrage present and set up the audience's expectations for the future. It is striking that her most dreadful violence in the earlier play, her tormenting of York and her relish in literally rubbing in the destruction of his child Rutland, is recalled now at the outset. Then

she enacted physically the traditional hostility of the witch to children—now she goes on with it by curses. Richard asserts that the
curse has been fulfilled which "my noble father laid on thee / When
thou didst crown his warlike brows with paper" and gave him to
wipe his eyes "a clout / Steep'd in the faultless blood of pretty
Rutland" (I.iii.173–74, 176–77). Margaret then spells out the blood-
feud logic, with the verbal symmetry that is to characterize its expression throughout the play:

> Did York's dread curse prevail so much with heaven
> That Henry's death, my lovely Edward's death,
> Their kingdom's loss, my woeful banishment,
> Shall all but answer for that peevish brat? . . .
> Edward thy son, that now is Prince of Wales,
> For Edward our son, that was Prince of Wales,
> Die in his youth by like untimely violence!
> (lines 190–93, 198–200)

Shakespeare does not, in his fully successful works, provide
supernatural resolution for human conflict. "Can curses pierce the
clouds and enter heaven?" (I.iii.194), as Margaret wishes, in this instance. *Richard III* is on an uneasy borderline in this respect. The
pattern of retribution, fueled by reciprocal injury and vengeance
and expressed as here in curses, is masterfully built into dramatic
and verbal structure. The language and action that develop this
web of curses are patterned far more than anything we get in other
history plays. For them Shakespeare uses masterfully the early
style of formal rhetorical and dramatic symmetry that Kyd used in
The Spanish Tragedy. Verbal play releases and seems to confirm aggression and destruction by uncanny power, suggesting an under-
the-surface or enveloping force beyond the control of will and ex-
ecutive intelligence.

So, for example, with Buckingham: Margaret makes a pointed
exception of him, after she has dealt out curses to the rest of the
"wrangling pirates," and warns him against Richard; only when he
rejects her "gentle counsel" does she doom him:

> O but remember this another day,
> When he shall split thy very heart with sorrow,
> And say poor Margaret was a prophetess!
> (I.iii.298–300)

Her vivid "split thy very heart" is not particularly appropriate for
Buckingham, who is heartless as Richard's accomplice, except for
his momentary hesitation about killing the little princes. Yet the

phrase is recalled verbatim after his rebellion fails and he is led off
to "the block of shame":

> Thus Margaret's curse falls heavy on my neck:
> "When he," quoth she, "shall split thy heart with sorrow,
> Remember Margaret was a prophetess."
>
> (V.i.25–27)

The accumulation of bad faith is scored off by this pattern of
retribution.

It is striking that Margaret is in symbiotic alliance with Richard,
like him even as she curses him. She warns Buckingham to "take
heed of yonder dog! / Look when he fawns, he bites." When she
adds "and when he bites, / His venom tooth will rankle to the
death" (I.iii.288–90) she all but describes her own curses. So with
her remonstrances to Queen Elizabeth: "Why strew'st thou sugar
on that bottled spider / Whose deadly web ensnareth thee about?"
(lines 241–42). Her own curses are a deadly web. When she turns
on Richard himself, the likeness is made explicit:

> Thou elvish-mark'd, abortive, rooting hog! . . .
> Thou rag of honor! thou detested—
>
> RICHARD: Margaret.
> MARGARET: Richard!
> RICHARD: Ha!
> MARGARET: I call thee not.
> RICHARD: I cry thee mercy then; for I did think
> That thou hadst call'd me all these bitter names.
>
> (lines 227, 232–35)

Richard's suave "I cry thee mercy" gives a superior, scornful accent
to his ploy. But the literalism of superstition about language is also
at work—here again a kind of out-in-the-open wit, words acting for
things. On this level, he eludes her curse by attaching it to her instead of to himself, as Queen Elizabeth makes explicit: "Thus have
you breath'd your curse against yourself" (line 239). Margaret cannot take violent action, cannot bite physically, but her curses cut off
lives, fall heavy on Buckingham's neck. She announces her final appearance with "So now prosperity begins to mellow / And drop
into the rotten mouth of death" (IV.iv.1–2). That mouth feeds her
hunger: "Bear with me; I am hungry for revenge, / And now I cloy
me with beholding it" (lines 61–62).

Margaret's role and this relationship to Richard make *Richard III*
a revenge play such as Shakespeare's sources only fitfully suggest.
She is the source, by her curses, of a feeling of helpless dread whose

taproot goes back to infancy, just as Richard's violence is rooted there. Through Margaret, Shakespeare creates what amounts to an inescapable external "conscience," a cruel and corrupt superego, rooted in infantile dread of maternal wrath, pronouncing vindictive fates that close in on others, who ultimately come to embody them. Although she only appears twice, near the opening and toward the close, she is repeatedly recalled as her curses are fulfilled. And the pattern her curses initiate is extended by people cursing themselves and in due course repeating their own words when each is "prov'd the subject of mine own soul's curse" (IV.i.80), as poor Anne puts it. As we read and reread the play, such returns can come to seem tedious, a verbal game too deliberately played out. But as we watch it happening on stage, the aura of menace colors our dismay about the step-by-step destruction of its people as people.

In the exchanges between the murderers as they prepare to kill Clarence, Shakespeare has them make conscience into an external thing:

> FIRST MURDERER: How dost thou feel thyself now?
> SECOND MURDERER: Faith, some certain dregs of conscience are yet within me.
> FIRST MURDERER: Remember our reward when the deed's done.
> SECOND MURDERER: 'Zounds, he dies! I had forgot the reward.
> FIRST MURDERER: Where's thy conscience now?
> SECOND MURDERER: O, in the Duke of Gloucester's purse.
> (I.iv.120–28)

Shakespeare mastered his synoptic use of clowning very early. The common men here treat conscience as something outside them, analogous to the curses that seem to hang in the air over the main characters as an external menace ready to drop on them. The murderers try to put conscience from them, becoming a version of Richard as he puts Margaret's curse from him:

> FIRST MURDERER: What if it come to thee again?
> SECOND MURDERER: I'll not meddle with it, it makes a man a coward. A man cannot steal, but it accuseth him. . . . It fills a man full of obstacles. . . . It beggars any man that keeps it. It is turn'd out of towns and cities for a dangerous thing, and every man that means to live well endeavors to trust to himself and live without it.
> FIRST MURDERER: 'Zounds, 'tis even now at my elbow, persuading me not to kill the Duke.
> (I.iv.133–46)

As they talk tough to keep conscience at bay, they are parodies of Richard: "I am strong-fram'd; he [conscience] cannot prevail with me" (lines 150–51). They too find that wit helps: "Take him on the costard with the hilts of thy sword, and then throw him into the malmsey-butt in the next room." "O excellent device! and make a sop of him" (lines 154–57). Richard keeps inveigling us to join him in escapes from conscience, as the murderers do here. The fullest expression in the play of the validity of conscience, its divine and civic sanctions, comes next, as Clarence wakes and the scene takes on strong poetic urgency. Second Murderer is dissuaded from the deed by the duke's moving appeals. First Murderer resists them in a way that also parallels Richard: "Relent! No: 'tis cowardly and womanish" (line 261).

Shakespeare makes Richard himself do battle with conscience, at least formally, before the play ends. In the pageant "dream" in the highly formalized scene that precedes the final battle, the ghosts of Richard's victims bid him "despair and die" and hearten Richmond. The device serves both to summarize the accumulating political consequences of violence and to embody, all too literally, the residual fear of violence from those whom he has violently destroyed. But it produces no feeling *in us* of dread, such as we experience in Clarence's dream earlier, or in the scene of Banquo's return as a ghost in *Macbeth*. Richard talks as he wakes of "cold fearful drops [that] stand on my trembling flesh," of "coward conscience" afflicting him, of his self-division and self-hatred, of "several sins" thronging "to the bar" (V.iii.181, 179, 198–99). But the speech is systematic rather than moving. He really has no conscience, in a fully developed sense, only fear of retribution.

This lack agrees with the stage of emotional development Shakespeare has inscribed, carefully, indeed systematically, as the psychological basis of his character. Richard lives by sadomasochistic structuring of relationships so as to enforce separateness and autonomy, a pattern shaped by fixation at what Abraham, Freud, and Erikson describe as the biting stage of infantile development.[9] To note this is surely not to force psychological theory on Shake-

---

9. See Karl Abraham, "A Short Study of the Development of the Libido, Viewed in the Light of the Mental Disorders" (1924), in *Selected Papers on Psychoanalysis* (London: Hogarth, 1948), pp. 418–50; Sigmund Freud, *Three Essays on the Theory of Sexuality* (1905), in *Standard Edition*, vol. 7, pp. 197–98; Erik Erikson, *Childhood and Society*, 2nd ed. rev. (New York: Norton, 1963), pp. 72–80, 247–51.

speare's dog, rooting hog, tusked boar. Sir Thomas More's sagacity
recognized that the idea of Richard's being born with teeth might be
a myth created because "menne [out] of hatred reported above the
truthe"—but their mythopoesis pointed to a psychology that Shakespeare elaborates tellingly and consciously. He sees the civil wars
as providing a social identity for this disposition.

Richard's own account of his unfitness for love turns on the fact
that he cannot look in a mirror:

> But I, that am not shap'd for sportive tricks
> Nor made to court an amorous looking-glass;
> I, that am rudely stamp'd, and want love's majesty
> To strut before a wanton ambling nymph;
> I, that am curtail'd of this fair proportion,
> Cheated of feature by dissembling nature.
>
> (I.i.14–19)

The pleasures of love as Richard imagines them are narcissistic—
the sort of loving we get in the show-off courting of *Love's Labor's
Lost*. "To strut before a wanton ambling nymph" is "to court an
amorous looking-glass." After he has won Anne he exclaims:

> Upon my life, she finds (although I cannot)
> Myself to be a marv'llous proper man.
> I'll be at charges for a looking-glass.
>
> (I.ii.253–55)

"Shine out, fair sun, till I have bought a glass, / That I may see my
shadow as I pass" (lines 262–63) symmetrically reverses the opening speech on his outcast role in the "glorious summer [of] this sun
of York," which can provide him with "no delight to pass away the
time, / Unless to see my shadow in the sun / And descant on mine
own deformity" (I.i.2, 25–27). In fact, as his tone makes clear,
Anne has given him no such flattering reflection—she has simply
been overwhelmed.

The mirror imagery of the Sonnets highlights a comparable symbolic and psychological dimension. There the beloved is taken as a
narcissistic mirror that saves the poet from what he feels himself to
be "when my glass shows me myself indeed" (Sonnet 62). Richard
moves about the stage as a version of the depreciating self-image to
which the poet of the Sonnets is vulnerable when without the resource of his mirroring love: "lame, poor, . . . despised" (Sonnet
37). Richard's constant verbal exploitation of his physical deformity—echoed by everyone else—obscures the fact that it is the

summation of his sense of self. In many of the sonnets, the poet takes over the maternal role, identifying with Nature as he makes the friend into a cherished and, he hopes, a cherishing mirror. Richard by contrast sees no way except violence to make up for being "Cheated of feature by dissembling nature."

Richard looks for nothing from his mother, the original mirror of earliest infancy, in whose face the child first sees reflected the self with which she endows him—a self more decisive in shaping his character than his body. As Richard maneuvers after Edward's death, he asks his mother's blessing and gets "God bless thee, and put meekness in thy breast, / Love, charity, obedience, and true duty!" (II.ii.107–8)—as much as to say, "Do not be what you are." His response provides a refreshing détente at this anxious moment:

> Amen!—[aside] and make me die a good old man!
> That is the butt-end of a mother's blessing.
> I marvel that her Grace did leave it out.
> (lines 109–11)

Margaret is much more obliging: she tells him to "snarl, and bite, and play the dog" (3H6 V.vi.77), as he has gleefully set out to do. Margaret corresponds to the image of maternal threat toward which the defensive structure of Richard's character is oriented.

In their relationship Shakespeare adumbrates the mother as imagined by projection of a child's earliest rage, provoked when he encounters the limits to the seeming omnipotence experienced during his initial symbiotic unity with her. In the process of early separation, as D. W. Winnicott understands it,[10] the hate and dread engendered in this relationship are transcended when "conscience is born of love" (Sonnet 151). As unity breaks down, love becomes possible because the mother's answering nurture, framed by newly acknowledged limits, brings the child to recognize her and himself as separate persons; the child can understand his anger in relation to the love she continues to supply and he continues to need, and so feel the possibility of restitution. In the working through of this recognition, there is an alternation between depressed feelings of guilt and isolation, generated by the child's rage at separation, and elated moments of merging, which restore lost union in fantasy. A deep structure of feeling about self and world continues this polarity throughout life for many people, perhaps everyone.

10. See especially "The Use of an Object and Relating through Identification," in D. W. Winnicott, *Playing and Reality* (New York: Basic Books, 1971), pp. 86–94.

Shakespeare's tragedies often bring into the struggles of their protagonists the infantile residues of the effort to fulfill conflicting needs for a separate identity and for merger with another. *Richard III* points toward those plays in which protagonists are overcome by such conflict at the core of their experience. But Richard's strength derives from the externalization of this conflict, his aggressive, brutal denial of its inner consequences. Hamlet must live in his own "sullied flesh," a body he perceives as contaminated by Gertrude's contamination of hers in an unnatural marriage. Richard flees defensively his imprisonment in a body he thinks of as unnaturally withered and broken by women. Feelings of shame and helplessness and deprivation, such as torment Hamlet, Richard transforms into contempt for and destruction of others. The threat grounded in fear of maternal abandonment or wrath, Richard transforms into his hatred of inconstant women. The curses of Margaret, which embody feared maternal malevolence; the "blessing" of an actual mother who would condemn him to a compliant son's role for all his life; the "conscience" that Hamlet, disgusted with his own inaction, thinks the source of all cowardice—all these remain outside Richard, in a world he can manipulate for self-aggrandizement. The protagonists of Shakespeare's mature tragedies alternately end in destructive engulfment or destructive isolation.[11] Richard *begins* in such isolation, turning its destructiveness outward with his savage playing until its recoil finally overwhelms him.

But, to repeat, Richard has the audience for a mirror. He *does* descant on his shadow, to us, and with relish. How well aware Shakespeare was of the relationship of this posture to infantile roots is apparent not only in the many accounts of Richard's loathed birth, but also in the dramatist's juxtaposing the cherishing of an infant to Richard's alienation. In the final scene of *3 Henry VI*, King Edward enters to triumph in state, with his Queen, his two brothers, Hastings, and a nurse with his infant son, Edward. After a chivalric summary of the Yorkist military victory, he turns to his wife:

> Come hither, Bess, and let me kiss my boy.
> Young Ned, for thee, thine uncles and myself
> Have in our armors watch'd the winter's night,
> Went all afoot in summer's scalding heat,

---

11. See Richard P. Wheeler, *Shakespeare's Development and the Problem Comedies: Turn and Counter-Turn* (Berkeley and Los Angeles: University of California Press, 1981), pp. 200–13.

> That thou mightst repossess the crown in peace.
> And of our labors thou shalt reap the gain.
> RICHARD: [*Aside.*] I'll blast his harvest, and your head were
> laid,
> For yet I am not look'd on in the world.
> This shoulder was ordain'd so thick to heave,
> And heave it shall some weight, or break my back.
> (V.vii.15–24)

There is something here that anticipates Milton's Satan respond-ing to Paradise—or recalls Judas, as Richard makes explicit in his aside after he kisses the child: "To say the truth, so Judas kiss'd his master, / And cried, 'All Hail!' when as he meant all harm" (lines 33–34).

"AND IN MY COMPANY MY BROTHER GLOUCESTER"

But there is something contrived about Richard's role, and about the counterpressures of the curses and laments, which makes com-parisons like those above seem too serious. The whole play, or much of it, works stunningly on stage. But when we read and re-read it, much of it goes dead—it is too stagey. The symmetries and iterations become tedious; the words sometimes are only loosely right, chosen as they are to fill out the formal patterns, match sound with sound, rhythm with rhythm. This is especially true of the women's condemnations of Richard and their mingle of laments and mutual recriminations. Richard's huge part keeps its vitality much better, buoyant as it is with wit, parody, shifts of diction and of tone, including those drops down into the colloquial that regu-larly distinguish the special people in the early work who can move outside the decorum of the main social group: Berowne in *Love's Labor's Lost*, for example, or the Bastard in *King John*. But even in performance or right after it questions remain. How seriously, fi-nally, can we take Richard? How seriously can we take the equation of his body and psychology with the whole evil of civil war, so that the large social evil is expelled when Richard is destroyed?

The play's official program calls for Richard's final defeat to work as a successful riddance. For E. M. W. Tillyard, who sees *Richard III* as a fully successful dramatization of the "belief that God had guided England into her haven of Tudor prosperity," ridding En-gland of the villain king purges "the great ulcer of the body politic into which all its impurity is drained."[12] But A. P. Rossiter finds that the play is disturbing in a way not to be fully contained by the Tudor ideas of history, as Tillyard would have it. Rossiter sees the play's unity in an "overall system of *paradox*, . . . a constant displaying of inversions, or reversals of meaning," the outcome of the conflict between the orthodox Tudor myth, which "made history God-controlled," and the myth of "Richard the Devil-king, . . . a ready-made Senecan tyrant."[13] Others have seen the play's resolution as still more problematic.

Rossiter finds that Richard's combination of histrionic appeal and repellent destructiveness makes sense if he is seen as a Scourge of God, an "Angel with Horns." He argues that the Tudor period's belief in this divinely ordained role for tyrants would have provided a way to appropriate for historical orthodoxy the tensions in Richard's attractive villainy. This argument, that Richard is serving a divine purpose by his villainy, would be more plausible if Shakespeare had unambiguously used the idea of a Scourge of God in his text. But though Margaret and others call on God to avenge wrongs through Richard's cunning savagery, their venal or pathetic motives as they do so are always underscored. A secular, dramatic understanding of what happens is always provided. Hence the way is left open for Jan Kott's subversive way of seeing and staging the ending.

Rossiter, insisting that the play's "overall system [is] paradox," has to neglect the ending, with its apparent movement beyond paradox to unqualified, optimistic affirmation. Kott proposes a completely ironic handling of Richmond's pious finale: the machine of ruthless state power, having used up Richard, merely finds a new facade.[14] Though this reading is clearly anachronistic as it is developed by Kott, his emphasis on "recurring and unchanging circles" (p. 6) of opportunistic violence is responsive to a dimension of the secular action that is missing from Tillyard's view of the play and that undermines the theological necessity of seeing Richard, with Rossiter, as a Scourge of God. Shakespeare's presentation of the sources of political action in the family, together with the cruel

12. E. M. W. Tillyard, *Shakespeare's History Plays* (London: Chatto and Windus, 1944), p. 204.

13. A. P. Rossiter, *Angel with Horns and Other Shakespeare Lectures*, ed. Graham Storey (New York: Theatre Arts Books, 1961), pp. 20–21.

14. Jan Kott, *Shakespeare Our Contemporary*, trans. Boleslaw Taborski (Garden City, New York: Anchor Books, 1966), pp. 3–55.

exigencies of dynastic struggle within a patriarchal society, is so cogent that, on reflection, we cannot entirely accept the ceremonial resolution that affirms Tudor orthodoxy by the marriage of the two houses, nor what comes to seem the scapegoat role given Richard. It is as if, at the end, the fully dramatized, secular, family-based determinants of the action are abruptly exchanged for a sacred, ceremonial causality.[15]

In putting family concerns to remarkable use in developing the historical plot, *Richard III* is exceptionally explicit in its reference back to childhood and in the development of maternal roles. After the death of Edward IV, mother and grandmother make comparisons between the two little princes as they await the arrival of the elder, now heir to the throne. In the younger brother, York, who is already with them, Shakespeare's often remarked tendency to make his children behave like miniature men is made plausible by a special precocity. The boy, hearing that he has "almost overta'en" his elder brother in growth, "would not have it so"—he has heard from Richard, his uncle Gloucester, that "'Small herbs have grace, great weeds to grow apace.'"

DUCHESS OF YORK: Good faith, good faith, the saying did not hold
In him that did object the same to thee:
He was the wretched'st thing when he was
young,
So long a-growing and so leisurely
That if his rule were true, he should be
gracious.
ARCHBISHOP: And so no doubt he is, my gracious madam.
DUCHESS OF YORK: I hope he is, but yet let mothers doubt.
(II.iv.16–22)

The exchange places the child, and Richard as a child, in the field of maternal approval and disapproval. Shakespeare dramatizes with telling precision the way the women set up rivalry between children: "I hope he is; but yet let mothers doubt."

Little York goes on to define himself, vis-à-vis his hostile uncle, in this field where mother and grandmother make growing up and growing up right into a competition. For this child, as for Richard, wit mobilizes the aggression thus engendered:

15. See Richard P. Wheeler, "History, Character and Conscience in *Richard III*," *Comparative Drama* 5 (Winter 1971–72): 301–21.

YORK: Now by my troth, if I had been rememb'red,
I could have given my uncle's Grace a flout,
To touch his growth nearer than he touch'd
mine.
DUCHESS OF YORK: How, my young York? I prithee let me hear it.
YORK: Marry (they say) my uncle grew so fast
That he could gnaw a crust at two hours old;
'Twas full two years ere I could get a tooth.
Grandam, this would have been a biting jest.
(lines 23–30)

The scene even includes the way the women think they hide crucial things and judgments—"I prithee, pretty York, who told thee this?" —yet talk about them in front of eagerly listening children:

QUEEN ELIZABETH: A parlous boy! Go to, you are too shrewd.
DUCHESS OF YORK: Good madam, be not angry with the child.
QUEEN ELIZABETH: Pitchers have ears.
(lines 31, 35–37)

The next moment a messenger enters to explode this peaceful domestic exchange with the news that the Queen's kindred have been arrested by Richard—a very biting jest indeed: "The tiger now hath seiz'd the gentle hind" (line 50). Shakespeare does not need Freud to tell him that what is played out with swords, dungeons, and scaffolds begins in the nursery.

The next scene opens with the arrival of Prince Edward and the queasy business of getting his younger brother out of sanctuary. When he is brought out by the Archbishop, the same theme of rivalry is played on, with remarkable boldness:

YORK: You said that idle weeds are fast in growth:
The Prince my brother hath outgrown me far.
RICHARD: He hath, my lord.
YORK: And therefore is he idle?
(III.i.103–5)

The limited destructive powers of children are then set against those of adults:

YORK: I pray you, uncle, give me this dagger.
RICHARD: My dagger, little cousin? with all my heart.
PRINCE EDWARD: A beggar, brother?
YORK: Of my kind uncle, that I know will give,
And being but a toy, which is no grief to
give.

RICHARD: A greater gift than that I'll give my cousin.
YORK: A greater gift? O, that's the sword to it.
RICHARD: Ay, gentle cousin, were it light enough.
YORK: O then I see you will part but with light gifts!
In weightier things you'll say a beggar nay.
RICHARD: It is too heavy for your Grace to wear.

(lines 110–20)

Immediately after acknowledging that his brother has outgrown him, York asks for Richard's dagger—as though he said in effect, "the dagger is my way to overtake him now"! The dagger is "but a toy," so he asks for the sword. He does so after the menacing double entendre that glints from Richard's "A greater gift than that I'll give my cousin," as though he understood the threat by his little pitcher's ears and sought to disarm his uncle of the "greater gift." But since in fact he cannot yet manage a sword, he moves on through plays on words, like Richard's, to make himself a monkey on Richard's back:

RICHARD: What, would you have my weapon, little lord?
YORK: I would, that I might thank you as you call
me.
RICHARD: How?
YORK: Little.
PRINCE EDWARD: My lord of York will still be cross in talk.
Uncle, your Grace knows how to bear with
him.
YORK: You mean, to bear me, not to bear with me.
Uncle, my brother mocks both you and me:
Because that I am little, like an ape,
He thinks that you should bear me on your
shoulders.

(lines 122–31)

Worsted for once in "sharp-provided wit" (line 132), Richard moves things along physically, to the tower—where we know that in due course he will deal with this little parody of himself. The child senses this too: "I shall not sleep in quiet at the Tower." Asked "Why, what should you fear?" by Richard, he throws back knowledge of the terrible adult world he has received from his grandmother: "Marry, my uncle Clarence' angry ghost. / My grandam told me he was murd'red there" (lines 142–45). The brittleness of his precocity accords with the fact that he is as helpless as the women to do anything about what he already knows from them.

His elder brother has a manly resolution—which will prove equally helpless:

PRINCE EDWARD: I fear no uncles dead.
    RICHARD: Nor none that live, I hope.
PRINCE EDWARD: And if they live, I hope I need not fear.
              But come, my lord; with a heavy heart,
              Thinking on them, go I unto the Tower.
                             (lines 146–50)

The chronicle tells how, after Richard's coronation and the princes' close imprisonment, Prince Edward anticipated his death: he "never tyed his pointes, nor any thyng roughte of hym selfe, but . . . lyngered in thoughte and hevines."[16] Shakespeare's rapid dramatic pace leaves this out; the murder takes place offstage. But he has already dramatized an equivalent in the murder of Clarence, whose telling of his premonitory dream brilliantly adapts accounts of the journey to the underworld after death from *De Casibus* tragedy:

I pass'd (methought) the melancholy flood,
With that sour ferryman which poets write of,
Unto the kingdom of perpetual night.
                    (I.iv.45–47)

The dream begins, appropriately, as a fulfillment of Clarence's natural wish to escape from England and his brother King Edward's power:

Methoughts that I had broken from the Tower
And was embark'd to cross to Burgundy,
And in my company my brother Gloucester,
Who from my cabin tempted me to walk
Upon the hatches. Thence we look'd toward England,
And cited up a thousand heavy times,
During the wars of York and Lancaster,
That had befall'n us.

                    (lines 9–16)

Brotherly solidarity, such as Richard has plausibly asserted, seems confirmed by the escape. But already "*tempted* me to walk" betrays what becomes manifest as the dream turns to nightmare; Clarence, asleep, knows the true malice of his brother, under the protestations he trusts when awake:

16. *Sources*, vol. 3, pp. 278–79.

> As we pac'd along
> Upon the giddy footing of the hatches,
> Methought that Gloucester stumbled, and in falling
> Strook me (that thought to stay him) overboard
> Into the tumbling billows of the main.
> O Lord, methought what pain it was to drown!
>
> (lines 16–21)

The dreamlike presentation of relationships is in physical imagery that conveys the menace of Richard's limp; bodily scuffling, such as boys engage in, turns suddenly to violence.

Wolfgang Clemen contrasts the imaginative power of Clarence's dream with the "well-drilled succession of ghosts" who "address themselves one by one first to Richard, then to Richmond, in morality play fashion."[17] His exhaustive discussion of Clarence's dream notes how the vision of the sea bottom, perhaps reflecting the recent wreck of the Armada, is a version of death's mockery of what is most valued in life reminiscent of the medieval "Dances of Death." It is "the most imaginatively and imagistically rich passage in the dream—indeed, in the whole play" (pp. 70–71). "Where eyes did once inhabit, there were crept / (As 'twere in scorn of eyes) reflecting gems" (I.iv.30–31), anticipates "those are pearls that were his eyes" (*Tmp*. I.ii.399), but without the same immediacy and suggestion of mysterious metamorphosis, the eyes turned into pearls, the bones to coral. The whole span of Shakespeare's development is in the difference, including the fact that it is Ferdinand's father who is so transformed, as the son, to his seeming, inherits his role—"Myself am Naples" (*Tmp*. I.ii.435). No such transformation is possible in the world of *Richard III*, where inheritance turns into brother against brother. Rossiter points out how elsewhere death at Richard's hands is falling "Into the fatal bowels of the deep" (Hastings at III.iv.101), or being wrecked in "a desp'rate bay of death" (Queen Elizabeth at IV.iv.233), or falling "Into the blind cave of eternal night" (Richard's threat about Stanley's son, at V.iii.62).[18] The incredible resonance—beyond full rationalization—of Shakespeare's handling of such fundamental imagery appears in the fact that a version is used by the questing brother in *The Comedy of Errors*, in the passage already emphasized: "like a drop of water / That in the ocean . . . / confounds himself" (I.ii.35–37). But the raft of

---

17. Wolfgang Clemen, *A Commentary on Shakespeare's "Richard III"*, trans. Jean Bonheim (London: Methuen, 1968), p. 73.
18. *Angel with Horns*, pp. 11–12.

comedy and romance floats him through to mother, father, and brother.

In *Macbeth* Shakespeare brings together in his protagonist what he keeps separate in *Richard III*—the sort of visionary torment by conscience in Clarence's dream, and the murderous energies which in Richard are distanced as stage villainy. There is also displacement of sexuality into violence as the great tragic villain responds to hopes from witches and demands from a witchlike wife. Macbeth's guilt centers on the gracious Duncan, the destruction of his kingly fatherhood. Clarence's guilt—through the givens of the historical situation and Shakespeare's way of working it up with Richard as the agent of his brother's actual punishment—does not involve a father; it is the legacy of violence on behalf of his brother Edward:

> The first that there did greet my stranger soul
> Was my great father-in-law, renowned Warwick,
> Who spake aloud, "What scourge for perjury
> Can this dark monarchy afford false Clarence?"
> And so he vanish'd. Then came wand'ring by
> A shadow like an angel, with bright hair
> Dabbled in blood, and he shriek'd out aloud,
> "Clarence is come—false, fleeting, perjur'd Clarence,
> That stabb'd me in the field by Tewkesbury:
> Seize on him, Furies, take him unto torment!"
>
> (I.iv.48–57)

Stephen Booth quotes Clarence's final lines to describe our experience when we "wake" from the poetic action of the more powerful sonnets:[19]

> I, trembling, wak'd, and for a season after
> Could not believe but that I was in hell,
> Such terrible impression made my dream.
>
> (lines 61–63)

In the great lines of the dream narrative, there is poetic density, fusions by sounds and rhythm, comparable to the Sonnets: the chiming vowel sounds spoken by "great Warwick"—"What scourge for perjury / Can this dark monarchy afford false Clarence." Similar physical reechoing continues, at a higher pitch, in the shriek of the "shadow like an angel, with bright hair."

19. Stephen Booth, *An Essay on Shakespeare's Sonnets* (New Haven: Yale University Press, 1969), pp. 167–68.

Clarence's account reaches to a depth of feeling and imaginative power beyond anything else in the play. The older brother's fear of a younger brother is realized with a fullness and an inwardness excluded by the sharply rendered outlines that hold Richard's fratricidal drive at a distance. Shakespeare's more limited imaginative participation in Richard's role is consistent with Richard's being a younger brother, dedicated to destroying older brothers, whom he sees merely as obstacles, objects of contempt and resentment. The lack of inwardness in the characterization suggests that Shakespeare, himself the eldest son in a family that included three younger brothers, imagines Richard from the outside, on the model of an external menace, an agent of fear at deep levels of the poet's sensibility, but not an inner potentiality. For the poet to endow Richard with many of his own powers seems on the face of it inconsistent. But at a deeper level, it makes sense to fear in a sibling what one relies on in oneself to be winning.

I have emphasized that the dramatist endows the protagonist with the potential disruptive power of his theater and with his genius for language, inviting the audience to identify with Richard in his self-conscious theatricality. Rossiter observes that Richard's role as an actor poses a serious question about the "*power* that would be in the hands of an actor consummate enough to make (quite literally) 'all the world a stage' and to work on humanity by the perfect simulation of every feeling."[20] This is one way of putting what I have been considering as the disruptive potential of theatrical aggression, of turning acting into action. Shakespeare converts the traditional tyrant figure into a "ruthless, demonic comedian" (p. 21); Rossiter's point is that the comic makes possible Richard's (and our) participation in destructive-heroic energy such as we get in the major tragedies.[21] In those tragedies we again get figures

---

20. *Angel with Horns*, p. 16.
21. Instead of writing "moral history" in *Richard III*, Shakespeare moved "toward writing *comic history*. The former would never have taken him to tragedy; the latter paradoxically did. Look the right way through the cruel-comic side of Richard and you glimpse Iago. Look back at him through his energy presented as evil, and you see Macbeth" (*Angel with Horns*, p. 22). In *Shakespeare and the Problem of Meaning* (Chicago: University of Chicago Press, 1981), Norman Rabkin sees *Richard III* as "the play in which Shakespeare discovers tragedy. . . . Shakespeare's Richard is both terrifying and like later tragic heroes—Macbeth in particular—because he is motivated not by the ambition of a Claudius or of his own materialistic father, but by a self-destructive and mysterious yearning which drives him to his glory and his death" (p. 84).

who, like Richard, dominate audiences with an imaginative force surpassing that of the characters around them. Disruptive wit and playing within the play give Hamlet his special superiority and Iago his insinuating command; Macbeth's heroism is against all moral odds, like Richard's. But in each of these cases the energies are galvanized by relation to a father or a male figure of authority whose identity the protagonist tries to take over for himself. There is no such figure of authority in *Richard III*. The protagonist is conceived (literally and imaginatively) as a mother's son, effectually without a father, despite the prominence of his father in the Henry VI plays. Edward is only a brother; we glimpse possible royalty in his son's boyish talk of imitating Caesar's undying fame, but it is undercut at once by Richard's aside, "So wise so young, they say do never live long" (III.i.79).

No feeling of royal dignity colors Richard after his accession, such as Macbeth partly achieves despite all the blood. Richard no sooner mounts his throne than he is asking "But shall we wear these glories for a day?" (IV.ii.5). Brother rivalry is continued, in effect, one generation down: "Shall I be plain? I wish the bastards dead" (IV.ii.18). Once he has achieved the empty crown, and the murder of the princes is a foregone conclusion, the play's dynamic structure of dread, and fulfillment of dread, is no longer at work. Richard has no heroic quality as he moves, in total isolation, and with increasingly uncertain control, to a tyrant's fall. After one last display of his histrionic power in wooing Elizabeth through her mother, the action is largely political and military. By contrast with the complete fusion of family and political action in the mature tragedies, something like a geological fault between the two comes to the surface as *Richard III* ends.

Shakespeare, like Marlowe, confronts ceremonial and ritual organization with experience that the new drama understands as historically and psychologically determined. But unlike Marlowe, Shakespeare feels allegiance to his society. In *Richard III* this allegiance carries with it elements of the traditional Elizabethan affirmation of divine purpose shaping history toward Tudor ascendency. *Richard III* pulls in two directions. It presents the disruptive and subversive—Richard's savage play and the web of curses as they shape the action—in historical and psychological perspective centered in familial tensions; the restoration of order is by ritual, which is presumed to reestablish ceremony. The combination does not fully work. The stress one feels in the work reflects the incongruity between the historical and ceremonial perspectives on the events in the play. In later plays, the opposition of these perspectives will be understood ironically, with the need for ritual meaning grounded in absolutist assumptions set against an action shaped throughout by the contingencies and limitations of historical experience. But one must add, finally, that Shakespeare's ideal of a gracious, organic society, not canceled by his ability to see through to the sources of conflict within it, will give his art its unequaled fullness, pathos, and comic and tragic intensity.

5

Titus Andronicus: Abortive Domestic Tragedy

Designed in obvious imitation of Kyd's *Spanish Tragedy*, *Titus Andronicus* has an aged, worthy pillar of social piety, who suffers outrage to his children, is driven to desperate, extravagant grief and protest, "takes false shadows for true substances" (III.ii.80) under the intolerable pressure of feeling, and finally, by turning dramatic fiction into physical action, achieves outrageous revenge. Much of the play is constructed with considerable dramatic skill and written with truly astounding verbal and imaginative energy. Shaping the whole is mythopoeic power which, far from being deficient, is too strong for the structure as developed. Because motives remarkably similar to those handled in *King Lear* are projected in symbolic action for which there is no adequate social matrix, there can be no control by ironic recognition, no clarification of what these motives mean as they are expressed in relation to a plausible community whose stability they disrupt. *Titus Andronicus* fails, by contrast with *The Spanish Tragedy* (let alone *King Lear*), because there is in effect no larger social world within which the outrage takes place, no ongoing business of state and private life within which the isolation and impotence of the injured hero can be presented, in the way that Hieronimo's desperate, helpless isolation is conveyed. The revenge motive as a struggle for vindication of what is at the core of society is only formally present in *Titus Andronicus*.

The limitation of *The Spanish Tragedy* lies in the fact that we have to take Hieronimo's emotions, his total absorption in Horatio, as given, and attend to the beautifully clear way this bond interacts with circumstances that develop in the ongoing social and political reality. We cannot know what the deeper roots of Hieronimo's attachment to Horatio are; Kyd's art does not go down or back to the level at which so nearly monomaniacal a dependence could be understood. In *Titus Andronicus* the circumstances are nearly absurd, while motives are explored far beyond the capacity of the plot to socialize them. From the outset, all that is artistically realized is family piety and pride concentrated in the aged hero's egotism. Shakespeare multiplies the outrages done to Titus by the destruction of two sons, not just one, by the useless sacrifice of Titus's hand, and by creating in the raped and mutilated Lavinia an always present, walking version of Hieronimo's murdered son, Horatio. The result is a father-daughter situation where total sympathy is demanded for an incestuous relationship expressed as suffering and violence. Those who commit the outrages are figures in whom sexual potency is fused with violence: Rape and Murder in the persons of Tamora's sons; Tamora herself, the overpowering Queen of the Goths; and her exotic lover, the Moor Aaron, to whom she bears a black child, and who is the arch-contriver of the villainies. The revenge is to turn nurturance into its opposite, to make "that strumpet, your unhallowed dam, / Like to the earth swallow her own increase" (V.ii.190–91).

Shakespeare finds dramatic equivalents for social realities much earlier in his comedies and histories. We have seen that in *The Comedy of Errors* an important part of the success of the farce is the author's skill in creating as a setting for the play's confusions an ongoing, credible mercantile world. He brings the whole family constellation into play by framing the farcical action with the romantic separation and final reunion of his twins' parents. In *A Midsummer Night's Dream*, a comedy with a surprising number of similarities in materials and style to *Titus Andronicus*, we can see him finding effectual, native embodiment in folk custom for erotic symbolic action. The early tragedy is abortive in dramatizing eros engulfed in family ties; the comic action of *Dream*, shaped by native, outgoing communal festivity, provides a way of leading eros out of family bonds into nature and its larger rhythms. The series of festive comedies follows; *Romeo and Juliet* starts out as a festive comedy, to turn into a tragedy of young love destroyed by family ties.

In his English history plays, Shakespeare enters on a long discipline in presenting complex social and national action where family ties and motives are seen as crucial. Here the central concern, however, is the nation as a whole, beyond any one destiny. Even in the two histories that center on tragic careers, *Richard III* and *Richard II*, the effort is to dramatize national history moving through and beyond the disruptive fates of their protagonists, though as we have seen, the action of *Richard III* is not fully assimilated to the context of historical destiny the play announces as a way of understanding its own events. Without the experience of writing the histories, Shakespeare could not have written the major tragedies as we have them. For the tragedies (with the partial exception of *Othello*) are histories centered in a new, total way on their individual protagonists. In dramatizing the interplay of individual and national destiny in the English history plays, Shakespeare developed the concept of a hero whose personal fulfillment might also be the consummation of a whole society. In the major tragedies, such concretely felt heroic possibility contributes a crucial part of the substance of tragic loss. *Titus Andronicus* lacks this felt social possibility; without meaning to be only that, it is abortive domestic tragedy.

"O SACRED RECEPTACLE OF MY JOYS"

The young author of *Titus Andronicus* is self-consciously literary. Perhaps partly to show that he does not need to be beautified by borrowing the feathers of university-trained wits, he brings in more than fifty references to Roman literature and its handlings of Greek myth. But he does not succeed in projecting a Roman state, probably not because he could not have done so but because his focus is so intensely on family matters, exalted and outrageous. The first scene is before "the Senate house"; the "Tribunes and Senators" enter "aloft"; Titus is invested with a "palliament" as "candidatus"; his grave brother speaks with large gesture on behalf of "the people of Rome." But the action begins with a family fight between sons of the late Emperor, their factions on the verge of blows over the succession. Then comes solemn ceremonial action as Titus, who with his twenty-five sons has been the terror of the Goths in ten years of war, returns in triumph with the Queen of the Goths and her sons as prisoners. He brings the black coffin of two more sons who are to join twenty-one already buried in the tomb of the Andronici.

The tomb dominates the action and presumably the stage. As it is solemnly opened, Titus directs that his sons be laid in it by their brethren:

> O sacred receptacle of my joys,
> Sweet cell of virtue and nobility,
> How many sons hast thou of mine in store,
> That thou will never render to me more!
> (I.i.92–95)

To balance this, shall we say, "tenderness," the "proudest prisoner of the Goths," the captured Queen Tamora's oldest son, is dragged off for sacrifice "*Ad manes fratrum*" (lines 96, 98), Titus blandly putting aside the passionate, eloquent protest of his mother. This sequence is an aggressive, aggrandizing ceremony, like Tamburlaine's ritual of white, red, and black tents on successive days of a siege, presented as though it were Roman custom, though it was in fact invented for the theater.

Like Lear's ceremony of dividing his territory in a contest of praise, the action progresses steadily, in the service of the egotism of a reverent, paternal protagonist, until it meets with an abrupt, devastating check. Where Lear is making the fatal mistake of giving up political authority, Titus, offered the empire, declines political power, also because of age, and makes the further error of choosing the former Emperor's cruel, weak son Saturninus to rule because he is the eldest. The sudden check in both plays comes over the issue of a daughter's independence. Saturnine, immediately after his election, announces that he will make Titus's daughter his empress. Titus at once agrees and his daughter complies; but Lavinia is already betrothed to Bassianus, the younger son of the former Emperor. When Bassianus steps forward to assert his right, Titus's noble brother, Marcus, and Titus's sons immediately support his claim to Lavinia. As they "convey her hence," the youngest son blocking the father's pursuit, Titus kills his son with a single blow: "What, villain boy, / Barr'st me my way in Rome?" (lines 290–91). One could scarcely imagine a more complete exhibition of oblivious parental egotism buttressed with civic service, ceremony, and pride—nor a more rapid confrontation of it. The oldest son remonstrates, and is rebuked by Titus:

> Nor thou, nor he, are any sons of mine,
> My sons would never so dishonor me.
> Traitor, restore Lavinia to the Emperor.
> (lines 294–96)

To cap it all, the new Emperor, who in asking for Lavinia seems to have tried to use his sudden new power merely to take away his brother's betrothed, no longer wants her:

> Was none in Rome to make a stale
> But Saturnine? Full well, Andronicus,
> Agree these deeds with that proud brag of thine,
> That saidst I begg'd the empire at thy hands.
> (lines 304–7)

Asserting his independence, he decides on the spot to marry the Queen of the Goths—a woman with grown sons, old enough to be his mother, as she makes clear in promising that she "will a hand-maid be to his desires, / A loving nurse, a mother to his youth" (lines 331–32). All the Andronici then plead with embittered Titus to let them bury in the sacred family tomb the son he has killed. His brother finally gains reluctant consent: "Well, bury him, and bury me the next" (line 386).

Up to this point, this opening scene is dramatically very well made, despite language that is frequently lame or merely cere-monial. Titus counting up sons dead in Rome's service is a male version of Volumnia counting up wounds on Coriolanus: "For two and twenty sons I never wept, / Because they died in honor's lofty bed" (III.i.10–11). His sons and the tomb provide for Titus a kind of family relationship that does without a wife as effectually as Volum-nia's does without a husband. The tomb is in effect a womb of death—in which he takes deep satisfaction! The strongest poetry in the act is in these first lines addressed to the "sacred receptacle" and the liturgy of committal, which he speaks as the coffin is placed in it:

> In peace and honor rest you here, my sons,
> Rome's readiest champions, repose you here in rest,
> Secure from worldly chances and mishaps!
> Here lurks no treason, here no envy swells,
> Here grow no damned drugs, here are no storms,
> No noise, but silence and eternal sleep.
> In peace and honor rest you here, my sons!
> (I.i.150–56)

The only verbal remonstrance to the death-directed tendency in all this piety is given by Tamora as she pleads against the sacrifice of her son:

> O, if to fight for king and commonweal
> Were piety in thine, it is in these.
> Andronicus, stain not thy tomb with blood!
> Wilt thou draw near the nature of the gods?
> Draw near them then in being merciful.
> (lines 114–18)

Titus overrules her eloquent and cogent protest with the blandness of an official explaining to a homeowner that the throughway must go through: "Patient yourself, madam, and pardon me" (line 121). It is clear that in a draft or earlier version the sacrifice was merely referred to as having happened; to dramatize it vividly enforces the motive for the Queen's later remorseless vengeance.[1]

It also opens up a perspective on Titus's ritual—"cruel, irreligious piety" (line 130), as she calls it—which the play completely fails to pursue. The ceremonial lynching of an enemy who might otherwise be a twin—an "enemy twin," as René Girard would phrase it—is necessary to maintain the crucial *difference* on which kinship ties are based.[2] The scapegoat ritual is necessary, the surviving sons must drag Alarbus off to "hew his limbs till they be clean consum'd" (line 129), to express potential hostility *among the Andronici*, which must be repressed if their total solidarity in family piety is to be maintained. But neither the opening scene nor the play reaches this latent motive—as *Macbeth* will later, where the violence of the heroic defender of Scottish society turns inward against its king.[3]

The opening scene abruptly leaves behind the division within the Andronici, by an exceedingly awkward transition. After all but Titus have joined in putting Mutius in the tomb, saying together, "He lives in fame, that died in virtue's cause," Marcus turns to Titus as if nothing had happened:

1. In the first quarto, Marcus's opening summary tells us that Titus has returned "bearing his valiant sons / In coffins from the field," and adds: "and at this day / To the monument of that Andronici / Done sacrifice of expiation, / And slain the noblest prisoner of the Goths." Sylvan Barnet comments in his edition (*The Signet Classic Shakespeare*): "These lines, omitted from the second and third quartos and from the Folio, are inconsistent with the ensuing action, in which Alarbus is sacrificed; perhaps Shakespeare neglected to cancel them in the manuscript after deciding to make Alarbus' execution part of the action."

2. In *Violence and the Sacred*, tr. Patrick Gregory (Baltimore: Johns Hopkins University Press, 1977), René Girard argues that a society uses its ritual forms, most notably sacrifice and derivative rites that carry on the logic of sacrifice, to reconfirm the differences, within itself and between it and other societies, upon which it is founded. For the mythic mind, "Any violent effacement of differences, even if initially restricted to a single pair of twins, reaches out to destroy a whole society" (pp. 63–64). "Tragedy tends to restore violence to mythological themes. It in part fulfills the dire forebodings primitive men experience at the sight of twins. It spreads pollution abroad and multiplies the mirror images of violence. . . . If the tragic poet touches upon the violent reciprocity underlying all myths, it is because he perceives these myths in a context of weakening distinctions and growing violence. His work is inseparable, then, from a new sacrificial crisis" (p. 65).

3. In "The Early Scenes of *Macbeth*: Preface to a New Interpretation," *ELH* 47 (1980): 1–31, Harry Berger, Jr., makes the telling point that this inward turning of violence is demanded by "the general psycho-structural dilemma of Scotland" as Shakespeare understands it in this play: "'revolt against the king' is simply another name for Scottish policy, and the killing of the king may be a recurrent feature of the political process by which the kingdom periodically rids itself of the poison accumulating within it as a result of normal institutional functions" (pp. 30, 24).

MARCUS: My lord, to step out of these dreary dumps,
How comes it that the subtile Queen of Goths
Is of a sudden thus advanc'd in Rome?
TITUS: I know not, Marcus, but I know it is. . . .
Is she not then beholding to the man
That brought her for this high good turn so far?
Yes, and will nobly him remunerate.
(lines 390–94, 396–98)

Of course the queen, who remembers her dead son though Titus apparently does not, repays him, not nobly but in kind, thrice over and more. As the scene ends she smooths things over, dissuading her new, young husband from acting on his resentment against his younger brother, now married to Lavinia, and Titus. "Yield at entreats," she tells him in aside, "and then let me alone, / I'll find a day to massacre them all" (lines 449–50). Her day comes immediately, in the extraordinary second act, during a hunt in a wood outside Rome, to which Titus has credulously invited the newly married couples.

Tamora and her illicit lover, Aaron the Moor, are now the villainous root of all evil, her two surviving sons the agents. By Aaron's contrivance and her encouraging presence, her sons Chiron and Demetrius stab the Emperor's brother and throw his body in a pit, then drag off Lavinia to rape her, cut out her tongue, and lop off her hands. Decoyed by Aaron, two of Titus's three remaining sons are brought to the edge of the pit; left alone, they fall into it in an inexplicable, half-mesmerized way. Then Aaron brings the Emperor to discover them in it and so convict them of the murder of his brother. Their execution follows in the next act. Titus pleads in vain for his sons and is tricked into sacrificing one of his hands, on the promise that they will be spared. When the mutilated Lavinia has been brought before grieving Titus by his brother Marcus, a messenger brings the heads of his two sons and "thy hand, in scorn to thee sent back" (III.i.237). Titus turns from remonstrance and complaint to ask "which way shall I find Revenge's cave?" (III.i.270).

One is tempted to dismiss all this bizarre violence as "mere melodrama." It is melodrama to the extent that the *particular circumstances and things done* are not motivated in such a way that we can understand them fully in social terms. A general motivation is provided in the injury done Tamora at the outset. But Aaron, the prime mover in these opening scenes, is a stock stage villain who tells us so with zest: "O how this villainy / Doth fat me with the very thoughts of it!" (III.i.202–3). We can understand what happens, however, when we see it as sexual potency conceived of only as violence and injury. On the one side, which the play from now on makes our side, there is family loyalty, centering on vertical relationship to Titus and, for a short time, on the chaste marriage of Lavinia and Bassianus, soon destroyed. On the other side, all the force is in illicit sexuality conceived and expressed as domination and violence. The sexually potent older couple forgo amorous delights proposed by Tamora to enjoy vicariously the sexual violence they abet in Demetrius and Chiron. Marcus and Titus, on their side, vicariously suffer the sexual violation of Lavinia.

The story Shakespeare seems to have dramatized sets up the situation in comprehensible historical and social terms as the infiltration of the Roman court by barbarians.[4] In the surviving eighteenth-century version of it, the opening chapters describe how Titus and his twenty-five sons raised a siege of Rome, winning the gratitude of Emperor and people; how they fought continual wars and killed the King of the Goths. But "those barbarous People still encreasing in their Numbers," the Emperor, in order to make peace, marries the Queen of the Goths, with the condition that "in case he should die without Issue, her Sons might succeed in the Empire." Her hostility to Titus is *politically* motivated, for "he opposed this very much, as did many other; knowing, through the Emperor's weakness, that she being an imperious Woman, and of a hauty Spirit, would govern him as she pleased, and enslave the noble Empire to Strangers" (p. 38). She banishes Titus with the help of the Goths she puts in office, but when a rising of the people forces the recall of their "Deliverer," she must plot her revenge "more secretly" (p. 39).

Of course there may have been another version of the story, which Shakespeare used. But his omission of all the reasonable political motivation for the violence is consistent with his imaginative design. The prose tale has nothing about the rivalry of a dead Emperor's sons, no reference to a tomb of the Andronici (Titus is *saddened* by the loss of sons in battle), no marriage of a young, newmade Emperor to the older Queen. Lavinia there is betrothed to the son and natural heir of the Emperor by a former marriage, whom he dearly loves; the Queen arranges for her sons to kill him to pro-

---

4. *The History of Titus Andronicus*, in *Sources*, vol. 6, pp. 34–44. "This work," Bullough judges, a chapbook "printed in mid-eighteenth century, probably goes back to a sixteenth-century original, . . . and may well represent a major source of the play" (p. 7).

tect their prospects of inheriting. The Queen in the story does have "a Moor as revengeful as herself." (When she gives birth to "a Blackmoor Child," she mollifies the aggrieved Emperor by "telling him it was conceived by Force of Imagination" [p. 39]!) The Moor and her two sons invite the Emperor's son to hunt in the forest, shoot him through the back with a poisoned arrow, and throw him into a deep pit dug for the purpose. Titus's sons soon join the murdered prince in the pit after Lavinia, "her heart misgiving her of some Treachery," has persuaded them to search for her husband (p. 40). The tricking of Titus out of his hand and sending it to him with his dead sons follows in the same brief chapter.

The rape and mutilation of Lavinia form a separate, subsequent episode. The Moor, observing that "she shunned all Company, retiring to Woods and Groves" to grieve the loss of her husband, informs "the Queen's two Sons, who, like the wicked Elders and the chaste Susanna, had long Time burned in Lust, yet knew her Virtues were proof against all Temptations, and therefore it could not be obtained but by Violence" (p. 42). There is no reference to Ovid or Philomela; the daughter reveals the identity of the ravishers without delay by writing with "a Wand between her Stumps" (p. 43). Titus's response is described, however, in a way that at once recalls Kyd's Hieronimo. Before he knows the villains' names, his "Grief . . . was so great, that no Pen can write or Words express; much ado they had to restrain him from doing Violence to himself" (p. 42). Afterwards he vowed revenge, "feigned himself distracted, and went raving about the City, shooting Arrows towards Heaven, as in Defiance, calling to Hell for Vengeance . . . ; and though his Friends required Justice of the Emperor against the Ravishers, yet could they have no Redress, he rather threatening them, if they insisted on it" (p. 43).

This description could suggest to a young dramatist that he had found material to match or outdo *The Spanish Tragedy*. *Titus Andronicus* dramatizes its protagonist's responses as described here in the story, except that Titus does not contemplate suicide, as Hieronimo does repeatedly, and there is no appeal to the Emperor for justice. Perhaps because of the disciplined military character of Shakespeare's injured old man he could not be shown in the Cave of Despair, toying with its dagger and noose; in any case, why reduplicate Kyd? The void of legitimate political power, established at the outset by choosing to open with sibling rivalry for the throne, excluded the possibility of dramatizing appeals to a ruler for justice such as we get in "Justice, O justice for Hieronimo," shouted out from the sidelines of the royal presence. Titus can only shoot his arrows to Jove and Mars. But Shakespeare wholeheartedly takes up the challenge to dramatize "grief so great, that no Pen can write or Words express."

MARCUS: O brother, speak with possibility,
And do not break into these deep extremes.
TITUS: Is not my sorrow deep, having no bottom?
Then be my passions bottomless with them!
MARCUS: But yet let reason govern thy lament.
TITUS: If there were reason for these miseries,
Then into limits could I bind my woes:
When heaven doth weep, doth not the earth o'erflow?
If the winds rage, doth not the sea wax mad,
Threat'ning the welkin with his big-swoll'n face?
And wilt thou have a reason for this coil?
I am the sea; hark how her sighs doth blow!
She is the weeping welkin, I the earth.
(III.i.214–26)

There is intense interest, as with Kyd, in turning passive suffering into active pressure of language on its limits as an agency through which the self negotiates relationship to the world. Shakespeare is more conscious of the process, as witness Marcus's remonstrances here. The moderate brother makes a similar comment in the next scene, where Titus mangles a dead fly after Marcus has suggested that, being black, it is like black Aaron:

TITUS: Give me thy knife, I will insult on him,
Flattering myself as if it were the Moor, . . .
There's for thyself, and that's for Tamora.
Ah, sirrah!
Yet I think we are not brought so low,
But that between us we can kill a fly
That comes in likeness of a coal-black Moor.
MARCUS: Alas, poor man, grief hath so wrought on
him,
He takes false shadows for true substances.
(III.ii.71–72, 74–80)

The self-conscious interest in displaced, projected images is like that of *A Midsummer Night's Dream*. Theseus's famous skeptical discussion of the process includes "the lunatic" as well as "the lover and the poet" among those whose "shaping fantasies . . . apprehend / More than cool reason ever comprehends" (V.i.5–6).

Titus's distraction does not actually reach the point of lunacy—it is more under the control of "as if" than Hieronimo's in its deep extremes: "as if it were the Moor." Theseus's madman "sees more devils than vast hell can hold" (V.i.9). Titus does not need to imagine devils, provided as he is with Tamora and the Moor to stab at. *Titus Andronicus* makes subjective projection by its hero less necessary (the rationalist perspective of the whole is reflected in Aaron's saying "if there be devils, would I were a devil" [V.i.147]). But the interest in the process of taking fiction for fact and fact for fiction is carried to an extreme in Tamora's final charade, when she relies on Titus's lunacy to make him believe she is in fact "Revenge, sent from below / To join with him and right his heinous wrongs" (V.ii.3–4). Titus is not taken in but pretends to be, reversing the way Kyd's finale works: where Hieronimo turns what is taken for playacting into actual killing of the villain, here the villains' playacting is seen through and made the means for actually trapping them. Tamora disguised as Revenge, and her two sons got up as Murder and Rapine, are utterly implausible, as Titus makes clear in sardonically pretending to be taken in:

> Good Lord, how like the Empress' sons they are!
> And you, the Empress! but we worldly men
> Have miserable, mad, mistaking eyes.
>
> (V.ii.64–66)

It is great fun to take off into the wild blue yonder of literalized allegory, a fitting liberation of the previous pressure of Titus's invention trying to deal with the actual horror. It permits wit to have free play, however crude. When Tamora, incredibly credulous, leaves her allegorized sons behind, promising to return for a banquet of reconciliation, Titus can keep up the joke as his friends emerge to help him:

> TITUS: Know you these two?
> PUBLIUS: The Empress' sons I take them, Chiron, and Demetrius.
> TITUS: Fie, Publius, fie, thou art too much deceiv'd.
> The one is Murder, and Rape is the other's name:
> And therefore bind them, gentle Publius. . . .
> Oft have you heard me wish for such an hour,
> And now I find it, therefore bind them sure,
> And stop their mouths if they begin to cry. [*Exit.*]
> CHIRON: Villains, forbear, we are the Empress' sons. . . .
> *Enter Titus Andronicus with a knife and Lavinia with a basin.*
>
> (V.ii.153–57, 159–62, 165s.d.)

In the source, there is of course no imaginative charade: the sons are surprised in an ambush while hunting in the woods, "and binding them to a Tree, . . . Andronicus cut their Throats whilst Lavinia, by his Command, held a Bowl between her Stumps to receive the Blood." [5]

"AND WORSE THAN PROGNE I WILL BE REVENG'D"

But what *is* the "reason for this coil"? In dropping all the political and dynastic considerations in the source, Shakespeare does without the sort of complex interpenetration of social with family and sexual action which he could control so marvelously later. Instead he shapes his material in symbolic, mythopoeic ways that ask for understanding, on the deeper levels, *only* in poetic or symbolic terms. Titus has a long speech of recapitulation and justification as he prepares to kill Tamora's sons:

> You know your mother means to feast with me. . . .
> Hark, villains, I will grind your bones to dust,
> And with your blood and it I'll make a paste,
> And of the paste a coffin I will rear,
> And make two pasties of your shameful heads,
> And bid that strumpet, your unhallowed dam,
> Like to the earth swallow her own increase.
> This is the feast that I have bid her to,
> And this the banket she shall surfeit on,
> For worse than Philomel you us'd my daughter,
> And worse than Progne I will be reveng'd.
> (V.ii.184, 186–95)

Titus's strongest line here echoes with Sonnet 19: "And make the earth devour her own sweet brood." Although there are constant references in the play to Ovid's Philomel and Procne and their revenge on Tereus, with a scene, on the whole quite effective, in which Lavinia dumbly takes up "Ovid's *Metamorphosis*" and "tosseth" it until she finds "the tragic tale" (IV.i.41, 47), the outrageous revenge in the play is directed primarily at *maternal* sexuality, conceived and represented symbolically as a ruthless, devouring power.

In Ovid we have the revenge of two women against the ruthless *male* violation of femininity. Procne's decision to kill her son is not

5. *Sources*, vol. 6, p. 43.

meditated but comes suddenly as she is thinking of other revenges: burning Tereus's palace with him in it, pulling out his tongue, putting out his eyes, castrating him:

> While *Progne* hereunto
> Did set hir minde, came *Itys* in, who taught hir what to doe.
> She staring on him cruelly, said, Ah, how like thou art
> Thy wicked father.[6]

The ensuing struggle between her maternal feeling and her overwhelming sense of outrage is very moving—and appalling. Looking right at the pleading child, she stabs him, Philomel cuts his throat, and the two women set about the women's work of preparing a solemn ritual meal for husband and wife alone together. The tale in Ovid is associated with women's ritual protest in the Bacchic rites. Informed of the outrage to her sister by the secret woven message, Procne frees her while running wild in the woods in animal disguise. The meal itself has a terrible immediacy in Ovid: Philomel reveals the boy's whereabouts by throwing Itys's bloody head in his father's face; Tereus screams, retches to cast his bowels out, seizes his sword, and pursues the women, only to find them turning into birds.

Shakespeare's handling of the final meal is ceremonial and theatrical: "Trumpets sounding, enter Titus like a cook, placing the dishes" (V.iii.25s.d.), sets up the situation almost as a joke. The horror of the meal as it takes place is not in verbal focus, for as soon as Tamora has tasted the food, Titus kills Lavinia, invoking the precedent of Virginius; Tamora has not time to respond after she is told that she has fed on her sons, for Titus immediately kills her, and is killed in turn by Saturninus, and he by Titus's son Lucius. Not only does Titus, as vindictive father, destroy the sexually voracious, alien mother figure in a reversal of the sexual roles of the Philomel story; along with his extroverted revenge against Tamora, his introverted erotic investment in his disfigured daughter reaches a climax when he destroys Lavinia, whose care and feeding he has taken over since her rape and mutilation:

> Die, die, Lavinia, and thy shame with thee,
> And with thy shame thy father's sorrow die!
> (V.iii.46–47)

---

6. Golding's translation, Bk. VI, lines 785–88; *Sources*, vol. 6, p. 56.

The masculine tie to the feminine as a potential source of vulnerability is as vital to the play as is masculine fear and violence toward woman as aggressor.

What is at work in this strange action becomes clearer if, following the talion logic backwards, we consider the symbolic content of the injuries done to Titus and his family. Shakespeare concentrates in the second act what is strung out in separate episodes in the source story, to make one sustained sequence of horrors in the woods, around the pit as a central symbol. The Moor, who has been only a silent presence in Act I, opens Act II with a triumphant salute to Tamora's elevation to power, and to his power through her and over her.

> Then, Aaron, arm thy heart, and fit thy thoughts,
> To mount aloft with thy imperial mistress,
> And mount her pitch, whom thou in triumph long
> Hast prisoner held, fett'red in amorous chains,
> And faster bound to Aaron's charming eyes
> Than is Prometheus tied to Caucasus.
>
> (II.i.12–17)

The assumption of these lines, that sexual potency is a cruel, dominating power, is to be acted out in what follows. Aaron goes on to relish the prospect that he will "wanton with this queen" while she in turn "will charm Rome's Saturnine, / And see his shipwrack and his commonweal's" (II.i.21, 23–24). The boy Emperor has married a woman not only old enough to be his mother, but who also comes equipped with a ruthless phallic lover intent with her on the young man's destruction. The play handles the infiltration of the Goths entirely in these sexual-family terms, with no suggestion of other barbarian qualities in them, and nothing of the "Roman" in Rome but military virtue and family loyalty.

Next in the wood, "Enter Chiron and Demetrius braving" (II.i.25 s.d.). What they are braving about is which brother should have Lavinia—Shakespeare has moved their lusting after her up from the period after her husband's death in the story version to the morning after her wedding and made it over into a second dramatization of sibling rivalry! It is a very homey exchange:

> CHIRON: Demetrius, thou dost overween in all, . . .
> 'Tis not the difference of a year or two . . .
> I am as able and as fit as thou
> To serve, and to deserve my mistress' grace. . . .

DEMETRIUS: Why, boy, although our mother, unadvis'd,
Gave you a dancing-rapier by your side.
They draw.
(II.i.29, 31, 33–34, 38–39)

Aaron steps forward, parts them, and brings up the little problem of how they plan to obtain Lavinia, to which Demetrius answers first in Richard III's machismo style, then in the idiom of *A Hundred Merry Tales!*

> She is a woman, therefore may be woo'd,
> She is a woman, therefore may be won,
> She is Lavinia, therefore must be lov'd.
> What, man, more water glideth by the mill
> Than wots the miller of, and easy it is
> Of a cut loaf to steal a shive. . . .
> What, hast not thou full often strook a doe,
> And borne her cleanly by the keeper's nose?
> (lines 82–87, 93–94)

This is the bragging talk of young men loitering about the village. Aaron picks it up as he intervenes, "Why then it seems a certain snatch or so / Would serve your turns" (lines 95–96). He then moves up to greater intensity, using the doe image as he goes through his program for them during the coming hunt. The forest is built up by contrast with the court as a place "Fitted by kind for rape and villainy. / Single you thither then this dainty doe" (lines 116–17).

> There speak, and strike, brave boys, and take your turns, . . .
> And revel in Lavinia's treasury.
> (lines 129, 131)

The young men's response almost ludicrously summarizes the assumption that—beyond poaching—sexual outrage proves manhood: "Thy counsel, lad, smells of no cowardice," says Chiron. The response of his older brother, Demetrius, is elevated into Senecan Latin: "Sit fas aut nefas, . . . Per Stygia, per manes vehor" (lines 132–33, 135).[7]

---

7. Later on, Chiron recognizes verses in Latin sent as a veiled threat by Titus: "O, 'tis a verse of Horace, I know it well, / I read it in the grammar long ago" (IV.ii.22–23). Though the scene is immature art concerned with immaturity, it uses a remarkable range of social experience as well as style, with a sure sense of underlying attitudes. The sexual initiation Aaron is arranging for the boys, even though

The hunt in the woods opens with "a noise with hounds and horns" (II.ii.0.s.d.) and poetry evoking the same dawn mood that ends the night's perplexities in *A Midsummer Night's Dream*. Hopeful, loyal Titus, urging his sons to "attend the Emperor's person carefully" (II.ii.8), directs the huntsmen:

> Uncouple here and let us make a bay,
> And wake the Emperor and his lovely bride.
>   (lines 3–4)

In the comedy, Theseus, about to waken the lovers, says "Uncouple . . . / And mark the musical confusion / Of hounds and echo in conjunction" (*MND* IV.i.107, 110–11).[8] Tamora in the next scene, where she and Aaron are alone, tries to lead him to amorous delights "whilst the babbling echo mocks the hounds / . . . As if a double hunt were heard at once" (II.iii.17, 19). She cites the example of "the wand'ring prince and Dido . . . curtain'd with a counsel-keeping cave" (lines 22, 24). But enclosure will be different in this forest. Aaron brings her back to business:

> Madam, though Venus govern your desires,
> Saturn is dominator over mine:
> What signifies my deadly-standing eye . . . ?[9]
>   (lines 30–32)

The serious business of course is to do in the Andronici and Bassianus: Aaron has already hidden a bag of gold and written a letter to incriminate Titus's sons. But this elaborately and emphatically villainous plotting is really irrelevant to the actual dramatic development; what we watch is sexuality as violence. Bassianus and Lavinia, coming up as the Moor leaves Tamora, taunt her in an exchange that moves through Diana and Actaeon's horns to

> Under your patience, gentle Emperess,
> 'Tis thought you have a goodly gift in horning,

---

they have the intelligence and sensibility of village toughs, does involve breaking through inhibiting moral restraints, plunging through repressive ghosts and hellish anxieties.

8. See also Howard Baker's observation that the poetry of the hunting scenes in *Titus* recalls the poetry of hunting in "Venus and Adonis," in *Induction to Tragedy* (Baton Rouge: Louisiana State University Press, 1939), pp. 135–37.

9. "Faced with the underlying danger of Tamora's seductive sexuality, Aaron," David Willbern writes, "rejects her proposition while simultaneously affirming his own threatened phallic potency." "Rape and Revenge in *Titus Andronicus*," *English Literary Renaissance* 8 (Spring 1978): 166.

And to be doubted that your Moor and you
Are singled forth to try thy experiments. . . .
BASSIANUS: The King my brother shall have notice of this.

(lines 66–69, 85)

The chaste couple's self-righteousness is met by the entrance of
Tamora's sons, for whom she concocts a vivid tale: "These two have
'ticed me hither to this place: / A barren detested vale you see it is"
(lines 92–93). The dreadful pit is first described as she develops a
tall story of threats by Bassianus and Lavinia (in the play nobody
digs the pit—it is just there):

And when they show'd me this abhorred pit,
They told me, here, at dead time of the night,
A thousand fiends, a thousand hissing snakes,
Ten thousand swelling toads, as many urchins,
Would make such fearful and confused cries,
As any mortal body hearing it
Should straight fall mad, or else die suddenly.

(lines 98–104)

Here, she says, they planned to bind her to a "dismal yew" to die,
and called her "foul adulteress, / Lascivious Goth . . . / Revenge
it, as you love your mother's life" (lines 107, 109–10, 114). Demetrius and Chiron at once stab Bassianus: "This is a witness that I
am thy son," says the elder, and the younger again announces that
he is grown up, with "And this for me, struck home to show my
strength" (lines 116–17). As they prepare to drag Lavinia off despite her anguished pleas, Tamora backs them all the way. She will
not consider saving another woman's honor by "a charitable murder," as Lavinia begs: "So should I rob my sweet sons of their
fee. / No, let them satisfice their lust on thee" (lines 179–80).

The two sons of Titus are next led on by Aaron and left at the
brink of the pit. While the bad boys are raping Lavinia offstage, the
good boys, onstage, are swallowed up. Their fall into the pit is ludicrous, viewed with detachment; but the author is working hard to
keep it tragical:

QUINTUS: What, art thou fallen? What subtile hole is this,
Whose mouth is covered with rude-growing briers,
Upon whose leaves are drops of new-shed blood
As fresh as morning dew distill'd on flowers?
A very fatal place it seems to me.

(lines 198–202)

The last line just asks, out of context, for the liberation of burlesque, such as we get in the clown's play of Pyramus and Thisbe: "I
kiss the wall's hole / Not your lips at all" (*MND* V.i.201). But there
can be no such fun with the "subtile hole" in *Titus Andronicus*. Martius, down in it, finds Bassianus "like to a slaughtered lamb,"
visible by the light of his precious ring: "So pale did shine the
moon on Pyramus, / When he by night lay bath'd in maiden blood"
(lines 223, 231–32). Quintus, "surprised with an uncouth fear,"
dares not look down: "ne'er till now / Was I a child to fear I know
not what" (lines 211, 220–21). Martius pleads that his brother help
him "Out of this fell devouring receptacle, / As hateful as Cocytus'
misty mouth."

> QUINTUS: Reach me thy hand, that I may help thee out,
> Or wanting strength to do thee so much good,
> I may be pluck'd into the swallowing womb
> Of this deep pit—
>
> (lines 235–40)

which is exactly what happens, just in time for Aaron to arrive with
the Emperor.

Now it obviously needs no Freud to tell Shakespeare what this
hole is.[10] The difficulty is with the dramatic mode in which he
is working. In a playful dramatic fantasy there would be no difficulty in developing such a symbol. In religious drama there was
Hell's Mouth, which Marlowe could use effectively at the end of
Dr. Faustus. Shakespeare here is developing a symbolism that *might*
be religious, but in resolutely non-Christian terms (there is I think
no Christian expression in the whole play); he is sticking strictly to
a symbolism he can use ad hoc to express family and sexual relationships. Such symbolism in the mature tragedies, where it is
placed in a fabric of familial and social action and characters, is
comprehensible, whether or not we stop over its physiological reference. Lear in his mad alienation can be explicit:

> Down from the waist they are Centaurs,
> Though women all above;
> But to the girdle do the gods inherit,

---

10. "Here is Freud's plenty," as David Willbern proclaims in response to Tamora's
account of the pit, which will "assume its central and over-determined symbolic significance as vagina, womb, tomb, and mouth, and all those 'snakes' and 'urchins'
(hedgehogs or goblins) and 'swelling toads' may plausibly be imagined as grotesquely distorted phallic threats." "Rape and Revenge," p. 169.

Beneath is all the fiends': there's hell, there's darkness,
There is the sulphurous pit—

(IV.vi.124–28)

and then go on in the next breath to recognize that his vision is unwholesome fantasy: "Give me an ounce of civet; good apothecary, / Sweeten my imagination" (lines 130–31).

It is the coherence of such symbolism as the pit, albeit in this isolated, unaccounted-for way, which makes *Titus Andronicus* something besides melodrama—indeed the work of genius, albeit an artistic failure to the taste of later generations. It also explains, I think, why the play is not only unsuccessful but so painful that most criticism has turned a blind eye to much of its content. C. B. Young, for example, commenting on Ravenscroft's version (designed to improve what its redactor called "rather a heap of Rubbish than a Structure") found that one of the "small improvements" the late Restoration rendition did make was that in it, Quintus and Martius, "instead of senselessly tumbling into the pit, . . . are found gazing into it after having been decoyed into the spot more naturally."[11] Shakespeare, however, has *very* firm structure motivating that fall symbolically; but it is too unmediated and so too troubling for Young to recognize it. From the distance of the celibate Friar's meditation in *Romeo and Juliet*, the key structural idea can be comfortably summarized: "The earth that's nature's mother is her tomb; / What is her burying grave, that is her womb" (II.iii.9–10). In *Titus*, the all-too-literal tomb-womb of Act I is matched by the devouring womb-tomb of Act II and the turning of the tables as Tamora devours her own sons in Act V.

Our difficulties with such an episode as this need to be considered in the light of the fact that *Titus Andronicus* was a successful play in its time, as witnessed by the three quartos, 1594, 1600, 1611, and by Jonson's Induction to *Bartholomew Fair* (1614), which pairs *Titus* with *The Spanish Tragedy* as plays whose continued popularity demonstrated the irksome constancy of judgment among unsophisticated playgoers. The fact that the play has never been successful since, until our own violent and symbolically minded time, suggests that its success depended on habits of mind or sensibility that did not survive. Shakespeare in this case was clearly writing for an age, not for all time. The crucial difference is not that Elizabethans

11. C. B. Young, "The Stage History of *Titus Andronicus*," in Cambridge ed., ed. J. Dover Wilson (Cambridge: Cambridge University Press, 1948), p. lxvii.

could tolerate more physical violence than later ages, though that must be a factor. There is just as much violence enacted on the stage in *Lear*, say, as in *Titus*. What we can infer from *Titus*, I think, is a greater habituation to seeing symbolic meaning in violence—or better, to feeling such meaning, consciously or not. Probably many of the play's first enthusiastic spectators came to demand more of the theater as it became more sophisticated; certainly those in later audiences who would still "swear *Ieronimo*, or *Andronicus*, are the best plays" drew Jonson's scorn. In Shakespeare's later work, the human meaning in social action of such violence is more clearly and compellingly conveyed, so that we accept it as we cannot easily accept the regressive erotic brutality in *Titus*.

Acceptance is partly a matter of aesthetic distance, partly the degree of intensity of the magnetic field of meaning established around the violence. The action that begins with Lavinia's entrance, taunted by the Empress's sons, "her hands cut off, and her tongue cut out, and ravish'd" (II.iv.o.s.d.), can be contemplated comfortably from the distance of Theseus's poetry about paternal power in the opening of *A Midsummer Night's Dream*:

> What say you, Hermia? Be advis'd, fair maid.
> To you your father should be as a god;
> One that compos'd your beauties; yea, and one
> To whom you are but as a form in wax,
> By him imprinted, and within his power,
> To leave the figure, or disfigure it.
>
> (I.i.46–51)

There is a frisson for us here, even though "disfigure" is a witty pun, suggesting that a daughter is a trope, as well as a face and a bodily shape. Of course in the comedy the penalty of "the sharp Athenian law" is promptly mitigated from death to entering a nunnery. And in the end—when by the night's accidents in the wood Demetrius has returned to his first love, Helena—the stubborn insistence of Hermia's father on "my consent that she should be your wife" is simply overruled by Theseus. The whole play, meanwhile, has been about imaginative transformations. Helena has wished at the outset that she could be "translated" into Hermia (and in effect she is); Bottom has been "translated" into an ass; and when Snout comes to "disfigure, or to present," Wall, Wall is disfigured back into Snout. *A Midsummer Night's Dream* puts such imaginative process into particularly conscious focus.

Rosalie Colie, in *Shakespeare's Living Art*, shows how Shake-

speare in his most successful works repeatedly translates metaphors back into enactment as events. She is particularly concerned
with his use of traditional tropes: in *Romeo and Juliet* "the spec-
tacular oppositions of the petrarchan rhetoric have been enlarged
into plot, as well as into the emotional and social structure of the
play." In her studies of that play, and notably also of *Othello* and
Antony and Cleopatra, she shows how Shakespeare's process of "un-
metaphoring" (an unhappily negative term) leads to the finding or
refinding of relationships between language and experience, the
"sinking of the conventions back into what, he somehow persuades
us, is 'reality.'" [12] The pit in *Titus Andronicus* is a case where the
common topos of womb and tomb (prominent of course in Christian iconography) does not persuade us that we are encountering
reality. One can contrast Romeo's use of it as he forces his way into
the tomb, the "womb of death" (V.iii.45), of the Capulets.

Lavinia is an "unmetaphored" version of Theseus's trope, a
daughter "disfigured" physically. The disfigurement is carried out,
of course, not by the father who "composed her beauties," but by
enemies, young brutes, and behind them, an overpowering, hostile
maternal force. So Titus is put in a situation of emotional isolation
with Lavinia in which he can experience her ravishment through
grief and protest. The properly poetic and dramatic powers by
which Shakespeare develops this situation are astonishing; in the
enjoyment of them he can envisage extreme human and inhuman
possibilities with a curious equanimity.

A great deal of Shakespeare's earliest work, when it deals with
tragic material—the death of Adonis or the rape of Lucrece, or the
outrages of *Titus Andronicus*—looks open-eyed at things from which
inhibition would ordinarily flinch. In the different mode of his
early histories, again we have situations worked up to poetic or
rhetorical extremes with, one feels, a workmanlike detachment.
Steadily increasing control of the overall design proves to be at
work as we get to know these earliest productions, but developing
from behind the surfaces rather than announcing itself with clear
signposts, as it does later. In the histories there are thematic preoccupations, especially in the area of sexuality and family, for
which he is only gradually finding public forms: *Richard III*, as we
have seen, is a breakthrough. In the narrative poems he is freer,

12. Rosalie Colie, *Shakespeare's Living Art* (Princeton: Princeton University Press, 1974), p. 145.

and to put it mildly, the subjects he chooses and the way he handles them are surprising. He is doing things of his own to traditional subjects and forms, and much of his autonomous artistic satisfaction must have been in that.

He shares with Ovid this equanimity in the enjoyment of active imaginative power. It is as though anything can be contemplated so long as it is being "translated" imaginatively into something else. Frequently in *Titus* the action halts as though it turned into a dumb show while the poetry elaborates it. As Stephen Lacey has shown, the poetry of *Titus Andronicus* frequently moves in this way out from or around a static spectacle.[13] After Demetrius and Chiron have left Lavinia, with cruel, crude taunts at her helplessness without tongue or hands, her uncle Marcus comes on and for forty-seven lines gives voice to what is literally a dumb show:

> Speak, gentle niece: what stern ungentle hands
> Hath lopp'd and hew'd, and made thy body bare
> Of her two branches, those sweet ornaments,
> Whose circling shadows kings have sought to sleep in,
> And might not gain so great a happiness
> As half thy love? Why dost not speak to me?
> Alas, a crimson river of warm blood,
> Like to a bubbling fountain stirred with wind,
> Doth rise and fall between thy rosed lips,
> Coming and going with thy honey breath.
>
> (II.iv.16–25)

What is so troubling here is not only the violence but the loveliness presented with it, the attraction along with revulsion, which is explicitly sexual attraction in the image of the lost hands as "circling shadows kings have sought to sleep in," and sexual also in a subliminal way in the imagery of the mouth as a rising and falling fountain of warm blood.

In a similar but more explicit passage in *Venus and Adonis*, the shocking sight of "the wide wound that the boar had trench'd / In his soft flank" (lines 1052–53) is dealt with at greater length and with more explicitly fanciful elaboration. At first, Venus's eyes withdraw altogether, like the "tender horns" of a snail shrinking "backward in his shelly cave with pain": "So at his bloody view her eyes are fled / Into the deep-dark cabins of her head" (lines

13. Stephen Wallace Lacey, "Structures of Awareness in Dante and Shakespeare" (Ph.D. diss., State University of New York at Buffalo, 1972).

1033–34, 1037–38). The narrative mode here permits a wonderfully flexible, compassionate control of aesthetic distance, control of the *reception* of violence, as in this celebrated stanza where we feel for Venus in feeling with the delicate vulnerability of the snail, "Long after fearing to creep forth again" (line 1036). The narrative mode also permits imaginative suggestions to be left hanging in the neutrality of hypothesis, envisaged without being asserted. So with Venus's fanciful development of the idea that, since wild creatures— lion, tiger, and wolf—all loved Adonis, the boar's violence was actually intended as love:

> "But this foul, grim, and urchin-snouted boar,
> Whose downward eye still looketh for a grave,
> Ne'er saw the beauteous livery that he wore—
> Witness the entertainment that he gave.
>   If he did see his face, why then I know
>   He thought to kiss him, and hath kill'd him so.
>
> "'Tis true, 'tis true, thus was Adonis slain:
> He ran upon the boar with his sharp spear,
> Who did not whet his teeth at him again,
> But by a kiss thought to persuade him there;
>   And nousling in his flank, the loving swine
>   Sheath'd unaware the tusk in his soft groin."
>   (lines 1105–16)

The tentativeness of Venus, trying on one conceit after another, permits the poet to present sexual fantasy shadowed by his poem—that such a late-maturing youth as Adonis is open to homosexual rape—without falsifying its status as fantasy. First the boar is entirely brutal, oblivious, and phallic, with his urchin snout and downward eye. Then his response is imagined as loving: he tries to dissuade Adonis with a kiss, but kills him because nature "pricked [him] out" with "one thing to [the] purpose nothing" (Sonnet 20). Then the aggressive goddess acknowledges: "Had I been tooth'd like him, I must confess, / With kissing him I should have kill'd him first" (lines 1117–18). Yet these disturbing possibilities are presented in a way that is basically playful. A tidy couplet ends the excursus by describing an untidy fall that "stains her face with his congealed blood" (line 1122), and the poem is ready for another elaboration of the new static situation.

By comparison with the flexibility and control in such a passage, one feels that in *Titus* the dramatic medium, incompletely mastered, is getting in the way; or to put it the other way round, that

Shakespeare in *Titus* is using this kind of *aria di bravura* in a way inappropriate to the dramatic mode. But *we* feel this difficulty to a degree that the original audiences well may not have felt it. The enthusiasm for elaborate complaints, or challenges, or vaunts, taking off from a static situation that demands expression, was part of the general excitement in the new theater for the new verse medium and for set speeches doing fine things. The Elizabethan audience was ready to listen to things like Hieronimo's "O eyes, no eyes, but fountains full of tears," or Marcus's leisurely description of Lavinia's missing hands. The dramatist had room for such rhetorical elaboration and for properly poetic development. The whole process is accepted as artificial, in a positive sense. In transforming disfigured Lavinia by figures or tropes, the play is taking imaginative action of the same kind that is eventually pressed beyond credibility altogether in Tamora's figuring herself and her sons as Revenge, Murder, and Rape, leaving Titus the opportunity to disfigure the two murderous rapists back into themselves, and then into a meat pie!

Titus Andronicus makes a special claim for such poetic elaboration of its materials by its emphatic use of classical precedents, especially Ovid.[14] Eugene Waith has suggested that its poetic development of horror has deep affinities to Ovid's imaginative transformations.[15] Violence, in Ovid, "is an emblem of the transformation," which "is itself transformed in the process into an object of interested but somewhat detached contemplation" (p. 43). Waith compares Marcus's description of Lavinia, "which has proved to be the most unpalatable passage in the play," to Ovid's descriptions of violence by extended comparisons: "In every case the visual image is exact and thus the horror more vivid, yet at the same time our minds are turned away from the individual as a whole to a minute contemplation of what has happened to one part of his body" (pp. 47, 42). A process of "abstracting and generalizing" eclipses the individuality of the body subjected to the violence, and "the suffering becomes an object of contemplation" (p. 47). The difficulty, as Waith sees it, is that this technique of description "is a narrative rather than a dramatic device." The change into a bird or a beast comes after "the unendurable emotional state robs the char-

---

14. Howard Baker sets *Titus Andronicus* in a medieval and Renaissance English tradition of adapting Ovid in his *Induction to Tragedy*, pp. 121–26.

15. Eugene Waith, "The Metamorphosis of Violence in *Titus Andronicus*," *Shakespeare Survey* 10 (1957): 39–49.

acter of his humanity and the story ends, so to speak, with a point of exclamation" (p. 47). Although the special emphasis in *Titus* on situations beyond human endurance asks for "the full Ovidian treatment, . . . the final transformation cannot take place. We have the description which almost transforms Lavinia, but in the presence of live actors the poetry cannot perform the necessary magic. The action frustrates, rather than re-enforces, the operation of the poetry" (pp. 47–48).[16]

"THOU MAP OF WOE"

Waith's beautiful essay focuses on the play's formal virtues and problems. But the play's specific erotic content is also a main reason for its difficulty in going on from the symbolic action of the poetry. Violence, after all, is what sexuality turns into when it cannot go on, cannot find properly sexual consummation. As Ovid abundantly testifies, violence is sexuality metamorphosed. Marcus's description of Lavinia repeatedly emphasizes that she has been deprived, not simply of the capacity to communicate the identity of her ravishers, but of means of sexual expression by the use of the hands:

> O, had the monster seen those lily hands
> Tremble like aspen leaves upon a lute,
> And make the silken strings delight to kiss them.
> (II.iv.44–46)

A similar image expresses the diffused eros of Cleopatra's barge:

> the silken tackle
> Swell with the touches of those flower-soft hands,
> That yarely frame the office.
> (*Ant.* II.ii.209–11)

When Marcus finally brings Lavinia to her father, Titus's first response is a rhapsody about her lost hands—and his hands:

---

16. Waith goes on to suggest that to attempt the kind of thing Shakespeare was after in *Titus Andronicus* was in line with sixteenth-century critics' emphasis on "admiration" as the proper effect of tragedy, in the sense of "wonder" or "astonishment." "Marlowe and Chapman each developed what might be called a rhetoric of admiration; one thinks of Marlowe's 'high astounding terms.'" From this perspective, "*Titus Andronicus* is Shakespeare's contribution to a special tragic mode. . . . The hero, in this respect like Tamburlaine or Bussy D'Ambois, is almost beyond praise or blame, an object of admiration" (p. 48).

> Speak, Lavinia, what accursed hand
> Hath made thee handless in thy father's sight? . . .
> Give me a sword, I'll chop off my hands too,
> For they have fought for Rome, and all in vain;
> And they have nurs'd this woe, in feeding life;
> In bootless prayer have they been held up,
> And they have serv'd me to effectless use.
> Now all the service I require of them
> Is that the one will help to cut the other.
>
> (III.i.66–67, 72–78)

When Lucius asks, "Speak, gentle sister, who hath mart'red thee?" Marcus again describes her mouth, its tongue ripped out by hands as yet unknown to Titus's family:

> O, that delightful engine of her thoughts,
> That blabb'd them with such pleasing eloquence,
> Is torn from forth that pretty hollow cage,
> Where like a sweet melodious bird it sung
> Sweet varied notes, enchanting every ear!
>
> (lines 81–86)

David Willbern, writing from a rigorously psychoanalytic vantage point, observes that symbolically Lavinia's mouth is an upward displacement of the female genitals.[17] It is perhaps significant that the full descriptions of the mouth, here and later, are given to Marcus rather than to Titus.

It is striking that Titus anticipates, as a desperate wish, the cutting off of his hand, which follows, initiated by Aaron! Here it expresses a wish to identify with Lavinia, along with the feeling that all the dutiful things he has done with his hands have been ill rewarded. Perhaps subliminally there is also a wish for punishment of sexual misuse of the hands; a psychoanalytic commonplace is the link of the hand with guilt about masturbation associated with Oedipal fantasies centering on the mother. The scene is to end—after the heads of his sons have been presented to Titus, with his severed hand, sacrificed in the promise of saving them—in the almost intolerable grotesquery of

> Come, brother, take a head,
> And in this hand the other will I bear;
> And, Lavinia, thou shalt be employ'd [in these arms];[18]
> Bear thou my hand, sweet wench, between thy teeth.
>
> (lines 279–82)

---

17. "Rape and Revenge in *Titus Andronicus*," pp. 171–72.
18. The bracketed words are omitted by Evans in the *Riverside* text. The quartos

To put his severed hand in her mouth could be the enactment, in a dumb-show way, of sexual fantasy. It is a fantasy so deeply forbidden, yet so baldly and cryptically presented, that a coherent social response is difficult to manage.

One can contrast, in *King Lear*, the control of the subliminal meaning of Gloucester's blinding as castration. Whether one attends to it or not, it is there in the text: "Out, vild jelly!" (III.vii.83). Earlier we have Lear lamenting his injustices with "Old fond eyes, / Beweep this cause again, I'll pluck ye out" (I.iv.301–2), and calling on the storm to "crack nature's moulds, all germains spill at once / That makes ingrateful man!" (III.ii.8–9). Later we have Edgar on his father and Edmund: "The dark and vicious place where thee he got / Cost him his eyes" (V.iii.173–74). But Gloucester's blinding and death point to far more than the "dark and vicious place" of Edmund's begetting, including what Edmund feels to be the vicious familial and social place bequeathed to him by his father's transgression and which lies at the center of *his* motive. Similarly, Lear's rage against his own eyes and his violent denunciation of the procreative process, released in the barren world engendered by Cordelia's banishment, link the tabooed dimension of Lear's love for Cordelia to the whole context of his need for her and hence to the whole imaginative design of the play. In the later tragedy Gloucester cannot see how he has created the circumstances that will lead to his blinding, and Lear cannot recognize the connection between his need and the chaos he brings into the world. In *Titus Andronicus* it is Shakespeare who does not connect the play's abundantly eroticized violence with motives integral to the situation of his protagonist.

The pathos of Lavinia as a wounded human being, which is at times poignantly realized, is conveyed rarely by Titus, but rather by Marcus, or by the grandson Lucius, or by the pathetic pantomime called for from the actor as Lavinia weeps or gestures or seeks to

---

read "in these Armes"; the Folio "in these things." Either version gives the line one foot too many; Dover Wilson omits the last word and substitutes "this" for "these" in the Cambridge edition. He explains that Aldis Wright "conjectured that 'the author, or some other corrector, to soften what must have been ludicrous in representation, wrote "armes" above "teeth" as a substitute for the latter'; that 'the printer of Q1 took "Armes" to belong to the first line'; and finally, that the scribe responsible for F 'made sense of the passage by substituting "things" for "Armes"'" (p. 132). But "armes" can make sense as a conceit that the heads and hand have become the armorial insignia of the Andronici; and the extra syllable can go with a retard in the delivery. Editorial ingenuity is here frankly in the service of the embarrassment which is frequently expressed about this *outré* piece of business.

hide herself, or tries by running after the frightened child, Lucius, to get Ovid's book from him. Titus in response to her keeps turning from her and her mutilated body, her sighs and tears, to himself, his body, his tears. Tears, especially, are made the medium of communication, in intense and elaborate developments of the familiar trope:

> She is the weeping welkin, I the earth . . .
> Then must my earth with her continual tears
> Become a deluge, overflow'd and drown'd.
> (III.i.226, 228–29)

Curiously grotesque but very imaginative passages center on tears as the only way open to the sufferers to act and so gain expression. The above passage continues from "overflow'd and drown'd" with the conceit that Lavinia's tears have become woes inside Titus:

> For why my bowels cannot hide her woes,
> But like a drunkard must I vomit them.
> Then give me leave, for losers will have leave
> To ease their stomachs with their bitter tongues.
> (lines 230–33)

Sitting down at dinner in the next scene, Titus develops a series of conceits on hands, hearts, and tears, which start from the physical gestures of the actors. Marcus is sitting with arms folded in grief, not eating. Titus begins by saying they must eat just enough to preserve strength for revenge:

> Marcus, unknit that sorrow-wreathen knot;
> Thy niece and I, poor creatures, want our hands
> And cannot passionate our ten-fold grief
> With folded arms. This poor right hand of mine
> Is left to tyrannize upon my breast,
> Who, when my heart all mad with misery,
> Beats in this hollow prison of my flesh,
> Then thus I thump it down.
> [To Lavinia.] Thou map of woe, that thus dost talk in signs!
> When thy poor heart beats with outrageous beating,
> Thou canst not strike it thus to make it still.
> Wound it with sighing, girl, kill it with groans.
> (III.ii.4–15)

This is effective, I think, in conveying compassion as well as an intolerable pressure of feeling that seeks to find an emblematic epiphany such as Waith speaks of. At the same time there is a submerged sexualization of death as an orgasmic consummation for the drown-

ing, beating heart, projected as an autoerotic rhapsody; a knife is
envisaged now between her teeth, rather than the severed hand:

> Or get some little knife between thy teeth,
> And just against thy heart make thou a hole,
> That all the tears that thy poor eyes let fall
> May run into that sink, and soaking in,
> Drown the lamenting fool in sea-salt tears.
>
> (lines 16–20)

When Marcus remonstrates at Titus's suggestion of violence—
"teach her not thus to lay / Such violent hands upon her tender
life"—he gives the dramatist, through Titus, another chance to deal
in puns on hands:

> How now! has sorrow made thee dote already?
> Why, Marcus, no man should be mad but I.
> What violent hands can she lay on her life?
> Ah, wherefore dost thou urge the name of hands, ...
> O, handle not the theme, to talk of hands,
> Lest we remember still that we have none.
> Fie, fie, how franticly I square my talk,
> As if we should forget we had no hands,
> If Marcus did not name the word of hands!
>
> (lines 21–26, 29–33)

The verbal and rhythmical energy of this is remarkable; isolated,
the punning is in bad taste—"O, *handle* not the theme"! But when
read so that the iterative rhythms support it, there is a telling effect
of near distraction in the circling repetition. The poetic energy is
greater than anything in Kyd, and looks forward to the circling, anguished iteration and wordplay of *Richard II*. Dramatically, the difficulty is that the situation is so claustrophobic; Kyd devises richer
social circumstances for Hieronimo to take up into his passioning.
But this self-enclosed quality is essential to what Shakespeare is
exploring. A scene of a family dinner, with only Titus, Marcus,
Lavinia, and the grandson present, Titus then mauling a fly on his
plate—this is part of an imaginative progress into domesticity that
ends with him spoon-feeding Tamora.

After another domestic scene, in which the grandson and Lavinia move about with some scope, and the murderers' identity is
learned, Shakespeare opens out his action by sending Titus, his
brother, grandson, and friends out into the open with bows to
shoot missives to the gods and to send an oration to the Emperor in
a clown's basket of pigeons. He also develops a subplot about the

"Blackmoor Child" who in the chapbook disappears after his conception has been so quaintly explained. The scenes in which Aaron
defends his black "tadpole" are regularly praised: "Aaron's strange
blend of villainy and engaging paternal affection" seems "beyond
the reach of any of [Shakespeare's] contemporaries" to R. F. Hill.[19]
The freedom of Aaron in his villainy is an immense relief after the
conflictual constriction we have experienced, and his language is
often wonderfully vital:

NURSE: O gentle Aaron, we are all undone! . . .
AARON: Why, what a caterwauling dost thou keep!
        What dost thou wrap and fumble in thy arms?
                                    (IV.ii.55, 57–58)

The two scenes in which Aaron protects his son from Chiron and
Demetrius and, after he is captured, from Lucius and his army of
Goths, show Shakespeare's sure feeling for opening out a tragic action before returning to its intense, deep-running channel—they
are like the shift out of Scotland to the court of England toward the
close of *Macbeth*. After so much displaced, submerged, and inhibited sexuality, it is delightful to have Aaron answer back to the
moral indignation of the Queen's sons (of all people!):

DEMETRIUS: Villain, what hast thou done?
    AARON: That which thou canst not undo.
   CHIRON: Thou hast undone our mother.
    AARON: Villain, I have done your mother.
                                    (lines 73–76)

The amoral mastery with which Aaron kills the nurse is a pleasure
after so much self-righteous moral frustration: "Weeke, weeke!—so
cries a pig prepared to the spit." "Shall she live to betray this guilt of
ours, / A long-tongu'd babbling gossip?" (lines 146, 149–50).

When captured, Aaron, with his gusty recitation of the villainies
he has committed or directed, recapitulates what we have witnessed with fascinated horror, freeing us from our complicity in
half enjoying outrage by *his* enjoying it so fully. Although he seems
clearly designed to out-Ithamore Ithamore, there is something in
him beyond Marlowe's Turk. He has a greater freedom to dip into

19. R. F. Hill, "The Composition of *Titus Andronicus*," *Shakespeare Survey* 10
(1957): 64. Hill's interesting essay assesses the play's blend of stylistic awkwardness
and strength to suggest that it may be Shakespeare's earliest work.

the vernacular for free-spirited common expressions: "That cod-
ding spirit had they from their mother" (V.i.99). His outsider's rela-
tivism about religion is gayer than Barabas's: "for that I know / An
idiot holds his bauble for a god" (V.i.78–79). To be sure, the whole
thing is stagey, but so fitted to serve our emotional need here that it
works very well indeed.

Aaron's "paternal affection" for his son also fits with the way
family and sexuality are structured in the play as a whole. Here is
frank sexual zest leading to unforced, committed parenting. But
the condition for it is that father and son be "black," beyond "a
thing . . . called conscience" (V.i.75), beyond, thanks to blackness,
the "treacherous hue, that will betray with blushing":

> Here's a young lad fram'd of another leer:
> Look how the black slave smiles upon the father,
> As who should say, "Old lad, I am thine own."
> (IV.ii.117, 119–21)

Aaron has plans for his son that anticipate Belarius with Guiderius
and Arviragus in *Cymbeline*:

> I'll make you feed on berries and on roots,
> And feed on curds and whey, and suck the goat,
> And cabin in a cave, and bring you up
> To be a warrior and command a camp.
> (lines 177–80)

It is a pleasant pastoral vision—of nurturance without women.

Earlier, to Tamora's sons' objection to letting the child live and so
betraying "thy noble mistress," Aaron has answered: "My mistress
is my mistress, this myself" (IV.ii.106–7). A father who would care
for his own son by himself, as an extension of himself, Aaron represents a vilified but actively potent version of Titus as a parent.
Titus the dutiful warrior is the nurturing male parent whose curious nurture is, for him and for his family, all there is: he leads male
children out to death and back into the family tomb; he cherishes a
daughter made sexually safe yet suggestive by disfigurement, only
finally to destroy her. After the engulfing Tamora is undone by
making her swallow her own sons in a hideous parody of nurturance, we are led through farewells to the hero, not as a stern
figure of authority, but as a tender, cherishing parent and grand-
parent. "Come hither, boy," Titus's surviving son urges his own son
at the end,

> thy grandsire lov'd thee well.
> Many a time he danc'd thee on his knee,
> Sung thee asleep, his loving breast thy pillow;
> Many a story hath he told to thee,
> And bid thee bear his pretty tales in mind,
> And talk of them when he was dead and gone.
>   (V.iii.159–66)

Aaron's great power expresses a fantasy of manhood beyond the reach of what makes Titus vulnerable: the cruel power of a domineering woman, Tamora, and Titus's investment of self in a bond of intimacy with another woman, his daughter. Within Titus's sphere, free sexual energy and procreative power are villainy outside the family and directed at its destruction. Yet the villainous outsider, Aaron, we admire to the verge of sentimentality for his freedom and his loyalty to progeny, even as he is morally reviled. Aaron's misogynous logic in dismissing his mistress is echoed in the new Emperor's final command:

> As for that ravenous tiger Tamora,
> No funeral rite, no man in mourning weed, . . .
> But throw her forth to beasts and birds to prey.
>   (V.iii.195–96, 198)

But whereas Aaron's misogyny has been based in a fantasy that denies masculine vulnerability, the Emperor's instructions reflect the desperate trend of Titus's vengeful action against an overwhelming threat: let the omnivorous mother, having devoured her own children, be devoured in turn by other beasts of prey.[20]

Titus's concurrent need for the caring intimacy of a feminine presence is expressed early when he greets Lavinia as the "cordial of mine age to glad my heart!" (I.i.166), anticipating Lear's "I lov'd her most, and thought to set my rest / On her kind nursery" (I.i.123–24). Like Lear leading Cordelia off to prison, Titus will end his life in a cherishing, sublimated bond with his daughter: "Gentle Lavinia, let me kiss thy lips / Or make some sign how I may do thee ease" (III.i.120–21). Cordelia's death is the tragic outcome of Lear's de-

---

20. As Willbern notes, Aaron's final punishment—"Set him breast-deep in the earth, and famish him; / There let him stand and rave and cry for food"—derives from the same matrix of fantasy. Willbern writes: "He is indeed like a baby, half-born and half-buried and half-devoured by the earth, crying for food. Anyone who would serve him as a mother will be killed" ("Rape and Revenge in *Titus Andronicus*," p. 181).

mand that she love her father all; Titus kills Lavinia himself after an interim in which the mutually disabled couple have lived in an all-absorbing intimacy. But unlike *King Lear*, the early tragedy does not comprehend the suppressed link between the need the father seeks to fulfill in the child and the destructive development of an action that engulfs them both.

Titus and the revenge play by Kyd that seems to have inspired it both fail in a measure because they lack control of a social perspective on the protagonist, or lose it toward the end. *The Spanish Tragedy* seems to me a much better play, despite the lower level of properly poetic power, because there is so much more social experience and meaning in it, until the final rampage of Hieronimo. *Titus* defines its hero (and heroine) almost entirely in domestic terms, and its antiheroes in antidomestic terms; there is no larger society, no larger human and social possibility, showing forth. And in trying to make extraordinary transpositions of usual family and antifamily roles and allegiances, the play tends to fall into sensationalism and sentimentality. The structure of the play substitutes paternal for maternal parenting and sentimentalizes Titus as it sensational-izes the malevolence of Tamora. In doing so it makes the destruc-tiveness that is recognized as such all come from the outside—from Goths and their Moor—and does not acknowledge the destruc-tiveness of Titus within his family, except in the moment, quickly passed over, of killing his youngest son. The revenge-play structure is used to avoid recognizing for what it is the underlying motive the play enacts.

6

Shakespeare in His Sonnets

The Sonnets are about, or rather, the Sonnets *are* Shakespeare's maintenance of a self at deep levels of need. Those to the young man involve the need, enormously significant for his whole sensibility, that self be realized selflessly in another. Among the last-numbered poems to or about this relation, there is increasing self-assertion and self-acceptance, reaching toward the independence of "No, I am that I am" in Sonnet 121. But in the great majority of the earlier poems, there is passionate dependence, initially and at intervals triumphant, but frequently precarious and desperate, the poet making himself nothing to make the beloved everything. The relationship that must be maintained at all costs is with a whole person, regarded as an all-sufficing presence. By steep contrast, the woman is a partner in sexual relations who must be denigrated to enable genital assertion and release. To understand fully both these groups of poems, and Shakespeare in them, it seems essential that we recognize that they are addressed to real persons. But it is equally essential that the action of loving is fulfilled, or maintained against odds, through the action of poetry. Any description of the relationships which neglects the poetic process is misleading, as is, for example, the description above: that the beloved man is made everything, the poet nothing. For the poet, even in the sonnets of complete self-abnegation, is masterfully conducting the sonnet.

"THIS POWERFUL RHYME"

The sheer poetic power has been brought out more fully than ever before by Stephen Booth's recent edition, with its 403 densely packed pages of analytic commentary.[1] The amount of attention

1. *Shakespeare's Sonnets*, ed. with analytic commentary by Stephen Booth (New Haven: Yale University Press, 1977); cited hereafter as "Commentary."

given in the past century to these 154 poems is staggering—and daunting to anyone undertaking to say more about them. After Hyder Rollins assembled all commentary and theories through the early 1940s in his fine, huge, two-volume *Variorum Edition*,[2] interpretations, editions, and "solutions" have continued to appear at a rate almost equaling studies of *Hamlet*. This witnesses to something inexhaustible about the poems which itself requires explanation. Booth insists that the poems are mind-boggling and that it is their great virtue to be so. "The relevant meanings of Shakespeare's words and phrases and the contexts they bring with them combine, intertwine, fuse and conflict,"[3] in an unparalleled concentration that "gives the whole sequence an illogically powerful aura of coherence,"[4] but must frustrate any effort to comprehend the whole. His own commentary does far more than any before to show the fantastically rich way that Shakespeare exploits the verbal resources of his culture. He holds firmly to the view that the poems are "satisfying to read, unsatisfying to think about, and likely to evoke critical analyses that satisfy only by *making* the poems satisfying to think about."[5] To do justice, not to limit and falsify, requires "pluralistically committed" commentary that does not try to say what the poetry means in other words and so violate it.

As with many others who care about the poetry, Booth excludes all consideration of the relationship between the Sonnets and Shakespeare as a man writing them out of human situations, the dimension that most concerns this study. In his view, the persons addressed may well have been fictions. To exclude consideration of the human context is an understandable, though misconceived, response to the quagmire of biographical speculations. Booth deals summarily with the "expeditions to find 'Mr. W. H.' and 'The Rival Poet,' and the games of pin the tail on 'The Dark Lady.'"[6] We can grant him that they have probably all been failures (and mostly bores). But it is one thing to read the Sonnets by thinking you have discovered their "story" (like so many—most vociferously A. L. Rowse) or by making it up (like Oscar Wilde), another thing to read

2. Hyder Rollins, ed., *The New Variorum Edition of Shakespeare: The Sonnets*, 2 vols. (Philadelphia: Lippincott, 1944).

3. "Commentary," p. xiii.

4. Stephen Booth, *An Essay on Shakespeare's Sonnets* (New Haven: Yale University Press, 1969), p. 14.

5. "Commentary," p. 507.

6. Ibid., p. 516.

them with awareness of what they themselves convey about the use Shakespeare is making of them, enigmatic as this use often is. To retell a poem as a personal "story" is to substitute the story for the action of the poetry. But the action of the poetry can be properly understood, I think, only by recognizing that it is working to transform or cope with "situations and relationships which," as J. B. Leishman put it, "cannot have been invented, if for no other reason than that they have been left so tantalisingly obscure."[7]

Although we do not know the persons involved, we can experience the gestures made toward them, and something of the roots of feeling in a particular temperament implied by the gestures. The poems' qualities, and Shakespeare's in and through them, are consistent with their not having been written for publication. We have Francis Meres's unambiguous reference in 1598 to "his sugred sonnets among his priuate friends."[8] Their private character is reflected in the circumstance that, except for the two sonnets (138 and 144) that were included in a piratical anthology in 1599, they were not published until 1609, late in Shakespeare's life, long after most of them must have been written. The only edition, brought out by a marginal publisher with no evidence of Shakespeare's permission or supervision, may well have been soon suppressed, for there is almost no notice of the Sonnets in the decades following their appearance. In 1640 they were so little known that a publisher ventured to pretend that he was bringing out unpublished poems of Shakespeare in issuing a rearranged version of the 1609 text.

Shakespeare's Sonnets are sometimes spoken of as his sonnet sequence, though they are not in fact such a production, indeed not one production at all. C. S. Lewis made the point that the typical Renaissance sonnet was a *public* form of poetry. "A good sonnet . . . was like a good public prayer: the test is whether the congregation can 'join' and make it their own, not whether it provides interesting materials for the spiritual biography of the compiler. . . . The whole body of the sonnet sequences is much more like an erotic liturgy than a series of erotic confidences."[9] In his Sonnets, as elsewhere, Shakespeare uses the current idiom and goes beyond

7. J. B. Leishman, *Themes and Variations in Shakespeare's Sonnets*, 2nd ed. (London: Hutchinson, 1963), p. 11.
8. *Palladis Tamia, Wits Treasury* (1598); quoted from *The Riverside Shakespeare*, p. 1844.
9. C. S. Lewis, *English Literature in the Sixteenth Century, Excluding Drama* (Oxford: Clarendon Press, 1944), p. 491.

it or puts it to new uses rather than rebelling against it. But though there are places where he seeks "to say / The perfect ceremony of love's rite" (23), most of the poems are drastic (and unparalleled) exceptions to Lewis's rule.

Written singly and in small groups, they were probably begun in 1593 or 1594, perhaps earlier, in the period when the rage for sonnets in private life was at its height and about to wane and when Shakespeare was making much of sonnets in his plays. There are many parallels in imagery and phrasing between those numbered below 97 and *Love's Labor's Lost, Romeo and Juliet, A Midsummer Night's Dream, Richard II*, as well as the two narrative poems published in 1593 and 1594. It seems to me that we can see in *Henry IV* and *Henry V, Twelfth Night* and the problem comedies, especially *All's Well That Ends Well*, Shakespeare rehandling and distancing the intense relationship to the highborn young man of the Sonnets. My assumption is that the sonnets to the young man are roughly at least in the order in which they were written—a sequence lived through rather than designed. What we find in them makes this clear in the large, though not in detail. The order of those to the mistress seems for the most part consistent with what they say.

What Shakespeare does with these poems is made possible by the special autonomous integration of the sonnet as a form for feeling and awareness: each sonnet is an action; and when successfully wrought, the action has a formal consummation. What he does was also possible because he was writing in the golden moment when, to call on C. S. Lewis once again, value seemed to be out there in the world, ready to be put into words, and words glowed with value ready to be put into poetry.[10]

The curious theme of the first seventeen sonnets works partly because to urge the friend to marry and have children provides occasions for saying simple things beautifully: how lovely April is; how fine it is that age, in spite of wrinkles, has windows through which to see its golden time renewed. The poet's vicarious interest in the young man's sexual fulfillment is not queasy, because it is realized by evoking the creative power generally at work in nature:

> Those hours that with gentle work did frame
> The lovely gaze where every eye doth dwell.
> (Sonnet 5)

10. Ibid., esp. pp. 64–65.

The phrase "gentle work" is typical of the direct cherishing of the processes of life. The feeling about the destructiveness of death is equally direct:

> For never-resting time leads summer on
> To hideous winter and confounds him there.
> (Sonnet 5)

There is no holding back from obvious words or metaphors: the sun's light is gracious, music is sweet, the buds of May are darling; death is winter, darkness, Time's scythe; beauty is all the usual things, for example a flower. But the meaning of the usual things is renewed:

> Since brass, nor stone, nor earth, nor boundless sea,
> But sad mortality o'ersways their power,
> How with this rage shall beauty hold a plea,
> Whose action is no stronger than a flower?
> (Sonnet 65)

That a flower is a fragile thing is familiar enough. But that a flower has its own kind of power too—this comes as a poignant realization. It often happens that the metaphorical vehicle in which Shakespeare conveys the tenor of his love absorbs our chief attention, so that the love itself is left behind or fulfilled in what it is compared to. We dwell on the fact that "summer's lease hath all too short a date," that the earth devours "her own sweet brood," that the morning flatters "the mountain tops with sovereign eye," that black night is "Death's second self," and "seals up all in rest." The world is full of value that can be looked at front-face. Shakespeare could get more of this gold into his poetry than anyone else in the golden age because he had the greatest power of admiration.

Every line or phrase of a sonnet is, in the act of reading, part of a single movement: when you know a sonnet well, an individual line, quoted alone, rings with the sound that it has in its proper place. Each sonnet is one utterance. Shakespeare's use of the form is simple and forthright and also delicate and subtle. He almost never varies from three quatrains followed by a couplet:

> Why write I still all one, ever the same.
> And keep invention in a noted weed,
> That every word doth almost tell my name?
> (Sonnet 76)

Other Elizabethan sonneteers showed more technical restlessness. Shakespeare not only uses nothing but the Shakespearean form (it *does* tell his name), but for the most part he uses it straight. Usually he does not run his syntax against the line endings or the rhyme scheme. There are a good many exceptions, but normally the sentences or clauses close with the close of each quatrain, or else are balanced symmetrically within the four-line unit. Within sentences, grammar and thought typically pause or turn at the end of the line; where they do run over, the enjambment is rarely emphatic. Shakespeare does not exploit the more outward forms of variation, because within the pattern he is making astonishingly beautiful designs with sound and syllable and cadence. He is like an accomplished figure skater who sticks to the classical figures because what he cares about is what he can make of each evolution. (Shakespeare had, after all, unlimited opportunities in the plays for free-style improvisations, swoops, spins, leaps.) Each sonnet is different, but the difference is achieved not by changing the framework of form but by moving in fresh ways within it.

It seems clear that Shakespeare wrote by quatrains. In coming to know a sonnet by heart, you find yourself recalling it one quatrain at a time and often getting stuck trying to move to the next, for lack of a tangible link. The imagery does not regularly carry through; what does carry through is the momentum of the discourse. The movement from quatrain to quatrain is usually a shift of some sort, though it can be simply a continuing with fresh impetus. The figure skater starts each evolution by kicking off from an edge, and can move from one evolution to another either by staying on the same edge of the same blade or by changing from inside edge to outside edge, or from left foot inside to right foot outside, and so on—each of these technical moves focusing a whole living gesture of the balancing, moving body. People praise Shakespeare's sonnets because each one is about one thing; one should add that each is *one motion* about one thing, the motion normally being composed of three large sweeps and the shorter couplet. (The very different serial movements of Sonnets 66 and 129 are revealing exceptions.)

We must recognize that in most of the Sonnets the couplet is *not* the emotional climax, nor indeed even the musical climax; where it is made so, either by Shakespeare's leaning on it too heavily, or by our giving it unnecessary importance, one feels that two lines are asked to do too much, especially in some of the sonnets involving conflictual attitudes. This letdown or overreach or turnabout in the couplet is the most common defect in the Sonnets; with tactful reading it usually can be kept from being troublesome (but not always). One needs to attend to the motion and the imaginative expansion which the sonnet achieves in the quatrains, realizing that the couplet is often no more than a turning around at the end to look from a new vantage at what has been expressed.

The main line of the sonnet as Shakespeare writes it is the patterned movement of discourse, not the imagery. The voice rides the undulation of the meter, gaining remarkable power and reaching out in ardent, urgent, solemn, or contorted gestures defined by rhythmical variations. This is not primarily a poetry that explores experience by carrying out the implications of a metaphor or a conceit, as is notable in Donne's work. Shakespeare in the Sonnets occasionally does something like this—most perfectly in the three paralleled metaphors of Sonnet 73: "That time of year . . . the twilight of such day . . . the glowing of such fire"; but this progression by extending metaphors is most definitely not typical. He is responsible to rhythmical, not metaphorical, consistency. The sonnet often starts with something like a metaphorical program, but usually the program is not carried through. There are, as Booth's annotation brilliantly demonstrates, many almost subliminal continuities or recurrences. Metaphors are picked up, changed, mixed, dropped ad libitum while the sonnet runs its strong course as an utterance. One often finds, as one penetrates the poetic texture of a particular poem, that it holds together by determinate rhythm and sound several almost independent strains of meaning, or a cluster of ambiguities that, worked out logically, are almost mutually exclusive. To ravel out such associations can of course be misleading. In an actual, live reading of a sonnet, clustering ideas, images, and words are felt together, not sorted; they are the mind and heart opening out into the plurality of the world's riches, or opening inward on complexly crossed purposes. What keeps us from coming to a standstill in walleyed contemplation is the flow of the poem's movement as it gathers in meaning in the service of the poet's love.

The poetry often makes a thick harmony out of what might be (sometimes indeed is) woolgathering multiplicity. The most famous instance is "Bare ruin'd choirs, where late the sweet birds sang," thanks to William Empson's discussion at the outset of *Seven Types of Ambiguity*.[11] As rich or richer than the interplay of imagery is the interplay of sound, the chord of vowels and of r's in "bare ruin'd choirs," sounded in three successive long, slow syllables—

11. William Empson, *Seven Types of Ambiguity*, 2nd ed. rev. (London: Chatto and Windus, 1947), pp. 2–3.

the mystery of the line comes from this music as much as from the wonderful complex of metaphors that Empson brought out. We need to consider, not a special case like Sonnet 73, but the much more common case where there is great richness of metaphor but no metaphorical consistency:

> O how shall summer's honey breath hold out
> Against the wrackful siege of batt'ring days,
> When rocks impregnable are not so stout,
> Nor gates of steel so strong but time decays?
>
> (Sonnet 65)

These are splendid lines—but it is the motion of the utterance, with the design of sound, that chiefly carries through, the open-breathing *o* and *u* sounds and flowing consonants of "how shall summer's honey breath hold out" followed by the battering lines, with "wrackful" and "rocks impregnable." One can understand summer's honey metaphorically as provision for a siege—but there is no question of carrying the metaphor further, for one cannot "batter" honey! And the summer-winter opposition, as well as the battering, has been lost by the time we get to "time decays."

The Sonnets often would be "witty" if it were not that the wit in them goes along with sound and cadences that hold feeling—the wit is rarely isolated to be felt separately, as Donne's so often is, but enters into the whole motion. If we were to read the lines in isolation, we would be amused by the virtuoso alliteration and assonance in lines like these:

> And with old woes new wail my dear time's waste.
>
> . . . .
>
> And heavily from woe to woe tell o'er
> The sad account of fore-bemoanéd moan.
>
> (Sonnet 30)

But when we read them as an integral part of the lovely sonnet "When to the sessions of sweet silent thought," the huddled sounds serve to convey the pressure of the past on the present as a thickening or troubling of speech. Where we feel a twinge of amusement, it is usually in combination with feelings dictated by the underlying rhythm, as with the ruefulness of "But, ah, thought kills me that I am not thought" (Sonnet 44). It would be wrong to suppose that the Sonnets are without humor. There are places where Shakespeare positively romps, but the fun is almost never unmixed with serious feeling. The gay whirl of "Let not my love be called idolatry" (Sonnet 105) is an extreme example of the repetition common in the Sonnets, the same words rolled round, each time with added life because they fall differently each time within the poem's progress. Here this sort of fun is indulged in almost by itself, in celebration of a moment's carefree confidence: "Kind is my love today, tomorrow kind, / Still constant with a wondrous excellence." But even this sonnet, which is as near to a jeu d'esprit as we come, has its serious side, for it raises a question about idolatry which it does not settle.

"LINES OF LIFE"

Many of the Sonnets are wonderfully generous poems: they give beauty and meaning. These are among the most familiar from anthologies. In Sonnet 18, "Shall I compare thee to a summer's day," the poet's art frees the young man from the effects of "chance or nature's changing course":

> But thy eternal summer shall not fade,
> Nor lose possession of that fair thou ow'st,
> Nor shall death brag thou wand'rest in his shade,
> When in eternal lines to time thou grow'st.
>> So long as men can breathe or eyes can see,
>> So long lives this, and this gives life to thee.

This poem comes just after Shakespeare has shifted from urging that immortality must come through children to promising it by his "eternal lines." The move comes after a characteristic *poetic* exploration of the relationship between "lines of life" and lines of poetry in Sonnet 16. Sonnet 15 has broached the shift with a pun on reproduction by husbandry and reproduction by art: "And all in war with time for love of you, / As he takes from you, I *engraft* you new" (italics added)—by writing I graft you to a new stock. Sonnet 16 returns to marriage, urging it as a "mightier way" to combat time than "my barren rhyme":

> So should the lines of life that life repair
> Which this time's pencil or my pupil pen
> Neither in inward worth nor outward fair
> Can make you live yourself in eyes of men.
>> To give away yourself keeps yourself still,
>> And you must live, drawn by your own sweet skill.

The suggestiveness of "lines of life" appears in the variety of commentators' paraphrases recorded in the *Variorum Edition*: the "lines

of life" can be the lines that life etches on a face, or the lines of descent in a genealogy, or the lines of the living pictures presented by
children, or the lines of children as living poems (as opposed to the
mere written lines of the "pupil pen"), or even, perhaps, as an echo
at the back of the mind, what one commentator defends in urging
unconvincingly that "lines of life" is a misprint for "loins of life"
(compare the sonnet's conclusion: "And you must live, drawn by
your own sweet skill"). Booth instances these lines in his preface
to exemplify the sort of multiplicity he is concerned to bring out,
noting that he is following Empson in suggesting, in effect, that all
the different glosses proposed are right.[12] It is characteristic that
even as Shakespeare urges the superiority of biological lineage, he
merges it with artistic reproduction.

After one more sonnet, the poet turns away entirely from reproduction that involves the triad of "sire, and child, and happy
mother" (8). The relationship becomes diadic. But the feminine is
kept in it, both in the youth—"A woman's face, with nature's own
hand painted, / Hast thou, the master mistress of my passion"—
and in the cherishing poet:

> And for a woman wert thou first created,
> Till nature as she wrought thee fell a-doting,
> And by addition me of thee defeated,
> By adding one thing to my purpose nothing.
>> But since she pricked thee out for women's pleasure,
>> Mine be thy love, and thy love's use their treasure.
>> (Sonnet 20)

The poet here is in nearly the same role as "nature as she wrought
thee," taking something of the same satisfaction in the young man's
sexuality that a mother takes in a man-child's. Ironically, he is like
Pygmalion in creating, more than he can acknowledge, the image
he adores. But Pygmalion created an age-mate of the opposite sex
whom he could finally possess as an object. Shakespeare, at this
stage at least, accepts an aim-inhibited relationship. What Shakespeare's metaphor of capital and interest here proposes is that he
should enjoy the whole identity of the friend, whereas women enjoy what "use" this capital yields of specifically sexual pleasure.

If the youth were "true" to the poet, his own relationships with
women would have to be of the same limited kind as the poet's with
his mistress. The poet frequently describes them as casual: "Those

---

12. "Commentary," p. xiii.

pretty wrongs that liberty commits, / When I am sometime absent from thy heart":

> Beauteous thou art, therefore to be assailed;
> And when a woman woos, what woman's son
> Will sourly leave her till she have prevailed?[13]
>
> (Sonnet 41)

This is the prologue to remonstrating about the young man's having taken on Shakespeare's own mistress: "Ay me, but yet thou might'st my seat forbear." We shall return to that situation. Meanwhile, we can notice that, with the exception of that relationship to his own mistress, the poet's attitude toward the young man's sexual adventures is sometimes remarkably like that of a concerned parent:

> Take heed, dear heart, of this large privilege;
> The hardest knife ill used doth lose his edge.
>
> (Sonnet 95)

But—as with some parents, especially a mother strongly attached to a son—concern keeps verging into feelings of neglect ("I am to wait, though waiting so be hell, / Not blame your pleasure" [Sonnet 58]), and resentment and condemnation ambivalently expressed.

Leslie Fiedler summarizes the shift from advocating immortality through "breed" to promising it through art: "In either case, love is the spur: either the love which attracts man to woman, body to body, thus ending in marriage and the family, or the love which draws man to man, soul to soul, thus ending in—literature."[14] Fiedler's bold and wide-ranging account is often illuminating about the problematic area dealt with here. But his view of the homoerotic strain in Shakespeare and the role of those "strangers," women, deals almost exclusively with the relationships as between adults, neglecting the factor of identification and the latent matrix of family feeling. The "love which draws man to man" in the Sonnets, though it ends, as he wittily says, in literature, begins in the family. The bar against physical relationship takes the place of the incest taboo underlying the "danger" of the adored mistress in the Petrarchan tradition.

The "danger" of the youth is also, in part, his higher social sta-

13. Booth keeps Q's *he* in this line; the emendation *she*, followed by most modern editors, originates with Malone (1780).
14. Leslie Fiedler, *The Stranger in Shakespeare* (New York: Stein and Day, 1972), p. 33.

tion. Shakespeare's worship includes his joy in "engrafting" himself
to an aristocratic heritage he cannot have in his own right. Sonnet 37
opens with a parental gesture of fulfillment through mirroring—
"As a decrepit father takes delight / To see his active child do deeds
of youth"—then moves from difference in age to difference in heritage. The poet, "made lame by fortune's dearest spite," takes all his
"comfort of thy worth and truth":

> For whether beauty, birth, or wealth, or wit,
> Or any of these all, or all, or more,
> Entitled in thy parts do crownéd sit,
> I make my love engrafted to this store.
> So then I am not lame, poor, nor despised,
> Whilst that this shadow doth such substance give.

With fine tact the poet matches the friend's inherited resources,
"birth," "wealth," with personal qualities, "beauty," "wit," then
combines social with intrinsic qualities again in a surge of vicarious
joy: "Or any of these all, or all, or more, / *Entitled* in thy parts."
(Italics added.) In his own middle-class situation, Shakespeare was
adroit, comparatively well off, admired: "lame, poor, . . . despised"
are obeisant to the aristocratic caste, compensatory for the drastic
claim made on a member of it. Yet the relationship is serving more
than social needs—"lame, poor, . . . despised" are metaphoric for
the enormous personal need served by this writing.

The concern to realize and live in the identity of another is just
what we should expect from the man who, beyond all other men,
created other identities. But in the plays there is freedom to use the
dramatist's power to limit and so define the others who are created.
The friend in the sonnets is sometimes rebuked, usually obliquely,
but he is never characterized fully; for the poet to do that would
limit the "all" which he requires of the friend. And in the sonnets
to him there is a difficulty that grows more and more obvious as
one reads and rereads the poems: the action, in such a love as this,
is almost all on the poet's side. Sonnet 61 recognizes this fact: "Is it
thy will thy image should keep open / My heavy eyelids to the
weary night?" The conclusion is a troubled recognition that it is the
poet's will, not the friend's: "For thee watch I, whilst thou dost wake
elsewhere, / From me far off, with others all too near."

There are sonnets which acknowledge that such identification as
the poet feels with his friend involves selfishness or self-love. Thus
Sonnet 62 exploits a double take as to who is who: "Sin of self-love
possesseth all mine eye, . . . / Methinks no face so gracious is as

mine, / No shape so true, no truth of such account." The turn comes with the third quatrain: "But when my glass shows me myself indeed / Beated and chopped with tanned antiquity." The same game is played in Sonnet 39, this time with "worth" and "self": "What can mine own praise to mine own self bring, / And what is't but mine own when I praise thee?" It is easy to dismiss this sort of reasoning as sonneteer's logic, when we read a sonnet in isolation. But when we come to understand the sort of relationship Shakespeare is expressing, we realize that these poems mean what they say in making equations. The poet's sense of himself hinges on the identification: elation in realizing himself in the friend's self is matched by desolation when he is left in the lurch of selflessness.

Freud in his study of Leonardo da Vinci described psychical processes in the origins of sublimated homosexuality which clearly have some relationship to what we encounter in Shakespeare in his Sonnets. He summarizes the pattern in general terms in an essay dealing with psychical processes in the formation of overt homosexuality in men. Central to what Freud sees as the "typical process" is an identification with the mother to whom the man, when a child, had been strongly fixated. The identification leads to a search "for love-objects in whom he can re-discover himself, and whom he might then love as his mother loved him. The characteristic mark of the process is that for several years one of the necessary conditions for his love is usually that the male object shall be of the same age as he himself when the change took place." The identification with the mother "enables the son to keep true to her, his first object choice," while the "narcissistic object choice" averts the difficulties of the "move toward the other sex." Freud associates the last of these factors with "the high value set on the male organ and the inability to tolerate its absence in the love object," and attributes the "depreciation of women, and aversion to them, even horror of them" to the "early discovery that women have no penis."[15]

We know, of course, that Shakespeare made the move toward the other sex early, with Anne Hathaway, at age eighteen if not before. His polymorphic sensibility did include in some contexts "high valuation of the male organ," but in displaced or sublimated forms. Fear and aversion to the female sexual organ is also expressed, in

15. "Some Neurotic Mechanisms in Jealousy, Paranoia and Homosexuality," in *Standard Edition*, vol. 18, pp. 230–31.

scarcely disguised form, in *Titus Andronicus*, as we have seen, and elsewhere. But again this is not a terminal attitude, but one which erupts at moments of special stress. The sonnets to the mistress make clear that genital relationship with her was crucial, if conflictual. W. H. Auden, a particularly trustworthy witness in this matter, mocked the eager claims of "the Homintern" on the Sonnets; he described the love for the young man as "mystical" and observed that such passionate devotion, enthralled by a special type of mortal beauty, rarely survives physical union.[16] To adapt Freud's description to Shakespeare's more inclusive sensibility, we should note also that often, again especially in the earlier work, cherishing fathers are set over against threatening, overpowering women.

The urgent, poignant concern about "never resting time" in so many of the sonnets accords with Freud's observation that "for several years one of the necessary conditions for his love" is the youth's being the same age as the older lover was when the mother was given up. The poet deals with a universal regret when he considers that "everything that grows / Holds in perfection but a little moment" (15), and that "thou among the wastes of time must go" (12). But the necessity of arresting the young man's *aging* is stressed almost obsessively, as the necessary condition for the saving identification: "My glass shall not persuade me I am old / So long as youth and thou are of one date" (22). This necessity for the relationship is insisted on especially as it is first set up on a flood tide of confidence:

> And do whate'er thou wilt, swift-footed time,
> To the wide world and all her fading sweets;
> But I forbid thee one most heinous crime,
> O carve not with thy hours my love's fair brow,
> Nor draw no lines there with thine ántique pen.
>
> . . . .
>
> Yet do thy worst, old time; despite thy wrong,
> My love shall in my verse ever live young.
>   (Sonnet 19)

The poet's power here is to confer not immortal memory but specifically eternal youth. Normal aging is an awesome threat, quite beyond usual human concern for a lover's moving out of the first

---

16. W. H. Auden, Introduction to the Sonnets, in *The Complete Signet Classic Shakespeare*, gen. ed. Sylvan Barnet (New York: Harcourt Brace Jovanovich, 1972), p. 1726.

bloom of youth. Sonnet 104, written after a separation of some duration, tries to deny any change:

> To me, fair friend, you never can be old,
> For as you were when first your eye I eyed,
> Such seems your beauty still.

The poem then faces up to the changes of three years in a wonderful metaphor that compares the moving hand of a clock to the imperceptible motion of the aging features:

> Ah yet doth beauty, like a dial hand,
> Steal from his figure, and no pace perceived;
> So your sweet hue, which methinks still doth stand,
> Hath motion, and mine eye may be deceived:
>> For fear of which, hear this, thou age unbred,
>> Ere you were born was beauty's summer dead.

The several tortured—or torturous—sonnets that deal with the young man's taking on Shakespeare's mistress are remarkable testimony to the fact that the poet's deepest sense of his identity is grounded—at this stage and in this situation—in his cherishing role toward the man and in identification with him, rather than in his relationship with the woman. The poems struggle to find a way of handling with words the injury the friend and mistress have done him in deeds. Sonnet 40 opens by insisting, through plays on the word *love*, that the woman's love is not "true" and so need not matter:

> Take all my loves, my love, yea take them all:
> What hast thou then more than thou hadst before?
> No love, my love, that thou mayst true love call;
> All mine was thine, before thou hadst this more.

Then, after a quatrain that moves a bit obscurely toward remonstrance, there comes a gesture of forgiveness that is almost more than the poet can make:

> I do forgive thy robb'ry, gentle thief,
> Although thou steal thee all my poverty;
> And yet love knows it is a greater grief
> To bear love's wrong than hate's known injury.
>> Lascivious grace, in whom all ill well shows,
>> Kill me with spites, yet we must not be foes.

In such a situation, failure of aggression, or the turning back of it upon the self, rouses disquiet: "Couldn't he be a man about it, at least." [17] This in spite of the urgent, poignant speaking voice present in these lines, peaking in the "all" of "Although thou steal thee all my poverty." Where most men would respond with rage or bury the event in silence, Shakespeare encounters this closed ruthlessness and remains open to it, turning injury into poetry. [18] The resentment one should expect against the man only finally bursts out in that one word "lascivious," so tellingly placed at the beginning of the line—and immediately taken back by what follows.

The strategy of denying dependence on the woman is combined, in the last of the sequence of Sonnets 40–41–42, "That thou hast her, it is not all my grief." The poem turns the two others into something between children (or wards) and actors in a play:

> Loving offenders, thus I will excuse ye:
> Thou dost love her, because thou know'st I love her,
> And for my sake ev'n so doth she abuse me,
> Suff'ring my friend for my sake to approve her.

After the third quatrain laments that their gain is the poet's loss, the poem concludes with a playful-ironic insistence on complete identity with the young man: "But here's the joy, my friend and I are one; / Sweet flatt'ry, then she loves but me alone." One could scarcely go further in living by identification! Yet the whole situation is eased in being distanced as a dramatic hypothesis that ends with a joke. In *The Winter's Tale* things will go differently after Leontes urges Hermione to treat Polixenes even as he would have her treat him: "How thou lov'st us, show in our brother's welcome" (I.ii.174). He then assumes, in the anguished fantasy of his jealousy, that she has played out the scenario Shakespeare endures passively in these sonnets. Shakespeare here can endure it because the maternal source of basic trust has been internalized; it can be preserved so long as he can go on with the relationship to the young man.

The sonnets about the triangle are disturbing and unsatisfying poems despite their great power, because they do not achieve a stable attitude toward the experience. They move toward control by moving in the direction of drama, but the poet here is twisted on

---

17. "Would you would bear your fortunes like a man!" (*Oth.* IV.i.61), says Iago, insuring that aggression born of jealousy will not yield to forgiveness or accommodation in the situation he has created as a binding illusion in Othello.

18. Sonnets 133 and 134 indicate that the poet remained, at least for a time after the betrayal was known, *also* attached to the woman, "mortgaged to [her] will."

the rack of an openness to life and a need for relationship, for love, which cannot let go of actual persons. The poet cannot forgo the cherishing parental bond that holds him in the relationship despite betrayal. In the plays such sympathy can flow into opposites and antagonists. In *Othello*—as later in *The Winter's Tale*—triangular relationships like that in the Sonnets are dramatized as totally disruptive because in these plays the implicit reference is not to a younger couple, envisaged from the poet's parental vantage, but to the original, older couple. Othello's and Leontes' experience of betrayal reanimates the rage of a child forced to recognize his exclusion by the sexual union of the parents.

"AS WITH YOUR SHADOW I WITH THESE DID PLAY"

Along with the poet's identity as cherishing parent there is also in the Sonnets a complementary relationship to the beloved as an object of love who is himself like the all-sufficing parent in infancy. To speak in this way falsifies of course the contingent way relationship to the friend is achieved. The positive poems characteristically evoke the friend's all-sufficing presence by synecdoche, parts taken for a whole that is beyond expression. Sonnet 53 dramatizes synecdoche:

> What is your substance, whereof are you made,
> That millions of strange shadows on you tend?
> Since everyone hath, every one, one shade,
> And you, but one, can every shadow lend.

Shakespeare here stands Neoplatonism on its head, as Leishman observes: the beloved is the Idea or "substance" of which things in the wide universe of becoming—Adonis, Helen of Troy, the "spring and foison of the year"—are but "shadows," even though the beloved is a living, actual person.[19] But the poem is of course not doctrine: it goes back through language used by Neoplatonism to the sort of experience out of which it may grow. Instead of defining the "substance" which "can every shadow lend," the poem asks in astonishment, "What is your substance, whereof are you made?" We experience the paradox that both Adonis and Helen are poor imitations, but the surprise and wonder point toward a unity that is the ground beyond sexual difference. The "strange shadows," the

19. *Themes and Variations*, p. 149.

"spring and foison of the year," convey the "you" which is "in every blesséd shape we know." They are "received together" with this presence, to use the Greek root of synecdoche.

Recent psychoanalytic studies of infancy, particularly the seminal thinking of the late D. W. Winnicott, provide a way of understanding, not simply the infantile roots of the "all," but the way the poetry achieves relationship to it.[20] In his view, playing in the presence of the mother, and the objects of play specially identified with that situation, are crucial in the infant's moving out from symbiotic unity toward separation. The child can endure periods of the absence of the parent by playing with "transitional objects." These are things originally "received together" with her, things that are synecdoches for her: "And you in every blesséd shape we know." Winnicott thinks of such play and its objects as existing in a "potential space," neither "objective" nor "subjective," which is resonant both with the maternal presence and with "things of this world"—to echo an apposite title of Richard Wilbur's.[21] The things of this world which are made into art, in this view, have been brought into such potential space as it expands beyond the nursery to include whatever each of us comes to make our own in the common culture.

Many of Shakespeare's sonnets can be seen, in this perspective, as play aimed at evoking, by way of the young man, a sense of the original maternal presence—and reckoning with its vulnerability to "never-resting time" (Sonnet 5) and other betrayals. The poems are transitional *objects*, for they are physical; meaning is made into "dulcet and harmonious breath" (*MND* II.i.151): "You still shall live—such virtue hath my pen— / Where breath most breathes, ev'n in the mouths of men" (Sonnet 81). The transitions the sonnets effect are back toward an original presence and at the same time out toward its new embodiment in the young man: a glow is cast upon him and on the world and reflected back upon the poet. Winnicott has a discussion of the way the mother's face mirrors to the infant what she sees in him or her, thus giving the infant an identity.[22] His discussion is illuminating for the mirror/face that bestows or confirms identity in the sonnets. He also describes the

---

20. D. W. Winnicott, *Playing and Reality* (New York: Basic Books, 1971); see esp. "Transitional Objects and Transitional Phenomena," pp. 1–25.

21. See "Love Calls Us to the Things of This World," from Richard Wilbur, *Things of This World* (New York: Harcourt, Brace, 1956).

22. "Mirror-role of Mother and Family in Child Development," in *Playing and Reality*, pp. 111–18.

stress for the child of a face that is indifferent or hostile, including situations where hostility within the frame of continued intimacy must be preferred to the nothing of indifference or rejection: "Bring me within the level of your frown, / But shoot not at me in your wakened hate" (Sonnet 117).

Sonnets 97 and 98, in describing poignant separation, embody and make explicit the resource of play for enduring absence. At the same time they adumbrate experience of loss in infancy.

> How like a winter hath my absence been
> From thee, the pleasure of the fleeting year!
> What freezings have I felt, what dark days seen!
> What old December's bareness everywhere!
> And yet this time removed was summer's time,
> The teeming autumn big with rich increase,
> Bearing the wanton burthen of the prime,
> Like widowed wombs after their lords' decease.
> Yet this abundant issue seemed to me
> But hope of orphans, and unfathered fruit;
> For summer and his pleasures wait on thee,
> And thou away, the very birds are mute;
> Or if they sing, 'tis with so dull a cheer,
> That leaves look pale, dreading the winter's near.
>
> (Sonnet 97)

Throughout, absence is creating even as it is lamented. The first four lines give intense life to the mouth and ear: the poignant sense of absence from "thee" is developed as we encounter the same sound in "fleeting" and "freezings"; the open *a* sounds in "What dark days" feel cavernous against the prevailing *e* tones; "December's bareness" includes three vowel sounds almost the same as those in "everywhere," so that the bareness seems to spread out "everywhere"—and the meter makes "everywhere" larger than it would be in prose by stressing two of its three syllables. Consonants of course are also put to work reinforcing the meaning—for example, by linking "fleeting" and "freezing" to "felt," "old" to "December," "December" to "bareness." In the imagery, similarly, orphaned nature is "teeming." Something enormously vital as well as "wanton" is going on, from which the poet feels cut off but which the poem makes present. The lines about gestation have the elusive richness of multidetermined association and suggestion characteristic of the sonnets at their most intense and expansive. "Bearing the wanton burthen of the prime" rehandles in a line of similar shape and sound what was relatively simple in Sonnet 3:

"and she in thee / Calls back the lovely April of her prime." Where the early poem urged the young man to bless some "uneared womb" with "the tillage of thy husbandry," now we look out through windows of age and separations at "abundant issue" which is "unfathered." Through the negative, "unfathered" says that the friend fathers the rich increase in the sense that it is only available to the poet when mediated by him. But playing with the thought of "widowed wombs" makes him a present absence.

Sonnet 98 continues the seasonal mediation exquisitely:

> From you have I been absent in the spring,
> When proud-pied April, dressed in all his trim,
> Hath put a spirit of youth in everything,
> That heavy Saturn laughed and leapt with him.
> Yet nor the lays of birds, nor the sweet smell
> Of different flow'rs in odor and in hue,
> Could make me any summer's story tell,
> Or from their proud lap pluck them where they grew.
> Nor did I wonder at the lily's white,
> Nor praise the deep vermilion in the rose;
> They were but sweet, but figures of delight,
> Drawn after you, you pattern of all those.
>   Yet seemed it winter still, and, you away,
>   As with your shadow I with these did play.

As the poem says "Nor did I wonder at the lily's white" it does so. The last four lines could not be more explicit in describing play with "transitional objects" as a way of coping with separation: lily and rose are "figures of delight, / Drawn after you"—"you away, / As with your shadow I with these did play." That the beloved youth and his absence are endowed with the meaning of an earlier situation is consistent with what seems a submerged reference in the two linked poems to the birth of a new, rival child.

In Sonnet 97 we move without transition from "this time removed was summer's time" to "teeming autumn big with rich increase"; the experience is like the fascination and dismay of a very young child who finds himself watching the mother grow pregnant, "big with rich increase," with the prospect of being himself orphaned, in effect, as her deepest attention is given to the new life. For that loss the friend's presence could be compensation, restoring "summer and his pleasures." In Sonnet 98 "proud-pied April" has arrived, "dressed in all his trim." Metrically, he bounces in on *four* trochees! He charms "heavy Saturn" to laugh and leap with him, and seems to sit and grow in a proud lap, from which the poet cannot or will not pluck him. But while the poet feels again the winter of being left out, with the spring for someone else, he in fact realizes its beauty, tells a summer story, even though a poignant one. Shakespeare's genius (and the capacity for growth that enabled it and was enabled by it) permits him to use the later relationship with the young man to keep alive by poetry his earliest relation to the grace of life.

"LOVE IS MY SIN, AND THY DEAR VIRTUE HATE"

In the sonnets to the mistress there is also a potential association of her with the ideal and taboo mother, from which it is usually the poems' business to escape. Where the ideal in the young man is propitiated, in the mistress it is exorcised, good-humoredly in "My mistress' eyes are nothing like the sun" (Sonnet 130). The idealization of the man is protected by the poet's turning the hostile component of a suppressed ambivalence back upon himself.[23] The hostile current is predominant with the woman. She seems to have given good cause. But this is convenient, for it gives a basis for degrading her and so making her sexuality accessible: "Love is my sin, and thy dear virtue hate"! (Sonnet 142). Hate is paradoxically a virtue because it is "grounded on sinful loving"—loving, not taboo. Shakespeare eagerly joins the mistress in this enabling animosity—"Canst thou, O cruel, say I love thee not, / When I against myself with thee partake?" (Sonnet 149)—which is abundantly complemented in his regard for her. The bawdy couplet of Sonnet 150 identifies the purpose served by his scorn for her: "If thy unworthiness raised love in me, / More worthy I to be belov'd of thee."

One of the few poems to her not dedicated to this "dear virtue," Sonnet 143 playfully casts her in the role of a mother neglecting her infant as she runs to catch "One of her feathered creatures broke away"—a hen, but so described as to admit recognizing it as another lover (or, by the shape of the experience, another child). The little domestic drama is a pleasant conceit, not to be leaned on heavily:

23. See Richard P. Wheeler, "Poetry and Fantasy in Shakespeare's Sonnets 88–96," *Literature and Psychology* 22 (1972): 151–62.

So run'st thou after that which flies from thee,
Whilst I, thy babe, chase thee afar behind;
But if thou catch thy hope, turn back to me,
And play the mother's part, kiss me, be kind.

It is striking that by setting up the relation in terms that so explicitly reflect its roots, Shakespeare arrives for a moment at a good-humored plea. The few other unhostile wooing poems, with the one exception of Sonnet 138, are similarly ingratiating and self-deprecating: in Sonnet 128 the poet envies the "saucy jacks" that "kiss the tender inward of thy hand." Much more commonly, he asks for favors in the same breath that he tells her he loves her in spite of his five wits and his five senses (Sonnet 141), spells out her falsehood, and exclaims at the paradox that "in the very refuse of [her] deeds" she somehow makes him love her more "the more I hear and see just cause of hate" (Sonnet 150). These are outrageous poems: one wonders whether in fact some of them can have been sent to the poor woman—whether most of them were not offstage exercises in hate and spite written from a need to get something out of the poet's system. To tell a woman that since she is promiscuous she may as well let you put in to her "will" among the rest, especially since your *name* too is Will (Sonnet 135), does not seem a very likely way to win even a hardened profligate.

Several poems, for example Sonnet 151, present a sequence in which degrading the woman and his relation to her frees the poet for impudent phallic self-assertion: "Love is too young to know what conscience is, / Yet who knows not conscience is born of love?" The "love" of the first line here is clearly Cupid.[24] The second line, as Shakespeare goes way beyond the usual clichés about help-lessness to resist Cupid's arrows that initiate passion, suggests the genesis of taboo in infancy: "conscience . . . born of love." The sonnet works to get past such conscience—"flesh . . . rising at thy

---

24. Brigid Brophy, in *Black Ship to Hell* (New York: Harcourt, Brace and World, 1962), pp. 463–72, explores the appropriateness of Cupid's youth as "the affirmation of infantile sexuality" (p. 467) in the development of adult sexual relations out of "the incestuous love between mother and son" (p. 466). She sees a hint regarding the "reduction of Cupid from a young man to a baby" in Apuleius's story of Cupid and Psyche, in which Venus is reluctant to recognize "that her son is grown-up enough to have a love-affair" (p. 466). Erich Neumann, in his commentary on Apuleius's tale, notes that it is Aphrodite herself, in her jealousy, who seeks to degrade sexually the mortal rival who becomes her son's lover (*Amor and Psyche*, trans. Ralph Manheim [New York: Harper and Row, 1962], pp. 60–61, 88).

name doth point out thee, / As his triumphant prize"—completing its action by changing the meaning of the key word: "No want of conscience hold it that I call / Her love for whose dear love I rise and fall." The whole relation to the mistress is a very clear-cut version of what Freud describes in his essay "A Special Type of Object Choice Made by Men": for a man to achieve potency the woman must be degraded, so as to disassociate her from the ideal presence founded on the early relationship to the mother.[25] The result of such symbolic action, repeated in poem after poem, is not simply despair—despite the wishful simplification of Sonnet 144: "Two loves I have of comfort and despair." On the contrary, as Sonnet 151 makes totally clear, denigration is sexually enabling. The poet often expresses bafflement that this should be so, even as he engages in the devaluing process.[26]

Where the sonnets to the woman do become completely grim, there is usually a certain falsifying simplification in resorting to unmeasured abuse, as in the couplet that ends but does not resolve the analysis of love's fever in Sonnet 147: "For I have sworn thee fair, and thought thee bright, / Who are as black as hell, as dark as night." But with the whole Sonnets situation in view, it does not seem cynical to observe that there is strength in Shakespeare's being able to have "relations," as we put it, with the woman. The positive value is recognized once very clearly, in Sonnet 138:

> When my love swears that she is made of truth,
> I do believe her though I know she lies,
> That she may think me some untutored youth,
> Unlearnéd in the world's false subtleties.

Consummation follows the laying out of lies, hers to him, his to her, tea for two, two for tea: "Therefore I lie with her, and she with me, / And in our faults by lies we flattered be." To be heavily moral about such a poem is to miss its positive function in getting beyond morality. For Patrick Cruttwell, Sonnet 138 is "perhaps the most terrible poem of the whole sequence," climaxed by the "grim se-

---

25. *Standard Edition*, vol. 11, pp. 165–75.
26. Cf. Robert Bagg ("Some Versions of Lyric Impasse in Shakespeare and Catullus," *Arion* 4[1965]: 64–95), who explores tensions between the poems' "recognition of a possible moral world where love has other habits" and "the world Shakespeare inhabits," where "love must absorb and comprehend many strange and ugly vicissitudes" with "protean transformations of feeling in the face of shifting truth" (p. 94).

riousness" of the pun on "lie"![27] I have felt that it is engagingly jaunty in defining the cheapness of the whole relationship—cheapness being one of the hardest things to get into poetry.[28]

Self-abasement in the relation to the young man reaches a climax in the Sonnets 87 to 94. This group follows the poems about the rival poet, where it is hard to sympathize with the queasy apologies for "my tongue-tied muse" (Sonnet 85) combined with disingenuous, covertly disabling praise for "the proud full sail of his great verse" (Sonnet 86). In Sonnet 87 we get the arresting opening: "Farewell, thou art too dear for my possessing, / And like enough thou know'st thy estimate"; the group is often called "the farewell sonnets." Numerically, they come before the retrospective descriptions of absence we have seen in Sonnets 97 and 98. It is reasonable to infer that a separation of some duration did follow the "farewell"; we shall see that many of the poems after 97 and 98 involve new, more self-affirming postures.

Of particular concern here are Sonnets 87 to 94 because of the connection one can see between the contorted gestures they make and infantile responses to the threat of intolerable loss. From a psychoanalytic vantage point the poet's predicament can be summarized as a struggle not to acknowledge a process of disillusionment that would erode the ideal image of the friend in which the poet's own identity is precariously anchored. These poems seek to sustain, at whatever cost to the self, a magical unity of poet and the beloved—something akin to "the hallucinatory wish-fulfillment Freud postulated of very young infants for whom the all-important mother is slow to reappear."[29] What is so strange in these posturings of a mature man is the assumption that the youth will profit from—and be grateful for—the moral masochism offered him as a transaction of devotion:

27. Patrick Cruttwell, *The Shakespearean Moment* (London: Chatto and Windus, 1954), pp. 13–14.

28. Edward Snow considers the lovers' lies in Sonnet 138 by reference to the way the love of Antony and Cleopatra moves through and beyond excellent falsehoods, and by contrast with the devastating exchange between Iago and Othello as they spiral down to sexual horror through the sonnet's key words, "know," "think," "believe." Following closely, through such comparison, the human implications of Sonnet 138's syntactic and semantic mutuality, Snow finds: "The grounds for cynicism and despair in Shakespeare's romantic vision are the stuff of the sonnet, but it manages to transform them into something workable, even strangely affirmative," ("Loves of Comfort and Despair: A Reading of Shakespeare's Sonnet 138," *ELH* 47 [1980]: 462, 479).

29. Wheeler, "Poetry and Fantasy," p. 156.

When thou shalt be disposed to set me light,
. . . .
Upon thy part I can set down a story
Of faults concealed, wherein I am attainted,
That thou in losing me shall win much glory.
(Sonnet 88)

The objective social situation that comes to mind as fitting this appeal is of a child placating a morally cruel parent by acknowledging ascribed wickedness in the hope of giving satisfaction and so winning acceptance: "The injuries that to myself I do, / Doing thee vantage, double vantage me." Of course in adult life lovers and intimate friends imitate every sort of child-parent scenario. But the scenario here is all, or almost all, Shakespeare's, as is apparent from his complaining of the youth's indifference. So in Sonnet 89 he pleads that the beloved at least give the attention involved in finding fault: "Say that thou didst forsake me for some fault." Then the poet would be able to play his game of self-reproof—which he plays anyway in promising to play it: "Thou canst not, love, disgrace me half so ill . . . / As I'll myself disgrace."

There are earlier poems of self-abasement where the class difference provides a social model of master and servant—or rather, slave:

Being your slave, what should I do but tend
Upon the hours and times of your desire?
I have no precious time at all to spend,
Nor services to do till you require.
(Sonnet 57)

The class or caste difference does in some measure motivate as well as shape expression in such cases. But making all allowance for the subservience expected in patronage, the energy of self-effacement is beyond any call of duty. And the language of complaint constantly strains against the tone of satisfied adulation—"the world without end hour . . . the bitterness of absence . . . though you do anything." The poem thinks ill even as it claims not to. If the friend were God! Milton's "They also serve who only stand and wait" comes to mind—and Jonson's comment on Donne's "Anniversaries" on the death of Mistress Elizabeth Drury, that "if it had been written of the Virgin Marie it had been something."[30]

These poems of abasement and farewell are so unsatisfying (are

---

30. *Notes of Ben Jonson's Conversations with William Drummond of Hawthornden*, ed. David Laing (London: F. Shorbel for the Shakespeare Society, 1842), p. 3.

any of them ever anthologized?) because the presence is missing which is evoked in the positive sonnets by synecdoche, drawing in "all things rare / That heaven's air in this huge rondure hems" (Sonnet 21). As transitional object and play fit the generous poems, so "hallucinatory wish-fulfillment" describes such gesturing in a void. "But do thy worst to steal thyself away, / For term of life thou art assuréd mine" (Sonnet 92)—the triumphant tone is almost absurdly incongruous with what is being said, "I cannot lose you because if you leave me I shall die."

When the poet turns to the youth as an actual person, in Sonnet 94, his complex ambivalence effectually pulls the poem apart. "They that have pow'r to hurt, and will do none," begins with a meditation on the lordly autonomy of those "who moving others are themselves as stone": "They are the lords and owners of their faces, / Others but stewards of their excellence." But the tone shifts abruptly when, after the first eight lines, the poem edges toward an expression of the youth's corruptibility:

> The summer's flow'r is to the summer sweet,
> Though to itself it only live and die;
> But if that flow'r with base infection meet,
> The basest weed outbraves his dignity.
>> For sweetest things turn sourest by their deeds;
>> Lilies that fester smell far worse than weeds.

The problem is not simply that the husbandry metaphor is radically transformed in moving from those who "husband nature's riches from expense" to the plight of the "summer's flow'r." We cannot put octave and sestet together in a single coherent reading—as attempts in the *Variorum* make clear—because Shakespeare's sensibility is confronting in the sonnet a situation in life which a sonnet cannot resolve.[31]

"MY DEEPEST SENSE, HOW HARD TRUE SORROW HITS"

The generalizing sonnets, which seek to express terminal attitudes—instead of a terminal event—are all among those after Son-

---

31. William Empson makes this sonnet the "crossroads" for very great criticism linking the Sonnets to the plays, particularly the Prince Hal-Falstaff relationship and the sense and sensuality of Angelo in *Measure for Measure*, in *Some Versions of Pastoral* (London: Chatto and Windus, 1935), pp. 85–111.

net 97: "Let me not to the marriage of true minds / Admit impediments" (116); "'Tis better to be vile than vile esteemed" (121); "Th'
expense of spirit in a waste of shame" (129); "Poor soul, the center
of my sinful earth . . . Buy terms divine in selling hours of dross"
(146). The first of these is often read at weddings; it is perhaps the
most commonly anthologized of all the sonnets, expressing as it
does the need all feel for unconditional love. Booth has an excursus
"on the special grandeur of the best sonnets," which exhibits its
marvelous range of meaning, instancing resonant contexts such as
the marriage service and the Psalms, and also bringing out ambiguous suggestions, some of them bawdy, which might undercut its
sweeping affirmation. He concludes that its absolute "love alters
not" is "absolutely strengthened by the self-contradiction engulfed
within it." [32]

But Booth's reading deals with the poem in isolation, and so neglects a frequent problem with the Sonnets, their uncertain or in-
determinate tone. When one reads Sonnet 116 in conjunction with
those immediately around it, it fits Robert Frost's definition of a
poem as "a momentary stay against confusion." [33] It is read in that
way, in conjunction with other generalizing sonnets, by Carol Neely,
who observes that these exceptional poems are "attempts to step
back and escape from the immediate painful situation" peculiar to
the parts of the sequence in which they appear. [34] She finds the precariousness of the attempt emerging *in* the poems, including in
Sonnet 116 the doubt underlying its final assertion: "If this be error
and upon me proved, / I never writ, nor no man ever loved." Then
she looks at the astonishing reversal of its affirmation about the
"ever fixéd mark" in the next following poem, where some of the
same imagery is used to acknowledge infidelities: "Accuse me thus:
that I have scanted all / . . . That I have hoisted sail to all the winds /
Which should transport me farthest from your sight." At the close,
Sonnet 117 attempts to justify infidelity by a couplet where we hear
the same rhyme words as those of the couplet in 116:

> Bring me within the level of your frown,
> But shoot not at me in your wakened hate,
>> Since my appeal says I did strive to prove
>> The constancy and virtue of your love.

32. "Commentary," p. 391.
33. "The Figure a Poem Makes" (1939), in *Robert Frost on Writing*, ed. Elaine
Barry (New Brunswick, N.J.: Rutgers University Press, 1973), p. 126.
34. Carol Neely, "Detachment and Engagement in Shakespeare's Sonnets: 94,
116, 129," *PMLA* 92 (1977): 83.

When we look now at Shakespeare dramatizing Shakespeare in Sonnet 116 (not a "speaker" uttering it in the house of language), it becomes the statement, verging on a plea, that the beloved should not "bend with the remover to remove" the poet, even though he has been a "wand'ring bark."

One has to accept the fact that Sonnet 116 can be read in two ways at least: one way, it makes unconditional love imaginatively real; the other way, it is a plea for such love. When one is concerned to encounter Shakespeare in his Sonnets, all the poems are gestures expressing need in an always open situation. Or one recognizes that they are all dramatic, though the dramatic situation is only clear—so far as it is clear—by implication. Those poems that seem to falsify the situation put one off: for example, the couplet of Sonnet 117 seems clearly specious after the confession "that I have scanted all / . . . Forgot upon your dearest love to call." If he *forgot* the love, how can his quasi-legal "appeal" be that "I did strive to prove / The constancy and virtue of your love"? If the sonnet were spoken by someone in a play—by Proteus, say, in *The Two Gentlemen of Verona*—we could enjoy seeing through the speciousness, cued by the dramatic situation (and by his servant Launce).

Another way to understand the protean meanings is to note that the Sonnets are poetry, not simply statements, though—and this can cause difficulties—they are statements as well as poetry. There is frequently an honesty by association, often to opposites. Booth does unprecedented justice to often subliminal counter-suggestions in his annotation. Even with Sonnet 116: though he observes that "it is one of the few Shakespeare sonnets that can be paraphrased without brutality," he brings out an "undercurrent of frivolous sexual suggestiveness." "Many of the metaphors and ideas of this sonnet seem just on the point of veering off towards puerile joking about temporary male impotence—loss of tumescence—after sexual climax. . . ; quatrain 2, for instance, is always ready to turn into a grotesquely abstruse pun on 'polestar.'" Whether one recognizes this sort of suggestion in "the star to every wand'ring bark, / Whose worth's unknown, although his highth be taken" depends on the reader and the occasion of his reading. The poem, because it is great poetry, is a thing one can walk around, so to speak, or a place one can walk in. Booth is certainly right that "a sense of straightforward simplicity" can emerge from "potentially dizzying complexity" in many cases or on many occasions.[35]

35. "Commentary," pp. 387, 391–92, xiii.

It is not plausible, with such poems, that a "final" attitude should be arrived at. Yet critics have taken Sonnet 146's hortatory advice to the "poor soul" as final, especially read in conjunction with Sonnet 129's devastating description of "lust in action." These are both powerful, moving poems. The torrential movement of Sonnet 129 scarcely pauses for twelve driving lines. In two lines of adjectives, "perjured, murd'rous, bloody" huddle like expletives. "Savage, extreme, rude, cruel" generate a reciprocal movement, "Enjoyed no sooner but despiséd straight," which concludes with "Before, a joy proposed, behind, a dream." Yet the couplet draws back:

> All this the world well knows, yet none knows well
> To shun the heav'n that leads men to this hell.

One need not notice the pun in "hell" from Elizabethan slang for female genitals; the recognition of the contingency of the denunciation is explicit. Is it too much to suggest, also, that in denouncing lust the poem has generated a violent pressure of frustration similar in structure to the driving pressure that can lead to "lust in action"? Such underground pressure, we know, frequently fuels denunciations—Angelo's, for example, as *Measure for Measure* demonstrates.

Even Leslie Fiedler takes Sonnet 146 as a final, conclusive turning away:

> Shakespeare, at the moment of writing the *Sonnets*, could not condone in himself the highest love he could conceive, but foresaw its dissolution in betrayal and lust, felt it deserved to be thus dissolved. And so he falls back, as generations of poets had before him, into the Christian palinode.[36]

Apart from considerations of context, Sonnet 146 cannot intrinsically bear the weight of such determinate reversal.

> Poor soul, the center of my sinful earth,
> . . . . these rebel pow'rs that thee array,[37]
> Why dost thou pine within and suffer dearth,
> Painting thy outward walls so costly gay?
> Why so large cost, having so short a lease,

---

36. Fiedler, *The Stranger in Shakespeare*, p. 38.

37. There is general consensus that the first three words of this line in the 1609 quarto—"My sinful earth"—were mistakenly supplied by the compositor. Several guesses have been made regarding what words were consequently lost, some quite plausible, all pure invention. In his note to this line, Booth offers "pressed with" as his own necessarily "arbitrary preference" ("Commentary," p. 504).

Dost thou upon thy fading mansion spend?
Shall worms, inheritors of this excess,
Eat up thy charge? Is this thy body's end?
Then, soul, live thou upon thy servant's loss,
And let that pine to aggravate thy store:
Buy terms divine in selling hours of dross;
Within be fed, without be rich no more.
 So shalt thou feed on death, that feeds on men,
 And death once dead, there's no more dying then.

The tenderness and beauty of diction in the octet are moving, but
the sestet becomes obtrusively hortatory. It is cast, moreover, in
prudential economic terms: buy long ages in heaven by "selling
hours of dross"—a bargain! The couplet about feeding on death is a
Q.E.D. that has not been very clearly demonstrated—though this
contributes to the somewhat hectic tone that is dramatized. The
poem does not establish any loving religious relationship, finds no
alternative object in God or Christ. One can contrast the widowed
Donne's expression of moving from the love of his wife to love
of God:

Since she whom I lov'd hath payd her last debt

· · · · · · · · · · · · · · ·
Here the admyring her my mind did whett
To seeke thee God.[38]

" 'Tis better to be vile than vile esteemed" (Sonnet 121) takes to
an extreme the self-knowledge of the poems around it and is like
them in making a declaration of autonomy within a social context:

For why should others' false adulterate eyes
Give salutation to my sportive blood?
Or on my frailties why are frailer spies,
Which in their wills count bad what I think good?

The third quatrain fuses self-assertion with self-acceptance, together with recognition of the final unknowable mystery of human
identity, by echoing, without any cue for a blasphemous tone,
Jehovah's self-description:

No, I am that I am, and they that level
At my abuses reckon up their own;
I may be straight though they themselves be bevel.
By their rank thought my deeds must not be shown.

38. "Holy Sonnets: XVII," *The Poems of John Donne*, ed. Sir Herbert Grierson
(London: Oxford University Press, 1933), p. 301.

The conclusion is tentative—and remarkable in that it does not abandon moral terms in spite of the way moral valuations have just been seen as contingent or projective:

> Unless this general evil they maintain—
> All men are bad and in their badness reign.

The poem shows Shakespeare enfranchising his identity without putting himself above "sinful earth" (Sonnet 146), but on the contrary accepting that he like everyone is down in it, and that the mysterious force of life may inescapably involve sources of vitality that are bad.

It is striking, by contrast with Marlowe, that Shakespeare can do without diabolism to support him in such exploration. Shakespeare's sensibility secularizes what in religious terms would be a tolerant recognition of original sin, a Catholic or broad Anglican sort of acceptance, as against the unforgiving terror that drives Doctor Faustus to the arms of Mephostophilis, or motivates other Marlowe protagonists to deny or subvert morality altogether. In psychological terms, Shakespeare's superego at this stage of his development is far less exigent and cruel. This relatively unthreatened openness to polymorphous pleasure is consistent with identification with the cherishing aspect of parental presences—with not having challenged and then internalized, as an alien and disabling inner directive, a threatening parental figure's potentially violent, feared antagonism to desire.

The sonnet just preceding 121, in expressing feelings of reciprocity, lets us see how Shakespeare's powers of sympathy come into play as he moves out from narcissism to recognition of his own experience in another person. Few poems have expressed so close to the heart and nerves the transformation of passion into compassion as does Sonnet 120, "That you were once unkind befriends me now":

> For if you were by my unkindness shaken,
> As I by yours, y'have passed a hell of time,
> And I, a tyrant, have no leisure taken
> To weigh how once I suffered in your crime.
> O that our night of woe might have rememb'red
> My deepest sense, how hard true sorrow hits.

Shakespeare's "deepest sense, how hard true sorrow hits" is the core of the generosity that animates the plays.

In considering how Shakespeare achieves a contingent mastery of the relationship to the young man, and increasing self-knowledge and acceptance, one runs into potential parallels, a number of them already made by critics, with *Henry IV* and *Henry V* and the festive and problematic comedies. Some relationships to the Sonnets will be explored in more detail in chapter 7 when we look at how the later history plays relate to the shift into the major tragedies. But we can note here something of the generous outgoing to life involved in Shakespeare's finding social and dramatic embodiment for the need which, in the Sonnets, is concentrated in the expression of the love for the friend. A striking instance is in the opening out of sexual possibilities in *Twelfth Night* in response to a young woman disguised as a young man.

The androgynous appeal of disguised Viola clearly reflects the fact, essential to the love for the friend in the Sonnets, that Elizabethan manners allowed the feminine aspects of men to be more fully expressed, without compromising their manhood, than in other epochs. *Twelfth Night* sorts out in a saturnalian, comic rhythm the Sonnets' congested response to the marvelous beauty and potentiality felt in a single young person, "the master mistress of my passion." Antonio, the infatuated rescuer of Viola's twin brother, Sebastian, carries on the directly charged friendship between men; like his namesake in *The Merchant of Venice*, he must at the end be content to look on while his protégé moves into a new stage of life through marriage. But meanwhile, the providential revelation that Cesario-Viola has an identical twin brother makes it possible for the misplaced infatuation of both Olivia and Orsino to be fulfilled. The master-mistress of their passion splits, at the last moment, into a master and a mistress.

In exploring Cesario-Viola's appeal to both Orsino and Olivia in *Shakespeare's Festive Comedy*, it seems to me now that I generalized ambiguously in saying that "with sexual as with other relations, it is when the normal is secure that playful aberration is benign."[39] The normal is never of course wholly secure; it is something that is maintained by culture against odds. The artist, in dealing with potentially disruptive situations, takes on the odds. Shakespeare's repeated use in the comedies of the boy actor playing a girl disguised as a youth permits him to show young womanhood emerging from the sexually undifferentiated beauty of early adolescence, and it

39. C. L. Barber, *Shakespeare's Festive Comedy* (Princeton: Princeton University Press, 1959), p. 245.

makes us realize anew how everyone who is fully alive to the grace of life has qualities of both sexes.[40] *Twelfth Night* finishes one way of working out the potentialities of the sensibility we see infatuated with a young man "for a woman . . . first created" (Sonnet 20) in the Sonnets. The verbal play with *master* and *mistress* in its final scene might conceivably signal Shakespeare's consciousness of doing so. The Duke says to Viola, who has yet to change from her masculine attire:

> Your master quits you; and for your service done him, . . .
> And since you call'd me master for so long,
> Here is my hand—you shall from this time be
> Your master's mistress.
>
> (V.i.321, 324–26)

But there was another thing to do, another way to go, subdominant in *Twelfth Night* but central, if not fully mastered, in *All's Well That Ends Well*, which splits off the "master" in Bertram while centering the passion for him in the "mistress," Helena.

In Helena's love for the elusive Bertram there is an uneasy alliance with the poet as he uses her to express passion reaching across class lines. Over against Helena—whose love, though largely silent after the beautifully poignant, hopeless love poetry of the opening acts, wins her way to a place in the aristocracy—Shakespeare exhibits in Parolles very voluble male-to-male sycophancy united with pretension to equality and tutelage. In the relations of Helena and Parolles to Bertram we have, I think, an attempt to work through, in art, aspects of Shakespeare's relation to the highborn young man of the Sonnets.[41] The love for the friend is vicari-

---

40. The culture's openness to androgynous coloration in the personal styles of men, and its relatively clear-cut definitions of the social roles of women, combine in the theatrical institution of boy actors for women's parts. The absence of any feeling that the role of boy actors is degrading, except as it accords with the general social status of common players, is notable in Hamlet's conversation about the children's companies and in his welcome of the players to Elsinore. As he greets the visiting company, it is striking that Hamlet pays considerable attention to the boy actor, playfully but not derogatorily addressed as though he were a young woman: "You are welcome, masters, welcome all. . . . What, my young lady and mistress! by' lady, your ladyship is nearer to heaven than when I saw you last, by the altitude of a chopine. Pray God your voice, like a piece of uncurrent gold, be not crack'd within the ring. Masters, you are all welcome" (II.ii.421, 424–29).

41. Muriel Bradbook first called attention to the resemblances between Helena's love and the Sonnets, in *Shakespeare and Elizabethan Poetry* (London: Chatto and Windus, 1951), p. 169. Roger Warren provides further exploration of this relationship in "Why Does It End Well? Helena, Bertram, and the Sonnets," *Shakespeare Survey* 22(1969): 79–92. Richard P. Wheeler considers the relationship of the Sonnets

ously invested in Helena; Parolles' attachment to Bertram is purely a social and military pretension, which turns out to be merely words. He is genuine only to the extent that he is not just a liar but a compulsive liar, so that his exposure and dismissal do not kill his heart at all—he can comfortably move down or over from pretended equal of Bertram to known buffoon for Lafew: "Simply the thing I am / Shall make me live" (IV.iii.333–34).

An emotional strategy recurrent in the Sonnets, to affirm the poet's love by distinguishing it from that of empty time-servers, is repeated over and over in *All's Well*: as Helena's masked pursuit of Bertram proceeds, Parolles is unmasked. In *All's Well* this strategy is not fully successful. The play dramatizes a scapegoat action by which Helena's search for heterosexual "mutual render, only me for thee" (Sonnet 125) is made up for by exposing Parolles' search for status by a male-to-male render of mere words. But the humiliation of Parolles cannot do what the deep scenario calls for it to accomplish: it cannot fully divert us from the real obstacles, and the humiliations, that never seem to be completely overcome in Helena's quest for Bertram. As Helena herself oscillates between gestures that proclaim her inadequacy to the aristocratic marriage and her insistent pursuit of Bertram through secret maneuvering and the expedience of the bed-trick, so the play, despite the ending, seems to extend more than resolve the persistent class tensions of the Sonnets. And the shallow and callous arrogance that peers out from behind the image of the friend in the Sonnets is so fully manifest in Bertram's behavior that our sense of Helena's final triumph is compromised by the nature of its object. Helena's love for a young lord who resembles in many ways the friend of the Sonnets presents one way in which the need for relationship to virile manhood finds expression at the beginning of the great tragic period. Although the comic form cannot fully master this mode of resolution, it is testimony of Shakespeare's commitment to the full range of possibilities that he should try this variation.

To turn to the relation of the Sonnets to the major tragedies, we need to go back to the earlier sonnets where the love is all-sufficing and to those where it becomes an all-or-nothing relationship, like Lear's with Cordelia or Othello's with Desdemona. Though the bio-

---

to *All's Well* in detail in *Shakespeare's Development and the Problem Comedies: Turn and Counter-Turn* (Berkeley and Los Angeles: University of California Press, 1981), pp. 57–75.

graphical chronology must remain inferential, it seems that Shakespeare made an investment in his own life which anticipated the
search for something like the divine in the human dramatized in
tragedy only some years later. Yeats wrote that man "is forced to
choose / Perfection of the life, or of the work."[42] In the worshipful
sonnets we see Shakespeare trying to choose perfection of the
life—but even here he seeks the perfection of another life and
seeks to realize it by poetry. The investment did not lead to personal tragedy or degradation, as it might well have done for a similar sensibility without Shakespeare's resources. The most important of these resources was of course his mastery as dramatist,
including the financial independence this yielded, which protected
him from abject practical need for patronage.

One way to focus on the relationship of the Sonnets to the major
tragedies is to consider likeness and difference with properly religious experience. J. B. Leishman does this in his fine study of the
poems, considered against a lifetime's reading in the poetry of the
whole Western tradition. Leishman, noting similarities between
Shakespeare's regard for the friend and attitudes that Herbert's poetry and Vaughan's reserve for addressing Christ, points out that
from a Christian vantage point many of the sonnets "seem in the
strict sense idolatrous, for in them the supreme object of the poet's
contemplation is a human life, regarded, not as the symbol or incarnation of something that transcends it, but as itself transcendent: all-supplying, all-restoring, all-sufficing."[43] Murray Krieger
has explored the way the Sonnets can recapture, by the action of
poetry, the equivalent of sacred time in a secular world, as mirror
becomes transforming window.[44] Leishman considers content rather
than poetics, and is not concerned with the familial roots of experience as poetry reaches back to and forward from them. Working
with religious analogy, he considers how the poems move between
doubt and faith—"there, where I have garner'd up my heart, /
Where either I must live or bear no life" (Oth.IV.ii.57–60):

Shakespeare's adoration is directed towards a mortal and visible beloved, whose worthiness and responsiveness he is sometimes com-

42. "The Choice," Collected Poems of W. B. Yeats (New York: Macmillan, 1956),
p. 242.

43. Leishman, Themes and Variations (n. 7 above), p. 217.

44. Murray Krieger, A Window to Criticism: Shakespeare's Sonnets and Modern Poetics (Princeton: Princeton University Press, 1964), pp. 165–90.

pelled to doubt, and one can never feel quite certain, and perhaps Shakespeare himself could never feel quite certain, whether what he is celebrating is the beloved or the love which the beloved has inspired. This continual oscillation between doubt at the heart of assurance and assurance at the heart of doubt is the dramatically tragic and tragically dramatic element in Shakespeare's sonnets, and it may well be that it was in it and out of it that some of the greatest moments in his tragedies arose.[45]

Of course, in struggling with the tragic potential of the love dramatized in the Sonnets, Shakespeare's resources included the sonnet itself, as he used it to evoke and live through an ideal presence and later to recover himself. A contingent but real mastery of the situation that pulls apart Sonnet 94 develops in many of the sonnets numbered from 97 up through the envoy in 126, including 120 and 121, discussed earlier. Among them are poems that recover the sense of wonder at the beloved's beauty as a resource, like Sonnets 97 and 98, or again, 106, "When in the chronicle of wasted time / I see descriptions of the fairest wights." But what is new is self-reference of an independent kind, beyond the efforts of the various generalizing poems to stand back from the relationship and so resolve its tensions—without, I feel, ever escaping contingency. The infidelities that the poet acknowledges and apologizes for are made occasions for Shakespeare to speak about himself in his own right, even while pleading for forgiveness. Self-knowledge becomes self-assertion and self-acceptance—again always contingent, as the poems are always in motion: "*though* in my nature . . ." "*No*, I am that I am" (Sonnets 109, 121).

Instead of falling into disabling disillusion, a possibility one feels in the farewell sonnets, Shakespeare in effect falls back into himself. In Sonnets 109 to 112 and 117 to 121 he confronts directly the polymorphic responsiveness of his own personality:

> Alas 'tis true, I have gone here and there,
> And made myself a motley to the view,
> Gored mine own thoughts, sold cheap what is most dear,
> Made old offences of affections new.
>
> (Sonnet 110)

Here "made myself a motley" suggests the actor's impulse and his humiliations, and in Sonnet 111 Shakespeare explicitly asks his

---

45. *Themes and Variations*, p. 230.

friend to forgive in him the "public manners" bred by the "public means" from which he must provide for his livelihood:

> Thence comes it that my name receives a brand,
> And almost thence my nature is subdued
> To what it works in, like the dyer's hand.

Commentators have emphasized, indeed exaggerated, the ignominious status of the acting profession in the Elizabethan age, seeing in this outward circumstance the source of Shakespeare's self-disabling humility toward his friend. No doubt it was a factor, just as part of the appeal of the young man was superior birth. But the temperament that made Shakespeare an actor and dramatist is more fundamental than the matter of status, as these sonnets make explicit: they describe a complex, resonant personality, which can be over-responsive, over-eager, drawn on to act unworthy parts and unable to avoid living out in new relationships what has already been found shameful. In Sonnet 109 ("O never say that I was false of heart"), Shakespeare subordinates an absence that "seemed my flame to qualify" to the overriding spiritual bond: "As easy might I from myself depart, / As from my soul, which in thy breast doth lie." His fluidity and his almost unbearable openness to life and desire are acknowledged in the sestet in a moving plea:

> Never believe, though in my nature reigned
> All frailties that besiege all kinds of blood,
> That it could so preposterously be stained
> To leave for nothing all thy sum of good—
> For nothing this wide universe I call,
> Save thou, my rose; in it thou art my all.

Though the couplet makes "this wide universe" nothing except the friend, in fact it is the poet in his own nature who occupies the whole poem.

The sort of knowledge of the heart and its turnings which finds expression in the plays appears in these sonnets with a special if limited intensity—the intensity involved in seeing, in one's single life, the broken lines made by Eros. In the same moment when he asks forgiveness for making "old offences of affections new," Shakespeare has the courage to recognize that there is value, as well as humiliation, in selling "cheap what is most dear":

> Most true it is, that I have looked on truth
> Askance and strangely. But by all above,

> These blenches gave my heart another youth,
> And worse essays proved thee my best of love.
>   (Sonnet 110)

There is no set posture in these poems against morality or convention: if they simplified things by adopting a romantic or bohemian rationale, they could not be so serious in exploring the way passion turns corners that it cannot see around and moves in directions contrary to the will.

The new, higher estimation of self—self-*regard*, with all that implies as against entire dependence on the regard of the friend—comes out in Sonnet 114, which deals in a new, detached way with projections of the friend's beauty, the "shadows" of Sonnets 53, or 97 and 98. This time they are explicitly recognized as projections and distortions and as the poet's action:

> Or whether doth my mind, being crowned with you,
> Drink up the monarch's plague, this flattery?
> Or whether shall I say mine eye saith true,
> And that your love taught it this alchemy—
> To make of monsters and things indigest
> Such cherubins as your sweet self resemble,
> Creating every bad a perfect best
> As fast as objects to his beams assemble?
> O 'tis the first, 'tis flatt'ry in my seeing,
> And my great mind most kingly drinks it up.

There is humor, surely, in speaking of "my great mind most kingly." But the concluding lines make clear that there is also serious self-assertion, and not to the credit of the whole relationship. Though the poet insists that he, not the friend, prepares the cup of specious similitudes, it still may be poisoned:

> Mine eye well knows what with his gust is greeing,
> And to his palate doth prepare the cup.
>   If it be poisoned, 'tis the lesser sin
>   That mine eye loves it and doth first begin.

This comes close to what we get in Sonnet 138 to the woman: here the poet's seeing flatters as mutual lies do there.

The next to last numbered sonnet to the man, 125, insists that that relation has become mutual, despite difference in social rank. The previous poem has asserted that "my dear love" is not "the child of state" but "all alone stands hugely politic"—the social references are cryptic (as in Sonnet 107, "Not mine own fears"), but the self-assertion is clear. Sonnet 125 insists, again with cryptic reference to time-servers, that the private tie can coexist with Shakespeare's being outwardly in the role of a gentleman-in-waiting in the service of the great:

> Were't ought to me I bore the canopy,
> With my extern the outward honoring,
> Or laid great bases for eternity,
> Which proves more short than waste or ruining?
> Have I not seen dwellers on form and favor
> Lose all and more by paying too much rent
> For compound sweet forgoing simple savor,
> Pitiful thrivers, in their gazing spent?
> No, let me be obsequious in thy heart,
> And take thou my oblation, poor but free,
> Which is not mixed with seconds, knows no art,
> But mutual render, only me for thee.
>   Hence, thou suborned informer! A true soul
>   When most impeached stands least in thy control.

Whatever happened to the social relationship later, it seems consistent with Sonnet 125 that the writing of sonnets to the young man should stop. For though it speaks of "my oblation," clearly the poem itself is not an oblation, as earlier sonnets had been. The relationship insisted on does not accept one-sided worship and so does not need to be made by sonnets.

In *All's Well That Ends Well*, the play that most closely dramatizes the social structure and its tensions as addressed in the Sonnets, the "love" of Parolles for Bertram is just such love as Shakespeare pours scorn on in Sonnet 125. Parolles dwells "on form and favor," obsequious only in his pretensions and pretenses; he becomes an informer when suborned by fear of supposed enemies, who delude this man of words by words—the wonderful gibberish Shakespeare invented for the exposure scene: "Portotartarossa"—"He calls for the tortures" (IV.iii.118–20). In attitudes developed toward Bertram we can see Shakespeare dramatizing something like the increasingly distanced perspective on experience characteristic of the later sonnets to the friend. One of the French lords, commenting on Bertram's flight from Helena and his behavior in Florence, exclaims: "As we are ourselves, what things are we!" (IV.iii.19–20). This reflection is in the mode of Sonnet 121 ("'Tis better to be vile than vile esteemed"), as is his summary statement of a "general evil":

The web of our life is of a mingled yarn, good and ill together: our virtues would be proud, if our faults whipt them not, and our crimes would despair, if they were not cherish'd by our virtues.

(IV.iii.71–74)

The sonnets to the friend come to a close in a comparable vein, mingling old admiration with an emergent sense of distance and limit. These sonnets end with a very different conclusion from "Farewell, thou art too dear for my possessing" (Sonnet 87). The twelve-line envoy, "O thou my lovely boy, who in thy pow'r," last-numbered of the poems to the friend, handles the familiar concern about the power of time and the youth's aging in a new way, with a new, detached attitude. The "lovely boy" is turned over to Nature, "sovereign mistress over wrack," who may, so long as she chooses, preserve his beauty as confirmation of *her* superiority to ravaging time. There is something verging on cruelty in the admonitory tone, which makes of the young man a kind of cat's paw in Nature's hands, serving her purposes while his lovers serve his:

> She keeps thee to this purpose, that her skill
> May time disgrace, and wretched minute kill.
> Yet fear her, O thou minion of her pleasure;
> She may detain but not still keep her treasure.
> Her audit, though delayed, answered must be,
> And her quietus is to render thee.
>
> (Sonnet 126)

In Sonnet 20 Nature doted on him as she made him, along with the poet. Now the "lovely boy" is only a "minion of her pleasure," and her quietus will be his. It is like Shakespeare to leave responsibility for this *Finis* with Nature: he does not, with Marlowe at the end of his great exploration of desire, *Doctor Faustus*, say "Terminat Author opus."

7

From Mixed History to Heroic Drama:
The *Henriad*

The two parts of *Henry IV* open out onto what seems to be the whole of English society, with a splendid development of Shakespeare's range, both in subjects and in the complexity of attitudes toward experience poised against one another. In *Shakespeare's Festive Comedy* I emphasized the way this richness, which the criticism of the last fifty years has variously recognized, is organized by the polarity of holiday and everyday in Shakespeare's culture.[1] "Mingling kings and clowns" in the native theatrical tradition Sidney deplored, the two plays are organized so that *Part One* balances Misrule against Rule, with Falstaff, as Holiday, asking to be Everyday; then *Part Two*, by a kind of Trial of Carnival, leads to the sacrifice of Falstaff, who is made to carry off bad luck and sin as the Prince makes atonement with his strong but guilty father. In my view, the dramatist resorts to magical action instead of dramatizing it, in inviting us to accept the ritual expulsion of Falstaff as scapegoat for the social and political ills of England. By setting the Sonnets against these plays, I think we can see how the expulsion of Falstaff, and with it the inhibition of Falstaffian ironies, is part of an effort to use the drama to establish a new relationship to manhood.

OLD OFFENSES AND AFFECTIONS NEW

Sonnet 146, "Poor soul, the center of my sinful earth," can serve as an entrance into a dramatic rhythm that uses the rejection of Falstaff to try to close over the ironic perspective on heroic action the two parts of *Henry IV* have opened up. After noting in chapter 6 that many regard this poem as a "Christian palinode" that resolves

---

1. C. L. Barber, *Shakespeare's Festive Comedy* (Princeton: Princeton University Press, 1959), pp. 192–221.

the conflicts engendered by the poet's search for fulfillment in human objects of love, we argued that this sonnet cannot be fully satisfying because it simplifies so drastically the complex sensibility engaged in the affirmations of human love. If we look at Sonnet 146 in relation to the Henry IV plays, we can see it as an effort by the poet to turn away from his former self, as Hal turns away from Falstaff:

> I know thee not, old man, fall to thy prayers.
> How ill white hairs becomes a fool and jester!
> I have long dreamt of such a kind of man,
> So surfeit-swell'd, so old, and so profane;
> But being awak'd, I do despise my dream.
> Make less thy body (hence) and more thy grace,
> Leave gormandizing, know the grave doth gape
> For thee thrice wider than for other men.
> Reply not to me with a fool-born jest,
> Presume not that I am the thing I was,
> For God doth know, so shall the world perceive,
> That I have turn'd away my former self;
> So will I those that kept me company.
>
> (2H4 V.v.47–59)

Here the newly crowned Henry V is "the soul of state" (*Tro.* III.iii.202), and Falstaff is synoptic for its corrupted body: "Then, soul, live thou upon thy servant's loss" (Sonnet 146) is the order of the day. Hal is doing what he advises Falstaff to do, and what the poet urges on himself in the sonnet: "Buy terms divine in selling hours of dross." "Make less thy body (hence) and more thy grace" recalls the poet's repudiation of his own body in the sonnet: "let that pine to aggravate thy store." As Henry V's heroic-Christian resolve replaces the passive-Christian resolution of the sonnet, the grave that gapes for "gormandizing" Falstaff displaces the death to which the poet turns with religious resignation:

> Within be fed, without be rich no more.
>   So shalt thou feed on death, that feeds on men,
>   And death once dead, there's no more dying then.

Behind the generalizing sonnets one can often hear echoes of other poems whose attitudes are in considerable tension with the sort of simplifying finality we get in Sonnet 146, as we saw in chapter 6. Just so, Henry's dismissive severity can recall Falstaff's characteristically ironic self-justifications, centered on the very surfeit-swelled excess now banished:

Dost thou hear, Hal? Thou knowest in the state of innocency Adam fell, and what should poor Jack Falstaff do in the days of villainy? Thou seest I have more flesh than another man, and therefore more frailty.

(1H4 III.iii.164–68)

The repudiation of Falstaff, however, is serious business. Shakespeare *is* exploring the soul of state and the exigencies of political action. In the last act of 2 *Henry IV* and in *Henry V* he is dramatizing the way a leader can become an organizing presence for a society by meeting needs cognate to those the poet has typically sought to fulfill, not in such Christian resignation as we find in Sonnet 146, but in the presence of the young man. In *Henry V* the Chorus gives explicit expression to the satisfaction the heroic presence of the young king provides:

> . . . every wretch, pining and pale before,
> Beholding him, plucks comfort from his looks.
> A largess universal, like the sun,
> His liberal eye doth give to every one,
> Thawing cold fear, that mean and gentle all
> Behold, as may unworthiness define,
> A little touch of Harry in the night.
>
> (IV.Cho.41–47)

Here the Chorus uses the same sort of imagery to describe the King's countenance, in the night before Agincourt, that the Sonnets use about the largess of the young man's countenance. On the social, historical side, the Chorus is describing the process Freud deals with in *Group Psychology and the Analysis of the Ego*, by which a charismatic leader can enter into the psychic economy of followers in a way comparable to what happens in falling in love.[2] The play *Henry V* both generalizes about this and localizes it in persons (Fluellen, for instance, as he puts his Welsh individuality in the devoted service of "your Majesty's manhood" [IV.viii.33–34]), while wrestling with what it involves in the person of the King.

Henry V also invites the audience to take its hero king in the same way that his society takes him. Just how far it goes in this direction, whether it is ironic about this, and if so, how, are questions that are perennially in dispute among good critics. In its incompletely controlled tone, *Henry V* is remarkably like such absolutely phrased but finally precarious sonnets as 146, or 116—"Let me not

---

2. *Standard Edition*, vol. 18; see esp. pp. 111–16.

to the marriage of true minds"—and, I think, for the same reason: the poet is using the work to meet *part* of his need as if it met the whole of it, with part of his need and sensibility kept out. But the drama provides a crucial resource that the Sonnets do not; it allows the dramatist to throw the stress, not on the need that seeks realization in a young man who cannot be brought into the utterance directed to him, but on the realization of that need in the character who meets it in a dramatic action.

The religiousness of Sonnet 146, as was emphasized earlier, has no object of worship; the poem does not turn to God or Christ in place of the young man or mistress, as Donne, for example, turns from his dead wife to Christ. At the close of 2 *Henry IV*, however, there *is* such an object, along with the prudential revulsion to piety of the sonnet; the object is Henry V, even as the dramatist rejects the part of the poet that has been in Falstaff. Although the scene of the rejection is a reprise of many similar gestures in the Sonnets, where the poet makes nothing of himself to make the beloved everything, it is taking place on the main line of Shakespeare's dramatic development, and with dramatic finality—for the moment at least. Because in the dramatic form Shakespeare can hypostatize what the Sonnets seek to hold together, it is possible to leave the Falstaff sensibility behind and still take as object a young man—in whom full manhood and authority are to be envisaged as being achieved. The sonneteer's role in realizing the life of the friend is taken over by the dramatist as dramatist. As in the Sonnets the all-or-nothing investment is not in a religious incarnation or transcendence but in a beloved friend, so here in *Henry V* Shakespeare invests in a secular hero king.

As we move from Falstaff's many-sided relationship with Hal to the celebration of Henry V's heroic virtues, the shift in dramatic perspective is akin to what we find in the Sonnets if we move from the action in poems that address Shakespeare's infidelity to the friend to the eloquent affirmation of unqualified love in Sonnet 116. I have already considered difficulties about the tone of the affirmation in this sonnet, "Let me not to the marriage of true minds," following Carol Neely in her analysis of the way certain of the sonnets attempt to stand back from the "motion in corruption" of the sequence and the way this attempt breaks down.[3] When viewed from

3. I am drawing here on Professor Neely's "Detachment and Engagement in Shakespeare's Sonnets: 94, 116, and 129," *PMLA* 92 (1977): 83–95, to which I am greatly indebted.

the perspective of sonnets that explicitly bring out other, more disruptive dimensions of the love for the friend, the unqualified affirmation of love in Sonnet 116 becomes precarious. The tension between the affirmation of this sonnet and the poems around it is similar to the tensions *inside* neighboring sonnets, between their hopeful finales and the stressful acknowledgments with which they begin.

We have considered the self-knowledge such poems convey, in chapter 6. Here it is the locked-in tension of these sonnets that contrasts with the similar but different things we get with Falstaff and his way of knowing and affirming himself in relation to Hal. Falstaff certainly fits in many ways the poet's self-description in Sonnet 110, written after an interval of separation:

> Alas 'tis true, I have gone here and there,
> And made myself a motley to the view,
> Gored mine own thoughts, sold cheap what is most dear,
> Made old offences of affections new.
> Most true it is, that I have looked on truth
> Askance and strangely.

But instead of suffering regrets about having "sold cheap what is most dear," with the strain this puts on the poet's effort to repudiate his past self and proclaim renewal, Falstaff rejoices in selling dear what, with his powers, comes cheap:

> I will devise matter enough out of this Shallow to keep Prince Harry in continual laughter the wearing out of six fashions. . . . O, it is much that a lie with a slight oath and a jest with a sad brow will do with a fellow that never had the ache in his shoulders!
>
> (2H4 V.i.78–84)

In this instance, the self-congratulatory enthusiasm belongs to Falstaff riding for a fall in *Part Two*. We can participate fully in Falstaff's gall as he relishes future prospects for opportunistic intimacy. We can also see, as he cannot, the movement of a dramatic action that is fast putting such wishful prospects, and the Prince, out of Falstaff's range, however great the imaginative powers through which he seeks to exploit them. But with Sonnet 110—which moves in an opposite direction to this action, from self-depletion and separation to wishful renewal through the friend's love—it is hard to settle what the tone is; as often with the Sonnets, the poet is using the poetry for special pleading that is not framed by anything comparable to the controlled interplay of perspectives the drama can provide.

Like Sonnet 110, Sonnet 109 ("O never say that I was false of heart") broods over absences that have "seemed my flame to qualify." Pairing these poems as "nimble apologia," Stephen Booth sees *comic* reference to perversion in 109:

> Never believe, though in my nature reigned
> All frailties that besiege all kinds of blood,
> That it could so preposterously be stained
> To leave for nothing all thy sum of good.

Of the travel simile by which Shakespeare understands his return to his soul lodged in his beloved's breast—"That is my home of love; if I have ranged / Like him that travels I return again"—Booth comments: "Shakespeare's purpose is presumably to display a Falstaff-like gall in solemnly making a logical-sounding equation between two non-comparable things: the journeys of a traveler and the promiscuous sexual liaisons of an unfaithful lover."[4] But surely the tone of this poem is ardently conflictual: it pleads, partly by the poet's acknowledging polymorphous temptation, for reconciliation that would accept the actual complexity of the poet's nature. Sonnets 109 and 110 are as moving in their way as Sonnet 116 is in its way. But there is no freedom for Falstaff-like gall in the relationship to the young man as these poems present it—the all-or-nothing bond precludes it: "For nothing this wide universe I call, / Save thou, my rose; in it thou art my all" (Sonnet 109). Hence, surely, part of the joy in creating Falstaff.

Where "Let me not to the marriage of true minds" works to submerge disruptive possibilities within a sweeping affirmation of love, Falstaff's incantatory denials of his disabling age, whoring, drunkenness, gluttony, obesity, and cowardice become an outrageous affirmation of himself:

> My lord, the man I know. . . . But to say I know more harm in him than in myself, were to say more than I know. That he is old, the more the pity, his white hairs do witness it, but that he is, saving your reverence, a whoremaster, that I utterly deny.
>
> (*1H4* II.iv.464–70)

What mock-king Hal, rehearsing his interview with his father, has denounced as scandalous "impediments" to the old ruffian's claims on the young prince, Falstaff denies or turns into virtues; all are

---

4. *Shakespeare's Sonnets*, ed. with analytic commentary by Stephen Booth (New Haven: Yale University Press, 1977), p. 351.

swept into the accumulating rhythm of his iterative prose, splen-
didly varied at the moment of climax:

> No, my good lord, banish Peto, banish Bardolph, banish Poins, but
> for sweet Jack Falstaff, true Jack Falstaff, valiant Jack Falstaff, and
> therefore more valiant, being as he is old Jack Falstaff, banish not
> him thy Harry's company, banish not him thy Harry's company—
> banish plump Jack, and banish all the world.
>
> (lines 474–80)

Shakespeare in Sonnet 116 ascends into poetry as though into a
waking dream: one can follow him into it and feel the marriage of
true minds without impediments; or, on reading it in relation to
more troubled sonnets, one can glimpse under its surface what in
Falstaff's waking dream is there for all to see. In the play we can,
with Hal, enjoy the contradictions, which are, "like their father that
begets them, gross as a mountain, open, palpable" (1H4 II.iv.225–
26). "Dost thou hear me, Hal?" "Ay, and mark thee too, Jack"
(II.iv.209–10). Instead of the tensions of anxious-pleading protestation, as in "Since my appeal says I did strive to prove / The constancy and virtue of your love" (Sonnet 117), there is delightful
release as we at once admire and dismiss Falstaff's excuses and
evasions:

> PRINCE HAL: Sirrah, do I owe you a thousand pound?
> FALSTAFF: A thousand pound, Hal? a million, thy love is worth a
> million; thou owest me thy love.
>
> (III.iii.135–37)

In the Sonnets there is a queasiness about the latent self-love displaced onto the highborn young man:

> Sin of self-love possesseth all mine eye,
>
> . . . .
>
> Methinks no face so gracious is as mine,
>
> . . . .
>
> But when my glass shows me myself indeed
> Beated and chopped with tanned antiquity,
> Mine own self love quite contrary I read;
> Self so self-loving were iniquity.
>   'Tis thee, myself, that for myself I praise,
> Painting my age with beauty of thy days.
>
> (Sonnet 62)

Falstaff's self-love is right out in the open, and at his most winning
"plump Jack" has all the charm of a little child:

CHIEF JUSTICE: Do you set down your name in the scroll of youth,
that are written down old with all the characters of
age? . . . and every part about you blasted with
antiquity? . . .

FALSTAFF: My lord, I was born about three of the clock in the
afternoon, with a white head and something of a
round belly.

(2H4 I.ii.178–80, 184, 187–89)

Self-disabling metaphor in the Sonnets is literalized in the drama—
and yet does not daunt Falstaff:

Speak of my lameness, and I straight will halt.
(Sonnet 89)

A pox of this gout! or a gout of this pox! for the one or the other plays
the rogue with my great toe. 'Tis no matter if I do halt, I have the
wars for my color, and my pension shall seem the more reasonable.
A good wit will make use of any thing.
(2H4 I.ii.243–48)

The marvelous autonomy of Falstaff goes with his constant relaxa-
tion into physical gluttony, as against the strain on the sonneteer's
psychic "gluttoning":

So are you to my thoughts as food to life,

. . . .

And by and by clean starvéd for a look;

. . . .

Thus do I pine and surfeit day by day,
Or gluttoning on all, or all away.
(Sonnet 75)

On one side, the sonneteer is getting his comeuppance. Decrepit
Falstaff takes delight in seeing his active Hal do deeds of youth in
killing Hotspur: "Well said, Hal! to it Hal! Nay, you shall find no boy's
play here, I can tell you" (1H4 V.iv.75–76). The merely vicarious enjoyment of manhood is explicit in "no boy's play here." A self-
interest in love that seeks to leap over caste difference is made obvious in Falstaff; so also is overestimation of what artful wit can do
across such difference: "I know the young king is sick for me. Let us
take any man's horses, the laws of England are at my commandement" (2H4 V.iii.135–37). A resentment, potential in the Sonnets,
at what belonging to a higher caste can do for someone actually
mediocre is expressed and then rebuked as the Prince overhears
Falstaff characterize him as "A good shallow young fellow. 'A
would have made a good pantler, 'a would 'a' chipp'd bread well"

(2H4 II.iv.237–38). Responding to Doll Tearsheet's question about Poins—"Why does the Prince love him so then?"—Falstaff speaks of roistering talents shared by Poins and the Prince: "gambol faculties . . . that show a weak mind and an able body, for which the Prince admits him" (2H4 II.iv.243, 251–52). "From me far off, with others all too near" echoes from Sonnet 61. As many have noted, Falstaff seems to carry a suggestion of Shake-speare. The buffoon's triumphant gluttonous and dramatic aggression is paid for by such playful self-mockery.

Sources of humiliation or helplessness for the Sonnets poet become resources of self-aggrandizement and (ultimately illusory) control for Falstaff.

> O for my sake do you with fortune chide,
> The guilty goddess of my harmful deeds,
> That did not better for my life provide
> Than public means which public manners breeds.
> (Sonnet 111)

"I am Fortune's steward," Falstaff exalts when Pistol brings news of the old king's death: "Blessed are they that have been my friends, and woe to my Lord Chief Justice" (2H4 V.iii. 130–31, 137–38). In the sonnet, "public means which public manners breeds" clearly refers to Shakespeare's gaining his livelihood in the theater:

> Thence comes it that my name receives a brand,
> And almost thence my nature is subdued
> To what it works in, like the dyer's hand.

Falstaff, for his public manners, receives one brand after another:

> SHERIFF: One of them is well known, my gracious lord,
> A gross fat man. . . .
> PRINCE: This oily rascal is known as well as Paul's.
> (1H4 II.iv.509–10, 526)

England is Falstaff's theater, and he takes heart that "Men of all sorts take a pride to gird at me" (2H4 I.ii.6).

Falstaff, within the plays, is always playing, freed by (and condemned to) a theatrical existence: "Out, ye rogue, play out the play, I have much to say in the behalf of that Falstaff" (1H4 II.iv.484–85). The poet, in writing the Sonnets, is freed and condemned in a different way to living by words and gestures, since it is by means of the poems that their author lives in his friend and his friend in him, as in Sonnet 81:

When all the breathers of this world are dead,
    You still shall live—such virtue hath my pen—
    Where breath most breathes, ev'n in the mouths of men.

Such immediate consummation in utterance, as we observed in the chapter on the Sonnets, gives something like an immediate experience of immortality. We have a similar experience in the great speeches where Falstaff eludes morality and mortality: "What is honor?" "The better part of valor." But the dramatic context places the experience within limits controlled by the dramatist; with the Sonnets it is only by our assessment of the potentially conflictual relationships between poems that *we* can place—never fully satisfactorily—the event that is such a poem as Sonnet 81. One must add that from Morgann on down to Roy Battenhouse in his essay "Falstaff as Parodist and Perhaps Holy Fool," Falstaff has been seen as triumphing in an unqualified way, or a way that somehow transcends qualification.[5]

As he relishes his role at the beginning of *Part Two*, Falstaff makes a brag that can fit his author:

> The brain of this foolish-compounded clay, man, is not able to invent any thing that intends to laughter more than I invent or is invented on me: I am not only witty in myself, but the cause that wit is in other men.

(I.ii.7–10)

Shakespeare of course was "the cause that wit is in other men" across the board, inventing all the parts for his fellows. There is good reason to feel uneasy in setting out to claim, as here, that Shakespeare is more in one part than in others. After all, as many have pointed out, Falstaff's role is compounded of several traditional roles: clown, fool, the Vice or Good Fellowship luring innocents to the tavern in the moralities, buffoon, Lord of Misrule, Carnival.[6] If there is Shakespeare in him, to be in everybody on stage was Shakespeare's professional job. One can add that, since Falstaff is a holiday figure, protagonist of saturnalian release, Shakespeare in animating him would be going on holiday—taking with him, as

---

5. Maurice Morgann, *An Essay on the Dramatic Character of Sir John Falstaff* (London: T. Davies, 1777); Roy Battenhouse, "Falstaff as Parodist and Perhaps Holy Fool," *PMLA* 90 (1975): 32–52.

6. See *Shakespeare's Festive Comedy*, pp. 67–73 and chap. 8, for one consideration of these roles. See also J. Dover Wilson, *The Fortunes of Falstaff* (Cambridge: Cambridge University Press, 1943).

revelers do, his own everyday powers now heightened by being free to express otherwise inhibited attitudes. Moreover, Shakespeare's whole controlling dramatic construction is using Falstaff, along with Hotspur, Henry IV, and the rest, in the rhythm of the polarized action, to present the development of Hal as an inclusive royal nature. By design, the two parts of *Henry IV* are centered on the Prince, not Falstaff.

Although one must grant all this, and *gladly*, in the perspective of Shakespeare's whole development something more is going on: Shakespeare is acting out the Falstaff relationship to life in order to try to banish it—"I do, I will." The goal is to disinvest in the vicarious enjoyment of manhood in order to reinvest in Manhood itself. The exigencies of the whole development are encountered (beyond full control) in the unsatisfactoriness of the hero king who emerges from the process. Hotspur, in the scene just before the Boar's Head revels, exclaims "I could divide myself and go to buffets" (*1H4* II.iii.32). Of course this is exactly what Hotspur cannot do. Shakespeare, however, is doing just such dividing, and while the divided parts are at play or at civil war, the drama has an inclusiveness which we can feel the Prince to be sharing from behind his circumspection. But the conclusion of *Part Two*, with its rejection of Falstaff, in effect tries for the simplification of such a sonnet as 110, which puts the "old offenses" of the poet behind in the renewed affiliation to the friend: "Then give me welcome, next my heav'n the best, / Ev'n to thy pure and most most loving breast." The play asks us to put Falstaff's perspective behind as we admire the heroic enterprise of King Henry V. Like "the star to every wand'ring bark" of Sonnet 116, the young king of *Henry V* becomes "this star of England" (Epi. 6), giving direction and inspiration to a whole nation that can be renewed in his presence, after having become mired in the old offenses of previous reigns. But in *Henry V*, without the full ironic interplay of perspectives that holds until the very end of *2 Henry IV*, we are back to such conflictual submission to an idealized figure as we have in the Sonnets.

"EV'N AT THE TURNING O' TH' TIDE"

The marvelous freedom of *Henry IV* depends on a redistribution outward of the aggression which in the Sonnets is so frequently turned inward on the poet. But it is striking that Shakespeare, in dealing for the first time with the transmission of heritage across tension between father and son, alters his sources to eliminate direct expressions of the Prince's hostile or defiant feelings toward his father. In the chronicles Hal and the large retinue he maintains burst in on the court dressed in strange, outlandish costume.[7] Shakespeare's Hal seeks other targets for hostile impulses engendered in a role and a bond that, by his own royal birth, are inescapable. In *The Famous Victories of Henry the Fifth*,[8] the Prince, until his sudden, unmotivated transformation, is a street bully who *does* undertake to abrogate the laws of England and to make one of his riotous companions a judge when he is crowned. This crude little play dramatizes the episode of Hal's striking the Chief Justice, an incident that is only referred to by Shakespeare in retrospect during the new Henry V's atonement with him at the close of *Part Two*. All explicit reference to the son's hostility is given to the father:

> PRINCE: I never thought to hear you speak again.
> KING: Thy wish was father, Harry, to that thought.
> (2H4 IV.v.91–92)

The scene of atonement with the Lord Chief Justice makes explicit an orientation that will be developed (if with some strain) throughout *Henry V*: the young king's aggression is wholly a function of his commitment to the sacramental political role he now embraces. Confronted by the new king, the Chief Justice apprehensively recalls the rationale by which he had imprisoned the rebellious Hal:

> I then did use the person of your father,
> The image of his power lay then in me,
> And in th' administration of his law,
> Whiles I was busy for the commonwealth,
> Your Highness pleased to forget my place,
> The majesty and power of law and justice,
> The image of the King whom I presented.[9]
> (2H4 V.ii.73–79)

Henry V responds by addressing the episode of striking the Chief Justice in a way that makes it part of an expectable pattern of

---

7. See *Sources*, vol. 4, pp. 179, 193–94, 216–17.
8. Reprinted in *Sources*, vol. 4, pp. 299–343.
9. The whole hopeful fusion of royal prerogative and constitutional law, which worked under Elizabeth and was to come apart under James, is invoked in Henry's reply to the Chief Justice, along with Shakespeare's respect for the institution of law and for the monarch as its sanction. The new king's response underscores the characteristically Elizabethan idea that he submits to the Justice voluntarily, that the monarch abides by law and Parliament by choice, with an absolute prerogative in reserve.

youthful wildness contained politically within harmless limits—
the pattern of the two Henry IV plays. He spells out, almost unc-
tuously, the extension of filial commitment to a more general allegiance to authority and law, here embodied in the Chief Justice:

> There is my hand.
> You shall be as a father to my youth,
> My voice shall sound as you do prompt mine ear,
> And I will stoop and humble my intents
> To your well-practic'd wise directions.
>
> (V.ii.117–21)

This is pure Henry V, as we come to know him in the next play,
always careful to keep righteousness on his side, consulting with
the Archbishop of Canterbury about his title to France, denying
that uncontrolled passion can have any part in his aggressive action, for "We are no tyrant, but a Christian king, / Unto whose
grace our passion is as subject / As is our wretches fett'red in our
prisons" (H5 I.ii.241–43).

When we see Hal at the outset of the Henry IV plays, the rebel-
liousness acknowledged in him only at the end is expressed by
Falstaff:

> But I prithee, sweet wag, shall there be gallows standing
> in England when thou art King? and resolution thus
> fubb'd as it is with the rusty curb of old father antic the
> law? Do not thou, when thou art king, hang a thief.
>
> PRINCE: No, thou shalt.
> FALSTAFF: Shall I? O rare! By the Lord, I'll be a brave judge.
> PRINCE: Thou judgest false already. I mean thou shalt have the
> hanging of the thieves, and so become a rare hangman.
>
> (1H4 I.ii.58–68)

As Ernst Kris pointed out in a pioneering psychoanalytic essay,
"Prince Hal's Conflict,"[10] the Prince's problem is like Hamlet's in
that he is in line to inherit from a usurper, but the Oedipal motive is
repressed and displaced onto Falstaff, who both covets the power
Hal will inherit when the father is dead and absorbs in his own person Hal's aggression toward a father. There is no need at this point
to labor the aggressive tendency of Hal's wit in undoing Falstaff's
pretensions, "dethroning" him at the Boar's Head during the extempore rehearsal of the interview with the king, enjoying a rhapsody of

---

10. Ernst Kris, *Psychoanalytic Explorations in Art* (New York: International Universities Press, 1952), pp. 273–88.

flyting about "that roasted Manningtree ox with the pudding in his belly, that reverent Vice, that grey Iniquity, that father ruffian, that vanity in years" (*1H4* II.iv.452–54). The aggression becomes deadly in the lines of rejection: "I know thee not, *old man.*"

It is dizzying to reflect that in that final scene Shakespeare is dramatizing the kind of rejection which the poet fears in the Sonnets. He gives Falstaff, in his opportunistic eagerness—to see the new king and to control the impression he will make on him—language like the Sonnets:

> I will leer upon him as 'a comes by, and do but mark the countenance that he will give me.
>
> (*2H4* V.v.6–8)

> But when your countenance filled up his line,
> Then lacked I matter, that enfeebled mine.
> (Sonnet 86)

> But to stand stain'd with travel, and sweating with desire to see him, thinking of nothing else, putting all affairs else in oblivion, as if there were nothing else to be done but to see him.
>
> (*2H4* V.v.24–27)

> For nothing this wide universe I call,
> Save thou, my rose; in it thou art my all.
> (Sonnet 109)

> Being your slave, what should I do but tend
> Upon the hours and times of your desire?
> (Sonnet 57)

Falstaff then calls out to the approaching king: "God save thy Grace, King Hal! my royal Hal! . . . God save thee, my sweet boy!" (V.v.41, 43).

Of course, the patterns of "worship" in Shakespeare's society, peaking in the kind of courtier courtship lavished on Elizabeth, made common idiom of expressions somewhat like these—Shakespeare skillfully insists on the breach of decorum by Falstaff's inappropriately personal and possessive phrasing, climaxing in "sweet boy!" ("What's new to speak, what now to register, / That may express my love, or thy dear merit? / Nothing, sweet boy" [Sonnet 108].) Falstaff thinks he is calling out to Hal, but it is Henry V who is coming from his coronation. By showing Falstaff, before the king appears, calculating what effects he can hope to produce, Shakespeare demonstrates beyond any doubt how impossible, morally and politically, Falstaff would be as a royal favorite. It is all handled impeccably in social-historical perspective.

Such similarities between the Sonnets and Falstaff's language when he contemplates or addresses Hal also reflect the homogeneity of Shakespeare's idiom, his repertory of tropes and situations, regardless of whether they also reflect changing ways of investing himself in his art. To see them as surveyor's reference points in his development from work to work depends on having the whole territory in view, and on one's sense of their place in the dynamic whole of each work in which they appear. So we need to be aware of the role of the Chorus and its tension with the dramatic action in *Henry V* when we compare

> Behold, as may unworthiness define,
> A little touch of Harry in the night . . .

with Falstaff's great lie about the action at Gadshill, when "it was so dark, Hal, that thou couldest not see thy hand":

> By the Lord, I knew ye as well as he that made ye. Why, hear you, my masters, was it for me to kill the heir-apparent? Should I turn upon the true prince? Why, thou knowest I am as valiant as Hercules; but beware instinct—the lion will not touch the true prince.
> (*1H4* II.iv.223–24, 267–72)

Falstaff's lie, which Hal heartily enjoys seeing through, is a burlesque of the mystique about magical royalty that undid Richard II, who imagined that the threat to his rule would dissipate when the night-reveler Bolingbroke "Shall see us rising in our throne, the east" (*R2* III.ii.50). One finds similar imagery, expressed with comparable seriousness, when the Sonnets celebrate the renewing presence of the friend. In Sonnet 27, the young man, "like a jewel hung in ghastly night, / Makes black night beauteous." "All days are nights" when the friend is absent in Sonnet 43, "And nights bright days when dreams do show thee me."

On confronting Richard, even Bolingbroke will respond to the grandeur of the king in terms of this imagery:

> See, see, King Richard doth himself appear,
> As doth the blushing discontented sun
> From out the fiery portal of the east,
> When he perceives the envious clouds are bent
> To dim his glory and to stain.
> (*R2* III.iii.62–66)

Yet it is, of course, Richard's magical identification of himself with such metaphorical equations that deflects him from full confrontation with political realities Bolingbroke knows how to manipulate. The same cluster of images is taken over by Hal in the soliloquy in which he explains for the audience how he is going to make Richard's imagery work, politically, by *using* his wildness and reformation:

> I know you all, and will a while uphold
> The unyok'd humor of your idleness,
> Yet herein will I imitate the sun,
> Who doth permit the base contagious clouds
> To smother up his beauty from the world,
> That when he please again to be himself,
> Being wanted, he may be more wond'red at
> By breaking through the foul and ugly mists
> Of vapors that did seem to strangle him.[11]
> (*1H4* I.ii.195–203)

By contrast, in the lines of the Chorus in *Henry V* about a magical sunlike presence in the night, the royal mystique is again being used seriously. In following out Hal's project to its heroic completion, with his "largess universal, like the sun, . . . / Thawing cold fear" among his soldiers, Shakespeare's search for idealized manhood carries on in a heroic mode the effort of the Sonnets poet to live through the life of his friend. It is essential to this project that Falstaff, and with him his ironic, mocking perspective on the mystique of royalty, be left behind.

From the vantage point of Shakespeare's development, it is exactly right that he did *not* carry out the program, suggested by the epilogue for *Part Two*, to "continue the story, with Sir John in it, and make merry with fair Katherine of France, where (for any thing I know) Falstaff shall die of a sweat, unless already 'a be kill'd with your hard opinions." Certainly Falstaff was not killed in the audience's opinions, as contemporary allusions to his role, and its rehandling in *The Merry Wives of Windsor*, make clear. What we learn in *Henry V*—that "The King has kill'd his heart" (II.i.88)—fits with the deeper levels of feeling underlying all the self-love and

---

11. William Empson, in his wonderful chapter on the Sonnets and *Henry IV*, observes that this is the same imagery as in Sonnet 33, "the earliest and most pathetic of the attempts to justify" the friend's infidelity: "Full many a glorious morning have I seen . . . / Anon permit the basest clouds to ride / With ugly rack on his celestial face." Empson notes that the attitude of the sonnet is "turned backwards" in Hal's soliloquy: "the sun is now to free itself from the clouds by the very act of betrayal." *Some Versions of Pastoral* (London: Chatto and Windus, 1935), p. 100.

self-aggrandizement of his buffoonery, the level of feeling in the Sonnets:

> But do thy worst to steal thyself away,
> For term of life thou art assuréd mine,
> And life no longer than thy love will stay,
> For it depends upon that love of thine.
>
> (Sonnet 92)

It is not so much that Falstaff loves Hal, but that Hal's love is for Falstaff the basis of his sense of self, however far he ranges in making himself a motley within the tavern world or sharking on Shallow in the country. On his side, Falstaff's love is as selfish *and* sincere as an infant's for its parent: "thy love is worth a million" in patronage, certainly, but also because "Thy sweet love rememb'red such wealth brings, / That then I scorn to change my state with kings" (Sonnet 29).

Sonnet 87 uses the poet's characteristic tendency toward self-effacement in an uncharacteristic reckoning with the prospect of losing the friend: "Farewell, thou art too dear for my possessing, / And like enough thou know'st thy estimate." At the end of *Part Two*, Falstaff finds that Henry V is too dear for his possessing, and very well knows his estimate. "Thus have I had thee as a dream doth flatter: / In sleep a king, but waking no such matter" (Sonnet 87) could serve to spell out the recognition we do not see banished Falstaff live to make. The poet, in the "farewell" sonnets that follow 87, can find consolation in the idea of dying if the young man abandons him:

> Thou canst not vex me with inconstant mind,
> Since that my life on thy revolt doth lie.
> O what a happy title do I find,
> Happy to have thy love, happy to die!
>
> (Sonnet 92)

But here the escape into a fantasy of dying seems too easy: by introducing the logical extreme of the self-negating tendency in the Sonnets, Shakespeare pulls back from such troubling awareness of conflict as we find in many, far richer poems that surrender self-concern to extend the relationship. The effort in Sonnet 92 to bury in death the burden of exploration and understanding contrasts sharply with the powerfully resonant dramatization of the response to Falstaff's death in *Henry V*.

But Mistress Quickly's account of that death involves us in a strange, consenting fascination:

> Nay sure, he's not in hell; he's in Arthur's bosom, if ever man went to Arthur's bosom. 'A made a finer end, and went away and it had been any christom child. 'A parted ev'n just between twelve and one, ev'n at the turning o' th' tide; for after I saw him fumble with the sheets, and play with flowers, and smile upon his finger's end, I knew there was but one way; for his nose was as sharp as a pen, and 'a babbl'd of green fields. "How now, Sir John? quoth I, "what, man? be a' good cheer." So 'a cried out, "God, God, God!" three or four times. Now I, to comfort him, bid him 'a should not think of God; I hop'd there was no need to trouble himself with any such thoughts yet. So 'a bade me lay more clothes on his feet. I put my hand into the bed and felt them, and they were as cold as any stone; then I felt to his knees, and so up'ard and up'ard, and all was as cold as any stone.
>
> (*H5* II.iii.9–26)

Arthur's bosom, the turning of the tide, and the green fields, with or without Theobald's emendation from "a Table . . . " to " 'a babbl'd of green fields," make Falstaff almost a mythological figure. One could go on about him in *Golden Bough* language: a fertility spirit, a dying god, or a scapegoat.

Shakespeare keeps it all believably within the Hostess's idiom, right through to her characteristically modest way of describing the final failure of his potency, a theme picked up in the talk that follows:

> NYM: They say he cried out of sack.
> HOSTESS: Ay, that 'a did.
> BARDOLPH: And of women.
> HOSTESS: Nay, that 'a did not.
> BOY: Yes, that 'a did, and said they were dev'ls incarnate.
> HOSTESS: 'A could never abide carnation—'twas a color he never lik'd.
> BOY: 'A said once, the dev'l would have him about women.
> HOSTESS: 'A did in some sort, indeed, handle women; but then he was rheumatic, and talk'd of the whore of Babylon.
>
> (II.iii.27–39)

The "mingled yarn" (*AWW* IV.iii.71) is beautifully woven here to include both Falstaff with Doll and the burlesque Puritanism in him that may go back to Oldcastle. The whole scene is an elegy, framed by the very unsavory life which, as Pistol says at the close of their previous scene, will go on:

PISTOL: His heart is fracted and corroborate.
NYM: The King is a good king, but it must be as it may; he passes some humors and careers.
PISTOL: Let us condole the knight, for, lambkins, we will live.
(II.i.124–28)

The group turn to fresh fields and pastures new at the end:

BOY: Do you not remember, 'a saw a flea stick upon Bardolph's nose, and 'a said it was a black soul burning in hell?
BARDOLPH: Well, the fuel is gone that maintain'd that fire. That's all the riches I got in his service.
NYM: Shall we shog? the King will be gone from Southampton.
(II.iii.40–46)

The acceptance of death as a way out of the tensions of all-or-nothing relationship, eroticizing death within a seasonal rhythm, is the burden of one of the greatest of the sonnets. Like Mistress Quickly's elegy, Sonnet 73 culminates with warm life's yielding to the cold of the deathbed:

That time of year thou mayest in me behold,
When yellow leaves, or none, or few, do hang
Upon those boughs which shake against the cold,
Bare ruined choirs, where late the sweet birds sang.
In me thou seest the twilight of such day,
As after sunset fadeth in the west,
Which by and by black night doth take away,
Death's second self, that seals up all in rest.
In me thou seest the glowing of such fire,
That on the ashes of his youth doth lie,
As the death-bed whereon it must expire,
Consumed with that which it was nourished by.
    This thou perceiv'st, which makes thy love more strong,
    To love that well which thou must leave ere long.

"Fare well, the latter spring!" Hal called out gaily after Falstaff's exit from their first scene together, "Fare well, All-hallown summer" (1H4 I.ii.158–59). He loves that well which he must leave ere long.

On Shakespeare's part: "Greater love hath no man than this, that a man lay down his life for his friends" (John 15:13)—or so vital a part of the life in him as animated Falstaff. To return to a significant point: the sacrifice of Falstaff's vicarious enjoyment of Hal within the Henry IV plays is made to permit vicarious realization of manhood by author and audience in admiring Henry V's "royalty of nature" (Mac. III.i.49). The fundamental reason that Falstaff could not go on to help us make merry with fair Katherine of France is that in *Henry V* Shakespeare shifts to using the whole theater as an "oblation" (Sonnet 125) to its hero: in Henry V's world there is no place for Falstaff as, in his strange way, a steward of his excellence. Despite the program, the sacrifice does not entirely work. However admirable the civic or patriotic commitment animating the enterprise, King Henry V, "all shining with the virtues of success," in Empson's phrase,[12] is not adequate to the possibilities for manhood Shakespeare comes to envisage in tragedy.

"I SPEAK TO THEE PLAIN SOLDIER"

In *Henry V*, as was noted, the Chorus continues the self-disabling attitude of the Sonnets, here directly tied to the theater. Like the Sonnets poet, the Chorus feels "subdued / To what [he] works in":

> we shall much disgrace
> With four or five most vile and ragged foils
> (Right ill dispos'd in brawl ridiculous)
> The name of Agincourt.
>
> (IV.Cho.49–52)

At the same time, the Chorus is full of wonderful poetry (the best, I think, in the play) about making "imaginary puissance" (Pro.25) in "the quick forge and working-house of thought" (V.Cho.23). There is an axis running from apology to assertion similar to that in the Sonnets:

> But pardon, gentles all,
> The flat unraised spirits that hath dar'd
> On this unworthy scaffold to bring forth
> So great an object.
>
> (Pro.8–11)

> Thus with imagin'd wing our swift scene flies
> In motion of no less celerity
> Than that of thought.
>
> (III.Cho.1–3)

So in the Sonnets we repeatedly get apology for "my barren rhyme" (16), but even more frequently assertions such as "Not marble nor the gilded monuments / Of princes shall outlive this pow'rful rhyme" (55).

---

12. *Some Versions of Pastoral*, p. 100.

In between on this axis are the many sonnets that express the tension between thought and physical circumstance: "If the dull substance of my flesh were thought, / Injurious distance should not stop my way; . . . / For nimble thought can jump both sea and land" (Sonnet 44). There is a hunger for the actual in such lines that the Chorus continues into *Henry V*:

> O, do but think
> You stand upon the rivage and behold. . . .
> Follow, follow!
> Grapple your minds to sternage of this navy, . . .
> Work, work your thoughts, and therein see a siege.
> (III.Cho.13–14, 17–18, 25)

Peter Erickson has observed that the concern of the Chorus about his theater's inability to present its actual subjects ignores conventions well recognized by common sense as well as by theory; as Sidney put it, "the poet . . . nothing affirms, and therefore never lieth."[13] In his hunger for the actual, the Chorus is the sonneteer transferred into the theater, asking it to do more than theater can do, as the poet often asks the sonnet to do more than poetry can do—or laments the impossibility of its doing so: "But, ah, thought kills me that I am not thought" (Sonnet 44).

But as Shakespeare dramatizes "the youth of England . . . / Following the mirror of all Christian kings, / With winged heels" (II.Cho.1, 6–7), he is obviously not drawing a portrait of the young man of the Sonnets. He is entering a world of male solidarity in aggression, presided over by a young man who has no use for mirrors. "I speak to thee plain soldier," Henry says to Katherine, "a fellow . . . whose face is not worth sunburning, that never looks in his glass for love of anything he sees there" (V.ii.149, 146–148). By the end of their encounter, he has arrived at

> I dare not swear thou lovest me, yet my blood begins to flatter me that thou dost—notwithstanding the poor and untempering effect of my visage. Now beshrew my father's ambition! he was thinking of civil wars when he got me; therefore was I created with a stubborn outside, with an aspect of iron, that when I come to woo ladies, I fright them. But in faith, Kate, the elder I wax, the better I shall appear. My comfort is, that old age, that ill layer-up of beauty, can do no more spoil upon my face.
>
> (V.ii.222–231)

13. Peter Erickson, " 'The Fault / My Father Made': The Anxious Pursuit of Heroic Fame in Shakespeare's *Henry V*," *Modern Language Studies* 10 (1979): 10–12.

Everything in this deliberate parade of bluff masculinity runs counter to the impression of the friend, his "woman's face, with nature's own hand painted" (Sonnet 20), exquisitely vulnerable to time, that "ill layer-up of beauty."

The wooing of Katherine is completed by an elaborate, displaced threat of violence. Love is blind, Henry agrees with Burgundy, in an exchange we will return to later:

> and you may, some of you, thank love for my blind-
> ness, who cannot see many a fair French city for one
> fair French maid that stands in my way.
>
> FRENCH KING: Yes, my lord, you see them perspectively: the cities
> turn'd into a maid; for they are all girdled with maiden
> walls that the war hath never ent'red.
>
> KING HENRY: Shall Kate be my wife?
>
> FRENCH KING: So please you.
>
> (V.ii.316–325)

Her father's consent is based on recognizing that the alternative to his daughter's marriage and loss of maidenhead is the rape of more French cities by war. We are reminded of Henry's threat in obtaining the surrender of Harfleur:

> in a moment look to see
> The blind and bloody soldier with foul hand
> Defile the locks of your shrill-shriking daughters;
> Your fathers taken by the silver beards,
> And their most reverend heads dash'd to the walls;
> Your naked infants spitted upon pikes,
> Whiles the mad mothers with their howls confus'd
> Do break the clouds, as did the wives of Jewry
> At Herod's bloody-hunting slaughter-men.
>
> (III.iii.33–41)

In the very next scene we first see Katherine, proper, protected, na-ive, learning English words:

> KATHERINE: Comment appelez-vous le pied et la robe?
>
> ALICE: Le foot, madame, et le count.
>
> KATHERINE: Le foot et le count! O Seigneur Dieu! ils sont les mots
> de son mauvais, corruptible, gros, et impudique, et
> non pour les dames de honneur d'user.
>
> (III.iv.50–54)

Oh, but English fuck and cunt *are* coming at this *précieuse*, the earlier scene makes us sure—with a male pleasure bordering on brutality.

No other Shakespeare play asks so insistently as *Henry V* for *us* to make ironic comments—and to puzzle over their pertinence for understanding the protagonist and the heroic action. We can note, for example, that "Once more unto the breach, dear friends, once more" is set up retrospectively as an invitation to gang rape:

> Stiffen the sinews, conjure up the blood,
> Disguise fair nature with hard-favor'd rage;
> Then lend the eye a terrible aspect;
> Let it pry through the portage of the head
> Like the brass cannon; let the brow o'erwhelm it
> As fearfully as doth a galled rock
> O'erhang and jutty his confounded base,
> Swill'd with the wild and wasteful ocean.
>
> (III.i.1, 7–14)

What is *the* appropriate response to the eye here as a cannon, all mutuality of regard left behind with "fair nature"? or to the brow as an overhanging cliff? Standing back, one can notice that this phallic imagery, deliberately ruthless, is not only fearful in the sense of inspiring fear, but also inspired *by* fear, the base of the rock "confounded." While "galled" is used in an obsolete, neutral sense, "washed away" (*NED*, 3), it carries suggestions of "made sore," exasperated—and this because its base has been "swilled" by the wild ocean, which wastes away form, structure.

What quarrel can one have with Henry's use of "sex-war imagery" here at the right time and the right place, a conscious use for the practical purpose of breaking through the breach in an actual war situation? He goes on, again for practical purposes, to remind his soldiers that they are "fet from fathers of war-proof! / . . . Dishonor not your mothers; now attest / That those whom you call'd fathers did beget you" (III.i.18, 22–23). The son's martial ruthlessness will attest to the father's virility. In his next scene, with the town's governors, Henry again has a practical objective in mind when he links the kind of incitement he has used at the wall to its potential consequences in sexual violence:

> The gates of mercy shall be all shut up,
> And the flesh'd soldier, rough and hard of heart,
> In liberty of bloody hand, shall range,
> With conscience wide as hell, mowing like grass
> Your fresh fair virgins and your flow'ring infants.
>
> (III.iii.10–14)

Such scenes happened and still happen in warfare. Henry, conducting a war, can say, "What is't to me, when you yourselves are cause"—and we get again the all but obsessive reference to sexual violation: "If your pure maidens fall into the hand / Of hot and forcing violation?" (III.iii.19–20).

In a fine chapter in *Shakespeare and the Problem of Meaning*, Norman Rabkin summarizes the radical disagreement *Henry V* has provoked among critics who tend to see its protagonist either as an ideal monarch or as a ruthless Machiavellian prince.[14] Rabkin sees *Henry V* as inviting opposed readings and leaving us "at a loss" because the two cannot be brought into a single "gestalt." His point of departure is the kind of irreducible doubleness that E. H. Gombrich, in *Art and Illusion*, has his readers demonstrate for themselves with a drawing that enables us to see now a duck, now a rabbit, without ever letting us see both at the same time. Rabkin concludes that in *Henry V*, "Shakespeare's habitual recognition of the irreducible complexity of things has led him, as it should lead his audience, to a point of crisis" (p. 61). As Rabkin sees it, Shakespeare "forces us, as we experience and reexperience and reflect on the play, as we encounter it in performances which inevitably lean in one direction or the other, to share his conflict" (p. 62).

I would agree, except that it seems to me that it is the play, rather than Shakespeare, that forces us to share his conflict. There is something not under control, I think, about the doubleness: the dramatist's powers, the sense of reality built by now into those powers, betray him into revealing in the round, or almost in the round, a figure and action programmed for two-dimensional admiration. But the metaphor of dimensions does not quite do. There is something intrinsic to Henry V and his enterprise that *requires* the inhibition of conscious awareness of moral cruelty, and sexual cruelty, as elements of his character, unless we, shifting the gestalt, stand outside. We are either with him or against him, depending on whether or not *we* supply the dissenting or qualifying perspective.[15]

---

14. Norman Rabkin, "Either / Or: Responding to *Henry V*," chap. 2 in *Shakespeare and the Problem of Meaning* (Chicago: University of Chicago Press, 1981), pp. 33–62.

15. The second, repellent "gestalt" that many see in *Henry V* owes a great deal to anachronistically modern resistance to war, and to our retrospective historical perspective on the separate national development of England and France. Sixteenth-century England accepted Henry's title to France as valid (see Bullough's discussion of the historical materials Shakespeare draws on, in *Sources*, vol. 4, p. 349) and regarded war as a necessary and glorious expression of a people's full humanity. This was all the more a matter of course in an England actively engaged in military resis-

We can see further into why this is so if we consider that the particular kind of political action dramatized in *Henry V* is the psychic mobilization for war and in war, with the galvanization of feeling and the inhibition of critical awareness this process involves. In mobilizing aggressive feeling behind Henry's cause, Shakespeare does not heavily emphasize hatefulness in the enemy army; more typically the French are made comically contemptible. There is no authority figure among them to be challenged. The French king's historical incapacity, along with Shakespeare's young-man-centered design, makes the fatuous Dauphin Henry's opposite. The war cannot be the occasion for an Oedipal victory over an older, threatening figure of power. But the play seeks to shape its auditors to "war psychology" by beginning with a succession of preparatory war rallies, then moving to the rallying of troops before Harfleur and then before Agincourt.

Prior to the departure for France, in the scene of the arrest of Cambridge, Scroop, and Grey, we in the audience are co-opted by figures on stage whose shocked sense of outrage we are to share. The play asks us to participate in the patriotic fellowship consolidated under Henry's aegis. The need for total solidarity is emphasized by the traitors' breach of it, especially by Scroop's: "Nay, but the man that was his bedfellow, / Whom he hath dull'd and cloy'd with gracious favors— / That he should, for a foreign purse . . . " (II.ii.8–10). The King enlarges on Scroop's breach of trust in a fifty-line rhapsody that begins "But O, / What shall I say to thee, Lord Scroop, thou cruel . . . " (lines 93–94). While participating in the scene's enactment—in the gestalt it demands when we are close-up—we are not going to notice how implausible it is that Scroop (or anybody else) should have had the intimate relationship to Harry that the king describes: "Thou that didst bear the key of all my counsels, / That knew'st the very bottom of my soul" (lines 96–97). Nor will we resist the appropriation of hell and God: "whatsoever cunning fiend it was / That wrought upon thee so preposterously / Hath got the voice in hell for excellence" (lines 111–13). Nor will we likely reflect that the King is close to blasphemy when he equates Adam's disobedience to God with Scroop's to him: "I will weep for

***

tance to Spain and in the "pacification" of Ireland. The Chorus equates the French campaign with Essex's in Ireland, and with the Roman imperialism of "conqu'ring Caesar," in describing Henry's triumphant return to England after Agincourt (V.Cho.22–34).

thee; / For this revolt of thine, methinks, is like / Another fall of man" (lines 140–42).

Along with the traitors, we have slackers and cowards and criminal camp-followers in Bardolph, Nym, and Pistol—Pistol a Miles Gloriosus such as Falstaff was not. As these "sworn brothers" (II.i.12) square off against one another in mock bravado, then come together again in shared greed, they travesty in advance the tensions that will bristle among individual soldiers and officers held together by loyalty to king and cause. The transformation of cowardly aggression into "military" camaraderie is exhibited at the outset as Nym and Pistol threaten each other and twice draw, only to be reconciled by Bardolph's "He that strikes the first stroke, I'll run him up to the hilts, as I am a soldier" (II.i.63–65). The shift from mutual hate to mutual alliance is sudden: "profits will accrue. / Give me thy hand" (II.i.112–13). After Falstaff's death we have another such parody of solidarity:

> Yoke-fellows in arms,
> Let us to France, like horse-leeches, my boys,
> To suck, to suck, the very blood to suck!
> (II.iii.54–56)

Shakespeare is using the ragged opportunists, as he has used the traitors, to focus our contempt on what cannot be taken up into the patriotic solidarity Henry forges in war.

Immediately after the King leads his followers once more into the breach, the slackers are shown *not* following, but mimicking heroics, and then singing a ditty about how they wish they were back in London. The boy is revealing here—he is too young for us to expect him to join in the battle, so we can sympathize with *his* cowardice. He spells out the shifts of the three amusingly different thieving cowards—and goes off in the end to the baggage train (to be killed in due course by the French cowards). These roles are very well handled indeed to show the seamy edge of war. But the comedy of Pistol and company does not provide any alternative perspective such as Falstaff provides at Shrewsbury. As foils they are completely self-disabling, and we cannot but be all with Fluellen: "Up to the breach, you dogs! Avaunt, you cullions!" (III.ii.20–21).

In the byplay that follows among the genuine captains—Fluellen with Jamy, Macmorris, Gower—Shakespeare broadens his canvas still further to suggest the consolidation of Welsh, Scots, Irish, and English through Henry's leadership. First he brings out the special pedantry and loyalty of real professional soldiers and the way their separate national cultures, with the aggressive set toward life active in their solidarity, can break the surface:

FLUELLEN: Captain Macmorris, I think, look you, under your correction, there is not many of your nation—
MACMORRIS: Of my nation? What ish my nation? Ish a villain, and a basterd, and a knave, and a rascal. What ish my nation? Who talks of my nation?
FLUELLEN: Look you, if you take the matter otherwise than is meant, Captain Macmorris, peradventure I shall think you do not use me with that affability as in discretion you ought to use me, look you, being as good a man as yourself, both in the disciplines of war, and in the derivation of my birth, and in other particularities.
MACMORRIS: I do not know you so good a man as myself. So Chrish save me, I will cut off your head.

(III.ii.120–34)

Then, with "A parley sounded" (s.d.) by the town under siege, they (and we) are united behind Henry as he stands before the gates of Harfleur and demands: "How yet resolves the governor of the town? / This is the latest parle we will admit" (III.iii.1–2).

In such scenes, Shakespeare is exhibiting the cranky parts of the military machine that is being put in honor's service. He is showing the battlefield equivalent of "the act of order [in] a peopled kingdom" (I.ii.189) described near the outset of the play in ideal terms by Exeter and Canterbury, its hierarchically ordered parts "Congreeing in a full and natural close, / Like music" (I.ii.182–83). Canterbury's exemplum from the bees adds the idea that "many things, having full reference / To one consent, may work contrariously" (lines 205–6). The contrariness on the battlefield includes the potentially disruptive aggression that keeps erupting into private quarrels or near quarrels, such as the sensitivity about his nation of the Wild Goose Irishman Macmorris.[16]

The quarrels take up a lot of stage time, and are surefire in performance, none more so than the encounter of plain soldier Williams with the disguised king in the long night before Agincourt:

WILLIAMS: Ay, he said so, to make us fight cheerfully; but when our throats are cut, he may be ransom'd, and we ne'er the wiser.
KING HENRY: If I live to see it, I will never trust his word after.
WILLIAMS: You pay him then. That's a perilous shot out of an

16. One can never do enough justice to Shakespeare's incidental observation, the sort of thing we get in Macmorris's "What ish my nation?" Seamus Heaney put

> elder-gun, that a poor and private displeasure can do against a monarch! You may as well go about to turn the sun to ice with fanning in his face with a peacock's feather. You'll never trust his word after! come, 'tis a foolish saying.
>
> KING HENRY: Your reproof is something too round, I should be angry with you, if the time were convenient.
> WILLIAMS: Let it be a quarrel between us, if you live.
> KING HENRY: I embrace it.
>
> (IV.i.192–206)

And so we are off on still another private quarrel that will be turned into mutual respect—through Fluellen's wearing the glove Williams gives the King for a gage, taking a box on the ear for his master, and coming round to admiration of Williams. After the King has teased the soldier, only to end by giving him his own gage, the royal glove, filled with crowns, Fluellen follows suit: "By this day and this light, the fellow has mettle enough in his belly. Hold, there is twelve-pence for you" (IV.viii.62–64).

It is a fine touch to have Williams's last words be "I will none of your money" (IV.viii.67). The whole episode is a version of pastoral, the king disguised as a common soldier instead of as a shepherd. Harry is engaged, as we are, in the sophisticated enjoyment of simplicity, both here and in relishing the would-be sophistication of Fluellen's verbosity. Fluellen is rather like a prose dialect version of loquacious Henry in assuming the stance of a plain man of few words while talking incessantly—even about the importance of not talking: "So! in the name of Jesu Christ, speak fewer. . . . If the enemy is an ass and a fool, and a prating coxcomb, is it meet, think you, that we should also, look you, be an ass and a fool, and a prating coxcomb, in your own conscience now?" (IV.i.65, 77–81). Where Fluellen is a military version of the shepherd speaking high poetry naively, like Sylvius, say, in *As You Like It*, Williams is a version of Corin, who when teased by Touchstone about the pastoral life comes on straight: "Sir, I am a true laborer: I earn that I eat, get that I wear" (*AYL* III.ii.73–74). In *Henry V*, the military pastoral does not involve any such questioning of the social structure as we are to get in the tragic version of pastoral in *Lear*. As with romance in *As You Like It*, the simplicities of captains and soldiers do not undercut the king, but support the authenticity of his difference,

---

him, "gallivanting / round the Globe," in a poem about Irish "Traditions" (*Wintering Out* [London: Faber and Faber, 1972], pp. 31–32).

which allows him, in his turn, to appreciate such as Fluellen from across this difference: "Though it appear a little out of fashion, / There is much care and valor in this Welshman" (IV.i.83–84).

"WE BAND OF BROTHERS"

The last of these quarrels converts aggression, not into mutual respect, but into solidarity by the expulsion of a pretender. Pistol eats Welsh leek under Fluellen's English cudgel and resolves to sneak back to London, where he will patch over his "cudgell'd scars" (*H5* V.i.88) and exploit them as war wounds. Fluellen's expulsion of the "counterfeit cowardly knave" (lines 69–70) completes the work of the series of quarrels, which has been to move us into participation in the all-male structure of relationships that dominates the play. Well rid of Pistol, we are ready to watch Henry woo Katherine. The emotional climax within this community of men at war comes not, however, in the decorous slow-motion conquest of Katherine, her marriage standing in the way of further rape of France's maiden cities, but in the battlefield death of York over Suffolk's body. It is here, still within the all-male structure, that we get the positive, idealized complement to Scroop's betrayal. Exeter describes it for the King:

> Suffolk first died, and York, all haggled over,
> Comes to him where in gore he lay insteeped,
> And takes him by the beard, kisses the gashes
> That bloodily did yawn upon his face.
> He cries aloud, "Tarry, my cousin Suffolk!
> My soul shall thine keep company to heaven;
> Tarry, sweet soul, for mine, then fly abreast,
> As in this glorious and well-foughten field
> We kept together in our chivalry!"
> Upon these words I came and cheer'd him up.
> He smil'd me in the face, raught me his hand,
> And with a feeble gripe, says, "Dear my lord,
> Commend my service to my sovereign."
> So did he turn and over Suffolk's neck
> He threw his wounded arm, and kiss'd his lips,
> And so espous'd to death, with blood he seal'd
> A testament of noble-ending love.
> The pretty and sweet manner of it forc'd
> Those waters from me which I would have stopp'd,
> But I had not so much of man in me,
> And all my mother came into my eyes
> And gave me up to tears.

KING HENRY: I blame you not,
For hearing this, I must perforce compound
With mistful eyes, or they will issue too.
But hark, what new alarum is this same?
The French have reinforc'd their scatter'd men.
Then every soldier kill his prisoners,
Give the word through.

                                   (IV.vi.11–38)

Does Henry command that every prisoner be killed in order to keep the "mother" from giving him up to tears? Here I am stepping back out of the all-male solidarity which, in the moment of death, can find such overt physical expression as Exeter describes—though in a successful performance I would likely go along with the king's sudden resolution for cruelty to share in the protection it provides him from further surrender to passive feelings. Those who find Henry cruel and ruthless point out that he has not yet heard of the slaughter of the boys and the pillage of the luggage, as he has not in the chronicles, where the move is prudential in view of the new French threat.[17] Whether or not he can be imagined as having heard about that offstage (Fluellen comes on immediately to tell about it), I think what repels us is not cruelty or ruthlessness as such, but the precarious sexual immaturity that motivates them. It is the use Henry makes of war in the service of unacknowledged inner conflict that puts us off, even as the play invites our assent. Shakespeare, to put it bluntly, is ennobling the psychology characteristic of an adolescent gang. All tenderness of feeling is turned back into primary male bonds that carry the latent erotic charge released in Exeter's account. The sanctity of these bonds is protected and validated by the directing of eroticized aggression outward against the common enemy, as with the rhetoric of sexual violation at Harfleur. Sexual relationship, in this case Henry's courtship of Katherine, is in turn shaped by the model of conquest.

The kind of group interaction mobilized in *Henry V* can provide a defense against the failure to have adequately internalized the father and with this the ability to deal in a whole human way with sexuality. What we have looked at as problematic elements in *Henry V* are consistent with the way Shakespeare dramatizes the young king's taking over royal authority from his father. On first meeting with his brothers after his father's death, Henry says, to reassure them (glancing as he does so at a recent notorious case of

17. See *Sources*, vol. 4, pp. 364–66, 397.

a Turkish Sultan who had, on his accession, strangled his five brothers):

> Brothers, you mix your sadness with some fear:
> This is the English, not the Turkish court,
> Not Amurath an Amurath succeeds,
> But Harry Harry. . . .
> For me, by heaven (I bid you be assur'd),
> I'll be your father and your brother too.
>
> (2H4 V.ii.46–49, 56–57)

The way he is a father to them is to lead them out to war, fulfilling in spirit his own father's dream of a holy crusade that would unite all England in a common cause. And in war he keeps insisting on being a brother as well as king. We can understand this as a way of dealing with anxiety about the situation of a new ruler: Henry diverts or converts potential fraternal hostility into allegiance. But there is, I think, a deeper level at work in Henry's attitude toward his royal inheritance.

Henry is particularly self-conscious about his role as king in the long night before the battle at Agincourt. In the encounter with Williams and Bates, for instance, after convincing them that the king is not responsible for the unpurged sins of his soldiers killed in battle, Henry seeks further satisfaction in announcing that "I myself heard the king say he would not be ransom'd" (H5 IV.i.190–91). His anger at the disbelief he encounters in Williams reflects an inner need, one that the play suggests but does not explore, animating Henry's heroic resolve. To take his chances of death along with all the English is to test manhood rather than to have it. Henry would deflect all hostility onto the French, including any suggestion of hostility toward him engendered among his troops by his own authority.

In the two soliloquies that follow his encounter with the soldiers, Henry addresses the burden of royal authority. These speeches reflect, I think, both the incompleteness of the internalization of his father, which *seemed* to be accomplished at the end of 2 *Henry IV*, and the incompleteness of that father. The first begins by expressing an agonized sense of the responsibility he seems to have just argued away:

> Upon the King! let us our lives, our souls,
> Our debts, our careful wives,
> Our children, and our sins lay on the King!
> We must bear all. O hard condition,

Twin-born with greatness, subject to the breath
Of every fool whose sense no more can feel
But his own wringing!

(IV.i.230–36)

This is part of the truth, and we can sympathize with the young king's feeling of the pressure. But his reaction is strikingly inconsistent with the immediate situation that has provoked it. Williams and Bates have been anything but such fools as he describes:

WILLIAMS: 'Tis certain, every man that dies ill, the ill upon his own head, the King is not to answer it.
BATES: I do not desire that he should answer for me, and yet I determine to fight lustily for him.

(IV.i.186–89)

Henry then goes on to another part of the truth, taken as the whole of it, as he weighs the "infinite heart's ease . . . that private men enjoy" against the king's bondage to the "idol Ceremony," the god that "suffer'st more / Of mortal griefs than do thy worshippers":

Art thou aught else but place, degree, and form,
Creating awe and fear in other men?
Wherein thou art less happy, being fear'd,
Than they in fearing.
What drink'st thou oft, in stead of homage sweet,
But poison'd flattery? O, be sick, great greatness,
And bid thy ceremony give thee cure!
Thinks thou the fiery fever will go out
With titles blown from adulation?
Will it give place to flexure and low bending?
Canst thou, when thou command'st the beggar's knee,
Command the health of it? No, thou proud dream,
That play'st so subtilly with a king's repose.
I am a king that find thee; and I know
'Tis not the balm, the sceptre, and the ball.

(IV.i.246–60)

This is such energetic rhetoric and, often, energetic metaphor—the "fiery fever" made still more incandescent by the wind of "titles blown from adulation"—that we cannot but be swept up in its special pleading. But Henry's complaint bears a striking resemblance to Richard's adaptation of *contemptu mundi* imagery in his "hollow crown" lament, with its assumption that if royalty does not transcend the human condition, it is worse than nothing:

Cover your heads, and mock not flesh and blood
With solemn reverence, throw away respect,

> Tradition, form, and ceremonious duty,
> For you have but mistook me all this while.
> I live with bread like you, feel want,
> Taste grief, need friends: subjected thus,
> How can you say to me I am a king?
>
> (*R2* III.ii.171–77)

Of course the differences in characters and circumstances are enormous. If Richard cannot "monarchize, be fear'd, and kill with looks" (*R2* III.ii.165), if he must also have human needs, he feels that he is "subjected." Henry's "I am a king that finds thee" asserts that he will not be "subjected thus"—even though his profuse listing of ceremonial appurtenances concludes with the complaint that "Not all these, laid in bed majestical, / Can sleep so soundly as the wretched slave" (*H5* IV.i.267–68). One must sympathize with a king's feeling in a moment of great stress that his royal predicament is a thankless trap. But one must also notice that Henry's rhetorical questions can be answered all too easily: besides ceremony, kings have authority. Along with being feared, they can have the satisfaction of being loved, revered. The balm, the sceptre, and the ball are not sleeping aids, after all, but embodiments of a sacramental role. One feels far more poignancy coming through the better poetry in which Henry's father regretted his sleeplessness; there the dying king's troubled reverie over the "dull god" that blesses the common bed and abandons the "kingly couch" is grounded precisely in the actual troubles that have ravaged both "the body of our kingdom" and its ruler (*2H4* III.i.15, 16, 38). The son's reviling ceremony as being merely external reminds one of the way the father manipulated it; the focus in the son's speech on fear and flattery, to the neglect of the grace in valid royal ritual, continues the assumptions of precarious legitimacy without bringing them directly into consideration.

Henry V's troubled inheritance does become the subject of the second soliloquy, his prayer to the "God of battles":

> Not to-day, O Lord,
> O, not to-day, think not upon the fault
> My father made in compassing the crown!
> I Richard's body have interred new,
> And on it have bestowed more contrite tears,
> Than from it issued forced drops of blood.
>
> (IV.i.292–97)

His prayer shows that the resolution his dying father thought might be accomplished in their moment of atonement has not entirely

happened: it has not proved true that "all the soil of the achievement goes / With me into the earth" (2H4 IV.v.189–90). (Shakespeare recalls the reign of Henry V as a glorious exception, not a
permanent resolution of the whole cycle of English history his
stage has shown: "Small time; but in that time most greatly liv'd /
This star of England" [H5 Epi.5–6].) Another way to put it is that
the son has after all not been able to escape the guilt he sought to
escape through avoidance of his father before their final atonement.
Henry gains in dignity by confronting this dynastic guilt, especially at such a time, and especially because he does not overesti-
mate the efficacy of the chantries he has built for Richard or of the
"five hundred poor" he has "in yearly pay" to pray for pardon: "all
that I can do is nothing worth, / Since that my penitence comes
after all, / Imploring pardon" (IV.i.298, 303–5). But even here the
son acknowledges only the guilt passed on from his father's fault;
there is no recognition of filial aggression toward the father from
whom he has inherited this burden.

Shakespeare should not, of course, be blamed for letting his
hero king deal as best he can with a potentially tragic situation! It is
a great achievement to have kept the tragic potential in view. What
we should focus on is the particular way that Henry V deals with
it—and the limitations of that way. He deals with it, in a word, by
brotherhood. He uses (or through him Shakespeare uses) allegiances
formed on the model of brotherhood as a way of avoiding confrontation with the Oedipal motives that we can see developing in
the Henry IV plays and that will come to full tragic expression
in *Hamlet*.

As we have noted, Henry IV makes the potential Oedipal motive
explicit only at the very end of *Part Two*, after Hal, thinking his father dead, has taken the crown. In his anger, the dying king thinks
of sons as wanting their fathers' wealth, which, in his analogy of
the murdered bees, he describes in a way that suggests the father's
sexual substance: "Our thighs pack'd with wax, our mouths with
honey, / We bring it to the hive" (IV.v.76–77). But what the prince
has picked up and tried on as the crown is his father's role and its
potency—as well as its awesome stress. As he addresses the father
he thinks dead, Hal articulates a pattern that ensuing developments
in this play and in *Henry V* will amplify:

> Thy due from me
> Is tears and heavy sorrows of the blood,
> Which nature, love, and filial tenderness
> Shall, O dear father, pay thee plenteously.

My due from thee is this imperial crown,
Which as immediate from thy place and blood,
Derives itself to me. [*Puts on the crown.*] Lo where it sits,
Which God shall guard; and put the world's whole strength
Into one giant arm, it shall not force
This lineal honor from me. This from thee
Will I to mine leave, as 'tis left to me.

(IV.v.37–47)

Hal sorts out his human indebtedness from his divinely sanctioned inheritance, his grief from his new imperial power. He looks to the legal institution of dynastic inheritance to contain or control potential conflict—forgetting, in "this lineal descent," the claims of Richard II, which will animate the Wars of the Roses after Hal's brief but glorious reign as Henry V. The crown here becomes in itself the embodiment of the fullest demands and possibilities of adult authority, apart from the human qualities of its bearer.

When they are again alone together, the dying king's misconceived rebuke and lament for England's future under a wastrel rouses his son to a further affirmation of filial commitment:

O foolish youth,
Thou seek'st the greatness that will overwhelm thee. . . .
O my poor kingdom, sick with civil blows!
When that my care could not withhold thy riots,
What wilt thou do when riot is thy care?

(2H4 IV.v.96–97, 133–35)

The prince's response insists on the reality of his grief:

God witness with me, when I here came in,
And found no course of breath within your Majesty,
How cold it strook my heart! If I do feign,
O, let me in my present wildness die,
And never live to show th' incredulous world
The noble change that I have purposed!

(lines 149–54)

To refute the idea that putting on the crown did "swell my thoughts to any strain of pride," Hal insists on the burden that royal authority involves: "I spake unto this crown as having sense, / And thus upbraided it: 'The care on thee depending / Hath fed upon the body of my father'" (lines 170, 157–59). He does not "affect" the crown except "as your honor and as your renown" (lines 144–45). That is to say, he will always be King as his father's son.

The simplifying, forcing tendency in the prince's summation of the rite of passage from grief to power is taken over by the symbolic action in 2 *Henry IV* and extended through *Henry V*. What is happening at Henry IV's deathbed is the sort of uncritical identification of son with father appropriate to a much earlier moment, the beginning of the latency period, not the end of youth and the assumption of manhood. As with the scene of atonement between Hamlet and the Ghost on the dark battlements, what we have here is total filial commitment to the good father.[18] There is no room, in either case, for the son's critical relationship to the father, for recognition of his human failings and the sense of separateness which permits the son to be his own man while still respecting the claims of filial piety. With Hamlet, that unfinished business of an earlier stage of life will come back to block his effort to give himself entirely to the Ghost's command. At the end of 2 *Henry IV* and in *Henry V*, Shakespeare uses the resources of the theater to absolve "this star of England" from such business, to cooperate with the King's simplification of a son's struggle to deal with the mixed heritage of a fully human father, including the disruptive heritage of a father's guilt:

> The breath no sooner left his father's body,
> But that his wildness, mortified in him,
> Seem'd to die too; yea, at that very moment,
> Consideration like an angel came
> And whipt th' offending Adam out of him.
> (*H5* I.i.25–29)

The Archbishop's description of the young king, which sees the prince's reformation as making him over into a kind of heroic saint, looks back to the assertion with which Henry concludes his reconciliation with his brothers and the Lord Chief Justice:

> And, princes all, believe me, I beseech you,
> My father is gone wild into his grave;
> For in his tomb lie my affections,
> And with his spirits sadly I survive,
> To mock the expectation of the world.
> (*2H4* V.ii.122–26)

18. In "'The Fault / My Father Made,'" Peter Erickson has shown how this process results in grave limitations on Henry V's humanity, creating a rift between the chivalric ideal he pursues and the human environment in which he pursues it. Erickson sees the play as a fully self-conscious exploration by Shakespeare of the "complex failure [of] Henry V's moral and psychological identity" (p. 24). Faced with guilt, depression, and uncertainty that derive from his ambiguous inheritance of the crown, Henry V follows his father's "model for evasion of moral issues by emphasizing tactics instead" (p. 22).

This scene of reconciliation concludes with imagery of "the tide of blood," the passions that had "proudly flow'd in vanity till now," being taken up into and merging with the energies of public life, to "flow henceforth in formal majesty" (lines 129–30, 133). In *Henry V*, however, unresolved passions—the fears, needs, and hostilities that animate Oedipal confrontation—do find expression, albeit in unamiable displaced forms, most obviously in the self-righteous threats of war's violent destructiveness that we have looked at— where the language relishes violence to the family, rape of "pure maidens" by "hot and forcing violation," the "reverend heads" of gray-bearded fathers dashed against the walls, "infants spitted upon pikes" in the view of howling mothers. But the play, like Henry himself, recognizes in these utterances only impersonal extensions of the hero's power, consolidated by the brotherhood of soldiers at war.

After the prayer that seeks absolution from "the fault / My father made," Henry gets up from his knees to join his nobles at his tent. His speech to them ends with the famous

> We few, we happy few, we band of brothers;
> For he to-day that sheds his blood with me
> Shall be my brother.
>
> (*H5* IV.iii.60–62)

It begins with the cult of chivalry, which the Elizabethan aristocracy enacted very seriously, and vainly, on such occasions as the Ascension Day tournaments. In the Henry IV plays, chivalry is placed within a larger, empirical understanding of social action. Here it is an unqualified value as the King opens his speech:

> By Jove, I am not covetous for gold, . . .
> Such outward things dwell not in my desires.
> But if it be a sin to covet honor,
> I am the most offending soul alive.
>
> (lines 24, 27–29)

Shakespeare's broad canvas in *Henry V* consistently puts the war machine in the service of this honor. The King's speech goes on to locate the military energies he is rousing in the larger structure of community by projecting this moment into the future as the basis for an annual festival:

> This day is call'd the feast of Crispian: . . .
> He that shall see this day, and live old age,

> Will yearly on the vigil feast his neighbors,
> And say, "To-morrow is Saint Crispian."
> Then will he strip his sleeve and show his scars,
> And say, "These wounds I had on Crispian's day."
> Old men forget; yet all shall be forgot,
> But he'll remember with advantages
> What feats he did that day.
>
> (lines 40, 44–51)

When we look at this moment in relation to the similar moment at Shrewsbury, where Hal meets the demand of chivalry to stand over the dead Hotspur, what is missing of course is Falstaff. To have left him behind has involved a great loss. But the narrower awareness of *Henry V* also accords with a movement away from a relationship to manhood that did not yet demand of Hal a resolution of the problem of taking on royal authority. Henry V's commitment to manhood requires the reinforcement of brotherhood, both as a protection against brotherly hostility and as a way of validating heroic identity in the absence of its validation by being the father. Such military fraternity is grounded in real social need and real social institutions and occasions—most notably an army in a battle. In the festive comedies Shakespeare created occasions like holiday, in which precarious sexuality, under a feminine aegis, could move, through a social rhythm of release, to clarification about its valid relationship to nature. So here, *mutatis mutandis*, in the almost all-male world of the later history plays, military campaigning provides a mode of self-realization. It is a far less amiable or complete rite of passage than green-world holiday provides. Pistol puts its underside into words in the one remark he makes that does have telltale bite: "The King's a bawcock, and a heart of gold, / . . . I love the lovely bully" (IV.i.44, 48).

The incompleteness that needs to bully comes out embarrassingly, from under the martially induced festivity, when Shakespeare makes the identity Henry has forged in battle do as a basis for his "plain soldier" wooing of Katherine. His almost sadistic sexual valor requires the sort of besotted feminine response Burgundy puts into words with uncanny precision:

> I will wink on her to consent, my lord, if you will teach her to know my meaning; for maids, well summer'd and warm kept, are like flies at Bartholomew-tide, blind, though they have their eyes, and then they will endure handling, which before would not abide looking on.
>
> (V.ii.306–11)

Katherine, as Henry's response makes clear, pays dearly, not only for being French but for being in a history play: "so I shall catch the fly, your cousin, in the latter end, and she must be blind too" (lines 313–14). Burgundy's "As love is, my lord, before it loves," confirmed by Henry's "It is so" (lines 315–16), exactly does *not* fit open-eyed Rosalind and Viola as they love in festive comedies of the same period.

That Shakespeare saw the incompleteness and hence the tragic potentiality of the manhood of a "band of brothers" appears in the fact that (within a few months apparently) he went on to write *Julius Caesar*. Here the men who come together in conspiratorial brotherhood find self-destruction in what they think will be the sacrifice essential to the validation of their manhood. In exploring the motives of men who are first united in their resistance to filial submission to monarchical authority, but who are ultimately diminished by the violent act at the core of their bonds, Shakespeare for the first time centers a whole play on all-or-nothing male-to-male conflict across generations. Not until *Hamlet* is such vertical stress centered on a single hero subjected to the stress involved in relationship to women. In *Henry V*, as we have seen, relationship to a woman becomes important only at the very end, and then Henry's battlefield logic is simply domesticated for use in the peaceful field of courtship: no need, no dimension of Henry's character emerges in the courtship which has not already taken shape in his quest for victory through all-male solidarity. With remarkable dramatic success, Shakespeare has shielded his hero king from direct confrontation with figures of authority, from the full burden of assuming in himself authority over the lives of others, and from conflicts engendered by relations to women and to his own sexuality. In *Hamlet*, the presence of the evil but commanding stepfather, Claudius, the Prince's struggle to take the place of his dead father, and the powerful attraction-repulsion in Hamlet's crucial bond to his mother (and by extension in his relation to Ophelia), open up tragedy to a much fuller range of family-based conflict, redefining in the process the conditions that can validate or destroy manly identity in the work that follows.

8

Sight Lines on *Hamlet* and Shakespearean Tragedy

The more successful Shakespeare's art is, the more arbitrary it may seem to suggest that he is meeting a personal need in his works. For the art consists precisely in finding in social life and language common experience that can be organized in dramatic rhythms, to be shared socially in the theater. The personal disappears into the social product. At some moments, like the rejection of Falstaff, however, there is wide agreement that we experience a strain. We have inferred a shift in the poet-dramatist's sensibility, centered in a new orientation toward an ideal of heroic manhood, which suppresses Falstaffian ironies in celebrating the newly crowned king. Where the play is a problem, as Rabkin and others agree that it is with *Henry V*, similar inference is invited. But the process of drawing such inferences without losing sight of the play's distinctive dramatic reality is delicate, uphill work.

In chapter 7 I argued that King Henry V embodies a willed assumption of authority and virility, and that the Chorus carries on something of the infatuation of an older man for a younger which we get in the Sonnets, changed now in the nature of its object in accordance with an increasingly urgent need to relate to virile adult authority. In working with that play, however, it was necessary to recognize how effectively the mobilization of group solidarity in war provides a social situation within which masculinity can envisage objects of conquest as women. That Henry protests so much in abjuring rapist intentions clues us to the precarious nature of the masculinity he achieves. But the situation justifying the sort of maturity to which he does gain access *is* very fully realized. Shakespeare could answer that he was only presenting the way things go in war for the son of a flawed, precarious father. The developmental perspective I am trying to bring into focus does not invalidate the direct vision of war that *Henry V* dramatizes. Yet when one stands back from the play, one can see the need for ruthless male assertion it is serving, and see how this need shapes and limits dramatic understanding.

The problematic triumph of masculine authority and solidarity in *Henry V* asks for the exploration of heroic manhood we find in the tragedies that follow. *Julius Caesar* dramatizes the tragic encounter of brotherly solidarity with emergent patriarchal authority. The given situation in *Hamlet* results from a fatal rivalry of brothers. In Shakespeare's earlier histories, brotherly rivalry among the new, younger generation is, in the absence of father-son confrontation, the dominant mode of male-to-male conflict. In *Hamlet*, as Joel Fineman has observed, it is a brother's murder in the older generation that reopens the whole filial struggle for the heir in the younger generation; his struggle is compounded by the mother who has abetted the brothers' conflict by making no difference between them.[1] In dramatizing the depth and complexity of feeling released into the play by this situation, *Hamlet* is equally impressive for the way it liberates Shakespeare as an artist and for the problem it creates for his art.

The place of *Hamlet* in Shakespeare's development is the concern of this chapter. With the appearance of his father's ghost to Hamlet, we can see the beginning of a new kind of dramatization of the hero—in relation to the hero's need and the need Shakespeare brings to his art. The Ghost who calls Hamlet from "unmanly grief" to heroic, vengeful action is the dramatization of a fantasy. So is the fable of the Bastard in *King John*, where the enterprising Faulconbridge supplies an ailing kingdom with the heroic manhood wanting in England's usurping ruler. It is striking that we find in this early history play many of the disruptive elements of the tragedy, though presented episodically, without their integration around a single protagonist. Hamlet's experience is determined throughout by the destructive concentration of disabling bonds to a dead, exalted father, a murderous, hated stepfather, and a mother who is wife to both; however roundabout the action, it is always shaped by these bonds toward the final tragic confrontation. The episodic structure of *King John* allows Shakespeare to balance and disperse instances of vertical relationship that complement each

1. Joel Fineman, "Fratricide and Cuckoldry: Shakespeare's Doubles," in *Representing Shakespeare: New Psychoanalytic Essays*, ed. Murray M. Schwartz and Coppélia Kahn (Baltimore: Johns Hopkins University Press, 1980), pp. 70–109; see especially pp. 89–90.

other: Queen Elinor and Constance struggle for dynastic heritage through their sons, the weak king and the unhistorically effeminate prince, while Faulconbridge—at once marginal to court and society and the son of a great king—embodies at the play's vital center the "dauntless spirit of resolution" (V.i.53). The enormous difference in the reality expressed by the fantasy in *Hamlet*, as well as the drastic alteration in its orientation toward the problem of manhood, is apparent when we set the tragedy against the earlier play's full-blown, uncomplicated family romance.

Like Hamlet, whose wit is his chief resource for coping, and who never seems more self-assured than when situating himself as an observer of the times, or toying with those who serve it, Faulconbridge is a shrewd court satirist. In negotiating his adoption into the royal family, as is proposed by the dominant Queen Mother Elinor, Faulconbridge opens up a special vein of colloquial, devil-may-care, down-to-earth talk, the kind of wit Berowne commands in *Love's Labor's Lost*, and Aaron uses when he wants to in *Titus*. The Bastard celebrates his "new made honor" with the mocking ironies of his soliloquy on "worshipful society" (*Jn.* I.i.205). His whole speech, which commends courtly "observation" as at once time-serving and knowing the times, *is* observation, one feels sure, of a very precise kind, about dimensions of court life that Shakespeare must have seen at first hand.[2] The freewheeling style the Bastard exercises, developed in the festive comedies chiefly in the roles of the heroines, will be further enriched when Hamlet turns his wit loose on the court of Claudius. But what Hamlet sees from an outside perspective, and speaks with wonderful, cynical detachment, he cannot help turning back against himself in the contempt that expresses his sense of his own corruption. For the Bastard, penetrating insight into "Mad world, mad kings, mad composition," all serving that "smooth-fac'd gentleman, tickling commodity" (II.i.561, 573), provides a resource for opportunistic

2. One could follow suggestions from Faulconbridge's speech out into the biographies of Elizabethan courtiers. The Bastard's "country manners" (I.i.156) can suggest Ralegh, who kept his West Country speech through all his meteoric career; the Bastard's verbal sparring with Queen Elinor in the opening scene is the kind of thing one can imagine, *mutatis mutandis*, between that actual arriviste genius of the times and his Queen Elizabeth. But though Ralegh was minor gentry, he was no bastard, and Shakespeare's Bastard entirely lacks dimensions of Ralegh for which one would need to look to other, far greater Shakespearean figures—and then not find them all. See Stephen Greenblatt's splendid exploration of the keen theatrical sense at work in Ralegh's self-conscious shaping of his own life (and death), in *Sir Walter Ralegh: The Renaissance Man and His Roles* (New Haven: Yale University Press, 1973).

self-sanctioning that he can put aside at will, going beyond it to serve "dear mother England" (V.ii.152) with robust manliness.

King John, like *Hamlet*, calls for heroic action. But unlike Hamlet, who spends most of the play not avenging his father's death, and who can complete that act only after he has himself been mortally wounded, Faulconbridge almost casually kills the murderer of his royal father in the third act, and then returns to the battlefield for more action. And unlike Hamlet, who feels sullied in his own person by his mother's adulterous union, the Bastard finds the source of his active strength in his mother's infidelity. Seeing his mother's yielding to Cordelion as the rightful "tribute to commanding love," Faulconbridge forces her to admit she was seduced by the hero king, and then, in dismissing her, congratulates her for it: "With all my heart I thank thee for my father!" (*Jn.* I.i.264, 270). Even when one grants the extraordinary differences in how these circumstances are developed in the two plays, conditions closely associated with the Bastard's manly power—a murdered father and an adulterous mother—have an almost uncanny kinship with the conditions that inhibit action in Hamlet. Why is it, in the early play, that a hero so situated can confront the vitiating bad faith of rulers, avenge the death of his father, and protect the royal heritage of a kingdom that has been forfeited to unscrupulous men, overpowering women, and generalized corruption?

King John takes us back, before the moratorium on mothers in the mature histories and the festive comedies, to a play that deals extensively with powerful women in relation to their sons: Elinor and the usurper, John, Constance and the legitimate heir, Arthur. It belongs with *Henry VI*, *Richard III*, and *Titus Andronicus* in its preoccupation with maternal domination and escape from it. We have looked at this preoccupation in connection with the civil strife that engulfs a weak king in *Henry VI*, the motives of a villain king in *Richard III*, and the victimization of an aging patriarch in *Titus*. The Bastard, with his undaunted autonomy, seems to recall the men of these plays chiefly by way of contrast. But *King John* is cut from the same cloth. It is Faulconbridge's bastardy that enables him to encounter success where others encounter destruction: he is not imagined as the son or husband or enemy of a figure of disabling female power; he is not imagined as a brother and thus engaged in rivalry with literal or figurative siblings. Instead he embodies an engaging fantasy of the autonomous manly force a figure might possess were he created free of the nets of fraternal and gender-based conflict that snare, and indeed define, his near contemporaries in Shakespeare's early work.

Shakespeare also imagines Faulconbridge as a character who is independent of the deep filial stresses that shape Hamlet's experience. Repeated references to Cordelion in *King John* make of the dead king a kind of legendary presence representing precisely what is consistently absent from the other early plays—the strong, heroic father. But though the heroic dead father is appropriated as a source of inspiration, there is no father, good or bad, spectral or sensual, whom the son must confront as an obstacle to his own fulfillment. Faulconbridge, who does not know himself as the king's son until long after the father's death, is further protected from disruptive filial conflict by his illegitimacy and the resultant incompleteness of his inheritance. For him there is effortless, almost magical participation in the heroic manhood of the royal, lion-hearted, undramatized father he has never known, but without the expectation that he must assume his father's place in his own person.

In relation to the tragic exploration of Hamlet's experience, Shakespeare's artistry in *King John* looks "but on the outside of this work" (*Jn*. V.ii.109). The historical materials from John's reign are handled so as to exhibit almost too systematically the worthlessness of political bonds, the universal opportunistic breach of faith complementary to the infidelities and moving fidelities dramatized in the family bonds. The detached, superior but bastard consciousness by which Faulconbridge is able to manipulate politics as a spectacle of out-there self-interests exemplifies a direction developed in *King John* which Shakespeare will not pursue, a mode of drama and an implicit relation to life tending toward the Jonsonian kind of drama, toward *Sejanus* rather than *Hamlet*. But the contrast between Faulconbridge, who easily repudiates one heritage to embrace another, and the situation of Hamlet, who is mired in the degradation of heritage forced on him by his father's murder and his mother's remarriage, reflects the profound shift that occurs as Shakespeare makes tragedy his principal dramatic form. The Bastard is endowed with manhood that owes its strength to conflicts he does not have to engage, but for Hamlet the struggle is to achieve manhood, and in this struggle he must confront a situation unlike those of any of the men in the early works.

Since Coleridge, discussion of Hamlet's problematic effort to achieve manhood has been focused on the problem of his delaying his revenge. It is in terms of this problem that most psychoanalytic interpretation has been framed, notably Ernest Jones's fine book, *Hamlet and Oedipus*, which developed skillfully the key insight Freud proposed in *The Interpretation of Dreams*.[3] In my judgment, the psychoanalytic interpretation of the problem of delay has significantly illuminated the conditions that obstruct Hamlet's access to heroic manhood. If we see the Ghost as a figure of the ideal father as conceived in infancy and childhood, and Claudius as a man who reanimates in Hamlet the other father of infancy, gross and dangerous, who possesses the beloved mother sexually and is the object of the son's death wishes, then Hamlet's anguished inability to revenge is a result of the repression established during childhood on murderous impulses toward this father. To kill Claudius would be to carry out the very motive that had been repressed. It is an act that threatens the basis of Hamlet's conscience, since it is the Oedipal impulse transformed, through identification, into the internalization of the father, from which develops the internal authority of conscience or superego.

This framework for an understanding of the relations among the key figures permits us to comprehend Hamlet's inability to act as a function of the new situation into which he is plunged. In *Hamlet*, for the first time in Shakespeare's work, the protagonist must reexperience the full stress of the Oedipal situation; the play makes the whole process problematic, opens up the whole complex. *Hamlet* dramatizes a crisis centered on identification with the murdered, heroic father who returns to demand that the son vindicate his heritage. Everything hinges on the protagonist's struggle to inherit, his effort to identify himself totally with his father's command. But identification with the father, instead of leading Hamlet out into the vengeful action to which he dedicates himself, blocks his purpose. In *Hamlet* Shakespeare sets up the problem of the transmission of heritage in a radically disruptive way, a way that blocks its own full expression, so that the play exemplifies the crisis it sets out to dramatize.

HAMLET AND THE BURIAL OF THE DEAD

When we consider Shakespeare's power of development, as it can be made out working to master his own family situation and adaptations to it in temperament, the shift into the major tragedies

3. Ernest Jones's *Hamlet and Oedipus* (New York: Norton, 1949), which earlier appeared twice in shorter essay forms (1910 and 1923), takes as its starting point a

comes home as marvelously daring. He is not willing to settle for unheroic, fractured heritage. The unheroic but secure internaliza- tion of a parent requires a process of gradually recognizing that the actual parent is only human; it is a process like grieving. Something of such grieving is in the passage about "particular men," spoken with the generous, humane sympathy with which Shakespeare en- dows Hamlet whenever the Prince's deeper and more immediate preoccupations do not interfere.[4] But in the larger movement of the play, Shakespeare has found a fable by which he can envisage the possibility of achieving heroic authority and manhood by atone- ment with a father in whom majesty is intact. That he should *need* to write *Hamlet* and the great tragedies that follow reflects an in- completeness. On the other hand, the writing itself is in its way a heroic enterprise, a refusal to settle for incompleteness.

Hamlet begins the play arrested in grief and depression. It is in- structive to set his movement from grief to vengeance against the symbolic action of grief as structured by religious ritual in the Book of Common Prayer. The Order for the Burial of the Dead is strik- ingly one-sided in its concentration on detaching the mourners from the particular life that has ended, except as the lost person may be taken up into life everlasting. Of course in practice it could be combined with a funeral sermon devoted to celebrating the de- parted. And naturally, since the order is designed to serve for any burial service conducted by the church, to include any praise at all might in particular cases prove embarrassing. But the one-sided emphasis is functionally right in any case, as it provides a rite of passage for the living as well as the dead, the beginning for the liv- ing of the necessary process of dissolving their ties to the dead. The service initiates detachment by emphasizing the universality of mortality: "He cometh up, and is cut down, like a flower"; "We . . . commit his body to the ground; earth to earth, ashes to ashes, dust to dust."[5] It also initiates the process of reinvestment in other ob- jects, not in other ordinary human beings but in Christ, as by the magnificent opening words: "I am the resurrection and the life, saith the Lord." Look to *me*, the line says in its ritual context, not to

---

footnote to Freud's *Interpretation of Dreams* (1900), which itself eventually made its way into the main body of Freud's text: see *Standard Edition*, vol. 4, pp. 264–66.

4. See the discussion of I.iv.13–38 in chapter 2, pp. 53–56.

5. Quotations are from the 1559 edition of The Book of Common Prayer in *Litur- gical Services of the Reign of Queen Elizabeth*, ed. William Keating Clay, Parker Society, no. 30 (Cambridge: Cambridge University Press, 1847).

the lost dead; look for the human dead to live again through me: "He that believeth in me, though he were dead, yet shall he live."

The function of grief as a process of relinquishing the bond to the dead and of reinvesting oneself in the living is taken up in *Hamlet* explicitly in the large throne-room scene of ongoing state business. The scene is ably and firmly conducted by Claudius, who addresses the awkward business of his marriage to the dead king's widow, sends ambassadors to deal with young Fortinbras, and gives gracious permission to Laertes to return to Paris. Hamlet, all the while isolated but prominent in his "inky cloak"—as Cordelia is isolated by her asides during the sweep of Lear's state business—is ready, like Cordelia, to stop the large movement in its tracks:

> But now, my cousin Hamlet, and my son—
> HAMLET: [*Aside*.] A little more than kin, and less than kind.
> CLAUDIUS: How is it that the clouds still hang on you?
> HAMLET: Not so, my lord, I am too much in the sun.
> QUEEN: Good Hamlet, cast thy nighted color off,
> And let thine eye look like a friend on Denmark.
> Do not for ever with thy vailed lids
> Seek for thy noble father in the dust.
> Thou know'st 'tis common, all that lives must die,
> Passing through nature to eternity.
>
> (I.ii.64–73)

His mother urges Hamlet to complete the work of mourning, to accept the burial of the dead. Gertrude's lines wonderfully summarize what the service says, except for its insistence on moving through Christ; she uses the familiar "dust to dust" image as the Prayer Book does, to insist that the dead person's soul is not there.

Claudius, in turn, develops at length the logic of giving up the lost object after appropriate mourning "for some term":

> 'Tis sweet and commendable in thy nature, Hamlet,
> To give these mourning duties to your father. . . .
>   But to persever
> In obstinate condolement is a course
> Of impious stubbornness, 'tis unmanly grief,
> It shows a will most incorrect to heaven,
> A heart unfortified.
>
> (lines 87–88, 92–96)

In other circumstances this would be good advice, in the tenor of the Prayer Book, and the characterization of Hamlet's grief as "unmanly," his heart "unfortified," hits home. It is all perfectly reasonable, right through to the offer of an alternative object: "We pray

thee throw to earth / This unprevailing woe, and think of us / As of
a father" (lines 106–8). It is also impossible for a stepson to accept
after the "o'erhasty marriage."

Claudius's apology for this marriage conveys what, by his elaborate rhetorical balancing act, he seeks to cover over—that it has violated the normal rhythms of ritual response to death and life:

> Therefore our sometime sister, now our queen,
> Th' imperial jointress to this warlike state,
> Have we, as 'twere with a defeated joy,
> With an auspicious, and a dropping eye,
> With mirth in funeral, and with dirge in marriage,
> In equal scale weighing delight and dole,
> Taken to wife.
>
> (lines 8–14)

Such a cross-purposed line as "With an auspicious, and a dropping
eye," if one stops over it, presents a downright ridiculous image—
but Claudius keeps going. His plea that Hamlet end his grief is like-
wise elaborated to a point where the appeal becomes involuntarily
ironic. When he offers himself as a substitute for the dead father,
Claudius's use of the royal plural—"think of us / As of a father"—
betrays the hollowness of his public offer of private solace. His reference to "the first corse" inadvertently alludes to Cain and the
"primal, eldest curse" of "a brother's murder," still secret though
perhaps half-guessed by Hamlet's prophetic soul.

As Hamlet stands by while the business of state proceeds, his
situation resembles in many respects that of Hieronimo in *The
Spanish Tragedy*, whose whole attention is riveted on his dead son
while the royal affairs of Spain move relentlessly on. But the situation in *Hamlet* differs importantly from that of *The Spanish Tragedy*
because the society is not intact at the outset. In *Hamlet*, the old,
honest world is gone before the play opens—though the full extent
of the destruction has to be discovered. The scenes of state in Kyd's
play center on monarchs who are genuinely responsible and benign;
social justice is vitiated by the young Machiavel working ruthlessly
to accomplish the dynastic marriage which in the older generation's
myopic eyes is a positive goal. In *Hamlet* the responsible ruler (and
he *is* responsible as a ruler)[6] is at the same time the hidden Ma-

---

6. G. Wilson Knight provides a persuasive account of Claudius as an "excellent
diplomatist," "a good and gentle king, enmeshed by the chain of causality linking
him with his crime," in "The Embassy of Death: An Essay on *Hamlet*," *The Wheel of
Fire*, 5th ed. rev. (New York: Meridian Books, 1957), pp. 33, 35.

chiavel. Claudius's long opening speech of state combines a sense of ongoing responsibility with queasy cover-up. Hamlet's first words satisfy the audience's accumulating need to challenge the King on this specious unction, initiating the identification with the Prince which the play invites in its audience throughout. The Prince's marvelous wit, in response to "my cousin Hamlet, and my son," summarizes the overintensification of familial relationships, "more than kin," in which the play's action centers, and which proves, to put it mildly, "less than kind"—unnatural and ruthless.

Against the ongoing concerns of managing the state, Shakespeare presents Hamlet first in a static condition of grievous, suicidal alienation; the world presents no object that the heart, imprisoned in "this too too sullied flesh" (line 129), can go out to. The vast energies knotted up in Hamlet begin to find social expression when Hamlet's quickened wit finds a sympathetic audience in the newly arrived Horatio.

HORATIO: My lord, I came to see your father's funeral.
HAMLET: I prithee do not mock me, fellow student,
I think it was to see my mother's wedding.
HORATIO: Indeed, my lord, it followed hard upon.
HAMLET: Thrift, thrift, Horatio, the funeral bak'dmeats
Did coldly furnish forth the marriage tables.
(lines 176–81)

The pressure toward some final solution is in Hamlet's "Would I had met my dearest foe in heaven" (line 182). He is about to meet the lost father toward whom he casts his mind, on earth: "My father—methinks I see my father" (line 184). Horatio thinks perhaps he has seen the Ghost already; his startled "Where, my lord?" is the first double take. Then comes Hamlet's turn for a beautifully meaningful double take.

HAMLET: In my mind's eye, Horatio.
HORATIO: I saw him once, 'a was a goodly king.
HAMLET: 'A was a man, take him for all in all,
I shall not look upon his like again.
HORATIO: My lord, I think I saw him yesternight.
HAMLET: Saw, who?
HORATIO: My lord, the King your father.
HAMLET: The King my father?
HORATIO: Season your admiration for a while.
(lines 185–92)

With the astonishing news from Horatio about the apparition, he is suddenly all animation, galvanized. The sudden release that comes

with his anxious questions—"Saw, who?" . . . "The King my father?"—initiates the movement toward Hamlet's total reinvestment
of self in the lost object that will be completed in his confrontation
with the Ghost.

In *Hamlet* the burial of the dead fails to work in the most drastic
way possible: the dead does not stay buried! At the Ghost's appearance to him, Hamlet is at first thrown back onto an appeal to the
old, ordered Christian supernatural: "Angels and ministers of grace
defend us" (I.iv.39). But Hamlet declares his filial allegiance to the
Ghost independently of any religious certainty:

> Be thou a spirit of health, or goblin damn'd,
> Bring with thee airs from heaven, or blasts from hell,
> Be thy intents wicked, or charitable,
> Thou com'st in such a questionable shape
> That I will speak to thee. I'll call thee Hamlet,
> King, father, royal Dane.

> (lines 40–45)

The open questions he goes on to ask, about where the Ghost
comes from and what it may mean, introduce the problematic situation of the whole play;[7] they confirm the Ghost's reality as a thing
that escapes the categories that control the perception of reality, including those of received religious tradition. Shakespeare uses all
the resources of his art to set the situation up that way, making it
unambiguously clear, by the Ghost's independent appearance in
the opening scene, that it is no hallucination or projection that
simply springs from the overwrought mind of Hamlet. The need to
bind an overwhelming emotional need by investment in an object
can lead to hallucination, as Shakespeare was well aware. Lady
Macbeth defines the process in rebuking her husband for his vision
of Banquo's ghost: "This is the very painting of your fear; / This is
the air-drawn dagger which you said / Led you to Duncan" (*Mac.*
III.iv.60–62). The Ghost of the elder Hamlet is objective in some
further sense, explicitly not mere fantasy: "Horatio says 'tis but our
fantasy, . . ." "How now, Horatio? You tremble and look pale. / Is
not this something more than fantasy?" (I.i.23, 53–54). C. S. Lewis

---

7. The play "leaves us wondering," writes Harry Levin in *The Question of Hamlet*
(New York: Oxford University Press, 1959): "It does not solve the problem of knowledge, the epistemological question, stated by the Ghost. . . . Shakespeare's development [of the Hamlet story] makes it a mystery in the more speculative sense, a rite of
initiation to painful experience, an exploration of stages of consciousness which
dazzle and elude the spectator 'With thoughts beyond the reaches of our souls'"
(p. 42).

says that Hamlet behaves like a man who has seen a ghost[8]—self-evident, yes, but crucial, all the difference between seeing "in my mind's eye" and "My lord, I think I saw him yesternight."

Everything hinges on the authenticity of the Ghost, both as an objective experience and as a legitimate source of moral strength. But in the play no one can fit it into categories. And modern scholarship has also determined that it does not fit into received Renaissance ideas of a ghost's status, neither those of Senecan stage tradition nor those of Catholic, Protestant, or popular imaginative lore.[9] In magical terms, the dramatist in creating the Ghost would be conjuring, would be like Faustus, whom Marlowe shows us summoning up Mephostophilis to meet an urgent need the discontented scholar cannot otherwise fulfill. The crucial difference is precisely that the Ghost is *not* contained by magical or religious terms. Hamlet looks at this possibility:

> The spirit that I have seen
> May be a dev'l, and the dev'l hath power
> T' assume a pleasing shape, yea, and perhaps,
> Out of my weakness and my melancholy,
> As he is very potent with such spirits,
> Abuses me to damn me.
>
> (II.ii.598–603)

---

8. "The Hamlet formula, so to speak, is not 'a man who has to avenge his father' but 'a man who has been given a task by a ghost'. Everything else about him is less important than that" (C. S. Lewis, "Hamlet: The Prince or the Poem?" in *Studies in Shakespeare: British Academy Lectures,* ed. Peter Alexander [London: Oxford University Press, 1964], p. 210).

9. Much modern debate about the Ghost's status takes its point of departure from J. Dover Wilson's *What Happens in "Hamlet"* (Cambridge: Cambridge University Press, 1937). Wilson saw the Ghost as "the linchpin in *Hamlet*; remove it and the play falls to pieces" (p. 52). He regarded the Ghost as an "epitome of the ghost-lore of his age" (p. 53), but in order to locate its habitat as Purgatory he had to posit a Catholic Ghost in a Protestant Denmark in which all the living characters—including the dead king's son, wife, and brother—are Protestant. In his carefully balanced review of contemporary ghost literature in relation to the play, Robert H. West has acutely pointed out that all efforts to pigeonhole the Ghost in one or another of the received traditions will (and have) run into such difficulties ("King Hamlet's Ambiguous Ghost," *PMLA* 70 [1955]: 1107–17). West notes: "The pneumatological evidence in the nature of the apparition seems, then, to point equally in three directions: to a Catholic ghost, a paganesque ghost, and a devil" (p. 1110). But he also notes that elements of the Ghost make it impossible to identify him fully with any of these possibilities: "We cannot decide formally, then, what the ghost is. In the last analysis all we have to go on is the dramatic impression derived from the bent and quality of the play as a whole and perhaps from the revenge tradition to which it belongs" (p. 1116).

But the apparition proves to be "an honest ghost" (I.v.138), confirming Hamlet's earlier conviction, in however complex a way. Shakespeare is presenting a figure of the heroic father that has, within the play, a reality that is ontological albeit frighteningly problematic.

But it is necessary, unless one believes in ghosts, to understand the dramatist's action in bringing the father back from the grave as expressing some process, not supernatural, in human life. In my view, the Ghost is a version of the father created under pressure of gathering need, visible in the immediately preceding plays, to reckon with the problem of achieving heroic male identity. The figure of Hamlet's father comes out of the unknown to meet an enormous need, at once terrifying and compelling to the son, to achieve full adult male authority by embracing a heritage that has been vitiated, but that might be vindicated by taking on the father's identity. In dramatizing a fully heroic embodiment of legitimate paternity in the Ghost, Shakespeare begins the series of tragedies in which heroic male identity either fails to find achievement or is destroyed. Later tragedies will present protagonists who, having already achieved what appears to be intact, powerful, socially validated manhood, are thrust back into destructive conflict when a new situation uncovers an existing vulnerability, a previously unacknowledged incompleteness. *Hamlet* is unique among the plays from the great tragic period in the Prince's being presented from the first in the role of a son seeking identity through his actual, lost father.

What Hamlet finds in the Ghost, however, is not the actual father. Nor does he find a paternal image that, in the son's development toward adulthood, has been subdued to realistic perception of the father's human limitations. The Ghost is so deeply disturbing, for Hamlet and for an audience that experiences the play through him, because it presents an embodiment of the father perceived, as in infancy, under the sway of omnipotence of mind. Blocked in his effort to internalize his father's heritage by his grief and by his mother's marriage to the hated, sensual stepfather, Hamlet confronts on the battlements a regressively constructed image of the idealized father whose overpowering presence demands the son's absolute dedication of himself to vindicating the paternal ideal.

For Hamlet, this archaic image—beyond subduing, appealing for love and obedience, and requiring a new act of identification that submerges the son's identity in the father's—is suddenly manifest *as an object*, out there in the world. In relation to the dramatist's need as well, the outsideness of the Ghost is essential; for him, the Ghost functions as a projection, the dramatic reality of which is vital to the play. Projection seeks to cope with an intolerable inner pressure, what Freud in his neoneurological vocabulary describes as a potentially traumatic inner excitation, by treating it as if it were outside and providing an object that can "bind" the disruptive psychic energy.[10] The expulsion process is conveyed in Hamlet's initial response to the Ghost by imagery that reverses the process of swallowing.

> Let me not burst in ignorance, but tell
> Why thy canoniz'd bones, hearsed in death,
> Have burst their cerements; why the sepulchre,
> Wherein we saw thee quietly interr'd,
> Hath op'd his ponderous and marble jaws
> To cast thee up again.
>
> (I.iv.46–51)

The imagery of terrible disruption here is exactly right for the undoing of the child's early introjection of the parent.[11] The resistance to this process is in "ponderous and marble jaws," while "cast thee up" suggests the physiological violence of vomiting—a process that wracks the whole physical body, as Hamlet's whole being is disrupted ("Let me not burst in ignorance"). The grave's casting up

10. In the language of *Beyond the Pleasure Principle* (*Standard Edition*, vol. 18), *binding* is the process of mastering unpleasurable sensations by subduing them to the service of the pleasure principle and the need for psychic equilibrium. Projection is a way "of dealing with any internal excitations which produce too great an increase of unpleasure: there is a tendency to treat them as though they were acting, not from the inside, but from the outside, so that it may be possible to bring the shield against stimuli into operation as a measure of defence against them" (p. 29). For Hamlet, however, within the play's dramatic reality, the Ghost is "outside" from the beginning, and endowed with "traumatic" force "powerful enough to break through the protective shield. . . . Such an event as an external trauma is bound to provoke a disturbance on a large scale . . . and to set in motion every possible defensive measure. . . . There is no longer any possibility of preventing the mental apparatus from being flooded with large amounts of stimulus, and another problem arises instead—the problem of mastering the amour.ts of stimulus which have broken in and of binding them, in the psychical sense, so that they can be disposed of" (pp. 29–30).

11. In "Mourning and Melancholia" Freud observes that the infant relates to an external object "in accordance with the oral or cannibalistic phase of libidinal development, . . . it wants to do so by devouring it" (*Standard Edition*, vol. 14, pp. 249–50).

again of the father, undoing the ritual work of civilization imaged as "canoniz'd bones . . . quietly interr'd," is the external equivalent of his becoming unburied in Hamlet.

In his encounter with the Ghost, Hamlet's investment in the family constellation is made total. As he makes his commitment, he explicitly calls in his spirit from participation in the larger world:

> Yea, from the table of my memory
> I'll wipe away all trivial fond records,
> All saws of books, all forms, all pressures past
> That youth and observation copied there,
> And thy commandement all alone shall live
> Within the book and volume of my brain,
> Unmix'd with baser matter.
>
> (I.v.98–104)

Hamlet here renounces all the growing out into the world by which a youth becomes a man, in his full social role, freeing himself from family bonds while remaining true to the core of his relationship to them. A radical withdrawal of investment in society is demanded by the total investment in the family ties—of love and loyalty to his lost father, and of hatred for those who have degraded the royal heritage, his mother and the grossly sensual parody of a father who has taken King Hamlet's place: "O most pernicious woman! / O villain, villain, smiling, damned villain!" (lines 105–6).

From the beginning Hamlet cannot but respond with disgust and submerged jealousy to Claudius's sensual possession of Gertrude. Even without the fact of the murder, the hurried marriage reanimates Hamlet's relation to his mother, and his fascination with her sexuality. To contemplate the marriage is so disturbing, even before the Ghost, that in his first soliloquy he alludes to it and circles about it for fifteen lines before actually coming out with "—married with my uncle" (I.ii.151). Yet, through the negative, his fascination animates the vivid language: "the flushing in her galled eyes," "to post / With such dexterity to incestuous sheets" (lines 155–57). A generalized revulsion at sexuality destroys his relationship with Ophelia—revulsion at his own sexuality ("virtue cannot so inoculate our old stock but we shall relish of it" [III.i.116–18]) as well as at women's: "you jig and amble, and you lisp, you nickname God's creatures. . . . Go to, I'll no more on't, it hath made me mad" (lines 144–47).

This revulsion and self-loathing is significantly complementary to Hamlet's retrospective idealization of a father "so loving to my mother / That he might not beteem the winds of heaven / Visit her face too roughly" (I.ii.140–42). The falling off from Hyperion to a satyr that Hamlet is here describing is repeated and amplified in the Ghost's rather troubling account of his queen's seduction:

> Ay, that incestuous, that adulterate beast,
> With witchcraft of his wits, with traitorous gifts—
> O wicked wit and gifts that have the power
> So to seduce!—won to his shameful lust
> The will of my most seeming virtuous queen.
> O Hamlet, what a falling-off was there
> From me, whose love was of that dignity
> That it went hand in hand even with the vow
> I made to her in marriage, and to decline
> Upon a wretch whose natural gifts were poor
> To those of mine!
> But virtue, as it never will be moved,
> Though lewdness court it in a shape of heaven,
> So lust, though to a radiant angel link'd,
> Will sate itself in a celestial bed
> And prey on garbage.
>
>   (I.v.42–57)

This apologia, when one pauses over it, seems strangely open to irony—one can imagine how Faulconbridge might respond were it offered as an account of his mother's seduction! Elsewhere in Shakespeare it is possessive fathers, pantaloons like Egeus or Brabantio, who complain of seductive gifts and spells and medicines. One can also wonder about certain "natural gifts" in Claudius that might not be poor in comparison with those of "a radiant angel . . . in a celestial bed."

But as the scene is played, and one listens to the Ghost in concert with young Hamlet, one does not think in this way. We respond in sympathy with the Prince's need. The disruption of his relationship to his father by the sexuality of his stepfather and mother makes a desexualized or prudish attitude in the Ghost right to meet the need for inhibition of awareness in that area, so that the identification can be renewed and intensified. The Prince's cruelty about sexuality with Ophelia and with his mother has a self-righteousness that accords with the identification established here. Hamlet's regard for Gertrude touches explicitly the child's attitude, normally helpful in inhibiting sexual curiosity, that after all the parents are too old for sex—"at your age / The heyday in the blood is tame" (III.iv.68–69). The desperate urgency with which Hamlet's

cruelty is expressed, or bursts out, makes us feel the necessity of
the Prince's all-important effort to identify himself with "the majesty of buried Denmark," and the restriction on his life that goes
with it.

The Ghost's appearance invites the hero to undertake again the
process of becoming a man. But instead of creating a situation that
would enable Hamlet to affirm his place in a world beyond the ties
of family, the Ghost puts him in a passive, childlike relationship to
an unassailable figure of paternal power. Laertes, repeatedly a foil
to Hamlet,[12] in these opening scenes is moving in exactly the opposite direction. "Take thy fair hour, Laertes" (I.ii.62), says Claudius
in granting permission for a return to learning the great world in
Paris; in the next breath he denies Hamlet permission to return to
Wittenberg. The scene immediately before Hamlet's meeting his father's Ghost is occupied with Laertes' taking leave of his father. Polonius is an old fool, perhaps, but one who urges and blesses his
son's departure, even as he loads him with "saws":

> Yet here, Laertes? Aboard, aboard, for shame!
> The wind sits in the shoulder of your sail,
> And you are stay'd for. There—my blessing with thee!
> And these few precepts in thy memory
> Look thou character. Give thy thoughts no tongue.
> (I.iii.55–59)

The precepts that Laertes is told to copy in "the book and volume of
[his] brain" are all about engaging the large world. The feeling for
growing outward that Shakespeare puts into the scene, poignantly
mixed with warnings by brother and father to Ophelia that she hold
herself back from Hamlet, is beautifully summarized by Laertes as
he speaks of the possibility of Hamlet's outgrowing his present affection, "a violet in the youth of primy nature" (line 7). To Ophelia's
dismayed "No more but so?" he answers:

> Think it no more:
> For nature crescent does not grow alone
> In thews and bulk, but as this temple waxes,
> The inward service of the mind and soul
> Grows wide withal.
> (lines 10–14)

---

12. In unfolding the analogical structure of the play, Francis Fergusson emphasizes Laertes' function as foil to Hamlet in *The Idea of a Theater* (Princeton: Princeton
University Press, 1949), pp. 138–39.

It is precisely this waxing, the full engagement of the "inward service of the mind and soul" with prospects for growth offered by a social world, that is blocked in Hamlet as his whole being is called back into the service of the "commandement [that] all alone shall live."

The Hamlet story was described earlier as providing what seems a second chance. It only *seems* so, however, despite all Hamlet's heroic struggles to get past "seems." For what happens on the battlements is the reverse of grieving. In the case of a loss through death, particularly the death of a father, the principle of *de mortuis nil nisi bonum* characteristically tends to protect conscious memory from hostile reflections, including resentment at having been abandoned, or the resentment one may feel toward a father who has proved unworthy or incapable of sustaining one's original investment in him. The work of grieving includes the working through of such unconscious hostility. But the split between Hyperion and the satyr Claudius, with the Ghost's sanction for unlimited hatred of the latter, rules out all realistic reassessment of the heroic good father, all humane compromise with the bad.

Freud has described a type of melancholia in which the normal process of grieving is prevented by the hostile component of an ambivalent tie to the person lost, whether by death or disenchantment or rejection.[13] Instead of a gradual withdrawal from the attachment, the lost person is kept by an identification that sustains the original ambivalence. Suppressed hostility in the relationship to the loved, lost person who is also hated is turned back upon the self and expressed as violent self-reproaches and self-loathing. Painful dejection goes with a sense of one's unworthiness as measured against an idealized image of the lost beloved, which becomes, through the identification, an unattainable ideal for the self.

We can understand more fully the enormous power of *Hamlet* if we consider Shakespeare's creation of the play as a partially successful defense against the self-destructive predicament of a melancholia. The play releases, in an action endowed with objective reality subject to the dramatist's manipulation of it, potentially disabling energies that are turned back against the self when the unresolved hostility of a deeply ambivalent bond blocks the work of grief. Put simply, the power of *Hamlet* arises from its dramatization of the figure of the father split into polar opposites, while the diffi-

13. "Mourning and Melancholia," *Standard Edition*, vol. 14, pp. 243–58.

culty comes with this split's putting the ghostly father beyond criticism. Hamlet can recover for an elated moment relationship to the ideal father. But the totalness of atonement also makes it impossible for him to escape his dependence by recognizing the limitations of this father as only a man. That Hamlet continues in the self-lacerations of melancholia for some time after the Ghost's revelation suggests that hostility toward the lost father remains, despite Claudius's availability as an object of hatred. And even the hatred licensed against the villainous version cannot find expression in action until Hamlet is himself mortally wounded. The splitting of the father in *Hamlet* is a way out of mourning which, tragically, does not work—except by accepting death as the consummation of self-hatred as well as the consummation of revenge.

PIETY, OUTRAGE, AND THEATRICAL AGGRESSION IN *HAMLET*

A psychological pattern is always an aspect of social life, an abstraction we make from observing an individual's way of coping with his relations to others. *Hamlet* is a play about disinheritance, experienced in its most drastic form, at the heart of a fully dramatized social world. It presents a hero who, though he should be the embodiment of the heritage—"The glass of fashion and the mould of form, / Th' observ'd of all observers"—is "blasted with ecstasy" (III.i.153–54, 160). Hamlet's struggle to cope with the desecration of heritage, his outrageousness in response to outrage, his piety in spite of it, his struggle for expression—it is these social realities and gestures that make the play's psychological configurations expressible, and that enable *Hamlet* to keep its relevance through changing historical situations.

Freud provided a bridge from individual to social development in observing that the individual conscience, the cultural heritage as reflected in one's system of values and sense of self, is formed through the child's internalization of the culturally shaped values of the parents.[14] So too are individual attitudes toward and concep-

---

14. In *New Introductory Lectures on Psychoanalysis*, Freud writes: "The child's super-ego is in fact constructed on the model not of its parents but of its parents' super-ego; the contents which fill it are the same and it becomes the vehicle of tradition and of all the time-resisting judgements of value which have propagated themselves in this manner from generation to generation" (*Standard Edition*, vol. 22, p. 67).

tions of the larger powers that sustain life. In a culture with an effectual religion, God is manifest in one's awareness of what validates and supports society, history, the universe. In a secularized culture, we still arrive, at maturity, at an awareness that the validating ground of individual life is larger than individuals. Acceptance of the parents' finitude and imperfection is part of the transfer of piety that recognizes the larger, culturally confirmed context as the source of the parents' being as well as the being of the child. A broader piety takes over from infantile dependence and, insofar as it does that, frees the child from the parents, permits him, in becoming a child of God, or a child of the times, to become a man.

Successful development permits the child to forgive the parents for not being gods; fixation along the road of development results in crippling investments of love and hate in idolatrous objects, parents or parent-substitutes. The deferred afflictions of the Oedipus complex, whether at the crisis of adolescence or erupting in later life, represent a crisis in the piety that normally sustains one's identity. In *Hamlet*, the father's return as a Ghost makes him the object of the son's idolatry. An idol is an inadequate image of the divine because it intervenes between the individual's worship and his awareness of the larger force in which he and his world are grounded. But his father's spirit is all that Prince Hamlet has. His lack of a stable, integrated image of the father at the core of himself makes the Ghost walk, creates the need to find him outside. And it allows filial piety to become an obsession. The Prince is trapped because his piety cannot get beyond the Ghost of his noble father, murdered by another father, ignoble, gross, revolting.

The Ghost, because it embodies the whole valid moral and social heritage, cuts off the protagonist (and to a large extent the play) from any wider allegiance. The nexus with what should be is almost entirely through Hamlet. Christian commentators, Roy Battenhouse, for instance, or Eleanor Prosser, point out that from a Christian point of view Hamlet embraces a sinful course in accepting the Ghost's charge to avenge his father's death, for "vengeance is mine, saith the Lord." [15] Hamlet pursues his ghostly father's will in place

---

15. For Battenhouse, "Hamlet's inability to discriminate this fact [that the Ghost is a "damned spirit"] is at the core of his tragedy, . . . a tragedy inseparable from his own decayed faith" (Roy Battenhouse, "The Ghost in *Hamlet*: A Catholic 'Linchpin'?" *Studies in Philology* 48 [1951]: 192). See also chap. 4 of his *Shakespearean Tragedy: Its Art and Its Christian Premises* (Bloomington: Indiana University Press, 1969), pp. 204–66. On the basis of extensive readings in both Protestant and Catholic writ-

of God's will. To see the play from this vantage point, however, is to let us, and Hamlet, out of the modern world that this play helps to usher in; it is to propose an alternative that simply is not present within the play's fable. The fact that Hamlet is the legitimate heir makes him, will he nill he, the final court of appeal and authority that should bring Claudius to justice. It is an appalling situation of aloneness, an appalling task.

Hamlet has to meet the dismaying isolation of his secret, which Shakespeare makes us realize as soon as the others rejoin him after the Ghost has gone:

> I hold it fit that we shake hands and part,
> You, as your business and desire shall point you,
> For every man hath business and desire,
> Such as it is, and for my own poor part,
> I will go pray.
>
> (I.v.128–32)

Already there is the sense that nothing ordinary—"business and desire, / Such as it is"—matters. Hamlet's "and for my own poor part, / I will go pray," in its terrible sense of aloneness, edges on ironic recognition of his situation, in which the religious dimension, the supernatural beyond the Ghost, is already out of range. We see the intensity of his suffering and isolation through the eyes of Ophelia in the next scene, where she reports that he has come to her closet looking "As if he had been loosed out of hell" (II.i.80). We feel his isolation too in the false diagnosis of Polonius, in Ophelia's helplessness, in his situation of being spied on, both by Rosencrantz and Guildenstern and by the King and Polonius—with Ophelia as bait. Hamlet's heroic identity, his greatness, is his power of maintaining himself in his relation to the Ghost and in the vision of the world's corruption that goes with it.

In dramatizing this heroic striving, *Hamlet*, more than any other play, invites identification with the hero and yet does not fully guide us in what we are to make of him. We identify with all the tragic protagonists, of course; but we also regularly feel horror, dismay, or even something like amusement:

---

ings on ghosts, Prosser finds a "definitive test": "No matter how convincing a spirit might be in every other respect, if it urged any action or made any statement that violated the teachings of the Church, it was an agent of the Devil" (Eleanor Prosser, *Hamlet and Revenge* [Stanford: Stanford University Press, 1967], p. 111).

LEAR: Dost thou call me fool, boy?
FOOL: All thy other titles thou hast given away, that thou wast born
with.

(*Lr*. I.iv.148–50)

We are aware, regularly, of more than the protagonist is, and this
awareness balances the claims of the protagonist on us. But once
Hamlet has seen the Ghost in the third scene, there is scarcely a
moment in the action when anyone in the play, or in the audience,
knows more than Hamlet knows. He even intimates that he sees
through to the King's purposes in sending him to England: "I see a
cherub that sees them" (IV.iii.48). Such judgments as are made on
Hamlet are pointedly not to the point. We see through others with
him, while the others are unable to see through him, to pluck out
the heart of his mystery.

A curious impunity surrounds Hamlet. Although he is outrageous, insulting, impudent, people do not call him on it. After
Hamlet has described the repulsiveness of old men to Polonius's
face, the old man diverts indignation into objective observation:
"Though this be madness, yet there is method in't" (II.ii.205–6). Or
again with Ophelia:

HAMLET: I did love you once.
OPHELIA: Indeed, my lord, you made me believe so.
HAMLET: You should not have believ'd me, for virtue cannot so in-
oculate our old stock but we shall relish of it. I lov'd you
not.
OPHELIA: I was the more deceiv'd.

(III.i.114–19)

The lack of direct response to Hamlet's outrageousness goes with
the assumption that he is mad or deranged. Ophelia, who does not
know how deeply his jilting has hurt her until she goes mad, says
"O, help him, you sweet heavens!" and finally, "O, what a noble
mind is here o'erthrown!" (lines 133, 150).

Even the King holds himself almost entirely in check, not taking
up Hamlet's insults and insinuations:

KING: How fares our cousin Hamlet?
HAMLET: Excellent, i' faith, of the chameleon's dish: I eat the air,
promise-cramm'd—you cannot feed capons so.
KING: I have nothing with this answer, Hamlet, these words are
not mine.

(III.ii.92–97)

Part of the other characters' helplessness, of course, comes from the sudden, shifting, half-hidden wit with which Hamlet attacks, as here, where he takes the would-be agreeable "How fares our cousin," *how do you do*, as though it were *how do you eat*, and answers "I eat the air" (*your promises*), implying *promises instead of the substance of the succession that you have taken from me*. "You cannot feed [even] capons so"—and, by implication, *I am no capon*. No wonder the King can say no more than "I have nothing with this answer, Hamlet, these words are not mine."

Only the Queen, in the pitch of excitement after the play-within-the-play, sets about wholeheartedly to rebuke her son, and she gets back, at once, better than she gives, as Hamlet turns her phrase: "Hamlet, thou hast thy father much offended." "Mother, you have my father much offended" (III.iv.9–10). When he has killed the man behind the arras, her natural humanity cries out: "O, what a rash and bloody deed is this!" only to be put down at once by "A bloody deed! almost as bad, good mother, / As kill a king, and marry with his brother" (lines 27–29). Part of the tragedy, of course, is that his mother has forfeited the moral authority that might provide a vantage point from which to grieve for the "unseen good old man" (IV.i.12). There is thus no one to comment on the frightfulness with which Hamlet dismisses the death of Polonius when he discovers whom he has killed: "Thou wretched, rash, intruding fool, farewell! / I took thee for thy better" (III.iv.31–32). Instead, Hamlet immediately returns to upbraiding his mother: "Leave wringing of your hands. Peace, sit you down, / And let me wring your heart" (lines 34–35).

As we watch the play, or are swept along in reading it, we are not invited to pause over the cruelty of Hamlet's taunts. The killing of Polonius makes more real the violence pent up in Hamlet; there is relief that he has reached to action, even if only in unpremeditated response, together with regret that it is not, as for a moment he thinks possible, the King he has killed. Polonius has been exhibited as something of a fool in his own right, a dotard version of the father-figure. The lack of compunction Hamlet feels about a man dead functions for us as a measure of the intensity of his deep sense of outrage about the people who matter. Indeed, his ruthlessness is somehow a testimony to his all-absorbing, heroic commitment to feeling the outrage done to life by the murder of his father and by what he perceives as his mother's infidelity.

The play is blind to Hamlet's faults except insofar as they are

expressed by Hamlet himself. To insist on them, to go beyond
Hamlet's own perceptions in dwelling on his destructiveness, his
egotism, his ineffectualness and irresponsibility, is in a curious way
discourteous, doing violence to an alliance with the sweet prince
that audiences enjoy. When Hamlet plays hide-and-seek with those
sent to find where he has hidden the body of Polonius, we enjoy
his exhilarated fun in baffling everybody:

ROSENCRANTZ: What have you done, my lord, with the dead body?
HAMLET: Compounded it with dust, whereto 'tis kin.

(IV.ii.5–6)

There is a curious beauty about Hamlet's answer: it puts the death
in the context of last things, suggesting a vision of mortality that
makes life scarcely matter. But at such a moment, what an evasion,
and how arrogant, how upstaging! That this is Hamlet's intention is
manifest in the sequel about the sponge and the son of a king. And
yet we are *with* Hamlet here as he puts the little eager terriers in
their place.

We are with him even more, of course, when at last he is brought
in, guarded, face to face with the King, who has seen the play, so
that the chips are down between them:

KING: Now, Hamlet, where's Polonius?
HAMLET: At supper.
KING: At supper? where?
HAMLET: Not where he eats, but where 'a is eaten; a certain con-
vocation of politic worms are e'en at him. Your worm is
your only emperor for diet: we fat all creatures else to fat
us, and we fat ourselves for maggots; your fat king and
your lean beggar is but variable service, two dishes, but to
one table—that's the end.

(IV.iii.16–25)

This is the high point in the antics of Hamlet's madness and worth
pausing over as a marvelous example of the way he keeps everyone
else off balance by the displacements of wit: "At supper." "At supper? where?" The King, who should be on top, is maneuvered into
the position of fall-guy. This technique of setting up the loaded
leading question is of course standard with the Shakespearean
clown or fool, and the discipline of writing such parts lay behind
Shakespeare's handling of Hamlet's antic disposition. In effect, the
Prince plays the fool's part as well as the hero's; his assumed madness gives him the equivalent of the court fool's license, which

Shakespeare had recently exploited as a dramatic resource in *As You Like It* and *Twelfth Night*. Part of the fool's stock in trade was the pithy sententious generalization, suddenly brought home by fitting it to present company. Hamlet turns Polonius into a supper for politic worms, with as much relish as disgust—leaving behind all question of his own particular responsibility for the old man's death as he rises to sweeping statement: "we fat all creatures else to fat us." And meanwhile his invisible fool's-bladder keeps bobbing the King, showing him "how a king may go a progress through the guts of a beggar" (lines 30–31). His direct access to aggressive action against the King blocked, Hamlet plays the fool to enable himself to maintain the integrity of his hatred.

If we stop to add up Hamlet's actions and inactions, we find a catalogue of outrage and failure. But the play does not situate us to stop, does not provide anyone to help in the process of evaluation. No one in the play observes that Hamlet fails Ophelia. We see her and can collect from the fragments of her madness an idea of her profound shock from the cruel disappointment of maiden ardor, along with her grief for the father Hamlet killed. Her loss of Hamlet, indeed, is partly expressed through grief for her father. But Hamlet is off at sea; he is not brought to confront anything of how he has failed her. On the contrary, at her grave he is able to say, without any environing irony:

> I lov'd Ophelia. Forty thousand brothers
> Could not with all their quantity of love
> Make up my sum.
>
> (V.i.269–71)

Hamlet arranges for Rosencrantz and Guildenstern to be "put to sudden death, / Not shriving time allow'd" (V.ii.46–47). "So Guildenstern and Rosencrantz go to't" (line 56) is the only comment, from Horatio, on the drastic expedience with which Hamlet deals with what are, after all, only ignorant agents. Again, no one comments on his complete lack of a viable plan of practical action, even after his return from England. The nearest thing to such a comment is Horatio's practical reminder, while Hamlet rails against the King, that time is passing: "It must be shortly known to him from England / What is the issue of the business there" (V.ii.71–72). Hamlet's response—"It will be short; the interim's mine, / And a man's life's no more than to say 'one'" (lines 73–74)—is one of the great, heroic moments of the play. The current of resolution, so long diffused and roiled, sweeps deep and silent through the magical word "interim," as that word opens up after the strong monosyllables. But the fact remains that he does not make any plan, accepting instead the initiative of the King and Laertes, with the result that it is not the King alone who dies, but also the Queen, Laertes, and Hamlet himself.

In creating the role of Hamlet, Shakespeare, exploiting fully the resources of the new theater, could define a new position with respect to heritage, expressing loss of heritage with all its doubts, uncertainty, loathing of self and life, but also exhibiting a hero with strength to protect integrity against acquiescence in the corrupt world, on one side, or acquiescence in self-loathing, on the other. Hamlet is a potentially great man protecting his greatness, the greatness of the demand he makes on life, even as life fails or betrays that demand. What Hamlet has to meet this challenge, to master the enormously disruptive energies it releases in him, is his power of expression. He must save himself from suicide, and he does this in part by expressing his need for it, both directly and in violent self-contempt. It is also essential that he turn aggression outward, affirming the reality of corruption and violence. His power of expression works to prevent or divert him from taking direct action even as it gives theatrical release, assertive and ironic in the terms he establishes, to his aggression; but without it Hamlet could not maintain his wounded identity at all.

It is Hamlet's need for expression that lightens his spirits as soon as he hears that the players are coming. He uses them at once, calling for a speech that serves to identify what is working inside him. As in 1 Henry IV, where we have a "play extempore" about a son's confrontation with his royal father, here we have a speech extempore, part of which Hamlet has by heart, about the destruction of a revered, aged king by a figure who is not restrained from action by any scruples whatever, "rugged Pyrrhus." It is a speech that, in its poised ambiguity, objectifies both Hamlet's feelings of grief and outrage "for a king, / Upon whose property and most dear life / A damn'd defeat was made," and Hamlet's wish that he could "make oppression bitter" by fattening "all the region kites / With this slave's offal" (II.ii.569–71, 578–80). We and Hamlet can experience both the horror of the killing of good old Priam and the terrible zest of it. It even swings around a moment of delay when Illium "stoops to his base," and Pyrrhus, distracted by the hideous crash, "like a neutral to his will and matter, / Did nothing" (lines 476, 481–82).

In developing Hamlet's preoccupation with the players, Shake-speare makes much of the use and abuse of expression and of its inadequacy as an answer to his protagonist's whole need. Hamlet's comments on acting rigorously subordinate the actors' need for ex-pression to "the purpose of the playing, whose end, both at the first and now, was and is, to hold as 'twere the mirror up to nature: to show virtue her feature, scorn her own image, and the very age and body of the time his form and pressure" (III.ii.20–24). Self is to be wholly absorbed in the discipline of playing as it looks beyond it-self. Hamlet's whole discussion notably leaves out the personal mo-tives, the need for self-preservation or reduplication, that animate the playing: "for in the very torrent, tempest, and, as I may say, whirlwind of your passion, you must acquire and beget a tem-perance that may give it smoothness" (III.ii.5–8). The individual's acting must fulfill, not disrupt, the team enterprise: no "necessary question of the play" (lines 42–43) must be neglected.

It is striking how fully *Hamlet* dramatizes the personal need for playing and formal theatrical action that is left out of Hamlet's ac-count of the process as a professional discipline. Hamlet has "that within which passes show," but he is preoccupied by "actions that a man might play" (I.ii.85, 84). He feels the pressure toward the-atrical violence that Kyd played on in *The Spanish Tragedy*, and he will often "tear a passion to tatters" (III.ii.9–10) in response to it. Dismayed by his own inaction, Hamlet laments:

> Yet I,
> A dull and muddy-mettled rascal, peak
> Like John-a-dreams, unpregnant of my cause,
> And can say nothing.
>
> (II.ii.566–69)

But in fact, of course, he is carried away in a torrent of words:

> Am I a coward?
> Who calls me villain, breaks my pate across,
> Plucks off my beard and blows it in my face,
> Tweaks me by the nose, gives me the lie i' th' throat
> As deep as to the lungs? Who does me this?
> Hah, 'swounds, I should take it.
>
> (lines 571–76)

Hamlet, as usual, is the only one who sees the irony about Hamlet. And, as usual, unaffected by it, he proceeds at once to a further use of expression:

> I'll have these players
> Play something like the murther of my father
> Before mine uncle. I'll observe his looks,
> I'll tent him to the quick. If 'a do blench,
> I know my course.
>
> (lines 594–98)

"The Murder of Gonzago" is intended by Hamlet to move acting to action by making the King proclaim his guilt. When it comes to the test, however, Shakespeare has Hamlet himself interrupt the necessary business of the play by aggressively summarizing its action instead of waiting for it to have its full effect on Claudius:

> 'A poisons him i' th' garden for his estate. His name's Gonzago, the story is extant, and written in very choice Italian. You shall see anon how the murtherer gets the love of Gonzago's wife.
>
> OPHELIA: The King rises.
>
> (III.ii.261–65)

That the poisoner is the "*nephew* to the king" (line 244), as Hamlet blurts out at his entrance, makes what is acted, while replicating the crime of Claudius, simultaneously present a figure in Hamlet's relationship to Claudius reenacting the murder, as though to fit the crime exactly to the punishment, to "re-venge by re-presentation."[16]

The enormous poetic and dramatic creativity achieved in *Hamlet* depends in good part on this pressure to turn speech and acting into action. The need to channel aggression through verbal and theatrical expression in turn depends on the initial, given situation of the two powerful fathers, one murdered by the other, with Hamlet identified with both. Hamlet asserts himself by loathing Claudius; he asserts his father by loathing himself, including the repressed part of himself identified with Claudius's double crime of murder and incest. The constant discharge of cruelty at others is Hamlet's relief from the hideous suffering of his aggression toward himself. Release reaches manic proportions in the rhapsody of elation that follows the play-within-the-play. But the deep movement of the aggression that occupies Hamlet looks toward death, so that by the fifth act the universalizing of death in the graveyard is

16. David Willbern, from whose work in progress this phrase is borrowed, observes that the need to do this is deeply grounded in the psychology of revenge and is a consistent feature of the revenge-play form, with its plays-(and audiences)-within-plays.

lyric release. The final havoc carries out the death-directed wish in action.

But whatever our conclusions when we add up Hamlet's actions, we are left with a sense of Hamlet as a moral hero in defeat, a sense of tragic loss, not just the sensational excitement of a revel in a blood bath. Why should this be so? Part of our high sense of Hamlet in death is Shakespeare's skillful manipulation. In the previous scene, the satiric-lyrical universals of the graveyard have opened the floodgates, and the burial of Ophelia has given occasion for a new sort of self-affirmation. Then in the last scene Hamlet's gracious, sociable self is recovered and brought home to us at moments—with Osric for foil, for example—together with the resolution born of the acceptance of death:

> If it be now, 'tis not to come; if it be not to come, it will be now; if it be not now, yet it will come—the readiness is all.
>
> (V.ii.220–22)

There is a staginess about some of it: Hamlet's apology to Laertes, for example, and Laertes' to Hamlet. But there is also Hamlet's concern, as he dies, about the succession, and about his "story," which Horatio must tell: "Report me and my cause aright / To the unsatisfied" (lines 339–40). And we do feel, through these gestures, the abortive effort of a younger generation to renew society, a striving toward health.

Yet the tragic dignity and loss must be more than these final heroics—must be something earned, on the basis of a deeper striving. It must be something beyond the meaning we get if we simply reduce Hamlet's problem to the Oedipus complex—and yet it must be consistent with the presence of that complex, for the Freudian explanation clearly works. T. S. Eliot puts us on the way to part of an answer, I think, in his famous criticism of the play as "an artistic failure." [17] Eliot observed that "Hamlet (the man) is dominated by an emotion which is inexpressible, because it is in *excess* of the facts as they appear. And the supposed identity of Hamlet with his author is genuine to this point: that Hamlet's bafflement at the absence of objective equivalent to his feelings is a prolongation of the bafflement of his creator in the face of his artistic problem" (p. 125). Eliot, responding to his own deepest preoccupations, as manifest later in

---

17. T. S. Eliot, "Hamlet and His Problems," *Selected Essays*, new ed. (New York: Harcourt, Brace and World, 1950), p. 123.

his dramatic version of the Orestes-Hamlet theme, *The Family Reunion*, concluded that "Shakespeare's *Hamlet*, in so far as it is Shakespeare's [and not an adaptation of a lost earlier version, probably by Kyd], is a play dealing with the effect of a mother's guilt upon her son, and that Shakespeare was unable to impose this motive successfully upon the 'intractable material' of the old play" (p. 123). Hamlet's disgust for his mother "envelops and exceeds her. It is thus a feeling which he cannot understand; he cannot objectify it, and it therefore remains to poison life and obstruct action. None of the possible actions can satisfy it; and nothing that Shakespeare can do with the plot can express Hamlet for him" (p. 125).

What Eliot ignores, focusing only on Hamlet's disgust in response to his guilty mother, is Hamlet's own sense of guilt—what the Freudian explanation makes central. Hamlet's guilt refers to his father not his mother; more accurately, it refers to his parricidal wish. It is this that cannot be given objective expression. The "possible action" that would correspond to this wish is not accessible, because the Ghost is a ghost. Hamlet cannot kill a ghost. Nor can he realize that the destructive force of his effort to serve the Ghost, to retrieve the heritage of his lost father, has its roots in the filial bond he struggles to keep intact by making it the entirety of his life. The given situation, Claudius's murder of the elder Hamlet, demands absolute loyalty to the memory of the idealized father and permits the diversion of the son's murderous wish from father to uncle. But since this repressed wish is unconsciously tied to the assumption that its enactment means death, Hamlet's hatred cannot be directed at Claudius without being deflected back onto himself as well. In the end, Hamlet is able to accept his destiny only when he has accepted death; he finally kills Claudius only when he himself has already received his death blow. It is Hamlet's "bafflement" in this situation that extends into the play the problem confronting its creator.

But *Hamlet* is, as Eliot said, a "puzzling" play, and "disquieting as is none of the others."[18] It is a play in which something gets out of hand. In it Shakespeare poses—and leaves open—the problem of control that later tragedies will master by an ironic balance. Fully

18. Ibid. In considering *Hamlet* in relation to Shakespeare's power of development, it is well to recall Ella Freeman Sharpe's telling distinction: "The poet is not Hamlet. Hamlet is what he might have been if he had not written the play of *Hamlet*" (*Collected Papers on Psycho-Analysis*, ed. Marjorie Brierly [London: Hogarth Press, 1950], p. 205).

achieved tragedy shows us, typically, a heroic protagonist rich in human values and commanding sympathy, but ultimately destructive. The action, in leading the protagonist to his death, moves us toward ironic awareness of his role in necessitating the tragic outcome. Poised against the hero's aggressive self-assertion, and shaping our understanding of it, irony is the aggressive assertion of a vantage point on the protagonist by means of the dramatist's control over the whole action. Ironic awareness enables us to see, from the outside, the limitations and the destructive force of a figure who, like King Lear, is simultaneously the object of our full sympathy. In *Hamlet* we are invited to identify with the hero at the expense of comprehensive ironic perspective; there is no adequate basis for an outside, controlling perspective. The single-sided attitude it creates toward its hero is one of the striking differences between *Hamlet* and the ensuing tragedies. What the play does not provide is ruthless awareness of Hamlet, such awareness as we are to get of Othello, Lear, Macbeth, Antony, Coriolanus.

The play's failure to situate us to see its protagonist from any vantage point beyond that which Hamlet provides on himself extends Hamlet's failure to see past the Ghost, to develop a perspective on his majestic father beyond his immediate and absolute dedication of himself to identification with the Ghost. We said earlier that the Ghost gives theatrical embodiment to the overwhelming pressure of a potentially disabling predicament. The Ghost is theatrical in the straightforward sense that it is the enactment of a fantasy possible only in the theater. The fantasy comes in answer to the wish Hamlet has earlier recognized as beyond fulfillment in remembering his father: "'A was a man, take him for all in all, / I shall not look upon his like again" (I.ii.188–89). But with the appearance of the Ghost to him, Hamlet is subjected, as we are with him, to a devastating theatrical power. The creation of the Ghost is an experiment in theatrical aggression that forecloses the possibility of ironic control. Shakespeare mimes omnipotence of mind to transform an impossible fantasy into theatrical actuality, unleashing the profoundly disruptive powers of the new theater in an open-ended way to engage and unsettle the audience as well as those who, within the play, encounter this "dreaded sight" beyond the reach of any controlling perspective.

The harrowing force of the Ghost's presence is registered fully, first in the responses of Horatio and the sentinels in the magnificent opening scene, then in Hamlet's agonized questions on the battlements:

What may this mean,
That thou, dead corse, again in complete steel
Revisits thus the glimpses of the moon,
Making night hideous, and we fools of nature
So horridly to shake our disposition
With thoughts beyond the reaches of our souls?
Say why is this? wherefore? what should we do?

(I.iv.51–57)

As the Ghost departs Hamlet thinks he can participate in this power, which answers to a deep need within himself:

My fate cries out
And makes each petty artere in this body
As hardy as the Nemean lion's nerve.
Still am I call'd.

(lines 81–84)

But despite the Prince's conviction here that the Ghost beckons to him with the call of enabling fate, and despite his subsequent absolute commitment to avenging his father's death, for Hamlet the Ghost's appearance puts out of reach the solution it seems at first to provide.

In Hamlet's confrontation with the spirit of his dead father, the overpowering pressure that Shakespeare copes with by creating the Ghost becomes the situation the protagonist must cope with within the play. Hamlet's means of coping is his use of theatrical aggression to engage and unsettle his audience within the play. In taking on a theatrical role like that of the licensed fool and adding to it the special heroic dimension of his extraordinary power to generalize skepticism and disillusion, Hamlet can keep his enemies at a distance while maintaining himself in the face of a potentially self-destructive predicament in which the inhibitions blocking direct action are insurmountable. And by using the players to stage "something like the murther of my father / Before mine uncle" (II.ii.595–96), he can give aggressive theatrical embodiment to the traumatic event revealed to him by the Ghost, releasing himself from its paralyzing force, at least momentarily, by directing it against Claudius.

In presenting the play-within-the-play, Hamlet is preoccupied with a motive and a cue for passion that come not from the fiction and the rhythm of an integrated dramatic performance but from within, and from offstage. To look at the place of *Hamlet* in Shakespeare's development is to consider how the cue for the whole play comes from Shakespeare, as the cue for the play-within-the-play comes from Hamlet. In *Hamlet* we can see the shift from the earlier work, with its base in a cherishing, parental sensibility that avoids full confrontation with fathers, to the confrontations with authority and heritage, grounded in relationship to the father, that characterize the great tragedies. The next section will take up the matter of how the hostility toward a good father not dealt with in *Hamlet* can be seen in what animates Iago in his enterprise of bringing out the weakness of a martial hero rather like Hamlet's father. Iago uses only what is potentially within his victim to make Othello destroy himself in the belief that he had been betrayed by his wife, as King Hamlet was betrayed. The naked parricidal motive against a gracious figure, in the attempt to become "no less than all" (*Lr.* III.iii.24), only finally gets physical enactment in the dagger that so horrifies Macbeth as he makes his way toward the murder of Duncan. In *Hamlet*, both Hamlet and Shakespeare understand as wholly separate objects of idolatry and hatred the single figure of a father who engenders the divided response of enduring loyalty and deadly opposition.

But if Hamlet's situation in the play reflects Shakespeare's predicament in constructing it, the play, in following out the destructive consequences of Hamlet's filial distress, also dramatizes the heroic and potentially paralyzing dimensions of a recurring cultural crisis that has its roots in Shakespeare's age and reaches into our own. *Hamlet* situates its hero, and its audience, at the node of despair and revolutionary protest, both of which draw perennially on heroic expectations whose roots are in infancy but whose definition is itself a heritage of culture:

> See what a grace was seated on this brow:
> Hyperion's curls, the front of Jove himself,
> An eye like Mars, to threaten and command,
> A station like the herald Mercury
> New lighted on a heaven-kissing hill,
> A combination and a form indeed,
> Where every god did seem to set his seal
> To give the world assurance of a man.
> This was your husband. Look you now what follows:
> Here is your husband, like a mildewed ear,
> Blasting his wholesome brother.
>
> (III.iv.55–65)

To vindicate the one, the other must be destroyed. Because in the almost four hundred years since *Hamlet* was written, Western men have repeatedly found themselves in predicaments akin to its hero's, the play's open-ended structure has taken up into itself unresolved energies of commitment and protest in successive generations. As Hazlitt put it, "It is *we* who are Hamlet. The play has a prophetic truth, which is above that of history."[19] This is a great destiny for a work of art, though there is a further kind of power in fully achieved tragedy.

In considering the radically disruptive, *potentially* revolutionary energies in *Hamlet*, it is crucial to recognize, however, that neither the hero nor the play envisages any alternative society. Marx pointed out how revolutionary groups have ennobled their goals by dressing themselves in the borrowed robes of earlier epochs, the English Puritans as Old Testament prophets, the French revolutionaries as Roman Republicans.[20] In Shakespeare's own time the revolutionary appeal of the Reformation to the primitive church was being urged by the radical religious minority—for example, in the Marprelate tracts.[21] The revolutionary impulse to think of innovation as the restoration of a pristine integrity clearly reflects psychological roots similar to those which animate Hamlet's expressions of disgust, protest, and the need for vindication. But there is no suggestion whatever in *Hamlet* of any alternative to established social forms, despite the Prince's drastic expression of their corruption and their limitations: "Then are our beggars bodies, and our monarchs and outstretch'd heroes the beggars' shadows" (II.ii.263–64).

19. William Hazlitt, *Characters of Shakespear's Plays* (1817), ed. Ernest Rhys (London: Everyman's Library, n.d.), p. 79.

20. Karl Marx, *The Eighteenth Brumaire of Louis Bonaparte* (New York: International Publishers, 1963), pp. 15–17. Marx distinguished such self-sanctioning by identification with a heroic past from his own call for a proletarian revolution: "The social revolution of the nineteenth century cannot draw its poetry from the past, but only from the future" (p. 18). In "The Resurrected Romans" (*The Tradition of the New* [New York: McGraw-Hill, 1965]), Harold Rosenberg turns Marx's observation back against the revolutionary optimism it was designed to serve: "The true image of the historical drama would be less *The Communist Manifesto*, with its symmetrical human movements, than *Hamlet*, in which those on stage are exposed at all times to the never-quieted dead" (p. 168). That *Hamlet* is no longer regarded as Shakespeare's preeminent masterpiece, as it was in the age of romantic and revolutionary enthusiasm, may be partly because we are more aware of the problematic character of revolutionary hopes.

21. Some of the common players, in the period when Shakespeare was starting in the theater, ventured to enter the Marprelate controversy on the establishment side, and after initial encouragement, were told firmly to leave religious matters alone. The Anglican establishment, under Archbishop Whitgift, was savagely repressing the radicals, resisting any further development of the reformation tendency. See E. K. Chambers, *The Elizabethan Stage* (Oxford: Clarendon Press, 1923), vol. 1, pp. 261, 295.

The hero's criticism of society is shaped by the tradition of Christian disillusion, *de contemptu mundi*, rather than Protestant protest:

HAMLET: A man may fish with the worm that hath eat of a king, and eat of the fish that hath fed of that worm.
CLAUDIUS: What dost thou mean by this?
HAMLET: Nothing but to show you how a king may go a progress through the guts of a beggar.

(IV.iii.27–31)

The Christian discipline of contemplation, as in, say, a representation of the Dance of Death, used such recognitions to turn the heart away from the world to allegiance to Christ.[22] One response to Hamlet's predicament would be to turn from the world to religious objects—the response that Eliot dramatized in *The Family Reunion*, or "Follow the Furies," as that play was first titled.

But Hamlet does not move from loss to the promise of resurrection in Christ, as the Burial of the Dead invites mourners to do. Part of the tremendous originality of *Hamlet* is to present what might have been a religious problem without a religious solution: in other words, a potentially revolutionary situation. For Hamlet, however, there is neither the hope of resolution of later centuries focused on revolutionary change, nor the traditional Christian hope of resolution through participation in Christ's sacrifice. Hamlet is a hero because he maintains the core of his commitment, even though he confronts the revolutionary potential of the Oedipal predicament without any way to know what it is, without benefit of clergy, so to speak. Instead, the Ghost provides a father in some ways godlike, in which the hero invests something like worship, while the hero, in going about his father's business, invites our participation in his involuntary and imperfect sacrifice.

Hamlet is not, I think, a fully achieved tragedy, but rather a heroic-prophetic play with a "tragical" ending—in its vastly more complex and meaningful way, a play like *Tamburlaine*. It differs from *Tamburlaine* in presenting, not heroic outrage by direct assault upon tradition, but a crisis in the transmission of heritage that leads to heroic outrage. In its concern with inheritance, and in its focus on desperation—on the need for revenge as the core of a need for expression and vindication, on passive vulnerability

22. Theodore Spencer explored Christian attitudes toward death in relation to the drama in *Death and Elizabethan Tragedy* (Cambridge: Harvard University Press, 1936).

struggling to become active, on language of magical expectation contorted into distraction, wit, or madness—*Hamlet* is remarkably like the one early play outside Marlowe's work that is both seminal and in its own right great, Kyd's *Spanish Tragedy*. Both plays call for an identification with the hero's alienation that excludes critical perspective. As with Hieronimo's dedication to avenging his son's death, Hamlet's tie to the Ghost of his father is so total, with no one there except him to evaluate it, that the play cannot dramatize an understanding of Hamlet's destructiveness from a tragic perspective larger than his own. My own feeling is that *Hamlet* is not fully under control, just because, as Eliot said, too much of the author is in the Prince—though its very open-endedness is what, *pace* Eliot, makes the play's distinctive greatness. But to bring under full artistic control what Shakespeare was dealing with, there was unfinished business, notably the business of seeing through the ideal father.

OTHELLO AS A DEVELOPMENT
FROM HAMLET

Iago is another figure who, like Hamlet, is endowed with his creator's special powers. Unlike Hamlet, Iago puts his theatrical intelligence and energy into a plan. As he monitors that plan's early progress, his language can call attention to a crucial difference between *Hamlet* and *Othello*: "The Moor already changes with my poison" (III.iii.325). The poison in *Hamlet* is actual: the Ghost tells us that Claudius poured it "in the porches of my ears," while the "whole ear of Denmark" is rankly abused by a forged tale of a serpent's sting (I.v.63, 36). The whole action hinges on this dreadful midnight revelation on the battlements. The poison Iago pours in Othello's ear is slanderous suggestion working in broad daylight:

> whiles this honest fool
> Plies Desdemona to repair his fortune,
> And she for him pleads strongly to the Moor,
> I'll pour this pestilence into his ear—
> That she repeals him for her body's lust.
> (II.iii.353–57)

In *Hamlet* Shakespeare uses all his own power as a dramatist to make the apparition objectively real, "something more than fantasy" (I.i.54). In *Othello*, Shakespeare invests Iago with astonishing dramatic powers to contrive situations and suggestions so that a "horrible conceit" (III.iii.115) shut up in his brain will come to seem real to Othello. Iago works "by wit, and not by witchcraft" (II.iii.372). In *Hamlet* we are astonished at the outset by the uncanny revelation of a dreadful reality. In *Othello* we watch in fascination and dismay as a "monstrous birth" is brought "to the world's light" (I.iii.404) and becomes a dreadful reality. The emphasis of the later play is all on the unreality of the fantasy: "Trifles light as air / Are to the jealous confirmations strong / As proofs of holy writ" (III.iii.322–24).

The disruptive motives and actions in the two plays are similar in many respects, despite the great surface differences between the plots. The difference in the way we encounter motives, the status they are given and the attitudes developed toward them, show us a development in Shakespeare's relationship to deep things working in him and in his art. In both plays a young man is out to destroy an older man, a figure of authority; in both, the young man is obsessed by the sexuality of the older man's wife. In *Hamlet* the young man is the hero, the older man the villain, though there are two father figures, the ideal, heroic figure of the Ghost, as well as Claudius. In *Othello* we have an older, large-gestured, martial hero, in many ways like King Hamlet, but alive; Iago sets out to destroy him by making him believe that the infidelity that happened to King Hamlet happened to him. So the later play says in effect that such infidelity may be merely an evil, destructive fantasy. Iago explicitly says that the fantasy amounts to poison:

> Dangerous conceits are in their natures poisons,
> Which at the first are scarce found to distaste,
> But with a little act upon the blood
> Burn like the mines of sulphur.
>
> (III.iii.326–29)

The possibility that the poison in *Hamlet* is something like a "dangerous conceit" is made explicit by Hamlet himself when he thinks the spirit he has seen "may be a dev'l," who "abuses me to damn me."

One way to see Hamlet's problem, which will connect with *Othello*, is to consider how the initial situation amounts to a "dangerous conceit," invested with reality by the dramatist, with which the Prince has to struggle. At first this situation "is scarce found to distaste"; it satisfies the son's great longing for atonement with his father. Yet it involves him in an overwhelming and isolating identification, a movement of self-surrender that no sooner reaches its climax in total commitment than the Prince turns to a complementary hatred, directed against the man who has taken sexual possession of his mother. This movement back and forth—"Look here upon this picture, and on this" (III.iv.53)—becomes a trap for Hamlet, as he himself becomes aware. While he remains in the trap the dangerous conceit will "burn like the mines of sulphur," obviating all expression of hostility toward his true father, and with it the full development of a self apart from his father. In Iago we come upon an appalling overt and intense hostility, directed this time against a good man, not an evil one, a man, as I have said, in many respects like Hamlet's father. Iago acknowledges that Othello "Is of a constant, loving, noble nature" (II.i.289). But among the declared reasons for his hatred is a sexual jealousy of the "lusty Moor," "the thought whereof / Doth (like a poisonous mineral) gnaw my inwards" (II.i.295–97). Along with Iago's hatred is his attachment to Othello, not expressed as such, but the condition of everything he does. He must live through Othello, become him by destroying him. It is as though he were a blasted, shrunken Hamlet, a Hamlet who has lost relation to the ideal father and is dedicated to demonstrating, by finding the fatal weakness of his commander, that such an ideal cannot exist. Iago is honest, beneath the outward pretense of openness and the wit that "speaks home" (II.i.165), in acknowledging a hatred normally suppressed. Shakespeare's extraordinary, new achievement is to express the complex of hostility and attachment together.

The fact that Othello is not Iago's father may be a reason why such frightful hostility can reach expression; similar total hatred directed at a father comes later, with Edmund, Iago's first cousin. The attachment has to be conveyed by indirection and implications, and by actions that contradict Iago's gospel of self-interest. Roderigo puts the question at the outset: "Thou toldst me thou didst hold him in thy hate." "Despise me if I do not" (I.i.7–8). Iago says he is not about to be overwhelmed by Othello (as Hamlet was by his father). He talks down "obsequious bondage"—"Whip me such honest knaves"—and talks of profit and self-respect: "Others there are, . . . when they have lin'd their coats, / Do themselves homage" (lines 46, 49, 53–54). In fact there will be no profit; fool Roderigo is his purse. His enterprise is spiritual: Auden got at its nature by likening him to the practical joker who has no meaning himself and so seeks meaning by tripping up someone who does.[23] "I follow

23. W. H. Auden, "The Joker in the Pack," in *The Dyer's Hand* (New York: Random House, 1962), pp. 246–72; see esp. pp. 256–57.

him to serve my turn upon him" (line 42). He does not say what the "turn" is except by implication: "Were I the Moor, I would not be Iago. / In following him I follow but myself" (lines 57–58). But he has no self: "I am not what I am" (line 65). What he seeks is to become the Moor by making the Moor enact his fantasies, fantasies that will destroy them both. When that is accomplished, he can stop: "Demand me nothing; what you know, you know: / From this time forth I never will speak word" (V.ii.303–4). At a deep level, beyond words, he has turned his equivalent of King Hamlet into his equivalent of Claudius and killed him. Strangely, and appropriately, his last words recall Hamlet's: "The rest is silence."

By comparison with the generosity of *Hamlet*, *Othello* is almost unbelievably tough. Consider the moment of atonement between Iago and Othello in comparison with Hamlet's atonement with his father on the battlements:

> IAGO: Patience, I say; your mind perhaps may change.
> OTHELLO: Never, Iago. Like to the Pontic Sea, . . .
> . . . my bloody thoughts, with violent pace,
> Shall nev'r look back, nev'r ebb to humble love,
> Till that a capable and wide revenge
> Swallow them up. [*He kneels*] Now by yon marble heaven,
> In the due reverence of a sacred vow
> I here engage my words.
> IAGO: Do not rise yet.   [*Iago kneels*]
> Witness, you ever-burning lights above,
> You elements that clip us round about,
> Witness that here Iago doth give up
> The execution of his wit, hands, heart,
> To wrong'd Othello's service! Let him command,
> And to obey shall be in me remorse,
> What bloody business ever.   [*They rise*]
> OTHELLO: I greet thy love.
>   (III.iii.452–53, 457–69)

It may seem farfetched to compare this dreadful business to the high-minded moment in *Hamlet*. But there are remarkable similarities. At one level Iago's gesture is pretense, but he is indeed surrendering himself to the older man, as Hamlet did to his father. This identification is the first stage of Iago's fulfillment. To be sure, the vengeance is directed not against a Claudius but against Othello's wife—whereas the Ghost warns Hamlet not to seek vengeance on Gertrude. But in fact Hamlet will degrade and indirectly destroy both Gertrude and Ophelia; he will be tormented in doing so, but he will do it. Again, though Othello is not overtly being marked for destruction, we and Iago are well aware that Othello must be destroyed by this pact with Desdemona's rival. Iago's diabolical line, which closes the scene, seals Othello's doom: "I am your own for ever."

Iago is playing the part of the devil whom Hamlet feared; that he is not a supernatural devil makes him all the more appalling for a modern sensibility. That an actual man can do the business of a devil is part of the play's revelation that nothing outside humanity is needed for spiritual horror. When Iago is brought on at the end, Othello confronts this modern situation, looking for a cloven hoof and not finding it: "I look down towards his feet; but that's a fable. / If that thou be'st a devil, I cannot kill thee" (V.ii.286–87). And he wounds Iago, trying to prove that he is not. Yet Iago has power over the soul: "Will you, I pray, demand that demi-devil / Why he has thus ensnar'd my soul and body?" (lines 301–2).

Othello releases violent tensions deeply rooted in historically shaped structures of relationship between men and women. Several recent commentaries have perceptively explored the religious, social, and philosophical contexts that inform the play's tragic development.[24] I shall consider here only those aspects of Othello's tragedy and Desdemona's—a complex, independent creation in its

---

24. Stephen Greenblatt sees in *Othello* the explosive confluence of a new historical situation and an old bias: individual identity liberated for "self-fashioning" by the Renaissance experience is made to serve an extreme form of traditional Christian distrust of the body's passions (*Renaissance Self-Fashioning* [Chicago: University of Chicago Press, 1980], pp. 222–54). Arthur Kirsch places the play in relation to the Pauline ideal of marriage as it is warped by Othello's failure to integrate "primitive" erotic energies into the spiritual fulfillment he seeks in his bond to Desdemona (*Shakespeare and the Experience of Love* [Cambridge: Cambridge University Press, 1981], pp. 10–39). Carol Thomas Neely and Edward A. Snow explore the insistent presence in *Othello* of an inflexible, repressive patriarchal order that seeks to defend itself against masculine fears of female sexuality (Neely, "Women and Men in *Othello*: 'What should such a fool / Do with so good a woman?'" in *The Woman's Part: Feminist Criticism of Shakespeare*, ed. Carolyn Ruth Swift Lenz, Gayle Greene, and Carol Thomas Neely [Urbana: University of Illinois Press, 1980], pp. 211–39; Snow, "Sexual Anxiety and the Male Order of Things in *Othello*," *English Literary Renaissance*, 10 [1980]: 384–412). Stanley Cavell, in the extraordinary meditation that closes *The Claim of Reason: Wittgenstein, Scepticism, Morality, and Tragedy* (Oxford: Clarendon Press, 1980), pp. 481–96, sees the protagonist's perverse conviction of Desdemona's faithlessness as an alternative more tolerable for Othello than the intolerable knowledge of himself forced upon him by Desdemona's otherness—dramatized for him in her sexual response to him. For Cavell the play reflects the philosophical problem of skepticism as it is shaped by the loss of the capacity for self-knowledge anchored in the certainty of God's existence: hence the worshipful strain in Othello's love, which swerves around Desdemona's humanness to his anguished perception of her as demonic.

own right—in which one can see the relationships of their roles to the structure of roles in *Hamlet*. Here we need to consider the glimpses we get in the earlier play of what King Hamlet was before his death—what the living people, especially his son, suggest about his life. For we are led to hope from the Moor for the same kind of heroic, integrating center which retrospects suggest King Hamlet provided when he overcame Fortinbras or "smote the sledded Polacks on the ice" (I.i.63), while maintaining a sacred marriage with his wife, "so loving . . . / That he might not beteem the winds of heaven / Visit her face too roughly" (I.ii.140–42).

Cassio's generous nature anticipates this while everyone on Cyprus waits anxiously for the general's ship:

> Great Jove, Othello guard,
> And swell his sail with thine own pow'rful breath,
> That he may bless this bay with his tall ship,
> Make love's quick pants in Desdemona's arms,
> Give renew'd fire to our extincted spirits,
> And bring all Cyprus comfort!
>
> (II.i.77–82)

The heroic expectation envisages the public, social world fulfilling the private, the private fulfilling the public: as Othello's tall ship will bless the bay that gives it haven, the heroic, virile husband, secure in his bride's arms, will bring comfort and renewed vitality to her, to himself, and to "all Cyprus."

But Othello loves Desdemona in an idealizing way, which we can also connect with the elder Hamlet, both through the son's memory and through the Ghost's account of his betrayal. With this idealizing tendency there is the same assumption in both plays that a woman's physical sexuality will express itself in infidelity. In the Moor this assumption agrees with some deep inability to cope with sexuality, implicit in his allowing the consummation of his marriage to be delayed and in his joining in the gross fantasies Iago offers. Horrified, jealous imaginations become a vicarious way of possessing Desdemona sexually through participation in the imagined virility of Cassio. Hamlet, in Gertrude's bedchamber, is similarly obsessed with thoughts of his mother's sensuality with Claudius; he cannot leave it alone even after his father's ghost interrupts him and after his mother, on her side, is contrite. "What shall I do?" she asks, and he goes ruthlessly on:

> Not this, by no means, that I bid you do:
> Let the bloat king tempt you again to bed,

Pinch wanton on your cheek, call you his mouse,
And let him, for a pair of reechy kisses . . .
                        (III.iv.180–84)

Hamlet's earlier degradation of Ophelia, after the disruption of his idealizing love, exhibits the same disassociation of tenderness from sensuality.

Desdemona is an Ophelia newly married, the same ingrained, gentle chastity embodying the intact heritage. Unlike Ophelia, she has the adventurous strength to go against her father, so that her destruction is not only pathetic but tragic. Othello's degraded view of her is not triggered, as Hamlet's is, by disillusionment with a mother. But Othello's tie to his mother is present in the play through the handkerchief. As he says in strange, highly charged lines, his gift of the handkerchief to Desdemona symbolizes his identification of her with his mother: "She, dying, gave it me, / And bid me, when my fate would have me wiv'd, / To give it her" (III.iv.63–65). The logic of the handkerchief, the "magic in the web of it" (line 69) which so completely escaped Rymer, is that a wife not identified with the mother must be a whore. The other side of this logic is that a wife identified with the mother cannot be physically sexual. No wonder the handkerchief was "dy'd in mummy which the skillful / Conserv'd of maidens' hearts" (lines 74–75). And no wonder Desdemona's healthy response is "Then would to God that I had never seen't" (line 77). Shakespeare is exploring relationships cognate to those in *Hamlet* without recourse to the drastic external events that precipitate Prince Hamlet's response. The fetishism of the handkerchief is consistent with the idealizing tendency of Othello's love, and with its vulnerability. His dependence on a binding magic suggests that he cannot trust a descent into the body. Yet this tie to the mother is also ground for the tender, spiritual and domestic quality of his devotion: "But yet the pity of it, Iago! O Iago, the pity of it, Iago!" (IV.i.195–96).

The play makes us confront a central, continuing dilemma of our culture: that such devotion, which we cannot but value, may not be capable of consummation and so is vulnerable to the degrading fantasies of jealousy and still more dreadful transformations into violence. It is this vulnerability which Iago sees in the moving moment when Othello greets Desdemona after he has landed:

If it were now to die,
'Twere now to be most happy; for I fear
My soul hath her content so absolute

That not another comfort like to this
Succeeds in unknown fate.
(II.i.189–93)

Iago has no need of a ghost come from the dead to help him with his business—this so absolute content bodes some strange eruption in the general:

[*Aside.*] O, you are well tun'd now!
But I'll set down the pegs that make this music,
As honest as I am.
(lines 199–201)

The transformation of love into violence is the last and most dreadful development of a potentiality in *Hamlet*. Iago accomplishes through Othello what Hamlet might have done in Gertrude's bedchamber. Gertrude thinks for a moment that her son is about to kill her. Hamlet guards himself against the possibility ahead of time:

O heart, lose not thy nature! let not ever
The soul of Nero enter this firm bosom,
Let me be cruel, not unnatural;
I will speak daggers to her, but use none.
(III.ii.393–96)

Iago specifically wants the thing to happen in the bed: "Do it not with poison; strangle her in her bed, even the bed she hath contaminated." "Good, good; the justice of it pleases; very good" (IV.i.207–10). That Othello actually does the deed accords with the fact that there is no father presence—as there is for Hamlet, initially warning against it and appearing a second time as things get out of hand in the Queen's chamber. And Desdemona is a wife, less taboo than a mother, though Othello has looked to her for the basic trust that a mother provides:

there, where I have garner'd up my heart,
Where either I must live or bear no life;
The fountain from the which my current runs
Or else dries up: to be discarded thence!
Or keep it as a cistern for foul toads
To knot and gender in!
(IV.ii.57–62)

Lonely Othello has put his whole identity into her keeping.

In the almost unbearable scene where the thing happens, Othello's self-righteousness in the bedchamber recalls Hamlet's. But the sexual imagery that precedes the violent consummation is utterly different from Hamlet's gross imaginations. It is a delicate, chaste imagery like that in which we might envisage or contemplate a bride before she is possessed: "that whiter skin of hers than snow, / And smooth as monumental alabaster" (V.ii.4–5). He approaches the rose diffidently—"O balmy breath" (line 16)—delicately kissing her that she may not wake. Then comes the irresistible flow of indignation, freeing swift action, by the powerful hands only, until the consummation: "Hah, no more moving?" (line 93). The inhibition about physical intimacy, Othello's isolation inside his majestic body, is manifest in the reverent emotional distance he struggles to keep even as he kills his wife.

Shakespeare the dramatist, conducting the play *Hamlet* and inviting identification with a hero who is an amateur of the drama struggling to use its resources to make what is hidden manifest, can be related to Iago as a dramatist conducting the action of *Othello*. Iago is an "amateur of tragedy in real life . . . getting up his plot among his nearest friends and connections," as Hazlitt observed.[25] Stanley Edgar Hyman explored this aspect of the figure, as well as Iago as Stage Villain, as Satan, as Latent Homosexual, and as Machiavel.[26] By looking at *Othello* in relationship to *Hamlet*, and at both in relationship to Shakespeare, I think we can see motivation in Iago which is not an "illusion," a variation of the Oedipal pattern manifest in the earlier play. And we can see, I believe, a motive *for* Iago. To create him was a way to objectify and master what in *Hamlet* is not fully recognized or under control—Shakespeare's use of his art for theatrical aggression, not just the aggressive use of the theatrical within the play (most obviously in the play-within-the-play), but aggression through the act of creating the fable of an ideal father betrayed by his wife and murdered by a gross father whose destruction the ideal father sanctions. In the whole journey of Shakespeare's development, we can see *Hamlet* as the expression of a crisis when the need for relationship to a strong father and his heritage takes theatrical illusion into its service.

Kenneth Burke, in an essay exploring the nature of symbolic action, saw *Othello* as a riddance ritual by which Shakespeare dealt with destructive potentialities in himself and his art.[27] His analysis

25. Hazlitt, *Characters of Shakespear's Plays*, p. 42.

26. Stanley Edgar Hyman, *Iago: Some Approaches to the Illusion of His Motivation* (New York: Atheneum, 1970).

27. Kenneth Burke, "*Othello*: An Essay to Illustrate a Method," *Hudson Review* 4 (Summer 1951): 165–203.

gets at the function I have been exploring in relation to the earlier play. But it also highlights a limitation of *Othello* which, again, has a similarity, across difference, with the earlier play. The ending of *Othello*, with its tendency to exonerate the protagonist at the expense of the antagonist, fails to achieve full artistic control precisely because it fits Burke's description, falling into ritual simplification in the scapegoating of Iago by the honest Venetians: [28]

> O Spartan dog,
> More fell than anguish, hunger, or the sea!
> Look on the tragic loading of this bed;
> This is thy work. The object poisons sight;
> Let it be hid. . . .
> . . . To you, Lord Governor,
> Remains the censure of this hellish villain,
> The time, the place, the torture, O, enforce it!
>   (V.ii.361–65, 367–69)

To hide what is on the bed and center only on the evil of Iago is to turn away from the full horror. The relation to *Hamlet* goes by contraries. The Prince is freed of all guilt at the end; at the end, all guilt is transferred to Iago. In neither play has Shakespeare yet achieved the complex balance that is to come in *Lear* and *Macbeth*, where sympathy is always present yet never distorts judgment, where the ruth and ruthlessness of tragedy are inextricable.

28. A. P. Rossiter attributes the tendency to "project on to Iago" the evil of the play to the psychological "make-up" of certain critics in need of a scapegoat (Coleridge and Bradley are his chief instances): they make Iago "the incarnation of their own unconscious *guilt*. Their guilt is his evil; and thus Othello and his jealousy are vindicated." But having deflated the ideal of a magnanimous Othello maliciously overthrown that Coleridge and Bradley struggle to affirm, Rossiter, though he admires the play's "artistic contrivance," is left only with "the peculiarly distressing effect of *Othello*," which "turns on this feeling of a hollowness at the centre, by the time the end is reached" (*Angel with Horns*, ed. Graham Storey [New York: Theatre Arts Books, 1961], pp. 200, 206).

9

Inextricable Ruthlessness and Ruth:
King Lear

"THE HOLY CORDS . . . TOO INTRINSE
T' UNLOOSE"

Although the Elizabethan Church set itself against vicarious participation in the Holy Family, as this had centered around the figure of
the Virgin Holy Mother in Catholic worship, it kept, of course, the
great Christian rites of passage: Baptism, Confirmation, Marriage,
and the Burial of the Dead. Each of these ceremonies is directed
toward freeing the individual from exclusive ties to family by putting him or her into relationship with God and the communion of
the church. Shakespeare's mature plays show people in passage
from one stage of life to another, succeeding in comedies, failing in
tragedies. Some tragedies start with the failure of ritual. In *Hamlet*,
as we have seen, it is burial as a rite of passage for those who survive the dead. Hamlet looks for the buried father in the dust; then
the father returns from death to ask for a total, uncritical commitment. As regularly happens in the tragedies, there is a swerve back
to the deepest family ties. And since on its positive side the tie to
his father is the core of his human and social values, Hamlet's Galilean turbulence is potentially creative as well as terribly destructive.

The rites of passage of the church are structured to take people
through threshold moments of losing or changing family bonds by
turning their need for total relationship to Christ and God; they
thus run counter to the isolating worship of family which takes over
in the tragedies with the break from the larger social investment of
self. The Prayer Book repeatedly insists that the achievement of a
Christian identity depends upon one's being reborn. The minister
in baptizing prays "that these infants may enjoy the everlasting
benediction of thy heavenly washing." "O merciful God, grant that
the old Adam in these children may be so buried, that the new man

may be raised up in them."[1] In Baptism the child is taken from the parents by godfathers and godmothers—in Elizabethan common parlance, gossips or "godsybs" of the parents, that is, fellow siblings as children of God. It is the minister, rather than the parents, who gives the child his name, after the name chosen by them is told to the sponsors: "[———]. I Baptize thee in the name of the Father, and of the Son, and of the Holy Ghost. Amen." The child's independent identity having been signified in this way, "*Then the Priest Shall make a cross upon the child's forehead, saying,* We receive this child into the congregation of Christ's flock; and do sign him with the sign of the cross" (p. 204). The godparents are to take care that in due time this child "be brought to the Bishop to be confirmed by him" (p. 205). Then he can take Communion as a godsyb of his parents, equally with them a child of God.

For an individual of intense religious vocation, total commitment to worship and the service of God would be a constant goal (and in some saintly persons an almost fully achieved transformation). But for the ordinary secular Christian, religious worship involves only a part of the whole self. Though the varieties of religious experience were in Shakespeare's age (as indeed in ours) enormously wide in range, one can venture the generalization that, for the secular Anglican, it was chiefly what we would now call the infantile roots of the self which would be invested in worship. In a relatively stable secular communicant of this kind, participation in the established religion would not be infantilizing, but on the contrary would serve to bind potentially disruptive infantile motives. For the successful communicant, eating and drinking the Lord's body and blood are actions symbolic of infantile dependence and of motives that are deeply disruptive when directed later at the human parents or parent substitutes; the ritual actions become a way of establishing relationship with society through communion with its ultimate source and sanction. Such communion also permits the child to see that his parents are not gods. The potential worship of them is directed away, by the sacred context, to its proper, transcendent object.

The "gossips' feast" that concludes *The Comedy of Errors*, with the Duke's validating participation in it, signifies the resolution of

1. *Liturgical Services of the Reign of Queen Elizabeth*, ed. William Keating Clay, Parker Society, no. 30 (Cambridge: Cambridge University Press, 1847), pp. 200, 203. All quotations from the 1559 Book of Common Prayer are from this edition.

the disruptive "errors" by the family's reunion and reconciliation with the society at large. But that is the conclusion of a comedy framed by a romance. *King Lear* begins with the failure of the passage that might be handled by the marriage service, as it is structured to persuade the father to give up the daughter. After the question "Who giveth this woman to be married unto this man?" the rubric in the Prayer Book spells out the hand gestures by which the groom "takes the plight" of the bride from her father or substituting friend: "And the minister receiving the woman at her father or friend's hands, shall cause the man to take the woman by the right hand, and so either to give their troth to other" (pp. 218–19). The ceremony of the father's giving away the daughter clearly serves to control, to mark an end of, his tendency to hold on to her. Put quite bluntly—but hardly more bluntly than Cordelia will put it— to have the father physically hand his daughter to the bridegroom is a defense against incest, which in *Lear* takes the form of the aged king's demand for his daughters' complete devotion and tenderness and his denial of their independent sexuality. The gesture in the marriage service implies consent to her independent development.[2]

From a social vantage point, then, the daughter is freed from family ties for another kind of allegiance, a new object of love, apart from parents. In religious terms, the rite works to keep separate the divine from the human, to avoid misplaced worship. Looked at psychologically, the ritual works, when it works, to avoid fixation or regression—in *King Lear* the regression the Fool specifies when he speaks of Lear having made "thy daughters thy mothers"

2. See the prayer for fertility as provided in the Elizabethan service: "We beseech thee assist with thy blessing these two persons, that they may both be fruitful in procreation of children, also live together so long in godly love and honesty, that they may see their children's children, unto the third and fourth generation, unto thy praise and honour: through Jesus Christ our Lord" (ibid., p. 222). One can compare Lear's terrible curse on Goneril (I.iv.275–82), where the implicit denial of Cordelia's sexuality in the opening scene is made explicit:

Hear, Nature, hear, dear goddess, hear!
Suspend thy purposes, if thou didst intend
To make this creature fruitful.
Into her womb convey sterility,
Dry up in her the organs of increase,
And from her derogate body never spring
A babe to honor her! If she must teem,
Create her child of spleen.

(I.iv.173). These perspectives come together when we consider that the genesis of worship is in the family constellation, as are the prototypes for sexual love. Lear overrides the social, religious, and psychological dimensions of the marriage rite as the need for a maternal presence is shifted for the first time in Shakespeare's drama onto daughters.

The opening scene of *King Lear* compresses into a single action the characteristic tragic shift from the hero's investment in the state to his all-or-nothing investment in family ties. Lear comes on stage, surrounded by his court, enjoying the very authority he says he is about to give up. The scene in the presence chamber sets out as solemn business of state—"to publish / Our daughters' several dowers, that future strife / May be prevented now" (I.i.43–45). Shakespeare, in marvelously understanding the folk motif of the test of affections, makes it clear that the business of state is really Lear's way of using the public realm for the private end of commanding his daughters' total love. He asks for worship, and from Goneril and Regan he seems to get it, in virtually incestuous terms:

> I profess
> Myself an enemy to all other joys
> Which the most precious square of sense possesses,
> And find I am alone felicitate
> In your dear Highness' love.
>
> (lines 72–76)

The stately march of ceremonial language proceeds—"To thee and thine hereditary ever / Remain this ample third of our fair kingdom" (lines 79–80)—until it is suddenly stopped short by Cordelia:

LEAR: Now, our joy,
    Although our last and least, to whose young love
    The vines of France and milk of Burgundy
    Strive to be intress'd, what can you say to draw
    A third more opulent than your sisters? Speak.
CORDELIA: Nothing, my lord.
    LEAR: Nothing?
CORDELIA: Nothing.
    LEAR: Nothing will come of nothing, speak again.
                              (lines 82–90)

Cordelia's resistance is not merely to his demand for flattery but, as she makes clear, to his underlying demand for a continuation of the total relationship of child to parent:

> Good my lord,
> You have begot me, bred me, lov'd me: I
> Return those duties back as are right fit,
> Obey you, love you, and most honor you.
> Why have my sisters husbands, if they say
> They love you all?
>
> (lines 95–100)

Her defense makes explicit reference to the giving-away of the marriage service:

> Happily, when I shall wed,
> That lord whose hand must take my plight shall carry
> Half my love with him, half my care and duty.
> Sure I shall never marry like my sisters,
> To love my father all.
>
> (lines 100–104)

The extraordinary explosion that follows is sparked by Lear's explicitly denying Cordelia a dower, the economic concomitant of giving the daughter away in the marriage service. The settlement of a dower provided material support for the daughter's separate ongoing life and life-giving in her turn; it was an obligation universally recognized, and it often involved very real financial sacrifices, even for the high nobility.[3] Lear perverts this custom, by which one generation endows the independence of the next, with his project of dividing his kingdom proportionally as "nature doth with merit challenge" (line 53).

Cordelia, in spelling out ordinary custom, has exposed Lear's demand that he continue to be everything to his children, even in the act of giving himself away entirely.

> LEAR: But goes thy heart with this?
> CORDELIA: Ay, my good lord.
> LEAR: So young, and so untender?
> CORDELIA: So young, my lord, and true.
> LEAR: Let it be so: thy truth then be thy dow'r!
> For by the sacred radiance of the sun,
> The mysteries of Hecat and the night;
> By all the operation of the orbs,
> From whom we do exist and cease to be;
> Here I disclaim all my paternal care,

---

3. See Lawrence Stone, *The Crisis of the Aristocracy: 1558–1641* (Oxford: Clarendon Press, 1965), pp. 595–99, 637–49.

Propinquity and property of blood,
And as a stranger to my heart and me
Hold thee from this for ever.

(lines 105–16)

Unable to endure the established process for the transmission of heritage, to maintain his own integrity while providing for the independent integrity of his daughter, Lear simultaneously invokes the mysterious generative powers that provide for new generations as he disowns the paternal relationship.

The next lines, in their strange reference to the most barbarous possible expression of greed in one generation's destroying the next by the devouring of their children, are a foretaste of the regression to infantile ways of relating that the action is to release:

The barbarous Scythian,
Or he that makes his generation messes
To gorge his appetite, shall to my bosom
Be as well neighbor'd, pitied, and reliev'd,
As thou my sometime daughter.

(lines 116–20)

Lear's language here—and from this point right on through his night of agony—desperately seeks to bind or alter or control reality in the moods of command, prayer, curse, commination. He covers his inability to give Cordelia away by throwing her away: "be gone / Without our grace, our love, our benison" (lines 264–65). But how little success the gesture or the words can have is clear from his own anguished admission even as he tries to make the separation final:

Peace, Kent!
Come not between the dragon and his wrath;
I lov'd her most, and thought to set my rest
On her kind nursery. Hence, and avoid my sight!

(lines 121–24)

"Hence" suggests that Cordelia has approached with some movement responsive to Lear's tender confession. There follows one of those sweeping statements, made early in the tragedies, where what is impulsively called for points ironically toward the play's final outcome:

So be my grave my peace, as here I give
Her father's heart from her.

(lines 125–26)

"UPON SUCH SACRIFICES"

Shakespeare presents social arrangements in the Christian terms of his society, and with a critical perspective that implies *part* of the Christian norm—but only part. The full Christian norm would deal with the need for a complete union in love—the need Lear looks for from Cordelia in his hope "to set my rest / On her kind nursery"—by redirecting it to divine objects, with the discipline of humility before God as the condition of being "one with Christ and Christ with us." What a father would give up in the marriage service would ideally be given compensation in the communion service that immediately followed. In Catholic worship, there would have been compensation also for him by relationship with the Blessed Virgin. The relationships toward which the incestuous love tends, to make the daughter a mother, whether by impregnating her or depending totally on her, are shown fulfilled in the traditional Christian scenes of the Annunciation and the Madonna and Child—fulfilled in a sacred way that expresses the latent wishes and protects against acting them out, against pursuing in human objects the total fulfillment reserved for divine persons. So a Christian Lear might be provided with the Presence whose lack drives him to madness; his daughters might be spared the demand that they be that presence, that all their tenderness be arrogated to a father who asks them to make him, in effect, their god.

Obviously Lear's world is not Christian in this full sense. On the contrary, in the opening acts Shakespeare emphasizes pagan, pre-Christian references: "by the sacred radiance of the sun, / The mysteries of Hecat"; "Hear, Nature, hear, dear goddess, hear!" But as we go through Lear's suffering with him, and the sufferings of Gloucester and Edgar, Christian *expectations* come increasingly into play.

> This shows you are above,
> You justicers, that these our nether crimes
> So speedily can venge!
> (IV.ii.78–80)

> Thou hast one daughter
> Who redeems nature from the general curse
> Which twain have brought her to.
> (IV.vi.205–7)

At the diabolical pole, we can recall Albany to Goneril when the scales have dropped from his eyes:

> See thyself, devil!
> Proper deformity shows not in the fiend
> So horrid as in woman.
> (IV.ii.59–61)

Albany's recognition of his wife in these terms locates Goneril within a frame of experience defined by Christian conceptions; it gives him, and us with him, a new kind of control, a way of placing the evil. We thrill with Albany's new determination: "Gloucester, I live / To thank thee for the love thou show'dst the King" (IV.ii.94–95).

And then the tenderness we have been feeling, generated from the night's horrors, has come back in the person of Cordelia. By the time she returns, significantly without her husband, we share with at least part of our sensibility the need in her father she comes to meet. There is a new kind of gentle, clear music in the verse as the gentleman tells about her, and benign light and soothing moisture: "You have seen / Sunshine and rain at once; her smiles and tears / Were like a better way" (IV.iii.17–19). Where during the night we were on an empty heath, Cordelia describes a world of natural growth: the idle weeds that deck Lear's madness grow "in our sustaining corn," and the soldiers are told to "search every acre in the high-grown field" (IV.iv.6–7). The whole effect is summarized when she says:

> All blest secrets,
> All you unpublish'd virtues of the earth,
> Spring with my tears; be aidant and remediate
> In this good man's distress!
> (IV.iv.15–18)

As regularly happens in Shakespeare's mature work, religious language comes into play to express the investment in the family bond:

> There she shook
> The holy water from her heavenly eyes,
> And clamor moistened.
> (IV.iii.29–31)

In Cordelia's "O dear father, / It is thy business that I go about" (IV.iv.23–24), there is a clear echo of Christ's words in Luke 2:49: "Wist ye not that I must be about my Father's business."[4]

---

4. I am focusing almost exclusively on the relationship of Lear to his daughters, particularly to Cordelia, because in the central part of the play the problematic relationship to the feminine, so important in the early work, is here given mature,

That Cordelia should echo Christ's words here is consistent with her practical purpose and with Shakespeare's control of the sympathies of his audience. She continues:

> Therefore great France
> My mourning and importun'd tears hath pitied.
> No blown ambition doth our arms incite,
> But love, dear love, and our ag'd father's right.
> Soon may I hear and see him!
>
> (IV.iv.25–29)

The whole speech is designed to legitimize her cause in English eyes by making clear that she does not serve an aggressive foreign purpose, but instead seeks to restore "our ag'd father's right." This passage has particularly appealed to those who want to give the play a Christian resolution. But the tragic irony of the situation is present for us here, as well as the sainted quality of the daughter's devotion. The play is a tragedy precisely because it is not God the Father whose business Cordelia goes about, but her finite father, Lear, who now compels by his helplessness what he has been unable to command from his daughter by his power.

By the same token, Goneril is not, finally, a devil, but the child of that same father. In her sexual jealousy over Edmund she will turn

---

understanding expression. But the complex interconnections among family bonds, religious feeling, and the constantly frustrated use of language (including, especially, religious language) to bind the terrible energies of life that move ruthlessly through one construction after another, are characteristic of the whole play. See Stanley Cavell's brilliant discussion ("The Avoidance of Love: A Reading of *King Lear*," in *Must We Mean What We Say?* [New York: Scribner's, 1969], pp. 267–353) of how the almost incessant efforts to postulate "kind gods," "the clearest gods," savage gods, and just gods, are attempts to turn away from recognition of the play's logic of human encounter. The helplessness to control life by language extends most notably to Gloucester and Edgar. Edgar as Poor Tom, with his lunatic bans, is often a parody of the effort to bind life with language. Janet Adelman argues persuasively that, in his own person, Edgar "constructs a world . . . populated only by general truths and abstractions" that serve to console him by rationalizing, distancing, and in effect denying the emotional suffering engendered by the play, including the suffering he undergoes as Poor Tom (Introduction to *Twentieth Century Interpretations of "King Lear,"* ed. Janet Adelman [Englewood Cliffs, N.J.: Prentice-Hall, 1978], p. 13).

Two exceptions or contrasts to the dreadful pressure of passion on language to accommodate what amounts to flight into incomplete, self-serving comprehension are revealing. The Fool's proverbial comments have a kind of detachment, based on folk wisdom or acceptance, in which language does not resist cruel realities but instead almost relishes them. And the villain Edmund puts no pressure of passion on language, because he is merely using it, working his schemes behind it, while even enjoying a comic zest as he manipulates.

as ruthlessly on Regan as the two of them have together turned on Lear: "I had rather lose the battle than that sister / Should loosen him and me" (V.i.18–19). The play does not move toward a Christian resolution, but unfolds the tragic consequences of Lear's investment in his youngest daughter and the investment in him that he has demanded of all his daughters. After initially domineering over them with tenderness and demands for tenderness, he has offered them the temptation of making himself helpless—like a baby: "Old fools are babes again" (I.iii.19). In the two older daughters, resistance to Lear's demand for their total love, in the situation of sibling rivalry—"He always lov'd our sister most" (I.i.290)—has atrophied their tenderness; they have become sexually avid and demonically vengeful, eager to destroy the impossible old man who has destroyed their full humanity. The psychiatrist Harold Searles has pointed out that people are often driven crazy by other members of the family through a process that amounts to seeking to get rid of them, to murder.[5] Lear's elder daughters drive him mad by depriving him of the sense of himself without which he cannot function: " 'Tis worse than murther / To do upon respect such violent outrage" (II.iv.23–24).

The play, in taking Lear into madness, takes him back to the source of the self in earliest infancy, to a deeper, more archaic level of being where self and world, child and parent, interpenetrate. With developments that accompany Lear's lapse into the madness he fears—"I prithee, daughter, do not make me mad" (II.iv.218)—the more general movement of the play unfolds as an experience of something like a world going mad. This is also the level of experience in which the need for the maternal, for the heritage of "basic trust" grounded in the earliest, cherishing bond to the mother, is substantive.[6] Lear's need for it is expressed not only in his demand on his daughters, but also in his effort to be or become the cherishing force he needs: by giving away the original inheritance (compare *Timon of Athens*), which makes him into a "sheal'd peascod"; by his solicitous regard for "my boy," his Fool; by the generous wave of feeling he finds in himself in thinking about the "poor

5. Harold Searles, "The Effort to Drive the Other Person Crazy," in *Collected Papers on Schizophrenia and Related Subjects* (London: Hogarth Press, 1965), pp. 254–83.

6. See Erik H. Erikson's discussions of "basic trust," the "cornerstone of a vital personality" formed in the early encounters of infant with maternal care and nurture, in *Childhood and Society*, 2nd ed. rev. (New York: Norton, 1963), pp. 77–80, 247–51, and *Identity: Youth and Crisis* (New York: Norton, 1968), pp. 96–107.

naked wretches" and Poor Tom; and finally by his eagerness, at the end, to give himself entirely to Cordelia, though he cannot see the destructive taking that is inseparable from this giving.

In his recognition of "unaccommodated man" in the guise of Poor Tom, in his savage railing at Dover—against "the sulphurous pit" of female sexuality, or against the "great image of authority: a dog's obey'd in office"—Lear envisages a universe stripped entirely of the kind of cherishing love that has its roots in the nurturant and nurturing experience shared by child and parent. But throughout his agonized repudiation of a world of savagery and corruption he remains the object of sympathetic, cherishing loyalty expressed by the Fool, Kent, Gloucester, Edgar, Albany, and others. Lear can hold the affection of so many characters, and of his audience, because he is so parental as well as childlike, embodying the impossible but loving parent who is forgiven and affiliated to—as Kent affiliates, after saying that he can get along without Lear, just as Lear has said that he can get along without Cordelia. It is because he has so much sense of self (however shattered by developments that he puts into motion), and with it so much self to give, for others who have anchored their own identities in his royal presence, that he can command the reverential compassion of those for whom his madness is "a sight most pitiful in the meanest wretch, / Past speaking of in a king" (IV.vi.204–5). There is a fuller love expressed *for* Lear than for any other Shakespearean character.

The most complete expression of that love, of course, is Cordelia. In the scene of Lear's reunion with her—for me as for many the most moving moment in Shakespeare—Lear's summary image on coming back into sanity is shaped by Christian conceptions: "Thou art a soul in bliss, but I am bound / Upon a wheel of fire" (IV.vii.45–46). He comes to himself after having gone through something like the letting go of life in Gloucester's imaginary fall, arranged by Edgar to prevent his own father's suicide:

> Pray do not mock me.
> I am a very foolish fond old man,
> Fourscore and upward, not an hour more nor less.
> (IV.vii.58–60)

For Lear, by contrast with Gloucester, the change leads not merely to acceptance of "affliction" but to the grace of Cordelia's love, a love beyond justice or deserts:

LEAR: Do not laugh at me,
For (as I am a man) I think this lady
To be my child Cordelia.
CORDELIA: And so I am; I am.
LEAR: Be your tears wet? Yes, faith. I pray weep not.
If you have poison for me, I will drink it.
I know you do not love me, for your sisters
Have (as I do remember) done me wrong:
You have some cause, they have not.
CORDELIA: No cause, no cause.
                                    (IV.vii.67–74)

The sort of love Cordelia expresses is the very ground from which love of God, transcending or fulfilling the love of parents, would develop in a fully Christian situation. Without the Christian development of the idea of radical love, beyond return, beyond law, I think that what we have here could not have found its way to expression, could not have been invented. In Cordelia's "No cause, no cause," we get a full expression of Christian love without the Christian supernatural.

How fully Shakespeare understood the destructive side of human bonds, the value of which he so movingly expresses, is manifest in his having changed the happy ending of all his sources. The English win, and among the English, Edmund. Lear's great speech in response to that situation is often quoted by those who, caught up in the Christian feeling, want to see the play's ending as wholly redemptive, with intimations of a reunion of father and daughter in a hereafter:

                   Come, let's away to prison: . . .
When thou dost ask me blessing, I'll kneel down
And ask of thee forgiveness. So we'll live,
And pray, and sing, and tell old tales, . . .
And take upon 's the mystery of things
As if we were God's spies.
                              (V.iii.8, 10–12, 16–17)

Lear has undergone a discipline of humility and achieved something like Christian disillusion with worldly things, together with a sense of the wrong he did Cordelia. He has seen through royal vanity. But he still wants his daughter "to love [her] father all." His vision of prison amounts, almost literally, to a conception of heaven on earth—*his* heaven, the "kind nursery" after all. A chasm of irony opens as we realize that he is leading her off to death. "Upon such sacrifices, my Cordelia, / The gods themselves throw incense" (V.iii.20–21). It is *her* sacrifice that the generous-hearted, loving old father is praising—the sacrifice she is to make, voluntarily, led on by love, but a sacrifice, finally, to his need for her. It is *her* sacrifice, made instead of the sacrifice that he in the first place refused, in refusing her dower, in refusing to give her away, in the deep sense outwardly symbolized by the marriage service.

To talk about what Shakespeare is appealing to (and controlling) in such a moment, one needs to understand the religious traditions or situation he is drawing on, and also the roots of potential religious feeling in the family. For the whole action of the play renews the springs of religious feeling, but without supernatural objects. He is presenting the modern situation where religious need, or need cognate to what has been dealt with by worship of the Holy Family, has no resource except the human family and its extensions in society, including the problematic ideal of kingship. William Elton's *King Lear and the Gods* shows how highly relevant the religious thought of the period is to the play—notably the idea of a *deus absconditus*.[7] The play's adumbration of religious ritual is exhibited in Herbert Coursen's fine study entitled *Christian Ritual and the World of Shakespeare's Tragedies*.[8] For my purposes, psychoanalysis is a useful supplement because it amounts, in some aspects, to a sociology of love and worship within the family, or derived from the family, especially as experienced in infancy.

The experiences of infancy were not, as such, a focus of much analytical attention in Shakespeare's period; our acute consciousness of them goes back to romanticism and develops along with the decreasing hold of religion. Infantile experience as such is also not a major concern of Shakespeare's art, since his culture little regarded it, except in displaced forms. Yet his plays find equivalents and shape action in ways that, with their central familial preoccupations, can be understood by reference to infantile residues. Thus it is useful, I think, to understand Lear's vision of prison as a regressive wish demanding that Cordelia join in it. In the large design of the play, this tendency connects with the childishness and

7. William Elton, *King Lear and the Gods* (San Marino, California: Huntington Library, 1966); see esp. pp. 171–263.

8. Herbert Coursen, *Christian Ritual and the World of Shakespeare's Tragedies* (Lewisburg, Pa.: Bucknell University Press, 1976), pp. 237–313.

playfulness, often charming and liberating in the midst of anguish, that floods through the Fool's part and flashes in moments in Edgar's impersonation of Mad Tom, as in Lear's own sprightliness in madness. The tendency also relates to Lear's confident assumption at the outset of relationship to a benign Nature, even as he asks the "dear goddess" to convey sterility into the womb of Goneril—with all the developing ambiguities: Edmund's "lusty stealth of nature" (I.ii.11), Lear's incredulous "Is there any cause in nature that make these hard hearts?" (III.vi.77–78).

It is surely because the plays are centered so much in family bonds that they can make comprehensible to the widest variety of auditors their enormous range of thought, lore, myth, and literary commonplace (as well as uncommon place). Such matters as the ambiguous status of Nature in the thought of the period, or again the fear that God has withdrawn from the world, need not be understood in systematic terms as we watch the play, fruitful as such understanding is in extending its significance. We understand distinctions that are potentially systematic by reference to the concrete social world and the family center of it: "Why brand they us / With base? With baseness? bastardy? base, base? / Who in the lusty stealth of nature . . . " (I.ii.9–11). So too with *deus absconditus*. The theological anxiety is brought home when God's representative on earth, the king, begins the play by in effect absconding. And he is first and foremost a father. The first, most important order of understanding is "close to home."

Lear looks to Cordelia for the fulfillment of needs that a child would find answered in a mother, or that a worshiper in the Old Religion could bring into compensatory relationship with the Blessed Virgin, Holy Mother. Shakespeare dramatizes the implications of Lear's need and the demand that issues from it as Cordelia's death—also the result, of course, of a whole complex social process that has been set in motion by Lear's abdicating and dividing authority, by Gloucester's sensuality and credulity, by the brute fact of chance in war. Those who insist on seeing the play as Christian rather than post-Christian have to ignore or "transcend" the fact that the heavens do not respond to the repeated appeals made to them, as by Albany:

> If that the heavens do not their visible spirits
> Send quickly down to tame these vild offenses,
> It will come,

Humanity must perforce prey on itself,
Like monsters of the deep.

(IV.ii.46–50)

Heaven's vault merely reverberates Lear's "Howl, howl, howl, howl!" as he enters with the dead Cordelia in his arms. And yet humanity does not simply prey on itself like monsters. We will not attempt here to describe the play's extraordinary final effect of affirmation along with tragic loss. But the argument needs to be completed by noting that Lear and Cordelia, while they are represented with marvelous understanding as human individuals, also become in effect icons. Lear with Cordelia in his arms is a Pietà with the roles reversed, not Holy Mother with her dead Son, but father with his dead daughter, whom he looked to for the divine in the human. In their dramatized lives, they are in time and in the human condition where Lear's demand and Cordelia's sacrifice to it lead to total, tragic loss: "She's gone for ever! / I know when one is dead, and when one lives; / She's dead as earth" (V.iii.260–62). But the realization of them in the theater takes them out of time, so that there is a kind of epiphany as we finally see them, a showing forth not of the divine but of the human, sublime and terrible as it reaches toward the divine and toward destruction.

Cordelia's love for Lear and Lear's for her are the most precious realities to which the whole anguished natural world of the play gives birth. In the new situation, where it was necessary to do without the supernatural figures and refind them in secular manifestations, Shakespeare's art finds new intensity of grace possible in human life, and new intensity of tragic loss; he makes us feel that human life is supremely valuable as well as terrible. The fact that Shakespeare could do this must be one main reason for the rise of bardolatry since the mid-eighteenth century. As the plays become part of the ongoing culture, particular figures within particular family constellations become themselves icons important for us, "Presences / That passion, piety or affection knows," as Yeats has it:

All perform their tragic play,
There struts Hamlet, there is Lear,
That's Ophelia, that Cordelia.

Or, as Lear himself has it, in dying words that express his final, complete absorption, beyond self, in Cordelia: "Look on her! Look her lips, / Look there, look there!" (V.iii.311–12).

In using the term "icon" about Lear and Cordelia, there is the difficulty that the Christian associations imply an image that stands for something holy which it only represents—for something beyond, transcendent. True, in a holy place an icon can come to be itself holy, something set apart—as with saints' relics, or the icons of the Eastern Orthodox tradition. But it does so in a context of worship and belief. In talking or writing about Shakespeare's use or adumbration of religious language and action, it is easy to slip into implying such a context. And so it is crucial to check the powerful tendency of the Christian vocabulary to imply the whole Christian situation—crucial because his tragic art does so.

Lear and Cordelia do not stand for transcendent persons beyond them—for God and the Virgin. They are themselves finite persons in a finite world. The play generates sacredness about them by the same development that makes their tragic destiny. The sacredness in Shakespeare's tragedy accords with recognition of the human impossibility of being divine, realized by the dread attempt, which brings destruction. The attempt is to have a total relationship, satisfying the assumption of omnipotence of mind—or better, in Lear's case, omnipotence of heart. What is lost is the sacred-in-the-human as humanity creates and destroys it.

10

"The masked Neptune and / The gentlest winds of heaven": *Pericles* and the Transition from Tragedy to Romance

In all of Shakespeare's development there is no change in dramatic style so striking as that between the final tragedies and the late romances. It is at first astonishing that Shakespeare, at the height of his power to explore the tight logic of character and circumstance, should have taken on, in *Pericles*, the writing or rewriting of a play based on Gower's wildly improbable romance about Apollonius of Tyre. In the late tragedies, particularly *Coriolanus* and *Timon of Athens*, Shakespeare works out a constricted, Hobbesian logic of political and social relationships. When he turns to *Pericles* he had possibly just written *Coriolanus*, in which political and psychological events are presented with an almost clinical rigor. Indeed, he may not have finished with that kind of play, and *Coriolanus* may have been yet to be written. But the romances are developed to express a very different kind of action in which the interplay of character and circumstance is much less important than in the tragedies.

As always in Shakespeare, a development of style has a profound inner logic. His unparalleled power of development obviously depends on his properly artistic ability to adapt and innovate dramatic and poetic form. But his shaping spirit of imagination creates new forms in the service of human needs. The shift from tragedy to romance comes to restore a sense of the magical and sacred in human experience. The late romances meet a need in Shakespeare for recovering benign relationship to feminine presences, accomplished by going through an experience of separation and loss that culminates in reunion—an experience which, in *Pericles* and *The Winter's Tale*, must have a visionary status. In both of these plays reunions first with the lost daughter and then with the lost wife involve an enhancement of the women's meaning beyond the merely human. One might call it religious, though the women are flesh and blood and the whole thing is art, as we are made emphatically aware. What is recovered is a sacredness that is grounded ultimately in charged memories within the bereft men—and in us, who as audience have shared in their loss and their longing and so are gathered up into the final raptures of reunion.

The final recognition scenes of these plays are arrived at by a dramatic movement, which I want to contrast, first with the movement characteristic of the earlier, festive comedies and then with developments in Shakespeare's use of tragedy. To consider what happens to deep family ties in the three kinds of plays can be useful for our understanding of the differences in form among them. It can also enable us to see changes in dominant attitudes and problems about similar family constellations in the whole journey of Shakespeare's development.

ROMANCE AND TRANSFORMATION

One can make the contrast with earlier comedy by referring to the sheep-shearing feast in *The Winter's Tale,* where the holiday moment renews our sense of the benign power of great creating Nature. Florizel, in a characteristic opening tableau, describes Perdita's transformation as queen of the feast:

> These your unusual weeds to each part of you
> Does give a life; no shepherdess, but Flora
> Peering in April's front.
> (IV.iv.1–3)

Those lines often make me think of the about-to-be-created Eve peering out over God's arm on Michelangelo's ceiling in the Sistine chapel. But this moment is framed by another kind of beginning, a traditional seasonal celebration. Perdita excuses the "transformations" of her royal lover to a shepherd and herself to a queen as the folly of holiday:

> But that our feasts
> In every mess have folly, and the feeders
> Digest't with a custom, I should blush.
> (lines 10–12)

The moment leads to the passionate avowal that concludes her flower speech when she regrets that she lacks spring flowers for

>   my sweet friend,
> To strew him o'er and o'er!
> FLORIZEL: What? like a corse?
> PERDITA: No, like a bank, for love to lie and play on;
> Not like a corse; or if—not to be buried,
> But quick and in mine arms. Come, take your flow'rs.
> Methinks I play as I have seen them do
> In Whitsun pastorals. Sure this robe of mine
> Does change my disposition.
>
>   (lines 128–35)

In the festive comedies, as here in the festivities that seem to release Perdita and Florizel to each other, holiday liberty moves young people away from family ties, out of the aegis of the older generation, freeing impulse from inhibition in the process of forming new ties in a new generation. Everyday decorum gives way to holiday liberty that licenses impudent wit, changes of role, girls playing at being boys, a change of allegiance from family and fortune to nature. It is important to emphasize that the comic machine has real work to do in freeing youth from family ties, including various kinds of family-derived adolescent or adult perversity or timidity. In the comedies of youth, the repressive and perverse are laughed out of court, whereas release leads to the embrace of passion, sanctioned by clarification as to its place in the natural cycle.

But in *The Winter's Tale* the holiday spirit of the sheep-shearing festival is exploded by the paternal wrath of Polixenes, who violently interrupts the young lovers' effort to "mark our contract," threatening to disinherit Florizel and to "devise a death as cruel for [Perdita] / As thou art tender to't" (IV.iv.417, 440–41). Perdita will not lie with Florizel on the bank of love until she is recognized by her own father and until the young couple's marriage is sanctioned amid the multiple reunions that take place in Leontes' court. These reunions will in turn serve as necessary preparation for the final recovery of Hermione as wife and mother. Here the festive movement is included within a larger movement where the center of feeling is in the older generation. One can generalize the difference between the festive comedies and the late romances by saying that where the comedies move out through release from family ties to the creation of new families, the romances, especially *Pericles* and

The Winter's Tale, move through experiences of loss back to the recovery of family ties in and through the next generation.

This emphasis, on recovering family relationships rather than on
freeing young people from them, engenders possibilities for incest.
Pericles opens to the incestuous bond of Antiochus and his daughter. Imogen and Posthumus finally achieve marriage in *Cymbeline*
against the odds of a brother-and-sister-like childhood relationship. In the source of *The Winter's Tale* Pandosto-Leontes does not
welcome the love of the young prince for his unrecognized daughter; on the contrary, when the young couple come to him for refuge, he throws the prince in prison and tries to win her sexually for
himself. Prospero alone in his cell with Miranda is in a situation
that Lear longs for in a prison with Cordelia. The incestuous potential of the father-daughter bond, averted in the youth-centered actions of the festive comedies, is intensified by the center of feeling
being in the older generation; for the old can participate in the new
energies of life only through the young. And so the romances move
not simply through release of sexual power but through transformation of it. Instead of the freeing of sexuality from ties of
family, as in the earlier comedies, the movement involves the recovering of family ties while freeing them from the threat of degrading sexuality.

In the tragedies family ties are the basis, directly or by participation in other motives, of heroic striving, of absolute demands on
life, which are realized as both sublime and, finally, destructive.
There is regularly a search for the holy in family-derived relationships; or complementary suggestions of the demonic—as in *Macbeth*—are engendered by such ties. This holy or demonic intensity
is characteristically related, as in the romances, to the possibility of
incest—Hamlet's unconscious participation in the sensual bond of
Claudius and Gertrude, the polarization of sexual and higher love
that follows Othello's effort to recover the deep maternal source of
"absolute content" in Desdemona. In these tragedies, complex social and historical demands are disrupted as they are taken over by
and used for sexual and familial ends. Lear gives away social power
and responsibility in his destructive search for total relationship to
Cordelia. Macbeth destroys the sacred king, Duncan, and the sacred bonds of the social order, only to end in barrenness and isolation even from the dominating wife-mother who has urged him on.

Like *Hamlet* and *Othello*, *Lear* and *Macbeth*, the late romances will look to the familial core of social relations in exploring compelling human needs. But first come three late tragedies, *Antony and Cleopatra*, *Coriolanus*, and *Timon of Athens*, which situate their protagonists very differently in relation to the range of experience shaped by deep family bonds. Although the three late tragedies, all in classical settings, extend many of the preoccupations of the tragedies that precede them, including the exploration of destructive conflicts attending the validation of male identity, these plays are characterized less by the loss than by the absence of the sacred in the human. Taken together, these late tragedies present a kind of impasse in Shakespeare's development of tragic form, which can help us understand the need for the sort of visionary relationship to women dramatized in the reunions of *Pericles* and *The Winter's Tale*.

Antony and Cleopatra is Shakespeare's most complete expression of human, fully sexual love. Antony's marriage to Octavia, proposed as the "hoop," the "unslipping knot" that would bind Antony and Caesar as brother and make the couple a crux for bonding together a whole social fabric, quickly gives way before the force of Antony and Cleopatra's love. Antony, "beguil'd . . . to the very heart of loss" when he thinks Cleopatra has betrayed their mutuality, declares that "the witch shall die" (IV.xii.28, 47). But whereas Othello must destroy Desdemona because of the intolerable confusion of needs—sexual, infantile, and sacred—that he invests in her, Antony is repeatedly renewed by Cleopatra's fusion in her own person of sexual, nurturant, and exotic dimensions of fulfillment. Cleopatra must be exotic to put their relationship beyond the patriarchal terms of Shakespeare's society—and Rome's: "In th' East my pleasure lies" (II.iii.41). Their bond is based not on fidelity but on mutual fulfillment and enhancement: "since my lord / Is Antony again, I will be Cleopatra" (III.xiii.185–86). After Antony's death, for all Cleopatra's immediate talk of suicide, the fifth act demonstrates that she would go on living if without Antony she could still be Cleopatra.

Antony and Cleopatra reaches toward a mode of fulfillment that poses a radical alternative to the dominant patterns of social and familial relationships. To the extent that Antony and Cleopatra are sacred, it is in a truly pagan way, Bacchus come to play with Venus for the good of all Asia. The finale is made possible by identification with Cleopatra and her dream—a dream of the hero such as we get in the tragedies of male affirmation. But in the end we

do not feel the sort of loss of the divine-in-the-human characteristic of earlier tragedies: in death Cleopatra "looks like sleep, /
As she would catch another Antony / In her strong toil of grace"
(V.ii.346–48). The historical sense of a moment when the heroic becomes archaic doubles Shakespeare's perception of Roman history
with his sense of the past heroic moment of Elizabeth's reign: "To
this great fairy I'll commend thy acts, / Make her thanks bless
thee" (IV.viii.12–13). It is Roman structure, not the serpent of
old Nile, that commands the historical moment and its civic logic.
Against that logic, *Antony and Cleopatra* points toward the late romances in its vision of human possibility "past the size of dreaming." But unlike the romances, it does not pursue this vision through
an intensification of those bonds that underlie the social order.
Antony and Cleopatra's intimacy is realized in an imaginative realm
outside the centripetal swerve toward family-centered bonds that
has shaped crucial relationships in the tragedies since *Hamlet* and
will shape key bonds in the romances.

Coriolanus and *Timon of Athens*, by contrast, present reciprocally
a crisis about relationship to the maternal powers in women. Mothers, as such, have been notably absent from the tragedies, with the
exception of Gertrude in *Hamlet*. But in *Coriolanus* we get what in
our time must be seen as an almost clinical study of a mother im-
posing an unbreakable symbiotic tie on a son who must live out for
her a role of unrivaled military preeminence. Volumnia imagines
with relish her son's exploits in battle:

> Methinks I hear hither your husband's drum;
> See him pluck Aufidius down by th' hair. . . .
>   His bloody brow
> With his mail'd hand then wiping, forth he goes.
>   (I.iii.29–30, 34–35)

When his wife, Virgilia, the chaste embodiment of Roman femininity, exclaims, "O Jupiter, no blood!" Volumnia responds:

> Away, you fool! it more becomes a man
> Than gilt his trophy. The breasts of Hecuba,
> When she did suckle Hector, look'd not lovelier
> Than Hector's forehead when it spit forth blood
> At Grecian sword, contemning.
>   (I.iii.38–43)

No wonder her son has no sympathy for the plebeians' hunger! In
feeding on his military heroics, Volumnia starves the son she has

shaped to her own martial ideal, as Janet Adelman observes in a searching study of what shatters brittle Coriolanus. Adelman connects Coriolanus's psychic starvation with his scorn for the hungry citizens, his fear of femininity in himself with latent hatred of his ungiving, overpowering mother, transformed in him to self-conflicting hate of Rome.[1]

Recent developments in psychoanalytic thought have stressed the need for the infant to gain a sense of the mother as a whole, separate person, and of himself as separate from his experience of psychic unity with her.[2] D. W. Winnicott has emphasized the importance, within the frame of the mother-infant bond, of the mother's capacity to absorb destructive fantasies directed at her; only thus, Winnicott argues, can she make possible reparation beyond the separation, which can be established because her actual nurturant presence survives the infant's psychic aggression.[3] The father contributes to this process of separation-individuation both as an essential alternative source for identification and as a rival whose own claim on the mother compels recognition of her separate identity. But Volumnia entirely enlists Coriolanus's aggression in the service of her own need, making her warrior son both the vehicle for her fulfillment—"I have lived / To see inherited my very wishes / And the buildings of my fancy" (II.i.198–200)—and indirectly the object of her rage: "O, he is wounded, I thank the gods for't" (II.i.121). Without a father (except for tolerant, avuncular Menenius) Coriolanus has no identity formed upon the model of a fallible man among men, a man who could provide an alternative to the rigid idealization of martial manhood by which the mother has formed him. Nor yet, of course, does he have a secure relation to his mother; her love is contingent on his fulfilling the ultra-masculine ego-ideal in which she has imprisoned him.

The shaping of the hero by his Roman mother is total, and his

1. Janet Adelman, "'Anger's My Meat': Feeding, Dependency, and Aggression in *Coriolanus*," in *Representing Shakespeare*, ed. Murray M. Schwartz and Coppélia Kahn (Baltimore: Johns Hopkins University Press, 1980), pp. 129–49. This essay first appeared in *Shakespeare: Pattern of Excelling Nature*, ed. David Bevington and Jay L. Halio (Newark: University of Delaware Press, 1978).

2. For examples of the work being done in this area, see the essays of Margaret Mahler in *On Human Symbiosis and the Vicissitudes of Individuation* (London: Hogarth, 1969) and *The Psychological Birth of the Human Infant* (New York: Basic Books, 1975).

3. See "The Use of an Object and Relating through Identifications," in D. W. Winnicott, *Playing and Reality* (New York: Basic Books, 1971), pp. 86–94.

bonding to her proves tragically inescapable. When he has Rome at his mercy, and his mother, wife, and child approach, he tries to "stand / As if a man were author of himself, / And knew no other kin" (V.iii.35–37). But this futile effort to establish godlike autonomy for himself breaks down when his mother turns her back:

> O my mother, mother! O!
> You have won a happy victory to Rome;
> But, for your son, believe it—O, believe it—
> Most dangerously you have with him prevail'd,
> If not most mortal to him.
>
> (V.iii.185–89)

Back at Corioli, Aufidius's exactly aimed taunt—"Name not [Mars], thou boy of tears!"—provokes "Cut me to pieces, Volsces, men and lads, / Stain all your edges on me. 'Boy,' false hound!" (V.vi.100, 111–12). In the scene just before his destruction in dreadful isolation, we have seen his mother pass over the stage with "Behold our patroness, the life of Rome! . . . / Cry, 'Welcome, ladies, welcome!'" (V.v.1, 6). The ironic and remorseless logic that silently counterpoints Volumnia's triumphant return to Rome with her son's death in an impotent struggle to deny his boyish dependence on her entirely excludes the range of sacred and demonic feeling characteristic of the tragedies from *Julius Caesar* and *Hamlet* to *Macbeth*.

Perhaps *Coriolanus* can be so clinical and sociological because the inflexible nature of its protagonist is so remote from the fluid responsiveness characteristic of its author's imaginative temperament. But Timon, in his giving himself to his countrymen, in involving himself in the lives of others, is in a sense like Shakespeare creating parts for his whole company, sharing in a brotherly enterprise for which he provides the words, the nurturant substance. Shakespeare, however, had the theater's saving balance between realizing life, on the one hand, and limiting it, ridiculing it, destroying it in the symbolic action of drama, on the other. Timon, who for his own fulfillment empties himself into others, has nothing like the resources of the theater for mastering and distancing through irony the violent aggression released by his abrupt disillusionment.

In *Timon* Shakespeare explores an extreme alternative to the overpowering of Coriolanus by his mother: Timon does without maternal nurturance by trying to be himself an all-providing patron. Timon's great wealth, his "plenteous bosom" (I.ii.125), is likened, by a half-submerged image, to an inexhaustible breast:

> His large fortune,
> Upon his good and gracious nature hanging,
> Subdues and properties to his love and tendance
> All sorts of hearts.
>
> (I.i.55–58)

Imagery of feeding and pouring out dominate the early scenes. But where a mother's milk has a biological source of renewal, Timon's wealth has not; where a wife has a husband to provide food to sustain her nurturing, Timon has none. After his bankruptcy, when friendly Alcibiades asks, "How came the noble Timon to this change?" Timon responds:

> As the moon does, by wanting light to give:
> But then renew I could not, like the moon;
> There were no suns to borrow of.
>
> (IV.iii.67–70)

As a result, Timon's giving proves to be his being eaten alive, as the cynic Apemantus comments during the first, lavish feast: "O you gods! what a number of men eats Timon, and he sees 'em not! It grieves me to see so many dip their meat in one man's blood" (I.ii.39–41).

There is in Apemantus's lines an adumbration of the Last Supper and of Judas: "the fellow that sits next him, now parts bread with him, pledges the breath of him in a divided draught, is the readiest man to kill him" (lines 46–49). But this is not, I think, to be registered consciously as parody or as an attempt to give Timon's fate Christlike significance. At one level the play is an extreme social history, its imagery of eating developed into traditional images of greed, wealth, and usury. Lucian used comparable imagery when he described Timon "having his liver eaten by so many vultures" who "when they had finally eaten him down to the bone, and sucked the marrow, . . . left him high and dry and stripped from top to toe."[4] But where Lucian's satire uses Timon to deal with the improper use of riches and the virtues of poverty, Shakespeare tries to deal with something far more fundamental. Shakespeare shows Timon trying to make up for insecurity about maternal nurturance by doing the nurturing himself.

Timon is engaged in a strategy of altruistic defense that joins potential rivals to him in apparent love; their threat to his security is

---

4. "The Dialogue of Timon," in *Sources*, vol. 6, p. 265.

denied in the precarious mutuality engendered by his feeding and giving.[5] In the first feast scene Timon's wish to believe in mutuality brings sentimental tears to his eyes:

> O, what a precious comfort 'tis to have so many like brothers commanding one another's fortunes! O, joy's e'en made away ere't can be born! Mine eyes cannot hold out water, methinks. To forget their faults, I drink to you.
>
> (I.ii.103–8)

After Apemantus's aptly cynical interjection—"Thou weep'st to make them drink, Timon"—a guest replies: "Joy had the like conception in our eyes, / And at that instant like a babe sprung up" (I.i.109–11). Timon's sentimental turn toward weeping, as checked by the guest's complementary assertion of joy "like a babe sprung up," presents an image complex that suggests the infantile roots of the insecurity underlying Timon's extravagant generosity.[6] Comfort, nurture, tears, and babe are yoked together, along with conception, birth, and the vanishing of joy—for Timon, joy is "made away" at the instant when the promise of nurturant fulfillment is imminent. The earlier discussion between poet and painter reflects even more directly the infantile situation of rivalry and precarious fulfillment, with the threat of losing the source of joy. The poet first depicts Lady Fortune "upon a high and pleasant hill," preferring Timon among all "That labor on the bosom of this sphere," then moves on to consider the time when Fortune, having found a new favorite, "Spurns down her late beloved," who is abandoned by all in his headlong fall into desolation (I.i.63, 66, 85).

The nature of the insecurity held in check by Timon's giving is further revealed in the incongruous fact that Timon's terrible curses as he turns from philanthropist to misanthropist are most intensely focused, not on flattery, usury, or even ingratitude, but on turning food into barren water or into poison and disease—and, most obsessively, on female sexuality. Wealth is insistently associated with

5. Anna Freud describes "altruistic surrender" as a defense in which a child overcompensates with exaggerated generosity for the hostility provoked in him by the appearance of a new sibling (*The Ego and the Mechanisms of Defense*, rev. ed. [New York: International Universities Press, 1966], pp. 123–34). The effort to hold onto the threatened security of the mother's love is made through an identification with her in her cherishing attitude toward the new arrival.

6. In connection with the "babe sprung up" amid this curious mix of melancholy and joy, compare the bouncing entry into Sonnet 98 of "proud-pied April, dressed in all his trim," as discussed in chapter 5 above, pp. 177–78.

whoredom as Timon gives his strangely found gold to Alcibiades' whores—the only women in the play besides those in the masque of Amazons—and urges them to "mar men's spurring" with diseases, to "defeat and quell / The source of all erection" (IV.iii.153, 163–64). As Timon urges Alcibiades to destroy Athens, one particular passage stands out:

> Strike me the counterfeit matron,
> It is her habit only that is honest,
> Herself's a bawd. Let not virgin's cheek
> Make soft thy trenchant sword; for those milk paps,
> That through the window-bars bore at men's eyes,
> Are not within the leaf of pity writ,
> But set them down horrible traitors.
>
> (IV.iii.113–19)

With the fear of rejection, earlier denied by compulsive generosity, now confirmed, Timon rages against pandering mothers, betrayers of the nurturant ideal with which he has identified himself, and against traitorous "milk-paps," here made agents (*they* "bore at men's eyes"!) of the volatile mix of desire and aggression they provoke. The surviving remnants of the longing for feminine tenderness are brought out, again incongruously, in Timon's response to his loyal steward Flavius:

> What, dost thou weep? Come nearer. Then I love thee,
> Because thou art a woman, . . .
>   Surely, this man
> Was born of woman.
>
> (IV.iii.482–83, 493–94)

But Timon goes on to counsel Flavius:

> Hate all, curse all, show charity to none,
> But let the famish'd flesh slide from the bone
> Ere thou relieve the beggar.
>
> (IV.iii.527–29)

Shakespeare does not develop a satisfactory way of turning the isolating infantile rage of Timon's response into a social and so dramatic action. (Editors agree that the play was left in rough draft.) In this respect *Timon* contrasts sharply with *Coriolanus*, where the whole play beautifully fuses the family and political constellations. It is crucial that Coriolanus's warp and his mother's influence are presented within a dramatic world fully realized in the two-sidedness of the political divisions, in the complex social activity of Rome, and in the male solidarity achieved in war. The isolation of women from the masculine military and civic concerns of Rome is established from the outset, with Volumnia's response to this exclusion shaping her demand on her son. *Coriolanus* is the last play in which Shakespeare presents this full interplay of the social and historical with individual and family life. *Timon of Athens* is like the romances in isolating its motivational theme from full social actuality. Timon is an abortive romance—unfinishable because there are no women who matter in the way that Thaisa and Marina will matter in *Pericles*. *Pericles*, with its protagonist who will nurture others, identify himself with feminine qualities, and withdraw into isolation prior to the recovery of his daughter and wife, is *Timon* with romance resources to fulfill rather than abort its action.

It is remarkable that *Coriolanus*, *Timon*, and *Pericles* all recall the movement of *King Lear* through an action of exile or banishment. Coriolanus's banishment and Timon's self-exile are both accompanied by violent rejections of what has rejected them; Pericles, also forced to leave his realm by threat, spends much of his life in exile-like wandering, withdrawing deep into apparently unreachable isolation before the final reunion. These three late plays, clustered together but very different from one another, with similar preoccupations poised in symmetrically different relationships, show Shakespeare, at a time of profound transition in his drama, moving restlessly around a problematic center—the maternal presence crucial to sustain his hero's identity. *Coriolanus* and *Timon* explore the destructive possibilities of such relationship. Coriolanus's exile ends when a reunion with his dominating mother, whom he has tried to deny, proves fatal to him. Timon's self-exile follows from the failure of his effort to make himself into the source of maternal nurture, an effort that is itself a flight from actual relationship to women and the vulnerability such relationship entails in the tragedies preceding *Timon*.

In *King Lear* it is out of Lear's need for the love he demands of his daughters that the play reaches its tragic encounter with the sacred in the human. But both *Coriolanus* and *Timon* turn away from the desire to establish actual relationship with women at the center of Lear's need. Timon's savage denunciation of women and the desire they provoke recalls the horror of female sexuality that bursts out in Lear when he has been betrayed by his sexually avid older daughters. But unlike Lear, who dies holding the dead body of Cordelia, peering into her face with inconsolable grief, Timon seeks his own death in total isolation. The dramatic worlds of *Coriolanus* and *Timon* have been emptied both of the gracious femininity embodied in

Cordelia and of the longing to live in relation to this feminine presence, manifested in Lear. But Lear's reunion with Cordelia, when he recovers his senses at Dover after the long ordeal of madness and rage—"Do not laugh at me, / For (as I am a man) I think this lady / To be my child Cordelia" (IV.vii.67–69)—anticipates, often point by point, the reunion of Pericles and Marina in *Pericles*. Later, when Lear holds his dead Cordelia in his arms, he thinks she may be alive:

> This feather stirs, she lives! If it be so,
> It is a chance which does redeem all sorrows
> That ever I have felt.
>
> (V.iii.266–68)

The redemptive feminine presence, which cannot be recovered in *King Lear*—"she's gone forever"—and is excluded from the outset in the tragic worlds of *Coriolanus* and *Timon of Athens*, Shakespeare will recover in the visionary comedy of *Pericles* and *The Winter's Tale*.

"THOU THAT BEGET'ST HIM THAT DID THEE BEGET"

In the shift to the new kind of drama made from the old romance form, Shakespeare's search for new relationship to the feminine brings into special prominence the threat of sexual degradation. *Cymbeline* and *The Winter's Tale* must move through and beyond Posthumus's conviction that the "woman's part" lies at the core of all human vice, Leontes' delusional insistence that Hermione's "actions are my dreams. / You had a bastard by Polixenes, / And I but dream'd it" (III.ii.82–84). *Pericles* makes the potential for degradation particularly clear because it begins with its hero's encounter with the overt incest of Antiochus and his daughter. The story that follows is shaped as though the shock of this encounter were a traumatic experience that Pericles can recover from only at great cost in depression, self-limitation, and avoidance.

With wonderful artistic tact Shakespeare respects the fairy tale or romance mode of his source in Gower's version of the centuries-old story.[7] He keeps the seeming arbitrariness of the ways things

---

7. The story of Apollonius of Tyre in *Confessio Amantis*, Bk. VIII; the relevant portions are reprinted in *Sources*, vol. 6, pp. 375–423.

happen to Pericles, gives dramatic and poetic actuality to the separate scenes, and motivates the strange vicissitudes largely by a marvelous running expression of the inscrutable power of the sea. The sea in *Pericles* causes most of the crucial events. When Cleon and Dionyza are saying goodbye to Pericles after he has left his motherless child, Marina, in their care, Cleon says, "We'll bring your Grace e'en to the edge a' th' shore, / Then give you up to the mask'd Neptune and / The gentlest winds of heaven" (III.iii.35–37).[8] The things that matter most in the play happen beyond "the edge a' th' shore" or on the edge. Neptune takes away, and again Neptune restores, without accountability, seemingly without reason, remaining "the mask'd Neptune."

> Alas, the seas hath cast me on the rocks,
> Wash'd me from shore to shore.
> (II.i.5–6)

> . . . the rough seas, that spares not any man,
> Took it in rage, though calm'd have given't again.
> (II.i.131–32)

It is on "the edge a' th' shore" that Leonine prepares to kill Marina on her foster mother's orders and she is rescued by pirates who sell her into a brothel. She opens that scene with a summary image of sea storm:

> Ay me! poor maid,
> Born in a tempest when my mother died,
> This world to me is a lasting storm,
> Whirring me from my friends.
> (IV.i.17–20)

She recovers her father when Mytilene is "honoring of Neptune's triumphs" (V.i.17), the city "hiv'd / God Neptune's annual feast to

---

8. The chapter title is taken from this quotation because the charged phrase, "the masked Neptune," suggests the inscrutable, hidden source in the play of mythic and visionary happenings. It is hard to know *what* we understand when we understand *Pericles*. And a feeling of the limits of our understanding is an essential part of the play's effect on us, along with an effect of distance promoted by the archaic remoteness of old Gower's choruses and his attitude toward his tale: "I tell you what mine authors say" (I.Cho.20). Shakespeare neglects most of the elaboration of circumstantial motivation added in the prose source he also used, Laurence Twine's *The Patterne of Painefull Adventures* (reprinted in *Sources*, vol. 6, pp. 423–82). Even though that source is often plausible on a surface level, it frequently displaces or obscures the tale's deeper logic. Instead, Shakespeare preserves and develops by poetry the motivations implicit in Gower.

keep" (V.Cho.16–17).[9] The great recognition scene turns on the meaning of her name and place of her birth:

> Where were you born?
> And wherefore call'd Marina?
> MARINA: Call'd Marina
> For I was born at sea. . . .
> PERICLES: O Helicanus, strike me, honored sir,
> Give me a gash, put me to present pain,
> Lest this great sea of joys rushing upon me
> O'erbear the shores of my mortality,
> And drown me with their sweetness.
> (V.i.154–56, 190–94)

At the beginning of the recognition, Marina answers Pericles' hesitant questions with a wonderful summary line:

> PERICLES: Pray you turn your eyes upon me.
> You're like something that—what country-woman?
> Here of these shores?
> MARINA: No, nor of any shores.
> (V.i.101–3)

The sea imagery of "the masked Neptune" makes us feel that our lives are lived through us, that we float on a surface that may engulf us and yet also may cast up to us what is most precious.

In the opening scene with Antiochus and his daughter, Pericles encounters masked incest and sees behind the mask. That a play centering on the loss of wife and mother should begin with incest makes drastic sense. Antiochus, having lost "a noble quene," for whom, Gower's original tells us, he "made mochel mone," now lives secretly with their daughter.[10] The riddle that describes the relationship emphasizes, even more explicitly than in Gower's original, that their sin is an intensification of family relationships which obliterates the crucial differences the incest taboo normally preserves: "He's father, son, and husband mild; / I mother, wife—and yet his child" (I.i.68–69). The dreadfulness of the violation of taboo, the menace of becoming involved in it, is concretely embodied by the heads of dead suitors impaled on the walls, in contrast to the inviting beauty of the daughter, "this glorious casket stor'd with ill" (I.i.77).

---

9. Here I follow the emendation of "striv'de" to "hiv'd" proposed by the eighteenth-century editor George Steevens. Evans follows the rather unsatisfactory Q1 reading.

10. *Sources*, vol. 6, p. 376.

Now to find the mother in the daughter, as Antiochus does in a fully sensual way, is what Pericles does in a sublime way when he recognizes Marina. In the recognition scene he describes her likeness to his lost wife with gathering rhapsody, before he knows her name or circumstances:

> My dearest wife was like this maid, and such a one
> My daughter might have been. My queen's square brows,
> Her stature to an inch, as wand-like straight,
> As silver-voic'd, her eyes as jewel-like
> And cas'd as richly, in pace another Juno;
> Who starves the ears she feeds, and makes them hungry
> The more she gives them speech.
>
> (V.i.107–13)

The play as a whole moves from the sexual degradation of family relationships in incest to this beautifully moving restoration of relationship through the new generation. After the riddle has regressively shaped the sexual bond into imagery of feeding—"I am no viper, yet I feed / On mother's flesh which did me breed" (I.i.64–65)—Marina's speech "starves the ears she feeds, and makes them hungry / The more she gives them speech."

In the opening scene, Pericles describes in terms of music what has been lost by the perversion of the daughter. This description, again, fits the later scene with a difference:

> You are a fair viol, and your sense the strings;
> Who, finger'd to make man his lawful music,
> Would draw heaven down, and all the gods to hearken.
>
> (I.i.81–83)

In Act V, after the recognition of Marina is fully achieved, Pericles hears supernatural music, which seems to draw down heaven. "The music of the spheres! . . . Most heavenly music! / It nips me unto list'ning, and thick slumber / Hangs upon mine eyes" (V.i.229, 233–35). He falls asleep, and Diana appears to him in a vision to tell him to go to her temple at Ephesus, where in the next scene he finds his lost wife, Thaisa. So the resolution avoids the potential perversion. Instead of finding the wife in the daughter and being left with her, the resolution moves under the aegis of chastity through the recovery of the daughter to the recovery of the wife. Pericles has fled from an encounter with Antiochus that seemed to poison his fate, nearly dooming him to a like destiny. In retrospect this doom is a special sort of blessing, for it leads to his achieving, in a sublimated way, the recovery of the wife through the daughter, which Antiochus tried to achieve physically.

Back at his own Tyre, after the initial encounter with Antiochus, Pericles is prey to a "change of thoughts, . . . dull-ey'd melancholy" (I.ii.1–2). His soliloquy opens with a remarkable account of melancholy anxiety: "Here pleasures court mine eyes, and mine eyes shun them" (line 6). He states explicitly that the menace experienced at Antioch has been internalized: although "danger, which I fear'd, is at Antioch, / . . . Yet neither pleasure's art can joy my spirits, / Nor yet the other's distance comfort me" (lines 7, 9–10). The initial fear is nourished and sustained by the resultant depressive cares that temptation may be resisted:

> the passions of the mind,
> That have their first conception by misdread,
> Have after-nourishment and life by care;
> And what was first but fear what might be done,
> Grows elder now, and cares it be not done.[11]
>
> (lines 11–15)

But no sooner has Pericles described an autonomous psychological state than he changes his mind, persuading himself that Antiochus is so great that he "can make his will his act," that Pericles and his Tyre are "too little to contend"; Antiochus advancing "with th' ostent of war will look so huge, / Amazement shall drive courage from the state, / Our men be vanquished ere they do resist" (lines 17–18, 25–27). Pericles concludes with a precise description of the internalization of Antiochus's threat: it "makes both my body pine and soul to languish, / And punish that before that he would punish" (lines 32–33).

The constellation here is an omnipotent older man who keeps

---

11. A propos of this extremely subtle passage, I agree with the hypothesis of Phillip Edwards in "An Approach to the Problem of *Pericles,*" *Shakespeare Survey* 5 (1952): 25–49, that the first two acts of the play, with their often turgid or lame language, are not the largely unrevised work of some minor dramatist whose last three acts Shakespeare far more fully revised. I think, with Edwards, that what we have is Shakespeare's work filtered through a reporter providing copy for the unauthorized quarto; that this reporter, instead of remembering verbatim, with lapses, like the reporter of the last three acts, "welds into mediocre verse the words, phrases and general sense of the original so far as he can remember them" (p. 45). This would account not only for the occasional exquisite late Shakespeare lines in the first two acts and for the fine first scene of Act II (in which the reporter may have had a part), but also for the depth and complexity of much of the thought, as in this passage, the uniformly fine dramatic design of the scenes, and the deep congruences of imagery between the play's opening and its ending.

the desired woman to himself, makes her guilty of sexual degradation, and threatens the life of the young man who desires her. One
can see here a variation of the Oedipal situation of the male child
barred from the "guilty" mother—a version of Claudius menacing
Hamlet, with the difference that the woman is a guilty daughter put
in place of the mother, rather than a guilty wife and mother. Unlike
Hamlet, Pericles does not struggle to fight back after the initial
traumatic experience. Instead, he takes refuge in flight on the seas.
The whole succeeding fable, shaped and reshaped over centuries
of retelling by projective, unrationalized imagination, can be summarized as painful adventures which end with the hero's achieving
on a sublime level what he fled from at the degraded level, and
achieving it without Oedipal confrontation with the corrupt father-
figure.

Pericles' finding a bride in Act II is a symmetrical reversal of his
failure to win Antiochus's daughter. In this case too there is a widowed king with a single daughter, for whose favor there is a competition of knightly suitors. The play adds the charged symbolic
circumstance that the shipwrecked Pericles, entering the lists
anonymously, is nevertheless wearing his dead father's rusty armor, cast up by the sea. Thaisa, with her father's blessing, does the
wooing: "All viands that I eat do seem unsavory, / Wishing him my
meat" (II.iii.31–32). Simonides' deliberate "trial" of the youth his
daughter has fallen in love with, a first version of Prospero's trial of
Ferdinand, elicits initially a characteristically submissive response
from Pericles. When, without comment, the king gives him Thaisa's
letter avowing her love of the stranger knight, Pericles believes it
is "the King's subtilty to have my life," and insists that he "never
aim'd so high to love your daughter, / But bent all offices to honor
her" (II.v.44, 47–48). When Simonides calls Pericles traitor, this
rouses a courageous response that Simonides admires in an aside.
But the king plays out the role of heavy father even as, with evident
pleasure, he suddenly reverses it:

> I'll tame you; I'll bring you in subjection. . . .
> Either be rul'd by me, or I'll make you—
> Man and wife.
> Nay come, your hands and lips must seal it too.
> (II.v.75, 83–85)

When, at long last, Thaisa finally asks if Pericles loves her, his answer is "Even as my life my blood that fosters it" (line 89).

This answer is deeply in character, for Pericles' way of responding to the original threat of incest and the potential vengeance of the powerful father has been, throughout, to identify with the fostering, nurturing side of life and with women as they embody the "blood that fosters" life. His first flight from Tyre had brought him to Tharsus, where he relieved a famine so terrible that the populace were resorting to cannibalism, the once doting mothers ready "To eat those little darlings whom they lov'd" (I.iv.44). This strangely intimate imagery of hunger in extremis recalls the dangerous eating imagery that defined the incest at Antioch. Cleon, the governor of starving Tharsus, expects conquest when he sees the Tyre fleet, but Pericles instead intervenes to provide nurture by supplying "corn to make your needy bread" (line 95). As Cleon, his wife, Dionyza, and the rest kneel in gratitude, Pericles asks them to rise: "We do not look for reverence but for love" (line 99). It is consistent with his uniformly abjuring aggression and with the quasi-magical power that the threat from Antiochus has over him, that, even after the grateful citizens have erected a statue to him, he flees the city on the news that Antiochus's Thaliard, commissioned to kill him, is pursuing him there. It is consistent also that later in Pentapolis, as the Chorus tells us, he does not reveal his princely station, even after he is happily married, until news comes that Antiochus is dead. He does not venture to love a woman until a generous father gives him his daughter. He does not assert his full identity until the jealous, incestuous father, Antiochus, is dead.

The problem about his character as a hero lies in the incongruity between the way he is described as a pattern of chivalric strength and talent—handsome, lusty, winner in knightly exercises, fabulously rich, a king—and his consistent avoidance of all aggressive self-assertions.[12] Pericles' holding back from confrontation by aggression accords with his special relationship to femininity. As he begins to tell his story to the still unknown Marina, he speaks in maternal terms: "I am great with woe, and shall deliver weeping" (V.i.106). All that we actually see of his marriage is the moment in the storm at sea when he grieves over his wife's travail, receives her newborn daughter with the news of Thaisa's death, and commits his bride to the sea. The marvelous scene presents a man's helpless, loving effort to participate in a woman's childbearing. The hus-

12. This inhibition of aggression is not necessarily an inconsistency of character; it is what we would call a neurotic compulsion, except that the term implies a failure of sublimation, whereas in fact Pericles succeeds in sublimation. If one uses the word "neurotic," one must add, using Freud's phrase, that the neurotic is a moral hero in defeat, and that Pericles, moreover, is such a hero who finally wins through.

band's exclusion from the travail of labor is conveyed by the storm's violence and noise. He calls to the nurse who is acting as midwife—"O, how, Lychorida! / How does my queen?"—only to realize that he cannot possibly be heard:

> The seaman's whistle
> Is as a whisper in the ears of death,
> Unheard.—Lychorida!—Lucina, O!
> Divinest patroness, and midwife gentle
> To those that cry by night, convey thy Deity
> Aboard our dancing boat, make swift the pangs
> Of my queen's travails!
>
> (III.i.6–14)

A cherishing delicacy of feeling for life is expressed along with the tempest. Pericles' greeting to his newborn child sets the two in repeated contrast:

> Now, mild may be thy life!
> For a more blusterous birth had never babe.
> Quiet and gentle thy conditions! for
> Thou art the rudeliest welcomed to this world
> That ever was prince's child.
>
> (lines 27–31)

His farewell to Thaisa's body is poetry like that which, later in *The Tempest*, makes the depths of the sea a region of mystery, of death, and of possible renewal—"Full fadom five thy father lies, / . . . Those are pearls that were his eyes" (*Tmp*. I.ii.397, 399). Pericles speaks of Thaisa's eyes, her "e'er remaining lamps":

> nor have I time
> To give thee hallow'd to thy grave, but straight
> Must cast thee, scarcely coffin'd, in the ooze,
> Where, for a monument upon thy bones,
> And e'er remaining lamps, the belching whale
> And humming water must o'erwhelm thy corpse,
> Lying with simple shells.[13]
>
> (III.i.58–64)

In the next scene we are on the edge of the shore, again with death and birth. The physician Cerimon is another cherishing, nur-

---

13. In line 62, I adopt the reading "*And* e'er remaining lamps," rather than "*The* e'er remaining lamps," which Evans takes from the Quarto, for the reference seems to me to be to Thaisa's eyes (compare *The Tempest*'s "Those are pearls that were his eyes"). It is difficult to imagine "e'er remaining lamps" as something already belonging in the sea along with "the belching whale / And humming water."

turant man, whose first words are "Get fire and meat for these poor men. / 'T'as been a turbulent and stormy night" (III.ii.3–4). We see him direct the opening of the great tarred chest containing Thaisa, which has been cast ashore by a huge billow. In succoring the queen back to life, he is in effect a midwife to a rebirth:

> Gentlemen, this queen will live. Nature awakes,
> A warmth breathes out of her. She hath not been
> Entranc'd above five hours. See how she gins
> To blow into life's flower again!
>
> (III.ii.92–95)

The essential power of life is realized as something so delicate that one can only reverently contemplate it. Its "action is no stronger than a flower."

Having lost his wife, Pericles alone with his daughter is potentially in the same situation as Antiochus. So in the next scene of Act III he gives his daughter to be brought up by Cleon and Dionyza:

> Till she be married, madam,
> By bright Diana, whom we honor, all
> Unscissor'd shall this hair of mine remain,
> Though I show ill in't.
>
> (III.iii.27–30)

In an essay entitled "Magical Hair," the anthropologist Edmund Leach describes religious cults where leaving the hair uncut expresses the celibate's renunciation of all sexual activity.[14] Pericles makes that significance explicit by his invocation of Diana. Wilkins's prose version, derived from the play as well as from earlier narrative versions, emphasizes the uncut hair repeatedly; it must have been a striking effect in the theater.[15] Pericles does not go to see his daughter for fourteen years, an avoidance unexplained and unremarked, though consistent with fear of repeating Antiochus's sin.

After Act III's evocation, in grief and cherishing, of delicate feminine powers of life, Act IV is countermovement. We see Pericles only in dumb show when he receives the overwhelming (false) news that Marina is dead. The Act opens with Dionyza hiring Leonine to kill Marina, out of jealousy of graces that put her own daughter in the shade. Here is a different, destructive side of ma-

---

14. Edmund Leach, "Magical Hair," *Journal of the Royal Anthropological Institute*, 88 (Pt. 2, 1958): 147–69.

15. George Wilkins, *The Painful Adventures of Pericles Prince of Tyre* (1608), in *Sources*, vol. 6, pp. 492–546.

ternal femininity. The fairy-tale motive for her murderousness, given in all sources, seems inadequate; Shakespeare does not go behind it. To go behind it by interpretation may seem to be forcing a pattern on the tale. But for what it is worth, one can observe that if Dionyza were a second wife to Pericles—and so the fairy-tale stepmother whose jealous role is more familiar—her deadly hatred would make sense as a response to Pericles' fixation on his daughter as the continuation of the life of his lost, first wife.

The second half of the act puts Marina in the brothel. This action, though presented entirely apart from Pericles, is the working through, at a distance, of the sexual potentiality that might tempt him. The stir among gentlemen "of all complexions" (IV.ii.80) at Boult's crying the new virgin about town is a long way from paternal incest. But the special attraction of a virgin, which at some level we cannot help but experience along with the bawd's customers, is a cognate impulse—one way to be in touch with "th' freshest things now reigning" (WT IV.i.13), even if you are "the French knight that cow'rs i' the hams" (IV.ii.105). The scenes are handled with a comic realism that is at once funny and dreadful enough to make not only the gallants but the audience feel that they want to be "out of the road of rutting for ever" (IV.v.9). "We have but poor three, and they can do no more than they can do; and they with continual action are even as good as rotten" (IV.ii.7–9). How matter-of-fact, reasonable, compassionate even, within the limits of business necessities. Marina is cunningly advised to exploit the moral and cherishing side of her customers: "To weep that you live as you do makes pity in your lovers; seldom but that pity begets you a good opinion, and that opinion a mere profit" (IV.ii.119–21).

After the false news of Marina's death, Pericles is plunged into a state of total depression, unwashed, unshaven, completely withdrawn from all objects:

> Behold him. [*Pericles discovered.*] This was a goodly person,
> Till the disaster that, one mortal night,
> Drove him to this.
>
> (V.i.36–38)

Pericles' condition here is close both to extremes of Christian asceticism—the renunciation of worldly experience for a complete inner concentration on the object of worship—and to deep depressions reported by modern clinical experience, where the loss of a primary love object, ultimately maternal, is a commonly ascribed etiology. The identification with maternal modes of relating, which we have noticed repeatedly in Pericles, accords with his responding so totally to the loss of Marina. The death of his wife in childbirth has deprived Pericles of the maternal presence with whose creativity he has so poignantly allied himself. But such a presence has remained for him in the potentiality of the girl-child.

In the intense concentration of his grief, Pericles pulls back from all connectedness with a world outside him. Prior to his recovery of Marina he has spoken to no one for three months, "nor taken sustenance / But to prorogue his grief" (V.i.25–26). He has become an embodiment of total valuation of what has survived of the inwardly preserved maternal presence on which we found our basic trust and sense of self. When Marina, as yet unrecognized, first approaches, he pushes her away, as if he is protecting what remains within him of his precarious tie to life. His fear of reinvesting his trust in actual objects punctuates his gradual taking in of Marina's identity throughout the long recognition process. In this recognition, the acceptance of the daughter's independent femininity is achieved, not by dramatizing her own self-realization as a woman, as is done with Perdita in *The Winter's Tale*, but by seeing in her a new embodiment of the generative powers of her mother. It is the renewed relation with these powers that brings Pericles out of his deathlike trance.

The delicate and precise complex of maternal and nurturant imagery is Shakespeare's contribution to the fable he took over: he poetically extrapolates the potentialities of relatively bare events in the story. Thaisa and Marina are associated repeatedly with precious possessions, as when Pericles, preparing to bury his wife, calls for "spices," "my casket and my jewels," the "satin coffin" (III.i.65–68). Or again when Cerimon opens the coffin:

CERIMON:	Wrench it open.
	Soft! It smells most sweetly in my sense.
2. GENTLEMAN:	A delicate odor.
CERIMON:	As ever hit my nostril. So, up with it.
	O you most potent gods! what's here? a corse?
2. GENTLEMAN:	Most strange.
CERIMON:	Shrouded in cloth of state, balm'd and entreasur'd
	With full bags of spices. A passport too!
	(III.ii.59–66)

Similar imagery of riches describes Thaisa as she comes back to life:

Her eyelids, cases to those heavenly jewels
Which Pericles hath lost, begin to part

> Their fringes of bright gold. The diamonds
> Of a most praised water doth appear,
> To make the world twice rich.
> (lines 98–102)

This reverend sense of Thaisa as a precious possession recovered
from the sea accords with the way the play has dramatized the moment of losing her (or rather seeming to lose her but preserving her,
"led on by heaven"). In the experience of early childhood, when
exclusive possession of the mother is lost, it is apt to be associated
with her bearing another child. There is no way to "prove" that
such experience is relevant, except that it is common, so that the
mythic imagining that shaped and preserved the tale of Apollonius
might well find the fable of losing a wife in childbirth appealing
as a way of reexperiencing the loss of a mother's whole love at the
time of her giving birth to a second child. The fable preserves that
mother, embalming her. Associations with the proximate sense of
smell fit with such early experience: "full bags of spices," as can
Pericles' way of describing the loss for himself:

> O you gods!
> Why do you make us love your goodly gifts
> And snatch them straight away?
> (III.i.22–24)

And still more his way of describing his child's loss:

> Even at the first
> Thy loss is more than can thy portage quit
> With all thou canst find here. Now the good gods
> Throw their best eyes upon't!
> (lines 34–37)

"Portage" makes a metaphor of Marina's life as a voyage, since it
meant what a sailor—"this fresh new sea-farer" (line 41)—could
put aboard as his own venture: nothing life can give in exchange for
her investment in it can make up for the loss of her mother. In
speaking for her, Pericles is clearly speaking also for himself.

When Marina is restored to him, Pericles is restored to himself,
and the loss that has left him bereft is requited. With this recovery,
the motive that in *King Lear* leads to tragedy finds resolution. How
is this possible? Of course the given facts in the two plays are
simply different: Pericles when he recovers Marina is a man in
middle age, and Diana directs him on from her to recover Thaisa,
whereas Lear is at the end of life and there is no wife, only his

daughters to look to. And where Lear is a superb, impatient egoist, Pericles is a figure who lives chiefly through his awareness of others. One can say, rightly enough and in the spirit of Gower's epilogue, that Pericles, "assail'd with fortune fierce and keen," earns the happy ending by patience, "Led on by heaven, and crown'd with joy at last" (V.iii.88, 90). By conscious fidelity to the sacred powers of life—"We cannot but obey / The powers above us" (III.iii.9–10)— Pericles preserves his relationship to wife and daughter intact; unconsciously or involuntarily "led on by heaven," he avoids degrading them sexually. On deeper levels, the final happy ending is earned by moving through a sequence of attitudes that have a spiritual and psychological logic and that make the seemingly random adventures a visionary exploration. Components of the motive in Lear are objectified, distanced, and so brought under control, with a generalized experience of suffering and misfortune that reflects the psychic cost of the process.

But why is not the romance, with its visionary restoration, merely a superbly realized wish-fulfillment? We may understand why the recovery of what is lost in *Pericles* is not simply a wish-fulfillment if we consider how visionary realization differs from mere wishful fantasy, a difference that is not easy to formulate, because it seems to involve the ontological status of what is envisaged. We can understand the difference by ascribing to what is known in vision an objective status as a Jungian archetype or a religious presence. Or we can focus on the process through which the vision is arrived at—the "way," as the term is used in the discipline of mystical devotion. My own understanding centers on the second possibility of seeing what happens: it seems to me that the *way* by which *Pericles* conducts us to the visionary realization is what gives it its strange reality.

T. S. Eliot in his poem *Marina* provides an extrapolation of the visionary experience in *Pericles*, and in his nearly contemporary essay on Dante, an illuminating commentary on the visionary process. In *Marina* Eliot translates the situation of the play into his own experience of recovering the sea and shore he knew during his boyhood summers on Cape Ann, together with a vision of a presence, a face "more distant than stars and nearer than the eye." [16] Building on Pericles' sailing about "in sorrow all devoured" after the false news of Marina's death, the poem creates a moment when his ves-

---

16. T. S. Eliot, *The Complete Poems and Plays: 1909–1950* (New York: Harcourt, Brace and World, 1962), pp. 72–73.

sel approaches land through New England granite islands, with "a breath of pine, and the woodsong fog . . . grace dissolved in place." One of the remarkable things about Eliot's handling of Shakespeare's action is the explicit recognition within the poem of the regressive character of the charged imagery: "Whispers and small laughter between leaves and hurrying feet," a place "Under sleep, where all the waters meet." Eliot situates the *Pericles* action in a twentieth-century rather than a Renaissance consciousness. "I made this, I have forgotten / And remember" recognizes that the images that return are recovered from or in an earlier composition, an earlier self or ship. And yet they are not merely memories but presences, albeit fugitive: "Given or lent?" And the whole motion is forward not back, the strange silent movement of a vessel sailing almost windlessly through fog, so that one can hardly tell whether it moves or things move toward it.[17]

Eliot's Marina is a daughter figure leading toward the Lady or Holy Mother of *Ash Wednesday*, who "moves in the time between sleep and waking":

> restoring
> Through a bright cloud of tears, the years, restoring
> With a new verse the ancient rhyme. Redeem
> The time. Redeem
> The unread vision in the higher dream
> While jewelled unicorns draw by the gilded hearse.

In the essay on Dante of this period, he speaks of "what I call the world of the *high dream*," adding that "the modern world seems capable only of the *low dream*."[18] He emphasizes Dante's having "a *visual* imagination . . . in the sense that he lived in an age when men still saw visions. It was a psychological habit, the trick of which we have forgotten. . . . We have nothing but dreams, and we have forgotten that seeing visions—a practice now relegated to the aberrant and the uneducated—was once a more significant, interesting, and disciplined kind of dreaming. We take it for granted that our dreams come from below" (p. 204). Much of Eliot's essay focuses on Dante's relationship to Beatrice, in the *Divine Comedy* and in the *Vita Nuova*.

---

17. "Marina" is the most exquisite of the Ariel poems in which Eliot moved toward Christianity through imagery for the most part not Christian but cognate, including, here and in "Animula," imagery of childhood and growing up such as we get in Shakespeare only adjunctively, though crucially. What we do not get in Eliot is the imagery of birth and earliest childhood in Shakespeare.

18. "Dante" (1929), T. S. Eliot, *Selected Essays*, new ed. (New York: Harcourt, Brace and World, 1950), p. 223.

Dante, meditating on an intense infantile experience, extended it "in a different direction from that which we, with different mental habits and prejudices, are likely to take," finding "meaning in *final causes* rather than origins" (pp. 235, 234). Eliot quotes the great recognition scene of Dante and Beatrice toward the end of the *Purgatorio*, where the poet's spirit, "broken with awe" in the long years bereft of her presence, finds, "through hidden power which went out from her, the great strength of the old love." As he turns to his discussion of the *Paradiso*, Eliot says parenthetically of the *Divine Comedy* as a whole, "You can compare it to nothing but the *entire* dramatic work of Shakespeare" (p. 225).

Eliot's *Marina*, with his essay on Dante, places *Pericles* as, on one side, a work of visionary art. In Jungian terms, as Elizabeth Drew pointed out, Eliot's Marina is an Anima figure, a feminine presence presiding over renewal or rebirth.[19] One could use the same terms about Shakespeare's Marina, but there is of course a more central Western symbolism. Beatrice leads Dante to the Virgin Mother, daughter of her own son, who stands at the summit of the *Paradiso*.

To see analogies with Christian ritual and symbolism in the plays can be illuminating, sometimes wonderfully so. But to substitute the Christian archetype for the dramatized human reality is to falsify the basic situation in which Shakespeare worked, where precisely the absence of the resource of Christian discipline, the necessity of dealing in another, secular, artistic way with needs worship might meet, is often the ground of the dramatic action. This mode of, as I see it, misconstruction, emerges very clearly in an interesting study by Roger Carson Price.[20] Price observes

19. Elizabeth Drew, *T. S. Eliot: The Design of His Poetry* (New York: Scribner's, 1949), pp. 127–29.
20. Roger Carson Price, "Pauline Perils: A Religious Reading of *Pericles, Prince of Tyre* (Ph.D. diss., University of California, Berkeley, 1974). Price pursues every emblematic or typological affinity he can discover for the text by referring its elements to the Book of Common Prayer, the Geneva Bible, and traditional Christian iconography. Pericles' name is construed as referring to the perils of the Christian vocation; Simonides alludes to Simon Peter; other names also yield suggestive allusions. When Pericles enters "wet" from shipwreck, he has undergone baptism; his father's rusty armor, which the fishermen draw up in their net, is St. Paul's armor of Christian faith. The death and burial of Thaisa at sea is so handled as to allude to the Dormition and Assumption of the Virgin, as is her revival at Ephesus, where " 'legend states that after the Crucifixion of Christ, his mother lived with the Apostle John'" (p. 239; quoted from George Ferguson, *Signs in Christian Art* [1954; rpt. New York: Oxford University Press, 1961]). The exhaustive assemblage of analogues is organized chiefly as a running commentary reconstructing a hypothetical Jacobean production "ventriloquizing the didactic Christian message"—"that except we be

that the conditions specified in the opening riddle about Antiochus and his daughter: "He's father, son, and husband mild; / I mother, wife—and yet his child," can "exist in *two* . . . only with the Godhead and the Virgin" (p. 340). The riddle, taken as a kind of cryptic ventriloquy, is thus seen as putting into Pericles' head "the *basis* of the knowledge the Hero needs to live a Christian life" (p. 341). But Price, though he points out an extraordinary number of Christian analogues and resonances to the moment-by-moment movement of the action, does not manage to show a Christian pattern emerging in the painful adventures of Pericles.

That there should be such analogues and suggestions is to be expected: Shakespeare is working with a tale saturated with Christian associations by centuries of retelling. One can go from the text of *Pericles* out to Christian parallels over and over again. But the "way" of Pericles is the symbolic action of poetic drama, not religious discipline. To identify the dramatic action with its religious analogues is to ignore the radically new situation of the Elizabethan drama in a secularizing cultural moment, developing alongside the new Protestant church. We have seen that this drama could be called upon to express and control human needs like those met in the Old Religion through worship of the Blessed Virgin Mary, a presence who could bind terrors associated with the maternal as well as hold intact its cherishing force. Shakespeare in his romances goes back to the form of medieval secular romance he had known in his youth. And within that form he pursues the symbolic satisfaction of needs that contribute to profound perturbations in his earlier work. What can best account for the deep inner coherence of *Pericles* is not the almost inevitable array of Christian analogues, but the way a symbolic action, centered on the recovery of lost bonds in a human family, is used to meet needs that, in different circumstances, are met in Christian worship of the Holy Family.

The great recognition scene in *Pericles* has such extraordinary

---

born again, we cannot see the kingdom of God; that [adapting Gower's closing lines] on our patience evermore attending new joy waits on us, though this particular play has ending" (pp. 357, 347). There is no reason to resist the validity of the symbolic equivalences Price discovers, at a general level, any more than there is a need to resist his assertion that the same words carry in richly complex ways similar meanings in the Shakespearean, classical, and biblical contexts. But the question for criticism is to be true to the *composition* of the work and so be free to enter into its consciousness, its detail, in a way that finds the logic of the parts in the unique whole. The "whole" must, of course, finally be in ourselves.

power because it recapitulates the process by which a human being establishes relationship to the world through the mother. At the beginning Pericles neither hears Marina's song nor looks at her. Only when he pushes her violently in response to her near approach, and she is roused to assert herself, does he begin to attend:

> She speaks,
> My lord, that, may be, has endur'd a grief
> Might equal yours.
>
> (V.i.86–88)

Pericles' coming back to life through Marina makes his relation to her like a child's to its mother: "O, come hither, / Thou that beget'st him that did thee beget." The deep source of what is happening is conveyed by the play's encompassing sea imagery: "this great sea of joys rushing upon me. . . . Thou that wast born at sea, buried at Tharsus, / And found at sea again!" (lines 192, 196–97). If Marina in one way bears him as a child, he in another way, because he has gestated the object recovered by his suffering, can say of himself also, "I am great with woe, and shall deliver weeping. / My dearest wife was like this maid" (lines 106–7). There is the suggestion of an exchange of roles:

> Tell thy story;
> If thine, considered, prove the thousand part
> Of my endurance, thou art a man, and I
> Have suffered like a girl.
>
> (V.i.134–37)

With this scene the process of recognition becomes the actualization of fantasy, or memory lived with as fantasy. The fear that it is all delusion is expressed in the text in spaced-out exclamations such as "O, I am mock'd" (line 142), or later, "This is the rarest dream that e'er dull'd sleep / Did mock sad fools withal. This cannot be" (lines 161–62)—until the final surge of joy, the moment of closure ("This is Marina" [line 199]), and the succeeding rapture:

> Now blessings on thee! rise, th' art my child.
> Give me fresh garments. Mine own Helicanus,
> She is not dead at Tharsus as she should have been. . . .
> Give me my robes. I am wild in my beholding.
> O heavens bless my girl! But hark, what music?
>
> (lines 213–15, 222–23)

The intervention of the music and Diana, goddess of chastity, just at this moment, to call Pericles to seek his lost queen, is exactly right in view of the identification he has made between daughter and mother. It leaves Marina with Lysimachus, a potential husband in a social world, who, before retreating from Pericles, provides "a pillow for his head" (line 236). The strange, wild, bearded figure subsides, saying "It nips me unto list'ning, and thick slumber / Hangs on mine eyes" (lines 234–35). "Nips" is one of those magically homely words that in the late romances so often accompany sublime moments. Though its Renaissance usage was much wider than present usage, in this context it carries suggestions of the intimate play of mother and child.

The lines given Diana are crisp, cool, authoritative, and somewhat cryptic, hiding from Pericles the key fact that Thaisa lives, so as to save the final recognition for the final scene. Structurally, that scene cannot but be somewhat anticlimactic: "Now our sands are almost run, / More a little, and then dumb" (V.ii.1–2), says the Chorus, relaxed after the great détente with Marina. The scene moves through ritual actions suggesting stages of initiation in a mystery cult, an emphasis that accords with the penetration, by a Prince with his male train, of a place sacred to feminine celibacy, under the aegis of "Celestial Dian, goddess argentine," with her "silver bow" (V.i.250, 248).

When Thaisa entered the temple fourteen years earlier, in a brief scene following close on her revival by Cerimon, she said:

> But since King Pericles,
> My wedded lord, I ne'er shall see again,
> A vestal livery will I take me to,
> And never more have joy.
> (III.iv.8–11)

The temple is like a convent, except that in Thaisa's case the "nun" is married not to Christ but to the memory of her lost husband. She insists on the commitment almost prudishly even as she recognizes him:

> O, let me look!
> If he be none of mine, my sanctity
> Will to my sense bend no licentious ear,
> But curb it, spite of seeing. O my lord,
> Are you not Pericles?
> (V.iii.28–32)

What Pericles says in response defines emotion that is cognate with religious worship—an impulse to lose himself totally in her or have her completely in himself. Showing the ring her father gave him, he exclaims:

> This, this. No more, you gods! your present kindness
> Makes my past miseries sports. You shall do well
> That on the touching of her lips I may
> Melt, and no more be seen. O, come, be buried
> A second time within these arms.
>
> (lines 40–44)

The rush of feeling toward identification—possible because the roles of father, husband, and son, mother, wife, and daughter, blurred by the opening incestuous bond, have been sorted out and made secure—is continued as Marina kneels, and it is completed in her beautiful lines "My heart / Leaps to be gone into my mother's bosom."

"IF THIS BE MAGIC"

In *The Winter's Tale* not only must relationship to the lost daughter be recovered, as in *Pericles*, but Leontes' bond with his estranged friend must be renewed before the final reunion of husband with wife is possible. I shall consider *The Winter's Tale* only in the baldest outline, focusing only on one of the relationships recovered en route to the final recovery of Hermione, that between Leontes and Polixenes. The analogy of *Pericles* can help to clarify the much more complex development of the later play. For where in *Pericles* we begin with overt incest and arrive at a sublime transformation of the motive, in *The Winter's Tale* we begin with the destruction of Leontes' affection for Polixenes by his pathological jealousy, and the action of atonement involves bringing the two kings back into amity *before* the recovery of the lost wife.

It is notable that the play begins with the relationship of the two men, not that of Leontes and Hermione. "Sicilia cannot show himself over-kind to Bohemia. They were train'd together in their childhoods; and there rooted betwixt them then such an affection, which cannot choose but branch now" (I.i.21–24). The affection does branch, for Leontes, in the "rough pash and the shoots that I have":

> Affection! thy intention stabs the centre.
> Thou dost make possible things not so held,
> Communicat'st with dreams.
>
> (I.ii.128, 138–40)

There is clearly a sense in which Leontes' jealousy continues his relationship with Polixenes in a terrible negative form. Some years ago J. I. M. Stewart replied convincingly to the common critical view that the jealousy is purely conventional and theatrical by referring to Freud's account of projective or paranoid jealousy as a defense against homosexual attraction.[21] The defense, in Freud's account, works according to the formula "*I* do not love him, *she* loves him." Leontes attributes to Hermione repressed elements of his love for his boyhood friend, brought to the surface when his wife's pregnancy and Polixenes' nine-months' visit come to term simultaneously. The dependent, affectionate, and erotic components that have been unstably distributed in marriage and idealized friendship violently collapse into Leontes' jealous delusion.

Beneath this level of psychological extrapolation there is another one, still less directly demonstrable, that relates Leontes' jealousy to very early levels of infancy. In his rigorous and imaginative psychoanalytic studies of *The Winter's Tale*, Murray Schwartz has seen in Leontes' boyhood affection for Polixenes an effort to recuperate through their inseparable twinship the essence of the infantile union with the mother.[22] The intense friendship centered on Polixenes is a substitute for and an extension of the early erotic investment in the mother, which the father interrupts. From this vantage point we can see that the idealization of the childhood intimacy has held in check not only the erotic component of that bond but also fear and resentment of the superior rival who possesses the mother sexually. When Hermione's appeal to Polixenes succeeds where Leontes' has failed, Leontes' projective jealousy puts the rival in the position of the intrusive, archaic father. His jealous delusion replaces the idealization of friendship with a more desperate effort to master an all-or-nothing childhood dependence. Leontes responds to a situation of infantile helplessness with rage,

---

21. J. I. M. Stewart, *Character and Motive in Shakespeare* (London: Longmans, Green, 1949), pp. 30–39. In a brief note, "Rooted Affection: The Genesis of Jealousy in *The Winter's Tale*," *College English* 25 (1964): 545–47, John Ellis makes the same argument, adding the suggestion that Leontes comes to himself with the news of the death of Mamillius (after being deaf even to the oracle of Apollo) by a mechanism of projection: "But it would seem not merely the shock which brings him to his senses, for now he has also sacrificed his victim. His sin has been carried away" (p. 547).

22. Murray Schwartz, "Leontes' Jealousy in *The Winter's Tale*," *American Imago* 30 (Fall 1973): 250–73; and "*The Winter's Tale*: Loss and Transformation," *American Imago* 32 (Summer 1975): 145–99.

both against the archaic rival who forces the child's renunciation of the erotic tie to the mother and against the faithless woman who appears to be the compliant object of the rival's sexual possession. One can thus connect the violent eruption of jealousy in *The Winter's Tale* to the action of *Pericles* by noting that Shakespeare's recovery of deep relation to the maternal presence in the earlier play would lead naturally to the recovery of deep hostility and jealousy toward a male rival. An accepted and accepting relation to the father is a condition of positive relationships to other men, so the onset of jealousy means as important a loss of relation to the crucial man as to the crucial woman.

One could pursue these speculations much further in the text of the opening scenes, in the memories of idyllic boyhood ("to be boy eternal . . . What we chang'd / Was innocence for innocence"), in the remarkable insistence on identification of the two kings with their sons, in the whole wonderful evocation of womanly, maternal strength in Hermione. But my interest here is structural, and my argument concerns the way the whole play moves. It seems to me that the primary motive that must be transformed before Hermione can be recovered in *The Winter's Tale*, as the father-daughter motive is transformed in *Pericles*, is the affection of Leontes for Polixenes, whatever name one gives it. The resolution becomes possible because the affection is consummated, as it could not otherwise be, through Perdita and Florizel. "How thou lov'st us, show in our brother's welcome," Leontes says to Hermione, and there follows the horrible sexual imagery of his wife "sluic'd in 's absence . . . by his next neighbor" (I.ii.174, 194–95). At the onset of "affection," he recoils with the exclamation (appropriate equally to his own relation to Polixenes and to that which he ascribes to his wife): "Too hot, too hot! / To mingle friendship far is mingling bloods" (I.ii.108–9). Through Perdita and Florizel the motive toward union can welcome the daughter's loving the son as Leontes loves the father; "mingling bloods" becomes possible.

The continuous presence of the unresolved Leontes-Polixenes relation, beyond its negative development while Leontes is in the grip of his delusion, is one of the manifest features of the play which supports this interpretation. Camillo describes Leontes' need for Polixenes as he makes plans for the flight of Florizel to Sicily, a flight that symmetrically reverses the earlier flight away from Sicily:

> Methinks I see
> Leontes opening his free arms, and weeping
> His welcomes forth; asks thee there, son, forgiveness,
> As 'twere i' th' father's person.
>
> (IV.iv.547–550)

When the encounter takes place, Leontes' first words identify son with father:

> Were I but twenty-one,
> Your father's image is so hit in you
> (His very air) that I should call you brother,
> As I did him, and speak of something wildly
> By us perform'd before.
>
> (V.i.126–30)

In the whole span of the action, we can see Leontes' jealousy and his recovery from it as the release of a motive that threatens a family tie with gross sexuality. The release leads to clarification in the third act, but the clarification is devastating not resolving. The trial scene makes clear what terrible violence Leontes has done to Hermione *and* to his children. It seems arbitrary and incredible because it lacks circumstantial support—there is no Iago to embody the energy of the destructive fantasy and provide circumstantial plausibility to support the delusion. If the whole thing seems unrealistic, one may consider the real horror of tyranny, as in Henry VIII's execution of Anne Boleyn and his treatment of other wives, who were entirely above suspicion, or what is actually done in private life by husbands and wives to each other, as well as the motives brought to expression by storytellers, writers of novels and novellas, and by Shakespeare himself. The very absence of mitigating circumstances makes Shakespeare's handling of this dread motive the more purgative. He masters it by knowing that it *is* irrational. He is able to deal with it in tragicomedy, mitigating its consequences short of the deaths of Perdita and Hermione, by knowing the irrationality for what it *is*, by not confusing the issue or blenching from its horrible potential.

In Act V the complex motive is transformed. Indeed, from one perspective we can see that the motive, with the need it serves and the fear it masks, cannot be fully embraced until it has been transformed. The sexual bond of Perdita and Florizel in the new generation makes possible the restoration of Leontes' friendship and the

recovery of family bonds purged of sexual degradation. The meaning of the recovered relation of Leontes to Perdita differs from that
of Pericles to Marina because what Leontes first recovers through
her is not his lost wife but his lost friend. He also recovers much
more through the discovery of Perdita, including relation to the
new life, which has been evoked in the great fourth act: "Welcome
hither, / As is the spring to th' earth" (V.i.151–52). But it seems to
me that he can find Hermione again because the energies of the tie
to Polixenes, which originally poisoned his love, have now been
transformed and fulfilled.

In the climactic moments of *The Winter's Tale*, where the recov-
eries take place, a great part of the poetry is occupied in describing
the principal people, praising them, doing them reverence, en-
hancing their meaning, while they present themselves, confront
one another at gaze, or form a center for the eyes of all beholders.
This mode of presentation accords with the special sort of dramatic
action, developed in *Pericles*, that turns on the transformation of
persons into virtually sacred figures who yet remain persons. Before he knows that she is his daughter, Leontes says to Perdita and
Florizel:

> O! alas,
> I lost a couple, that 'twixt heaven and earth
> Might thus have stood, begetting wonder, as
> You, gracious couple, do.
> (V.i.131–34)

This might be a description of a moment in a court masque where
some noble couple are presented in the role of mythological deities;
at court, the real identity of Prosperina and her consort would be
known; the heaven and earth would be the work of Inigo Jones.
One can think of more serious parallels in baroque religious painting, where the principals are highlighted in a large space defined
by streams of light connecting heaven and earth while secondary
figures come from the presence chamber with wonder and awe. In
The Winter's Tale secondary figures come from the presence chamber to report to us the recognition of Perdita; some of their description might fit a painting by El Greco:

I make a broken delivery of the business; but the changes I perceiv'd
in the King and Camillo were the very notes of admiration. They
seem'd almost, with staring on one another, to tear the cases of their
eyes. There was speech in their dumbness, language in their very

gesture; they look'd as they had heard of a world ransom'd, or one destroy'd. . . . There was casting up of eyes, holding up of hands.

(V.ii.9–15, 46–47)

In the final scene of *The Winter's Tale*, Hermione is presented to bereft Leontes as a statue in a chapel, to which people kneel in awe; Perdita has kneeled to her in prayer. Suggestions of a sacred or taboo figure surround the seeming statue, along with an ecstacy that "transports" Leontes. Audrey Stanley's masterful production at Ashland, Oregon, in 1975, which bathed this whole scene in blue and white light, with all costumes also in blue and white, brought out how much Hermione's return to life is like a medieval miracle when a statue of the Holy Mother moves in response to prayer. But only *like*: after Hermione "stirs," and before Leontes is able to speak, Paulina presents the moment as a new wooing: "When she was young, you woo'd her; now, in age, / Is she become the suitor?" (V.iii.108–9).

The fulfillment of the scene is her coming down into humanity to embrace him:

O, she's warm!
If this be magic, let it be an art
Lawful as eating.

(V.iii.109–11)

Along with the transformation in the direction of the sacred, the recovery of the particular human identity of the long-lost one is crucial. The enhancement of Hermione as she is recovered, the sanctification, expressed in her appearing first as a sacred statue and then coming alive as the warm, actual wife, has been earned by freeing Leontes' perception of the maternal in her from the perverse dependence expressed in his jealousy. One can place the spiritual process involved in such sanctification of a particular individual by imagining, for contrast, a medieval Leontes who, after similar aberration, might recover his relation to his wife through the intercession of the Holy Mother. The Shakespearean situation requires the discovery of the Holy Mother in the wife.

The late romances, in seeking such recovery, can be casual about coincidences, about divine intervention or white magic introduced to help along the symbolic action, for they are frankly fiction, "Like an old tale still" (*WT* V.ii.61). And this is because the presences restored, though they are presented as natural human beings, really matter, have their actuality, as internal objects at the core of the self but apperceived as neither self nor other by the grace of maternal and filial love. They are restored to the visionary reality of these plays by way of "the grave where buried love doth live" (Sonnet 31), the grieving heart in which their memory is kept intact, made sacred as they are made a part of the self. The benignity of this process, though it unfolds with insistent, self-conscious artifice, is itself rooted in nature. The actions of *Pericles* and *The Winter's Tale*, for all their artistry, are as natural as the action of successful mourning, in which the lost beloved is recovered as an inner presence and the mourner is freed to turn anew toward worldly objects to meet the need that had been met by the object of his grieving. The particular way that these plays, like the work of mourning, confront ambivalence and potential perversion and work through them permits it to be said of their art that

> Nature is made better by no mean
> But Nature makes that mean. . . .
> This is an art
> Which does mend Nature—change it rather; but
> The art itself is Nature.
> (*WT* IV.iv.89–90, 95–97)

It is tempting to adapt a line already quoted from the recognition of Marina in *Pericles* to describe what happens in Paulina's chapel. This strange line, spoken by Pericles to his recovered daughter, summarizes both the effect of the beloved figures on the protagonists, in bringing them back into life, and the thing that is most emphasized in the feminine figures—their power to create and cherish life, their potential or achieved maternity. When Hermione's statue comes alive, "Thou that beget'st him that did thee beget" might read, referring now to the dramatist himself: "He that begets her that did him beget." Of course such reference is pure speculation, in one sense, or something utterly obvious, in another. One particular feature of the scene points, not to Shakespeare's particular life, but at least to his particular art: the statue's coming to life is dramatized by moving from the wonder of Julio Romano's sculptor's art to, literally, Shakespeare's own art. "What fine chisel / Could ever yet cut breath?"

"GENTLE BREATH OF YOURS"

In sharp contrast to *The Winter's Tale*, *The Tempest* is centered in a dominant male figure, a manipulative, all-but-all-powerful magician, sometimes troubling for a certain arrogance or egocentricity, even at times a smugness. From beginning to end, Prospero is the consummate artist in firm control of his plot. He jealously maintains for himself all the power there is on the island, including the power to provide his daughter with the husband he has chosen for her. The plot he designs to culminate when he bestows "this my rich gift" (IV.i.8) on Ferdinand—so different from the movement toward marriage in *The Winter's Tale*—reflects the very different circumstances of this play. For Prospero, as for Lear, there is no wife to recover through his daughter. His anxious control over the fate of Miranda's sexuality is the way this play protects its action from the threat of incest, which it shares with the tragedies and the other late romances. In *The Tempest* this threat is given expression in the libidinal danger posed by Caliban, the degraded representation of the father's incestuous impulse; in the symbolic connection of Ferdinand with Caliban as Prospero's log-carrier; and in the extreme insistence on chastity before Prospero's difficult, highly charged surrender of Miranda to marriage.

The dominance Prospero exercises, however, reflects yet deeper currents in Shakespeare's imagination. We have looked at how a crucial identification with nurturing, parental modes of relating in Shakespeare's temperament shapes not only the development of his drama but his relationship, as dramatist, to his creations. *The Winter's Tale*, the culmination of this orientation, gives embodiment to the cherishing feminine figure who is lost but whose presence is restored, even in her physical warmth: the play participates in the gracious maternal powers it evokes. But poised against this identification is the threat of female power as destructive, manifest in its most extreme form as witchcraft or the demonic—Joan de Pucelle and Queen Margaret in the early histories, Lady Macbeth and the witches in *Macbeth*, Regan and Goneril in *Lear*. Women who embody sinister power in the late romances—Dionyza in *Pericles*, the wicked Queen in *Cymbeline*—have a diminished stature when compared with the great tragic figures. And of course there is no such woman character in the action proper of *The Tempest*. But in order to establish his power on the island, Prospero has had to supplant a legacy of black magic left behind by the foul witch Sycorax, who was banished from Argier "For mischiefs manifold, and sorceries terrible / To enter human hearing" (I.ii.264–65).

Ariel, who has become the agency of Prospero's imaginative faculty, had earlier been forced to serve Sycorax. When he refused to perform "her earthy and abhorr'd commands," he was subjected to "her most unmitigable rage," confined in a cloven pine, where he vented his groans "as fast as mill wheels strike" (I.ii.273, 276, 281). The perversion of the imaginative faculty by Sycorax suggests an art that has been given over to the destructive side of the powers Shakespeare associates with women. After evoking the full range of benign, creative, female powers in *The Winter's Tale*, Shakespeare in *The Tempest* sketches out the dangers of an art that participates totally in his whole imagination of the feminine. Ariel's unwillingness to carry out the loathsome commands of Sycorax fixes a limit, while his consequent inhibition by her indicates the potential malevolence of such an art: "It was a torment / To lay upon the damn'd" (lines 289–90). Prospero, by his liberation of Ariel and his reappropriation of the "delicate spirit" to enact his own "most potent art," subdues to patriarchal mastery the dread potential within Shakespeare's imagination of women—at the cost of a severe constriction of feminine powers in the play and a deep mistrust of sexuality in Prospero's own imagination.

Prospero's own art, however, incorporates the threatening aspect of maternal powers, as when the sumptuous banquet provided for Alonzo and company is made to vanish when Ariel appears as a harpy, inducing madness in the guilty parties. But in the whole movement of the action, such elements are taken up into the affirmation of Prospero's manhood and the ultimately restorative, reparative cause his art serves. As Prospero guides the play to its outcome in marriage and a renewed social order, Shakespeare in effect endows the figure of the cherishing father from the very early works with the triumph of aggressive masculine assertiveness, which in the early histories is subverted by the disabling presence of overpowering women. Indeed, Prospero succeeds precisely where these early figures fail: by establishing his magical dominion he overcomes the legacy of destructive femininity bequeathed by Sycorax; by recovering his dukedom from his usurping brother and frustrating Antonio and Sebastian's plan to kill Alonzo he resolves without violence the pattern of brother-to-brother rivalry predominant in the early histories; by arranging the marriage of Miranda and Ferdinand he secures the stable transmission of authority and heritage to the next generation.

But Prospero's mastery of these enduring themes through his art—his manipulation of the island world as if it were his theater—is a highly self-conscious dramatization of the power of the theater as Shakespeare came to understand it at the very close of his career. We can see what is distinctive about this understanding by reference to *A Midsummer Night's Dream*, written some fifteen years before *The Tempest* when the festive form of comedy was coming into its own. The earlier play is a gathering-in of the resources of drama and ritual that had been spread out in Elizabethan society, spread out around the year in the saturnalian festivities of holidays, in the casual performances of visiting troupes, and in the improvisations, usually classically inspired, of aristocratic and royal entertainments. In *Dream*, Shakespeare gathers all this up and makes it part of his theater; he thus makes us conscious as such of magical assumptions, which in an actual folk festival would be taken literally. Shakespeare makes such assumptions a function of the theatrical moment, the fancies shaped by the influence of the forest of his creation. *Dream* makes us conscious of the imaginative design of a kind of experience that in its original holiday statement would not ask for self-consciousness.

Whereas *Dream* brings the saturnalian rhythm of holiday festivals into the ironic awareness of the theater, *The Tempest* is a making conscious of, and a reckoning with, the power of the theater as an established institution. The point of departure for the later play is an occasion that is already theater. *The Tempest* is a version of a masque in which members of the court, disguised as visitors from a world far away, would come to salute the reigning monarch. As Enid Welsford has shown, the masque form is reflected in the arrival on the island of the shipwrecked visitors; in what amounts to an anti-masque conducted by Stephano, Trinculo, and Caliban; and finally in the revels that celebrate the marriage, in prospect, of Ferdinand and Miranda.[23] Of course in this instance the visit is involuntary, and the Prince who receives the visitors has been wronged by them; the anti-masque itself is a threat to the Prince as well as a burlesque of the serious threat posed by Antonio and Sebastian. And though Shakespeare is partly imitating the structure of the masque, he is critical of monarchs in ways that the courtly form would not allow. *The Tempest* puts the artist as magician in control of a plot aggressively designed to bring about a change of heart in Alonzo, King of Naples. Prospero makes Alonzo one of the visitors, puts him totally within the artist's power, and

23. Enid Welsford, *The Court Masque* (Cambridge: Cambridge University Press, 1927), pp. 335–49.

forces him to suffer for the past wrongs he has committed. Instead of subordinating its art to the monarch's power, *The Tempest* explores the power of the theater itself.

Shakespeare uses the play to test what a dramatist might do, how far his power might extend, if he were to make this rule—that any event can take place short of an event that destroys the subjects who participate in it—and then see how much these subjects can be changed at deep levels by putting them inside the plot the dramatist invents for them. He finds an equivalent for the theater in the island, a space within a boundary, set off from the rest of the world. On the island things can happen that are experienced as wholly real to feeling and imagination, and yet at the same time, as with the "direful spectacle" of the shipwreck, "Not a hair perished; / On their sustaining garments not a blemish, / But fresher than before" (I.ii.26, 217–19).

The play begins by situating us among the people on the deck of the ship that is about to wreck, with the boatswain shouting: "What care these roarers for the name of king?" (I.i.16–17). And then we are immediately with Prospero and Miranda as he responds to her sympathetic, auditor's response to the wreck she has seen:

> Had I been any god of power, I would
> Have sunk the sea within the earth or ere
> It should the good ship so have swallow'd, and
> The fraughting souls within her.
>
> (I.ii.10–13)

"Tell your piteous heart / There's no harm done" (lines 14–15)—the storm, the wreck, these "fraughting souls" belong to Prospero's plot. After having been first put inside the dramatic illusion, we are abruptly made to realize that on the island the dramatic illusion is presented by, represented by, Prospero's magic. *The Tempest* is an experiment in drama, with Shakespeare asking: What is my theater after all? What is this enchanted space and how much can be done in it? And what are the limits of its power, beyond which it violates or falsifies the human materials on which it is based?

This experiment in theater reflects the great social experiment of colonization.[24] The early colonist went out with the assumption

---

24. O. Mannoni reads *The Tempest* in relation to the psychology of colonialism, in *Prospero and Caliban*, trans. Pamela Powesland, 2nd ed. (New York: Frederick A. Praeger, 1964), pp. 105–9. In "*The Tempest* and the New World," *Shakespeare Quarterly* 30 (Winter 1979): 29–41, Charles Frey convincingly demonstrates "the extent to

that he, like Prospero, was to be lord of an island or a territory. Where others were exploring and appropriating geographical territories, within which they could conduct their own social experiment in managing human relations, Shakespeare sets up the theater as his territory. Assuming that one could make for the new colony not only a social constitution or set of laws but also a plot, which the drama can envisage because it has its freedom from the exigencies of the actual—what would the series of events reveal about the redeemability and the irredeemability of human nature? Gonzalo's dream of an idealistic plantation mirrors the dream of some at the time that the colonial might be freed from the old exigencies of the actual in Europe. The plot, as conducted by Prospero, brings the old exigencies to the forefront, balancing Alonzo's change of heart against the recalcitrance of Antonio and Sebastian, understanding Miranda's "brave new world" as the precarious reconstitution of the old one, finding in Caliban first a childlike generosity and dependence and then an inner core of viciousness deeper than the corruption induced by society and beyond the reach of society's mitigating nurture.

At the heart of the play are rites of passage that have organized Shakespearean drama from the first, just as they have ordered the society that is represented in it. But the dramatic center of these rites has undergone the shift to the older generation characteristic of the late romances. Again, *A Midsummer Night's Dream* can help put the later play in perspective. *Dream* is a rite of passage from adolescence out into commitment in love, supervised by the mature marriage of Theseus and Hippolyta and by the recommitment to love after childbirth dramatized in the reconciliation of Titania and Oberon following the dispute over the changeling boy. Similarly, the action of *The Tempest* is organized around the courtship of Miranda and Ferdinand, their passage into adult lives. Ferdinand, even as he grieves for the father he believes dead, moves through his royal version of a young man's assumption of paternal heritage: "I am the best of them that speak this speech, / Were I but where 'tis spoken" (I.ii.430–31). He reaches toward fulfillment in Miranda as she gives herself to the brave new figure that he makes. But the experience of courtship as a rite of passage is dramatized most

which some themes, situations, incidents, and even phrases in *The Tempest*" participate in responses to the exploration and colonization of the New World which had become "the common coin of Shakespeare's day" (p. 38).

forcefully, not in the youthful movement toward marriage, but in the father's giving away of his daughter, counterpointed by Alonzo's loss and recovery of his son.

So experienced, this rite of passage becomes a recognition by the older generation of the place of death in the great cycle of life beginning anew in the marriage. The experience of the parent who feels that the child's life is more important than his own is very movingly rendered in the last scene when Alonzo, questioning Prospero on the "particulars of thy preservation," is struck anew with grief for the son he thinks drowned: "Irreparable is the loss, and patience / Says, it is past her cure" (V.i.135, 140–41). Prospero, in his smug mode, insists that Alonzo has not sufficiently sought the "soft grace" and "sovereign aid" of patience—as he has done in losing his own daughter. Then we get the splendid moment when Alonzo says:

> O heavens, that they were living both in Naples,
> The King and Queen there! That they were, I wish
> Myself were mudded in that oozy bed
> Where my son lies.
>   (lines 149–52)

The sense of a giving up, for the younger generation, of the life that has been led nearly to its conclusion by the older generation is also reflected in Prospero's asides as he plays the heavy father to Ferdinand and Miranda's courtship:

> So glad of this as they I cannot be,
> Who are surpris'd withal; but my rejoicing
> At nothing can be more.
>   (III.i.92–94)

When he finally surrenders her to Ferdinand, it is as "a third of mine own life, / Or that for which I live" (IV.i.3–4). After the nuptial is solemnized, Prospero will "retire me to my Milan, where / Every third thought shall be my grave" (V.i.311–12). One cannot have lived to be older than Shakespeare when he died without that thought coming home.

Prospero's surrender of his daughter to the large sustaining rhythms of life, his firm but tense recognition that such rhythms are beyond the power even of so potent an art as his own, accords with what all the while seems to be the most important reference in the play. The epilogue refers us back to Shakespeare himself and to his dependence on the audience, which alone can release the artist from his cell of self, which can provide fulfillment for the artist by way of those who, in receiving his art, make it possible, complete it. Prospero, like Leontes watching the statue of Hermione emerging into life, refers explicitly to the "breath" that animates Shakespeare's dramatic art. Prospero affirms, not the theater's autonomous, life-giving power, however, but the dramatist's audience, for whom his life and art are shaped:

> Gentle breath of yours my sails
> Must fill, or else my project fails,
> Which was to please.[25]
> (Epi.11–13)

As *The Tempest* reflects on the theater's powers and on the limits of those powers, it does so as a valediction to their use—the play's most crucial rite of passage. After its astonishingly aggressive display of the dramatist's power to subdue life to his own purposes, the play finds its most moving moment in this epilogue, where the artist relinquishes the art that has shaped the play and sustained the artist, to turn for sustenance to the audience.

When one recognizes the potential of social aggression that is transformed in the art, it seems almost a matter of prudence for Shakespeare, at the close of his most aggressive fantasy, where the fable has fused the poet-producer with the prince, to insist that he and his fellows are only artists in the service of their public:

> Now my charms are all o'erthrown,
> And what strength I have's mine own,
> Which is most faint.
> (Epi.1–3)

There is of course far more to this than simply a social deference—there is deference to the magic-like process of art itself. And in the following conceit about releasing Prospero from his cell, there is recognition of the profoundly social process involved in dramatic art, recognition of the audience's cooperation in the actors' project, by which the isolation of individual sensibility is transcended:

---

25. The differences between Prospero's epilogue and the end of *The Winter's Tale* extend tensions we have encountered before, as in the Sonnets. To move from the recovery of Hermione in Paulina's chapel to the emptied stage from which Prospero delivers his final lines to his audience is akin to moving from those exultant sonnets that celebrate the life-giving capacity of the poet's art to those deferential poems that regard the friend as the indispensable but elusive source of life, both for the poet and for his verse.

> Let me not,
> Since I have my dukedom got,
> And pardon'd the deceiver, dwell
> In this bare island by your spell,
> But release me from my bands
> With the help of your good hands.
>
> (Epi.5–10)

The concluding lines, with their use of religious ideas, can be read in many ways:

> Now I want
> Spirits to enforce, art to enchant,
> And my ending is despair,
> Unless I be reliev'd by prayer,
> Which pierces so that it assaults
> Mercy itself, and frees all faults.
>
> (Epi.13–18)

Certainly a primary reference in "faults" to be "reliev'd by prayer" is simply to faults in the play, which the epilogue's petition asks the audience to excuse. There is possibly also a plea to be forgiven any blame for using magic, albeit white magic. Perhaps at a still deeper level there is concern about the guilt attaching to the aggressiveness of the fable of an artist as mercifully avenging prince. And perhaps also there is a need for expiation after having bodied forth, in *The Tempest* and throughout the unprecedented diversity and power of the work prior to it, motives underlying life—"this thing of darkness I / Acknowledge mine" (V.i.275–76)—even though they have been brought under the control of art:

> As you from crimes would pardon'd be,
> By your indulgence set me free.

Index

Aaron, 134, 135, 138–42, 150, 154–55, 239; cherishing fatherhood of, 4, 154, 155; sexuality-violence of, 126, 131–32, 138–42, 155, 156
Abbess, 5, 21, 70, 72, 73, 75–76
Abraham, Karl, 110
Adelman, Janet, 290n, 304
Adonis, 4, 147, 174
Adriana, 68–79 passim
Aemilia, 68, 72, 76, 84–85
Aggression: in Comedy of Errors, 81–82, 83–84; in Coriolanus, 304; in Hamlet, 262, 264; in Henriad, 108–211, 218, 222, 224, 226, 227, 231; Pericles and, 316; in Richard III, 95–96, 101; Shakespeare's, 61–64; Sonnets and, 172–73. See also Theatrical aggression; Violence; War
Aging, 171–72
Alarbus, 130
Albany, 288–89, 295
Alcibiades, 306, 308
All's Well That Ends Well, 15, 16, 17, 18, 161, 190, 196
Alonzo, 336, 337–38, 339, 340
Androgyny, 189–90
Angelo, 16, 17, 183n, 186
Anglicanism, 23, 270n, 282, 283, 284n. See also Prayer Book; Protestantism
Anne, 4, 102–3, 104, 109, 111
Antiochus, 301, 310–18 passim, 325
Antipholus of Ephesus, 68–84 passim
Antipholus of Syracuse, 72, 74–75, 77–80, 82
Antonio, 189, 336, 337, 339
Antony, 181n, 302
Antony and Cleopatra, 18, 37, 145, 302–3
Apemantus, 306, 307
Aphrodite, 179n
Apollonius, 298, 321
Apuleius, 179
Archbishop, 91, 117, 233

Arden, Mary. See Shakespeare, Mary Arden
Ariel, 335–36
Aristocracy, 62–63, 234; in All's Well That Ends Well, 190; Sonnets and, 52, 60, 61, 64–65, 169. See also Court life
Aristotle, 71
Art and Illusion, 221
Arthur, 4, 240
Ash Wednesday, 323
As You Like It, 6, 7, 225, 261
Auden, W. H., 171, 274
Audience: Lear's, 37–38; Prospero's, 37, 340–42; Richard III's, 87, 91, 101, 113
Aufidius, 305
Authority, male, 3, 4, 11, 13, 14, 24–25, 36, 64, 65; in All's Well That Ends Well, 16; in Comedy of Errors, 85; in Hamlet, 12, 123, 238, 243, 249; in Henriad, 210, 228–30, 232, 235, 236, 237, 238; in Julius Caesar, 238; in King Lear, 128, 285, 292; in Macbeth, 123; in Measure for Measure, 16; Richard III and, 123; of Shakespeare's father, 50–51; in Titus Andronicus, 128

Bagg, Robert, 180n
Baker, Howard, 140n, 148n
Banquo, 33, 247
Baptism, 282–83
Barabas, 91, 92
Bardolph, 223
Barnet, Sylvan, 130n
Bartholomew Fair, 143
Barton, Anne, 75–76, 77, 80
Bassianus, 128, 132, 140–41, 142
Bastard, 4, 238, 239, 240, 241
Bates, 228, 229
Battenhouse, Roy, 207, 256
Beatrice: in Dante, 323–24; in Much Ado about Nothing, 7

Benedick, 7
Berger, Harry, Jr., xx, 130n
Berowne, 5, 239
Bertram, 15, 17, 18, 190–91, 196
Betrayal, 174, 269
Bevington, David, 93n
Binding, 250n
Birth, Shakespeare's, 22
Bishop of Ely, 97, 99, 103
"Black Rubric," 29n
Boleyn, Anne, 331
Bolingbroke, 212–13
Book of Common Prayer, 29n, 243–44, 282, 284
Booth, Stephen, 121, 158, 159, 164, 167, 184, 185, 186n, 203
Borges, Jorge Luis, xviii–xix
Bottom, 58, 144
Brenner, Charles, 82
Brophy, Brigid, 179n
Brothers, 26; in Comedy of Errors, 74, 85, 120; in Hamlet, 231, 238; in Henriad, 228, 231, 234, 235, 236; in Julius Caesar, 238; in Richard III, 5, 86, 92, 101, 119–20, 121–22, 123; Shakespeare's, 44, 47, 122; in Tempest, 336. See also Male solidarity
Brower, Reuben A., xxii, 26n
Brutus, xxi, 11, 36
Buckingham, 102, 103, 107–8
Bullough, Geoffrey, 69, 132n
Burckhardt, Sigurd, 101–2
Burgundy, 219, 235, 236
Burial of the Dead, 243–44, 271, 282
Burke, Kenneth, 280–81

Caesar, xxi, 36, 302
Caliban, 335, 337, 339
Cambridge, 222
Camillo, 330–31
Cassio, 35, 277
Cassius, 36
Catesby, 90
Catholicism, xx, 20, 23–24, 26, 32, 282, 288; ghost's status in, 248; of Shakespeare's father, 48–49, 50
Cavell, Stanley, 276n, 290n
Cerimon, 317–18, 320, 327
Cesario-Viola, 6–7, 189, 190, 236
Chapman, George, 149
Cherishing, 3, 7–8, 13, 15, 46–47, 61, 65; in Henriad, 10, 12, 49–50; in King Lear, 47, 292; in Pericles, 317–18; in Sonnets, 3, 8, 9, 10, 12, 49, 61, 112, 172, 174, 188; in Tempest, 336; in

Titus Andronicus, 4; in Winter's Tale, 335
Chettle, Henry, 59, 60–61
Chief Justice, 209–10, 233
Chiron, 131, 132, 138–39, 141, 146
Chivalry, 234–35
Chorus, in Henry V, 10, 12, 14, 200, 212, 213, 217–18, 222n, 237
Christ, 23–31 passim, 192, 271, 289–90
Christianity, xx–xxi, 1, 14n, 21–38 passim, 282–83; in Comedy of Errors, 21, 75–76; and Hamlet, 29–32, 247, 256–57, 271, 282; in Henry V, 199; King Lear and, 38, 288–91, 292–93, 294, 297; Othello and, 34, 276n; Pericles and, 319, 324–25; psychoanalysis and, xxiv, xxv, xxvi, 24, 25–26, 29; Sonnets and, 192, 198–99, 200. See also Catholicism; Protestantism
Christian Ritual and the World of Shakespeare's Tragedies, 294
Clarence, 5, 88, 89, 91, 96; dream of, 119–20, 121–22; murder of, 92, 109, 110
Class differences: Falstaff–Prince Hal, 64–65, 205, 211, 212–13; in Sonnets, 52, 60, 61, 64–65, 169, 182, 190, 191, 194. See also Aristocracy; Middle class
Claudio, 6, 7, 17
Claudius, 30, 53–56, 236–57 passim, 266, 275; marriage of, 12, 244–45, 251, 252, 277, 301; poisoning by, 272; theatrical aggression against, 264, 268
Clemen, Wolfgang, 120
Cleon, 311, 316, 318
Cleopatra, 149, 181n, 302–3
Coleridge, Samuel Taylor, 241
Colie, Rosalie, 144–45
Colonization, 338–39
Comedies, xv–xvi, 4n, 5–8, 62, 63, 126; feminine modes in, 3, 5, 7, 9–10, 15–16, 17; festive, 5–8, 9–10, 17, 23, 126, 189, 235, 236, 239, 299, 300–301, 337; New, 6, 75, 80; problem, 10, 17–18, 161, 189; vs. romances, 300–301; Roman vs. Elizabethan, 71; sexuality in, 16, 17–18, 235, 236, 300; Sonnet themes in, 161, 189, 191; worship in, 23. See also Farce; names of individual comedies
Comedy of Errors, 67, 68–85, 86, 88, 89, 120–21, 126; family in, 5, 67, 80,

126; gossips' feast concluding, 72, 85, 283–84; religion in, 21, 75–76
Comic history, 122 n
Conscience, xxiii, xxiv, 109–10, 121, 179–80, 242, 255
Constance, 4, 239, 240
Cordelia, 18, 38, 151, 156–57, 244, 284, 285–97, 301, 309–10
Cordelion, 4, 240, 241
Corin, 225
Coriolanus, 129, 303–5, 308–9
Coriolanus, 35, 37, 298, 302, 303–5, 308–10
Countess of Auvergne, 93, 99–101
Couplets, 163–64
Coursen, Herbert, 294
Court life, 20, 45–46, 62–63, 66, 211; in *Hamlet*, 64–65, 239; in *Henriad*, 64–65, 211, 212–13; Richard II and, 212–13; in *Richard III*, 91
Courtship, 339–40
Cressida, 16
Cruttwell, Patrick, 14–15, 180–81
Cupid, 179
Cymbeline, 155, 301, 310, 335

Dances of Death, 120, 271
Dante Alighieri, xvii, 32, 188, 322, 323–24
Daughters: in *King Lear*, 38, 284–97; in *Pericles*, 301, 320; Shakespeare's, 58; in *Tempest*, 38, 340; Virgin Mary as, 32; in *Winter's Tale*, 301, 328
Dauphin, 93, 222
da Vinci, Leonardo, 170
Death: Christ's, 25–26, 27–28; Falstaff's, 214–16; in *Hamlet*, 243–44, 247, 254, 255, 264–65, 266, 282; Renaissance attitudes toward, 64 n; Sonnets and, 214; *Tempest* and, 340
Debts, in *Comedy of Errors*, 82, 83
Dedalus, Stephen, 25 n, 47, 57
Delaying revenge, in *Hamlet*, 241–42
Demetrius, 131, 132, 138–39, 141, 144, 146
Depression, 319
Desdemona, 21, 34–35, 36, 276–77, 278–80, 301, 302
Deus absconditus, 294, 295
Diabolism, 188, 276, 288–89, 301
Diana, 313, 318, 321, 326, 327
Dionyza, 311, 316, 318–19, 335
Discourse, in Sonnets, 164
Disfiguring, 144, 145, 148
Divine Comedy, xvii, 32, 323–24

Doctor Faustus, xx, 188, 248
Doctor Faustus, 20, 29, 142, 197
Dominance, male, 4, 10–11, 138, 334–36. See also Female dominance
Donne, John, 59, 164, 165, 182, 187, 201
Dreams: Clarence's, 119–20, 121–22; farces like, 81, 82; Richard's wit like, 88
Drew, Elizabeth, 324
Dromios, 69, 72, 74, 78, 79–80
Drury, Elizabeth, 182
Duchess of York, 104–5
Duke (Solinus), in *Comedy of Errors*, 72, 79, 84, 85, 283
Duncan, 13, 121, 269, 301

Edgar, 151, 288, 290 n, 292, 295
Edmund, 151, 274, 290–91, 293, 295
Edward, Prince, 113, 117, 119, 123
Edward II, 94
Edward IV, 102; Clarence and, 92, 96, 119, 121; Edward, son of, 113–14, 117, 119, 123; queen of, 88–90, 95, 96, 101, 103–4, 108
Edwards, Phillip, 314 n
Egeon, 68, 71, 72, 78, 80–81, 82–84
Elinor, 4, 239, 240
Eliot, T. S., 1–2, 40, 265–66, 271, 272, 322–24
Elizabeth, Queen, 14, 32, 303; and law, 209 n; Prayer Book of, 29 n; Ralegh and, 46, 239 n; worship of, 45–46, 211
Elizabeth, queen to Edward IV (*earlier* Lady Grey), 88–90, 95, 96, 101, 103–4, 108
Elizabethan culture, 14–15, 20, 51–52 n, 71, 337; androgyny allowed by, 189, 190 n; chivalry in, 234; Church in, *see* Anglicanism; law in, 209 n; sonneteers in, 162; violence tolerated in, 143–44, 148. See also Court life; Elizabethan theater
Elizabethan theater, xx–xxi, xxvi, 19–38, 63, 194, 325, 337; economics in, 58–63, 64, 65, 194; violence tolerated in, 143–44, 148
Elizabeth of York, 103, 104, 123
Ellis, John, 329 n
Elton, William, 294
Ely, Bishop of, 97, 99, 103
"Embassy of Death," 31
Empson, William, 64, 164–65, 167, 183 n, 213–14, 217
Ephesus, 69

Epistle to the Ephesians, 69
Erickson, Peter, 11n, 218, 233n
Erikson, Erik, 110, 291n
Erotium, 70, 71
Evans, G. Blakemore, 151n, 312n, 317n
"Everything," xix, 47
"Everything and Nothing," xviii–xix
Execution, public, 63, 63–64n
Exeter, 226, 227

Falstaff, 10–17 passim, 91, 183n, 198–
    217 passim, 237; and class differ-
    ences, 64–65, 205, 211, 212–13;
    male solidarity after, 223, 235, 237
"Falstaff as Parodist and Perhaps Holy
    Fool," 207
Family, 1–24 passim, 32, 145, 282, 299,
    301–3; in *Comedy of Errors*, 5, 67, 80,
    126; in *Coriolanus*, 35, 302, 308–9; in
    Hamlet, 35, 236, 246, 251, 282; in
    King Lear, 35, 38, 285, 294, 295; in
    Othello, 34, 35; in *Pericles*, 300–301,
    312–13, 316; in *Richard III*, 86, 115–
    16; Shakespeare's, 40–64 passim,
    76–85 passim, 122, 170; Sonnets
    and, 46, 168; in *Titus Andronicus*,
    126, 132, 155, 157; in *Winter's Tale*,
    300–301, 332. *See also* Brothers;
    Daughters; Heritage; Incest; Infants/
    Infantilism; Marriage; Parents/
    Parental modes; Reunions; Sons
Family Reunion, 266, 271
Family romance, 4n, 29, 239
Famous Victories of Henry the Fifth, 209
Farce, 69, 72, 81–82, 85, 126
Fathers, 3, 4–5, 11–12, 35n, 36, 301,
    330; Christ's, 24–25, 29–30; in *Com-
    edy of Errors*, 5, 80, 83, 85; *Coriolanus*
    and, 304; in *Hamlet*, 11–12, 29–31,
    52, 53–56, 64, 123, 236–82 passim;
    in *Henriad*, 11, 208–11, 227–28,
    230–32; in *King John*, 240, 241; in
    King Lear, 38, 156–57, 284–97; in
    Macbeth, 123; in *Othello*, 34, 123,
    278, 279, 280; in *Pericles*, 301, 316;
    Richard III and, 123; Shakespeare's,
    40–56 passim, 61, 64, 78, 79, 80,
    83–84; in Sonnets, 171; in *Tempest*,
    37, 38, 340; in *Titus Andronicus*, 4,
    137, 155–57; in *Winter's Tale*, 301, 329
Faulconbridge, 238, 239, 240–41, 252
Faustus. *See* Doctor Faustus
Female dominance, 3–4, 6–8, 10, 46,
    61, 85, 335–36; in *Comedy of Errors*,

5, 84–85; in *Coriolanus*, 37, 303–5; in
    King John, 240; in *Macbeth*, 12–13; in
    Richard III, 99, 105–9, 112, 113
Feminine modes. *See* Women/Feminine
    modes
Fenichel, Otto, 81
Ferdinand, 120, 315, 335, 336, 337,
    339–40
Fergusson, Francis, 253n
Fiedler, Leslie, 168, 186
Finances, Shakespeare's, 43, 48, 58–61,
    64, 192
Fineman, Joel, 238
Flavius, 308
Florizel, 299, 300, 330, 331–32
Fluellen, 200, 223, 225, 226
Foakes, R. A., 68, 84n
Fool: Hamlet as, 260–61, 268; in *King
    Lear*, 290n, 291, 295
Form, in Sonnets, 162–64
Fortinbras, 244
Freedman, Barbara, 81–83
Freud, Anna, 307n
Freud, Sigmund, xxii–xxvi, 35n, 36,
    200; on Christ's death, 25; on con-
    science, 255; on delay, 242; on
    dreams, 82n, 88; on homosexuality,
    170, 171, 329; on identification,
    xxiii–xxiv, 9, 170, 254; on infant de-
    velopment, 110, 181; on jealousy,
    329; on melancholia, 254; on neu-
    rotics, 27n, 316n; on projection,
    250, 329; on sex objects, 180; "thing
    presentation" of, 30. *See also*
    Psychoanalysis
Frey, Charles, 338–39n
Frost, Robert, 184
Frye, Northrop, 5

Games, Richard's, 86–87
Gertrude, 303; Hamlet's mourning
    urged by, 244; Hamlet's reactions to,
    113, 251, 252, 275, 277–78, 279, 301
Ghost, 29–31, 53, 233, 242, 254–55,
    258, 266; appearance of, 55, 246–53;
    on Gertrude, 252, 275; heroic man-
    hood influenced by, 238, 242, 249,
    253, 257, 268, 271; idolatry of,
    256–57; poisoning described by,
    272; theatrical aggression with, 29,
    267, 268
Girard, René, 26, 35, 130
Gloucester, Earl of (*King Lear*), 151, 288,
    290n, 292, 295

Gloucester, Humphrey, Duke of (*2H6*), 50, 93, 94
Gloucester, Richard, Duke of. *See* Richard III
Gombrich, E. H., 221
Goneril, 284n, 285, 288–89, 290–91, 295, 335
Gonzalo, 339
Gossips' feast, 72, 85, 283–84
Gosson, Stephen, 23n
Gower, John, 223, 298, 310, 311n, 312, 322
Grandmother, in *Richard III*, 116–17
Greenblatt, Stephen, 276n
Greene, Robert, 59, 60, 61
Grey, 222
Grey, Lady, 95, 96, 101. *See also* Elizabeth, queen to Edward IV
Grief, 232–33, 243–45, 254, 255, 334
Group Psychology and the Analysis of the Ego, 200
Guildenstern, 257, 261
Guilt, 83, 121, 231, 233, 266, 281

Hair, 318
Hal, Prince, 10, 11, 64–65, 183n, 202–16 passim, 231–33, 235. *See also* Henry V
Hall, Edward, 96n, 97
Hamlet, 11–12, 29–32, 52–65 passim, 91, 233, 236, 241–81; and boy actor, 190n; and Claudius-Gertrude bond, 12, 113, 244–45, 251, 252, 277–78, 301; and father's burial, 244, 271, 282; Hal compared with, 64–65, 210, 233; Richard III compared with, 113, 123; wit of, 123, 239, 246, 259, 260–61
Hamlet, 11–12, 35, 53–56, 64–65, 236, 238–81; brothers in, 231, 238; burial in, 243–44, 271, 282; Christianity and, 29–32, 247, 256–57, 271, 282; father figures in, 11–12, 29–31, 52, 53–56, 64, 123, 236–82 passim; mother in, 113, 236, 238, 240, 244, 251–52, 259, 266, 277, 303; and theater companies, 58–59, 62, 190n, 262–65, 268–69, 280
Hamlet and Oedipus, 242
Handkerchief, in *Othello*, xxi, 34, 35, 278
Hands, 149–51, 153
Harvey, Gabriel, 56
Hastings, 90, 97, 98–99, 100

Hate. *See* Hostility/Hate
Hathaway, Anne (Shakespeare's wife), 56, 76, 170
Hazlitt, William, 270, 280
Heaney, Seamus, 224–25n
Helena, 15–16, 17, 18, 144, 190–91
Helen of Troy, 174
Henry IV, 10, 11
Henry IV, 11, 12, 15, 198–235, 262; love in, 45n, 200, 202, 203, 204–5, 213–14; Sonnets related to, 12, 161, 189, 198–219 passim
Henry V, 11, 12, 94, 199–200, 201, 208–37 passim
Henry V, 10, 11, 200–236; Chorus in, 10, 12, 14, 200, 212, 213, 217–18, 222n, 237; heroics of, 12, 94, 200–201, 208, 213, 228, 234, 235, 237–38; love in, 45n, 200; Sonnets related to, 10, 161, 189, 200–219 passim, 237
Henry VI, 3, 4, 49–50, 92, 93, 94
Henry VI, 50, 87, 93–102 passim, 113, 123, 240
Henry VIII, 331
Herbert, George, 192
Heritage, 3, 11, 13, 243; in *Hamlet*, 64, 241, 242, 249, 255, 256, 262, 269, 271; in *Henriad*, 11, 208–9, 230, 232, 233; in *Julius Caesar*, 11, 36; in *King John*, 239, 241; in *King Lear*, 11, 291; in *Richard III*, 120; Sonnets and, 9, 60, 169; in *Tempest*, 339
Hermia, 144
Hermione, 18, 173, 300, 310, 328–34 passim, 341n
Hero, 6, 7
Heroes/Heroics, 3, 13, 14, 16, 18, 21, 32–33, 127; Christian, 26n, 27–28; in *Hamlet*, 11–12, 52, 54, 238, 240, 242, 243, 249–62 passim, 268, 269, 271; in *Henriad*, 12, 94, 200–201, 208, 213, 228, 234, 235, 237–38; in *King John*, 238, 240, 241; Marlowe and, 20; in *Othello*, 277; in *Pericles*, 316; in *Titus Andronicus*, 4, 127. *See also* Authority, male
Hieronimo, 148; *Hamlet* compared with, 245, 272; *Titus Andronicus* compared with, 125, 133, 135, 153, 157
Hill, R. F., 154
Hippolyta, 339
Histories, 4n, 94, 100, 126–27, 145, 189; cherishing in, 3, 9–10; female domi-

Histories (*continued*)
   nance in, 3, 10, 85, 99; heroic mode
   in, 12, 94, 127; male-to-male conflict
   in, 238. *See also names of individual
   histories*
History of Richard III, 91
Holidays, 300
Holland, Norman, 57n, 77
Holloway, John, 31n, 63–64n
Homilies, 22, 23–24
Homosexuality, 170–71, 329
Horatio (*Hamlet*), 30, 246, 261, 265, 267
Horatio (*Spanish Tragedy*), 125, 126
Hostility/Hate, 269; in *Hamlet*, 53, 254,
   255, 266, 269; in *Henriad*, 209, 228,
   235; in *Othello*, 274; in Sonnets, 176,
   178, 179
Hotspur, 205, 208, 235
Huguenots, 65
Humanism, 14n, 19
Hundred Merry Tales, 139
Hyman, Stanley Edgar, 280
Hyperion, 252, 254

Iago, 17, 35, 91, 122n, 123, 173n, 269–
   81 passim
Icons, 22–23, 296–97
Identification, xvii–xix, 3, 7–9, 15–16;
   Christ's, 25; Freud and, xxiii–xxiv, 9,
   170, 254; in *Hamlet*, 242, 252, 257,
   272, 273–74; in *Henriad*, 233; in
   Othello, 275; in Sonnets, xviii, 3, 8,
   9, 46, 49, 169–70, 172, 173, 188; in
   Spanish Tragedy, 272
Identity: Christian, 282–83; in New
   Comedy, 75; in Sonnets, 175. *See
   also* Male identity
Idolatry, 22–24, 29n; in Hamlet, 256–
   57, 269; Sonnets and, 166, 192
Illium, 262
Imogen, 301
Impersonal theory of poetry, 40
Incarnation, 28–29
Incest, 18, 288, 301; in *Pericles*, 301,
   312–13, 316; *Tempest* and, 335; in
   Titus Andronicus, 126
Infants/Infantilism, 20–27 passim, 35,
   256, 283, 294–95; in *Comedy of
   Errors*, 83; *Coriolanus* and, 304; in
   Hamlet, 242, 250, 256; in *King Lear*,
   291; *Richard III* and, 86, 101, 112–13;
   in Shakespeare's life, 47, 51; in Son-
   nets, 175–77, 178–79, 181, 182; in
   Timon of Athens, 307; in *Winter's Tale*,
   329–30

Inheritance. *See* Heritage
Internalization (of parent), 9, 13, 255–
   56; *Hamlet* and, 242, 243, 249, 255–
   56; in *Henriad*, 11, 227–28; in
   Winter's Tale, 173
Interpretation of Dreams, 242
Irony, 63, 252, 266–67, 290
Isabella, 16

James, King, 209n
Jamy, 223
Jealousy, 329–30
Jewell, Bishop, 22n
Jewish religion, xxiv–xxv, 25
Jew of Malta, 91–92
Joan de Pucelle, 33, 93, 94, 335
John, 4n, 240
John Bon and Mast person, 28n
Jones, Ernest, 242
Jonson, Ben, 67, 143, 144, 182, 241
Joyce, James (*Ulysses*), 25n, 47, 57
Judas, 114, 306
Juliet, 6
Julius Caesar, xxi, 11, 12, 35–36, 236,
   238
Jungian terms, 322, 324

Kahn, Coppélia, 4n, 76n, 101n
Kate, 5, 7
Katherina, 5
Katherine, 218, 219, 226, 227, 235–36
Keats, John, xviii, 47
Kent, 292
King John, 4, 238–39, 240–41
King Lear, 35, 38, 281, 284–97, 335; *Cor-
   iolanus* compared with, 309–10; her-
   itage in, 11, 291; ironies in, 63, 290;
   "nothing" in, xix, 47; pastoral in,
   225; *Pericles* compared with, 309,
   310, 321; reunion in, 18, 293, 310;
   Timon of Athens compared with,
   309–10; *Titus Andronicus* compared
   with, 125, 151, 157
King Lear and the Gods, 294
Kirsch, Arthur, 276n
Klein, Melanie, xxvi
Knight, E. Nicholas, 53–54n, 58
Knight, G. Wilson, 31, 245n
Kohut, Heinz, 51
Kott, Jan, 115
Krieger, Murray, 192
Kris, Ernst, 210
Kyd, Thomas (*Spanish Tragedy*): and
   Hamlet, 245, 263, 272; *Richard III*
   and, 91, 107; theatrical aggression

of, 62, 91, 263; *Titus Andronicus* and, 67, 125, 133, 134, 135, 143, 153, 157

Lacey, Stephen, 146
Laertes, 244, 253, 262, 265
Lavinia, 126–57 passim
Law, 209n, 210
Leach, Edmund, 318
Lear, 37–38, 142–43, 151, 244, 284–97, 301, 309; authority of, 128, 285, 292; Pericles compared with, 310, 321–22; reunion of, with Cordelia, 18, 293, 310; Timon compared with, 309–10; Titus compared with, 156–57
Lear. See *King Lear*
Leishman, J. B., 160, 174, 192
Leonine, 311, 318
Leontes, 173, 174, 301, 310, 328–32, 333
Levin, Harry, 75n, 247n
Lewis, C. S., 160, 161, 247–48
Lewis, Wyndham, 63–64n
Lies, 180–81
"Lines of life," 166–67
London, 58, 65–66, 78, 85
Lord Mayor, 91
Lord's Supper, 28–29, 283
Love: in *All's Well That Ends Well*, 16, 190–91, 196; in *Antony and Cleopatra*, 302; of Christ, 25; Donne on, 187; Freud on, 170; in *Henriad*, 45n, 200, 202, 203, 204–5, 213–14; in *King Lear*, 288, 292–93, 296; in *Measure for Measure*, 16; in *Othello*, 274, 279; in *Richard III*, 111, 112; in Sonnets, 44–45, 46, 162, 168–74 passim, 180n, 184–93 passim, 199, 201–2, 204, 213–14; in *Twelfth Night*, 189
Love's Labor's Lost, 5, 7, 111, 161, 239
Lucian, 306
Luciana, 75, 78, 82
Lucio, 16, 17
Lucius, 4, 137, 150, 152
Luther, Hans, 30n
Luther, Martin, 30n
Lysimachus, 327

Macbeth, 12–13, 33, 122n, 123, 269, 301
Macbeth, 11, 121, 130, 154, 281, 301, 335; female violence in, 12–13, 121, 335; witches in, xxi, 33, 121, 335
Macbeth, Lady, 12–13, 33, 247, 335
Machiavels, 91, 245–46
Macmorris, 223, 224
Madonna cult, xxvi

Magic, xix–xxi; in *Comedy of Errors*, 69–70; in *Hamlet*, 29, 248; in *Henriad*, 198; in *Midsummer Night's Dream*, xx, 337; *Tempest* and, 37, 341, 342. See also Sorcery
"Magical Hair," 318
Male identity, 3, 13, 14, 24, 36; in *Hamlet*, 30–31, 236, 249; in *Measure for Measure*, 16. See also Manhood
Males. See Men
Male solidarity: in *Coriolanus*, 308–9; in *Henriad*, 94, 100, 101, 218, 222–36, 237, 238; in *Love's Labor's Lost*, 7
Male-to-male confrontation, 3, 5, 6, 26, 64, 85, 238; in *All's Well That Ends Well*, 16; in *Hamlet*, 238; in *Henriad*, 101; in *Julius Caesar*, 236; in *Measure for Measure*, 16; in *Richard III*, 5, 85, 86; in *Tempest*, 336
Mamillius, 329n
Manhood, 3, 14, 16–17, 237, 249; in *Hamlet*, 11, 52, 239, 241, 242, 243; in *Henriad*, 10, 198, 200–201, 205, 208, 213, 216–17, 228, 235, 236, 237–38; in *Julius Caesar*, 236, 238; in *King John*, 240–41; in Sonnets, 201; in *Tempest*, 336; in *Titus Andronicus*, 156. See also Authority, male; Heroes/Heroics
Man-woman relationships, 6–8, 10, 18, 31–35, 170–71; in *All's Well That Ends Well*, 16; in *Hamlet*, 12, 236; in *Henriad*, 11, 99–101, 236; in *Macbeth*, 12–13; in *Measure for Measure*, 16; in *Othello*, 34–35; in *Richard III*, 99–101, 102–9; in Sonnets, 158, 170–71, 172, 173, 178–80; in *Titus Andronicus*, 137–38; in *Troilus and Cressida*, 16. See also Dominance; Marriage; Sexuality
Marcus, 128, 130–31, 132, 134, 146–53 passim
Margaret, Queen, 3, 4n, 86, 92–93, 95, 105–9, 112, 113, 115, 335; Shakespeare likened to, 61
Marina, 309–34 passim
Marina, 322–23, 324
Marlowe, Christopher, xxiii, 22, 123, 188; *Doctor Faustus* of, xx, 20, 29, 142, 188, 197, 248; Henry VI plays and, 94–95; theatrical aggression of, 63, 91–92; *Titus Andronicus* and, 142, 149n, 154
Marprelate tracts, 270
Marriage: in *All's Well That Ends Well*,

Marriage (*continued*)
15, 16; in *Comedy of Errors*, 68, 72–
73; in *King Lear*, 284–86; in *Measure
for Measure*, 16; *Othello* and, 35,
276n, 278, 279; Shakespeare's, 41,
56–58, 76, 78, 85; in *Tempest*, 336,
340
Martius, 142, 143
Marx, Karl, 270
Mary. *See* Virgin Mary
Masque form, 337
Maternal modes. *See* Mothers/Maternal
modes
Measure for Measure, 15, 16, 17, 18,
183n, 186
Melancholia, 254–55
Melodrama, 131
Men, 6, 13–14, 189–90; in Sonnets,
158, 170, 172–73, 178, 181–82, 188–
89, 201, 237. *See also* Authority,
male; Brothers; Fathers; Male iden-
tity; Male-to-male confrontation;
Man-woman relationships; Sons;
Vulnerability, male
Menaechmi, 70, 75. *See also* Plautus
Menander, 75
Mephostophilis, 188, 248
Merchant of Venice, 6, 189
Mercutio, 5, 6
Meres, Francis, 160
Merry Wives of Windsor, 68, 73, 213
Metamorphosis, 136
Metaphors, 145, 162, 164, 165
Middle class, 39–66, 169
Midsummer Night's Dream, 126, 134,
140, 144, 161, 339; financial patron-
age addressed in, 58; magic in, xx,
337
Milton, John, 114, 182
Miranda, 37, 301, 335, 336, 337, 338,
339–40
More, Thomas, 91, 96n, 97, 98, 99, 100,
111
Morgann, Maurice, 207
Morton, Bishop of Ely, 97, 99, 103
Mother Church, 26, 32–33. *See also*
Christianity
Mothers/Maternal modes, xxvi, 3, 4, 8,
31–35, 46, 179n, 304, 335; in *Comedy
of Errors*, 83, 84–85; in *Coriolanus*,
303–5, 309; in *Hamlet*, 31–32, 113,
236, 238, 240, 244, 251–52, 259, 266,
277, 303; Holy, *see* Virgin Mary; in
King John, 240; *King Lear* and, 291; in
Macbeth, 12–13; in *Othello*, 34–35,

278, 279; in Ovid, 136–37; in *Peri-
cles*, 85, 309, 316, 318–20, 326, 330;
Richard III and, 4, 86, 105, 112, 113,
116–17, 123; Shakespeare's, 43–44,
47, 48, 83–84; in Sonnets, 112, 175,
177, 178; in *Tempest*, 336; *Timon of
Athens* and, 303, 305–7, 308, 309; in
Titus Andronicus, 4, 136, 137; in
Winter's Tale, 85, 329–30, 335. *See
also* Cherishing
Much Ado about Nothing, 6, 7
Mutius, 5n, 130
Mytilene, 311–12

Narcissism, 46, 111–12
Nashe, Thomas, 94
Navarre, 5
Neely, Carol Thomas, 184, 201, 276n
Negative capability, xviii–xix, 47, 57n,
64, 102
Neoplatonism, 174
Neptune, 311
Neumann, Erich, 179n
Neurotics, 27n, 316n
New Comedy, 6, 75, 80
New Place, 64, 66
"Nothing," xviii–xix, 47. *See also* Nega-
tive capability
Nym, 223

Oberon, 339
"Ocean to Cynthia," 46
Octavia, 302
Oedipus complex, 3, 24, 35n, 38, 64; in
Comedy of Errors, 83; in *Hamlet*, 29,
242, 256, 265, 271; *Henriad* and, 210,
222, 231, 234; in *Othello*, 280; in *Peri-
cles*, 315; in *Titus Andronicus*, 150
Olivia, 189
Ophelia, 236, 251–58 passim, 261, 265,
275, 278
Order for the Burial of the Dead, 243–
44, 271, 282
Orgel, Stephen, 65
Orlando, 6, 21
Orsino, Duke, 6, 189, 190
Othello, 21, 34–35, 36, 173n, 174, 269–
80 passim, 301, 302
Othello, xxi, 34–35, 145, 174, 272–81
Ovid, 136–37, 146, 148, 149, 152

Padel, John, 49
Paganism, 23, 288, 302
Pandarus, 17
Pandosto-Leontes, 301. *See also* Leontes

Paradiso, 324
Paradox, 115
Parents/Parental modes, 3, 25, 35–36, 243, 335; in *Comedy of Errors*, 83–84; in *King Lear*, 35, 292; Shakespeare's, 40–56 passim, 61, 64, 78, 79, 80, 83–84; in Sonnets, 8, 9, 168, 174, 188. *See also* Cherishing; Fathers; Internalization; Mothers/Maternal modes
Parolles, 17, 190–91, 196
Pastoral, 225
Patronage, financial, 58–60, 192
Paul, Saint, 69
Paulina, 333, 334, 341 n
Perdita, 299–300, 320, 330, 331–32, 333
Pericles, 309, 310–28, 332, 334
Pericles, 37, 76, 85, 309, 310–28, 335; reunion in, 18, 37, 76, 85, 298–302 passim, 310; *Winter's Tale* and, 18, 37, 298–302 passim, 310, 320, 330, 332, 334
Petruchio, 5, 7
Philomel, 136, 137
Pinch, Dr., 69, 70
Pistol, 206, 215–16, 223, 226, 235
Plautus, 5, 67, 68, 70, 71, 73, 75
Poins, 206
Poison, 272, 273
Polixenes, 173, 300, 328–30, 332
Polonius, 253, 257, 259, 260, 261
Pompey, 17
Poor Tom, 290 n, 292, 295
Portia, 6
Post-Christian art. *See* Religion; Secularism
Posthumus, 301, 310
Power. *See* Dominance
Power of development, Shakespeare's, 1–2, 11, 15, 242–43, 266 n, 298. *See also* Temperament, Shakespeare's
Prayer Book, 29 n, 243–44, 282, 284
Priam, 262
Price, Roger Carson, 324–25
Procne, 136–37
Projection, 250, 329
Prospero, 17, 18, 37, 301, 315, 335–41 passim
Prosser, Eleanor, 256, 257 n
Protestantism, xx, 20–29, 325; ghost's status in, 248; *Henry VI* and, 50; and Virgin Mary, 23, 32–33. *See also* Reformation
Prynne, William, 23 n
Psyche, 179 n

Psychoanalysis, xxii–xxvi, 40–41, 304; of Christ's death, 25–26; of farce, 81–82; of *Hamlet*, 241–42; of *Henriad*, 210; of *King Lear*, 294; of Sonnets, 175, 181; of *Titus Andronicus*, 150. *See also* Oedipus complex
Punch, 90
Punishments, 25–26, 82, 83, 121
Purgatorio, 324
Pygmalion, 167
Pyrrhus, 262

Quatrains, 163
Quickly, Mistress, 215, 216
Quiney, Adrian, 42
Quintus, 142, 143

Rabkin, Norman, 122 n, 221, 237
Rainolds, John, 22 n
Ralegh, Walter, 46, 239 n
Rape of Lucrece, 4
Ravenscroft, Edward, 143
Reformation, xx, 19, 20–24, 28–29, 33–34, 270
Regan, 285, 291, 335
Religion, xxiii–xxv, 19–38, 256, 270, 283, 299; *Hamlet* and, 29–32, 256–57, 271; in *Henry VI*, 50; Jewish, xxiv–xxv, 25; *King Lear* and, 38, 288–91, 292–93, 294–97; *Pericles* and, 325; Sonnets and, 188, 201. *See also* Christianity
Renaissance, 19, 20, 22, 64 n, 65–66, 276 n; ghost's status in, 248; magic in, xx; sonnets public during, 160. *See also* Elizabethan culture
Resurrection, Christ's, 28, 30
Reunions, 18, 300; in *Comedy of Errors*, 75–76, 85; in *King Lear*, 18, 293, 310; in *Pericles*, 18, 37, 76, 85, 298–302 passim, 310; in *Winter's Tale*, 18, 37, 85, 298–302 passim, 310
Revenge: in *Hamlet*, 241–42, 255, 264, 271; in *Richard III*, 108–9; in *Titus Andronicus*, 67, 125, 126, 131–37 passim, 152, 157
Revolutionary situation, 270–71
Richard II, 212–13, 232
Richard II, xx, 126, 153, 161
Richard III, 4, 5, 62, 86–124, 231–32
Richard III, 67, 74, 85, 86–124, 126–27, 145, 240
Richmond, 103, 115
Rites of passage, 76, 233, 282–83, 284–85, 339–40, 341

Rivers, 88–89
Roderigo, 274
Rollins, Hyder, 159
Romances, 67; late, 18, 37, 298, 300–
302, 303, 333–34, 335, 339. *See also*
names of individual romances
Romeo, 5–6, 145
Romeo and Juliet, 5–6, 126, 143, 145, 161
Rosalind, 236
Rosenberg, Harold, 270 n
Rosencrantz, 257, 261
Rossiter, A. P., 115, 120, 122, 281 n
Royalty. *See* Aristocracy; Authority,
male; Court life
Rutland, 106
Rymer, Thomas, xxi

Sacredness, 1, 24, 36–37, 302, 333–34;
and Desdemona, 35; and Hamlet,
30; in *King Lear*, 38, 288, 297, 309; in
Pericles, 299, 332; in *Winter's Tale*,
299, 332–33. *See also* Religion
Sacrifice: Christ's, 24–26, 27–29, 271;
Hamlet's, 271; in *King Lear*, 288–97;
in *Titus Andronicus*, 129–30
"Saints' plays," 67
Salingar, Leo, 62–63, 67
Saturninus, 128, 137, 138
Schlatter, Richard, xxiii
Schoenbaum, Samuel, 39, 41–42, 43, 49
Schwartz, Murray M., 18, 329
Scotland, 33, 130 n
Scroop, 222, 226
Searles, Harold, 291
Sebastian, 189, 336, 337, 339
Secularism, 19–20, 27, 36–37, 50, 256;
in Anglican church, 283; in *Comedy
of Errors*, 76; *Hamlet* and, 30; in Son-
nets, 188
Sejanus, 241
Self: Falstaff's sense of, 214; Iago and,
275; in *King Lear*, 292; in Sonnets,
xviii, xix, 9, 158, 182–83, 193,
195–96
Self-abasement, in Sonnets, 182–83
Self-assertion, 26 n, 158, 193, 195–96
Self-love, 169–70, 204, 213–14
Senecan stage, 248
Seven Types of Ambiguity, 164
Sexuality, xxiii, 17–18, 145, 179 n, 189–
90, 235, 301; in *All's Well That Ends
Well*, 16, 17, 18, 190; in *Cymbeline*,
301, 310; in *Hamlet*, 32, 251, 252,
277–78; in *Henriad*, 220–21, 227,

235, 236; in *King Lear*, 142–43, 284,
288, 292, 301, 309; in *Macbeth*, 121;
in *Measure for Measure*, 16, 17, 18;
in *Much Ado about Nothing*, 7; in
Othello, xxi, 35, 274, 276 n, 277,
279–80; in *Pericles*, 301, 312–15, 316,
318, 319, 322; in *Richard III*, 96–97,
99, 100, 102–3, 104; in Sonnets, 158,
161–62, 167–68, 170–71, 178–81; in
Tempest, 301, 335, 336; in *Timon of
Athens*, 307–8, 309; in *Titus Andronicus*, 126, 132–56 passim, 171; in
Troilus and Cressida, 17; in *Venus
and Adonis*, 147; in *Winter's Tale*,
301, 310, 329–30, 331, 332. *See also*
Marriage
Shakespeare, Anne Hathaway (wife),
56, 76, 170
Shakespeare, Gilbert (brother), 44, 47,
122
Shakespeare, Hamnet (son), 49 n, 58
Shakespeare, Joan (sister), 43
Shakespeare, John (father), 40–56 pas-
sim, 61, 64, 78, 79, 80, 83–84
Shakespeare, Margaret (sister), 43
Shakespeare, Mary Arden (mother),
43–44, 47, 48, 83–84
Shakespeare, William: birth of, 22, 43;
family of, 40–64 passim, 76–85 pas-
sim, 122, 170; finances of, 43, 48,
58–61, 64, 192; in London, 58,
65–66, 78, 85; temperament of,
xvi–xvii, xviii, 46–47, 194, 335
Shakespeare and the Problem of Meaning,
221
Shakespearean Meanings, 101
Shakespeare's Festive Comedy, xv–xvi, xx,
71, 189, 198
Shakespeare's Lives, 39
Shakespeare's Living Art, 144–45
Sharpe, Ella Freeman, 266 n
Shore, Mistress, 98, 102, 105
Shylock, 6
Sidney, 198, 218
Siegel, Paul, 14 n
Simonides, 315
Sisters, Shakespeare's, 43
Skepticism, 276 n
Snout, 144
Snow, Edward A., 181 n, 276 n
Sonnets, 14, 44–45, 52, 74, 158–97,
341 n; and *All's Well That Ends Well*,
15–16, 161, 190, 196; cherishing role
in, 3, 8, 9, 10, 12, 49, 61, 112, 172,

174, 188; class differences in, 52, 60, 61, 64–65, 169, 182, 190, 191; and *Henriad*, 10, 12, 161, 183n, 189, 198–219 passim, 237; identification in, xviii, 3, 8, 9, 46, 49, 169–70, 172, 173, 188; love in, 44–45, 46, 162, 168–74 passim, 180n, 184–93 passim, 199, 201–2, 204, 213–14; *Richard III* and, 111–12, 121; self in, xviii, xix, 9, 158, 182–83, 193, 195–96
Sons, 4–5, 35n; in *Comedy of Errors*, 80, 83, 84–85; in *Coriolanus*, 303–5; in *Hamlet*, 11, 31, 249–50; in *Henriad*, 11, 94, 208–9, 230–33; in *Richard III*, 86; Shakespeare's, 49n, 58; in *Tempest*, 340; in *Titus Andronicus*, 4, 155–56. See also Heritage
Sorcery: in *Comedy of Errors*, 69, 77. See also Witches
Sound, in Sonnets, 164–65
Spanish Tragedy. See Kyd, Thomas
"Special Type of Object Choice Made by Men," 180
Stanley, 90
Stanley, Audrey, 333
Status. *See* Class differences
Steevens, George, 312n
Stephano, 337
Stephen Dedalus, 25n, 47, 57
Stewart, J. I. M., 329
Stone, Lawrence, 50
Stratford, 58, 65, 66, 78, 80, 81, 85
Subjective interpretations, 39–40
Suffolk, 93, 94, 226
Superego, 83, 188, 242, 255n. *See also* Conscience
Sycorax, 335–36
Sylvius, 225
Synecdoche, 174–75

Talbot, 4–5, 93, 94, 99–102
Tamburlaine, 22, 91, 95
Tamburlaine, 91, 271
Taming of the Shrew, 7
Tamora, 4, 126–43 passim, 148, 155, 156, 157
Tears, 152
Temperament, Shakespeare's, xvi–xvii, xviii, 46–47, 194, 335
Tempest, 3, 37, 38, 317, 334–42
Tereus, 136, 137
Thaisa, 18, 309–21 passim, 324n, 327–28

Thaliard, 316
Theater, new. *See* Elizabethan theater
Theatrical aggression, 61–64; in *Hamlet*, 29, 62, 262–65, 268, 276, 280; Marlowe's, 63, 91–92; in *Othello*, 280; in *Richard III*, 62, 86, 91, 122; in *Tempest*, 37, 336–42
Theseus, 134, 135, 140, 144, 145, 339
"Thing presentation," 30
Thomas, Keith, 33
Tillyard, E. M. W., 114–15
Times, 68
Timon, 305–8, 309
Timon of Athens, 37, 298, 302, 303, 305–10
Titania, 339
Titus, 4, 5n, 125–57
Titus Andronicus, 3, 4, 67, 125–57, 171, 239, 240
Toby Belch, 6
Tom, Poor, 290n, 292, 295
Totem and Taboo, xxiv, xxv, 25, 36
Tragedies, xvi, xxi–xxii, xxiv, 11–38 passim, 64–65, 113, 145, 189; family in, 5–6, 14, 18, 21, 35, 38, 282, 299, 301, 302; heritage in, 3, 11, 13, 36, 64; heroic in, 3, 11–21 passim, 127, 249, 267; and history plays, 12, 122–23, 126–27, 236; irony in, 63, 266–67; male-to-male confrontation in, 3, 64, 85; rites of passage in, 282; romances related with, 18, 37, 298, 299; sacredness in, 1, 24, 36–37, 302; Sonnets related to, 191–92; theatrical aggression in, 63, 122–23; violence in, 18, 130n. *See also names of individual tragedies*
Trinculo, 337
Troilus, 16
Troilus and Cressida, 15, 16, 17
Trojan war, 16
Tropes, 144, 145, 148
Twelfth Night, 6, 7, 15, 161, 189, 190, 261
Twine, Laurence, 311n

Ulysses (Joyce), 25n, 47, 57
University Wits, 59, 60

Variorum Edition, 159, 166–67, 183
Vaughan, Henry, 192
Venus, 3–4, 146–47, 179n
Venus and Adonis, 146–47
Vincentio, Duke, 16, 17

Viola, 6–7, 189, 190, 236
Violence, 6, 18, 26, 35 n, 81–82, 85,
130 n; in *Henriad*, 106, 219, 220–21,
234; in *Macbeth*, 12, 121; in *Othello*,
278, 279–80; in Ovid, 148; in *Richard
III*, 5, 85, 86, 95, 102, 105, 109, 112,
115; in *Titus Andronicus*, 126, 131–
32, 137–38, 144, 146, 148–49, 153; in
Venus and Adonis, 146–47. *See also*
Male-to-male confrontation; War
Virgilia, 303
Virgin Mary (Holy Mother), 26, 288,
295, 325, 333; Queen Elizabeth and,
46; Reformation changes with, 23,
31–34, 282
Visionary realization, 298–99, 302,
322–24, 334
Vita Nuova, 323–24
Volumnia, 129, 303–5, 309
Vulnerability, male, 4, 32, 47, 57 n; in
Hamlet, 249, 271–72; in *Othello*,
278–79; in *Titus Andronicus*, 138, 156

Waith, Eugene, 148–49, 152
Wall, 144
War, 94, 221 n, 222–37 passim
Wars of the Roses, 94, 232
Weird Sisters, 33
Welsford, Enid, 337
West, Robert H., 248 n
Whitgift, Archbishop, 270 n
Whoredom, 32–33
Wilbur, Richard, 175
Wilkins, George, 318
Willbern, David, 140 n, 142 n, 150,
156 n, 264 n
Williams, 224–25, 228, 229
William Shakespeare: A Documentary Life,
41
Wilson, J. Dover, 151 n, 248 n
Winnicott, D. W., 112, 175, 304
Winter's Tale, 173, 174, 298–301, 310,
328–34; *Pericles* and, 18, 37, 298–302
passim, 310, 320, 330, 332, 334; re-
union in, 18, 37, 85, 298–302 pas-
sim, 310; and *Tempest*, 334–35, 336,
341 n

Wish-fulfillment, 322
Wit: in *Hamlet*, 123, 239, 246, 259, 260–
61; in *Henry IV*, 205–6; in *Richard
III*, 88–89, 116–17; in Sonnets,
165–66
Witches: in *Comedy of Errors*, 77; in
Macbeth, xxi, 33, 121, 335; *Richard III*
and, 99, 101, 105–7; in *Tempest*, 335
Wives: in *Othello*, 35, 278, 279; Shakespeare's, 56, 76, 170
Women/Feminine modes, 9–18 passim,
31–35, 43, 47, 170, 298; in *All's Well
That Ends Well*, 17, 190; in *Antony
and Cleopatra*, 18, 36; *Coriolanus* and,
36, 308–10; in *Henriad*, 10–11, 99–
101, 236; in *King John*, 240; in *King
Lear*, 18, 309–10; in *Othello*, 36; in
Pericles, 298–99, 302, 310, 316; in
Richard III, 92–93, 99–101, 102–9,
112–13, 116–17; in Sonnets, 158,
167, 170–71, 172, 173, 178–80; *Tempest* and, 335–36; in *Timon of Athens*,
36, 307–8, 309–10; in *Titus Andronicus*, 137–38, 170–71; in *Twelfth
Night*, 189–90; in *Winter's Tale*, 298–
99, 302, 310, 335, 336. *See also*
Daughters; Female dominance;
Man-woman relationships; Mothers/
Maternal modes; Witches; Wives
Worship, xxiii–xxiv, 13, 34, 239, 284–
85; of Elizabeth, 45–46, 211; in
Hamlet, 31, 256, 271; in *Henriad*, 201,
211; religious, 19, 20–23, 26–27,
283. *See also* Sacredness
Wright, Aldis, 151 n

Yeats, W. B., 192, 296
York (Richard's father), 4–5, 61, 93, 94,
95, 106, 226
York (Richard's nephew), 91, 116–19
Young, C. B., 143
Youth, 171–72

Zenocrate, 22

Compositor: G&S Typesetters, Inc.
Text: 10/12 Palatino
Display: Palatino
Printer: Maple-Vail Manufacturing Group
Binder: Maple-Vail Manufacturing Group